# South of Lobber Point

*This book is dedicated to the memory of my father,*
*Ernest William (Bill) Platt, RN*
*(1918–1974)*

Africa Star and Bar
Burma Star
Atlantic Star
1939–1945 Star
War Medal
Defence Medal

*There was things which he stretched,*
*but mainly he told the truth.*

Mark Twain (1835–1910)
*The Adventures of Huckleberry Finn*

James Platt

# SOUTH OF LOBBER POINT

*More Stories from Port Isaac, North Cornwall, 1944–1950*

First published in Great Britain in 2005 by
Creighton Books
www.creightonbooks.nl

ISBN 90 807808 3 9

British Library Cataloguing in Publication Data
A catalogue record for this book is available from the British Library

Designed in the UK by
Special Edition Pre-Press Services

Printed and bound in Great Britain by
Lightning Sources UK Ltd

*Front cover picture painted by Maria Platt*

# Contents

# List of Illustrations

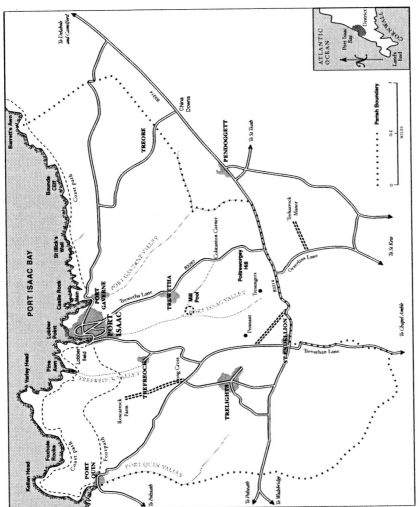

*Sketch map of Port Isaac district*

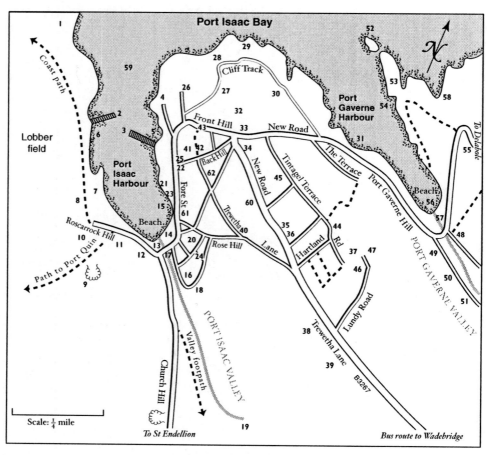

*Sketch map of Port Isaac village*

## Key to numbered locations

1. Lobber Point
2. Western breakwater
3. Eastern breakwater
4. Residence of Mr and Mrs Hillson
5. Hillson's dump
6. Lobber cliff
7. Allotments
8. Khandalla
9. May's Quarry
10. Poplar trees
11. Residence of Capt (retd) Roy May
12. Roscarrock Chapel (Methodist)
13. Pawlyn's cellars
14. Town Platt
15. The Pentice and Mr Altair Bunt's fruiterer's shop
16. Middle Street
17. Black Doors
18. Wesleyan Methodist Chapel
19. Old mill
20. Dolphin Street
21. Port Isaac County Primary School
22. Liberal Club
23. Old Lifeboat House, Little Hill and Chapman's grocery shop
24. Temple Bar
25. Old Drug Store
26. Old Coastguard Station
27. New Coastguard Station
28. Coast Watcher's Hut
29. Shillingstones cliff and adits
30. New Vicarage and Castle Rock Hotel
31. Moon's Grave
32. Rivoli cinema
33. Trelawney Garage (Prout Bros)
34. J. N. Hicks and Son Family Butchers
35. National Bus Garage
36. Co-op
37. New council houses
38. Prefabs
39. Mr Hillson's Farmyard
40. Carlenice (residence of Mr and Mrs Carveth Brown)
41. Canadian Terrace
42. St Peter's church
43. Residence of Miss Jinny Hills and Mr Wilfred Hills
44. Residence of Miss Maud Lark
45. Police Station
46. Residence of Mr and Mrs Steve Bate
47. Mr Tom Saundry's field and pigsty
48. Port Gaverne Hotel
49. Fort and residence of Commander and Mrs Llewellyn Davis
50. Granfer Creighton's garden
51. Flat-roofed residence of Mr and Mrs Tom Honey
52. Castle Rock
53. Port Gaverne Main
54. Tagg's Pit
55. Headland's Hotel
56. Port Gaverne beach tank traps
57. Mrs Strout's café
58. Cartway Cove
59. Kenewal Rock
60. Residence of Miss Cassie Saundry
61. Port Office
62. Residence of Mr William Auger

Also by James Platt (jim.platt@planet.nl)
and published by Creighton Books

**East of Varley Head**
*Stories from Port Isaac, North Cornwall, 1944–1950*

Published in 2003, ISBN 90 807808 1 2

**Your Reserves or Mine?**

Published in 2004, ISBN 90 807808 2 0

www.creightonbooks.nl

# Foreword

*South of Lobber Point* (*SOLP*) is not intended to be as much of a sequel to its predecessor *East of Varley Head* (*EOVH* – published by Creighton Books in 2003) as it is a complement to the latter, containing as it does further stories and reminiscences of life as lived in the north Cornish village of Port Isaac in the late 1940s.

The respective compass orientations that characterise the pair of titles may have changed as if they were assuming the style of the fickle winds of Port Isaac Bay, but the human spirit of the time they deal with has deviated not a whit from the one to the other. The way of life, the colour, the texture and the individuality of the village characters, of whom there was such proliferation that we were spoiled for choice, are forever enduring.

One difference that *SOLP* has with respect to *EOVH* is in an increased autobiographical emphasis that is placed on the events and escapades described. I hope that this may add to the enjoyment of readers (if there are any!).

However, not all is sweetness and light.

An elderly lady, making a holiday visit to Port Isaac from a foreign country in the early summer of 2004, parked her car on the area of beach designated for the same at the head of the harbour (the tide being out at the time) and set her feet to crunch the shingle in order to proceed towards the Town Platt above.

She had recently purchased (and moreover read!) a copy of *EOVH* and carried the book in one hand, intending to use its maps as a guide (of sorts) for a stroll through the village prior to retrieving her car before the inevitably rising tide could place its future in jeopardy.

A local institution in the person of the keen-eyed beach car parking attendant, ever alert to his responsibility for the prevention of motorised traffic chaos on the streets leading to his personal fiefdom (the streets having been designed for the movement of one-at-a-time light horse drawn vehicles at best), spotted the book in her hand. He approached her and pointed at it.

"You don't want to believe anything you read in that!" he told her.

*EOVH* damned without the benefit of even faint praise!

Now read on...

# 1

# The Best Place in the World

*Myself when young did eagerly frequent*
*Doctor and Saint, and heard great argument*
*About it and about; but evermore*
*Came out by the same Door wherein I went.*

Edward Fitzgerald (1809–1883)
*The Rubaiyat of Omar Khayyam*

PORT ISAAC WAS the best place in the world. Everybody knew that! Port Isaac was no more and certainly no less than the only place in the world that was worth either coming from or living in.

> 6 Canadian Terrace,
>   Port Isaac,
>     St Endellion Parish,
>       North Cornwall,
>         Cornwall,
>           England,
>             Europe,
>               The World,
>                 The Universe.

That was my address, laboriously inscribed at the regulatory descending slope to the right with pen and ink on the cover of an exercise book. I was then in the Second Class (one up from the Infants) at the County Primary School in Fore Street.

I managed to write the address without (for once) dropping a single blot.

The Second Class's teacher was the redoubtable Mrs Morman. Her pupils pronounced her surname as "Merman". By direct association they suspected that her voluminous skirt and thick stockings covered up fish-scaled legs. It was she who gave the class the address-writing exercise and she who didn't care too much for my contribution, but there was nothing new in that, as Mrs Morman's reaction to my exercise output seemed to me to be ever thus. She crossed out all the lines of my address from England downwards and then went higher up and crossed out St Endellion Parish and North Cornwall as well.

I looked at the results of Mrs Morman's savage editing and felt only sorrow. I put my hand up. "But Miss," I asked (we called Mrs Morman "Miss" even though she was a Mrs), "Port Isaac is the best place in the world so shouldn't "The World" be in my address?"

"That", she replied, "is neither here nor there!"

I couldn't let that one go.

"I know it's not there Miss, but it is here."

That earned me a crack over the knuckles from the edge of the one-foot long wooden ruler that Mrs Morman consistently carried and wielded as a badge of office with all the majesty she could muster from the not insignificant avoirdupois carried along by her presumably scaly legs.

"Port Isaac is only a tiny village!" she declared to the class, and then, pointing the ruler at me again as if to endorse this disparaging assertion with an implied threat, "Tell me the name of the capital of Cornwall," she demanded.

I had to think about that for a bit. Outside of Port Isaac there wasn't much in Cornwall worth bothering about in my opinion, but I couldn't tell her that.

In a flash of inspiration I ventured the response, "Please Miss, is it the letter C?"

That got me two cracks of the well-tempered wooden ruler on my held out hand. Mrs Morman knew precisely where to bring the ruler's edge into contact with forcibly poised knuckles to the maximum detriment of her victim. The ruler never missed. Any attempt to pull my hand back as the ruler made its descent were thwarted by Mrs Morman's grabbing hold of my wrist with her free hand so as to anchor my knuckles firmly in position.

"What is the capital of Cornwall?" she hissed at me through a set of tightly clenched false teeth. I knew that her false teeth were clenched because they didn't shift and clack around as they usually did when her temper was less inclement. The customary bits of white spit in the corners of her mouth were still there, though.

Hands shot up into the air from some of my fellow pupils who sat up at the front of the class. It was as if they were waving energetic goodbyes to someone or other. The front was where the clever ones were put. Resigned dunderheads like me were exiled to the back where we formed an appropriate coconut shy-like line of targets to be picked off at will by Mrs Morman for the encouragement of the others.

Once the initial show of hands by those in the know was complete, a few more hands came into play, although the latter rose both slowly and not without reluctance. It was a matter of timing, getting your hand up at the very instant that another pupil was being selected to provide an answer to the question of the moment. By this device, those of us who didn't know the answer were able to give (we thought) an impression that we could easily have answered if we had been the chosen ones.

In common with several others I learned from experience that it was folly to be too wise. An expression of willingness made all the difference between being singled out by a teacher for the purposes of general class entertainment or of being left alone at the back where ignorance was bliss.

Some teachers demonstrated every indication of obtaining

great personal pleasure out of regularly picking on specific pupils for the kind of focused ridicule that was sure to get a cheap laugh from the rest of the class. As a member of the ranks of the afflicted, I found that the counter was to play along as a straight foil to the teacher's comedic talent. I knew what I was, and the teacher, who could then continue to work under the delusion that she (or he) had the situation under control, could stand easy in the sure knowledge that her opinion of me was confirmed.

Such a teacher was Miss Phyllis White, better known as Polly, who taught me English (Language and Literature) at Sir James Smith's Grammar School at Camelford, which I went on to attend after I had left Port Isaac CP School as a result of passing the Eleven-Plus exam.

Polly was (probably) a little younger than she looked. At least, for her sake I hoped she was. She was quite tall, more or less slim and absolutely severe of dress, demeanour and attitude towards the pupils she taught. Polly was the kind of lady on whose feet sensible shoes were destined to be worn. Tightly drawn hair, thick-lensed spectacles and overly pink cheeks that all too often became flushed with combative fire completed her ensemble.

Polly appeared to entertain an aversion to me and take comfort from the same. I couldn't fathom out its root cause, but there must have been something about me that rubbed her up the wrong way, as I wasn't especially bad at the subject she taught. I didn't speak the language part of it particularly well, as my Port Isaac accent was one of broad dimensions, so perhaps that was it. Polly may simply not have liked Port Isaac people, which, if so, must only have been a result of jealousy because Polly herself didn't come from the best place in the world (or even the universe for that matter).

Polly jumped on my accent as if it were manna sent to her from heaven. She both mimicked it and mocked it. Stimulated by her attention, I was induced to involuntarily intensify its breadth

4

and so make matters worse. Accents hadn't counted for anything in the primary school at Port Isaac – we were even proud of the way we spoke; after all, that was a part of who and what we were. It defined us.

Under Polly's regularly needling machinations I slipped into maintaining a silent vigil in her classes, a prototypically low profile that, in the climate of the time, was considered by most brands of authority figures, not least Polly herself, as representative of dumb insolence.

I adopted a tightly shielded facial expression suggesting a sabre-like mind behind it being swung in glittering arcs in the search for an answer. The answer was in there, somewhere, merely evading contact with the blade. By this mute subterfuge Polly's attention could only be diverted elsewhere.

Throughout this ritual pantomime, the curious thing was that I knew many of the answers to Polly's questions but was unwilling to risk exposure to scorn by providing her with them. I whispered the answers to Pat ("Slim") Sleeman (from Tintagel, a much lesser place than Port Isaac) who shared a desk with me. Slim sometimes volunteered my answers to Polly, much to his credit with her and also with me.

I should have done reasonably well in the English exams set and marked by Polly at the end of each school year, but even though I knew in my heart that I had completed the set papers well enough to pass, the dismal marks that Polly awarded me invariably failed to reflect the fact. Eventually, the so-called O-level examinations came along. External examiners marked O-level papers. At O-level I somehow received the best grade of marks possible for English.

Polly was thereby furious with me at the commencement of the subsequent school year, but by then, not only was I no longer scheduled to be in her classes but I was also getting to be old enough not to give a bugger about things like that. I came from the best place in the world and Polly didn't, and "QED," as Miss

Violet Jones (known as "Jonesie") said in geometry lessons, the theorem was proved.

As to the identity of the capital of Cornwall, under Mrs Morman's figurative rule (or ruler), that was a question that set up a potentially much more tricky hurdle to surmount.

"Well?" Mrs Morman asked me yet again, "What is the capital of Cornwall?"

The two strokes of the wooden ruler had taught me that it wasn't the letter C. An association of "capital" with London thrust its masts into view above the dull horizon of my mind.

"Please Miss," I said, "is it London?"

"London? No, Cornwall, the capital of Cornwall! C-O-R-N-W-A-L-L."

I could have spelt Cornwall for her if she had asked me to do that.

I thought again.

"Please Miss, London."

"No, no, no! Hold out your hand."

Two more strokes of the ruler were delivered.

"Now, what is the capital of Cornwall?"

"I don't know Miss, but I think it's London!"

That did me no good either; however, it shifted Mrs Morman's attention to one of the eager hand wavers at the front of the class, who, naturally enough, was one of the girls.

"You tell us then!" said Mrs Morman to the girl, knowing that the girl knew whatever there was to know of the rote.

"Please Miss, Launceston because it used to be, Truro because it ought to be, and Bodmin because it is!"

Turning again to me, Mrs Morman said, "There! Now you tell me what the capital of Cornwall is!"

I didn't really care what Cornwall's capital used to be or should be, or even what it was. I had never been to Truro, and all I knew about it was that it had a Bishop that we had to pray for every

Sunday in church, and I hoped he was grateful to us even though I thought he probably wasn't.

Launceston (or "Lanson" as we pronounced it), was another place that I had yet to visit, though it was unlikely that I would ever want to. I had heard of Lanson jail of course. Everyone knew about Lanson jail, which must have made an exceptional sight since the expression "looking like Lanson jail" signified an ultimate state of squalid untidiness.

I had once been on a trip to Bodmin and hadn't thought much of what I saw. Bodmin was where a looney bin was located behind a threateningly high wall. Bodmin and the looney bin were irretrievably linked in my mind. My elders and betters, balking at my behaviour, regularly informed me, "You should be in Bodmin!" Since they were my elders and betters, it was not my prerogative to doubt them.

Out in the school playground the stock answer to any question as to what or where something or someone was when the pupil being asked didn't have a clue was, "Up Jack's ass in America!" I was pretty sure that Mrs Morman wouldn't have welcomed that home truth coming from me.

London, however, was a capital. I had seen pictures of parts of London so I was to that extent reliably informed. London was a much better choice for the capital of Cornwall than any of the three ritually chanted options that Mrs Morman liked so much, and I was ready to go down defending London's right.

Without hesitation I replied once more, "Please Miss, London!"

The one-foot long wooden ruler rose and fell with consummate accuracy.

As an additional penalty adding insult to injury I was required to remain in the classroom at playtime, where I had to write out the name of the capital of Cornwall, in the gospel according to Mrs Morman, a total of fifty times in my abortively self-addressed exercise book.

I took my pen in hand, dipped it in the inkwell and wrote across the top of a clean page, "and the cabin boy pissed in the captain's eye", for no other reason than, backed by a sense of outrage, it simply seemed to be the right thing to do at the time.

It took no more than the blink of an eye for a feeling of the utmost horror at this consequence to replace the satisfaction of the impulse that caused it. I flicked blots of ink at the offending assertion of the cabin boy's misdemeanour with the intention of covering it over, but I must have pressed too heavily with the pen-nib when I wrote the damning statement, as blots of ink alone formed an ineffective mask to my penmanship. Desperate for a solution I lifted the inkwell out of its hole and poured its contents over the incriminating page. That worked far too well as the overflow of ink swamped more than a few innocently clean pages of the exercise book.

Mrs Morman was predictably incandescent. She asked me in strident tones if I thought that paper grew on trees. Actually, I thought that that was where paper did grow, because she once told us that it did, but discretion dictated that it might not be wise of me to remind her.

The question of seeking an identity for the capital of Cornwall, which I accepted wasn't Port Isaac, while continuing to ponder on London as being the most likely city, gave me a first great experience of involvement in a quiz coupled with the unpleasant aftermath of giving what the questioner believed to be the wrong answer. It was just as well that the experience was realised in the best place in the world, where as a rule I never came to be afflicted with any more or any less than I justly deserved.

It wasn't always easy to be right. When I was presented with a question, either I knew the answer or I didn't, and in the case of the capital of Cornwall it appeared that I didn't, even when I knew that I did. Yes, the capital of Cornwall was London, because it had to be.

—

Of course in Port Isaac we were by no means strangers to quizzes. There were some terrific quiz programmes on the wireless that we listened to every week without fail. The philosophy behind such quizzes was that a contestant was asked a question, and if he or she got the answer right a reward would be forthcoming. That kind of thing never seemed to happen at school.

In the perennially popular *Have a Go!* programme presented on the wireless by Mr Wilfred Pickles, contestants were more or less given the answers to questions by virtue of Wilfred's prompting, so that when Wilfred declared, "Give 'em the money, Barney!" Mr Barney Colehan was able to hand over a quid or so of winnings in good conscience.

Wilfred presented "the people to the people" in "a spot of homely fun", broadcast live from village halls all around the British Isles. He specialised in interviewing a succession of rustic hayseeds in a manner that it would be unfair not to describe as somewhat patronising. Wilfred didn't elicit answers with the aid of a one-foot ruler, although given the astounding wooden-headedness of certain of his interviewees, the thought of doing so may well have crossed his mind.

Although Wilfred never brought *Have a Go!* to the Port Isaac Temperance Hall, a version of the programme once took place on the stage of that institution, with Mrs Joe Knight taking the role of Wilfred. She gave a performance of such consummate bravura that anyone who didn't know that it was Mrs Knight up there could easily have believed that Wilfred had appeared in person.

———

*Ask me Another* was a rather more serious wireless quiz programme presented by Mr Franklin Engelman, known as "Jingle". Like Wilfred, Jingle also came *Down Your Way* to undertake local interviews.

*Ask me Another* demonstrated that those who took part in competitive quizzes did not have to have village idiot pretensions in order to provide entertainment for half an hour to rural

9

audiences whose members by and large knew the answer to at least one question per programme.

———

*Top of the Form* was a knockout quiz competition between schools, broadcast usually in the early evening on Sundays. Two schools took part in each programme. The teams consisted of four members respectively drawn from four separate forms in each school. The team captains were invariably sixth-formers. It seemed, to judge from the accents of the contestants, that Cornish grammar schools were forever destined to be conspicuous by their absence as programme contestants.

For many of us who listened, the real fun of *Top of the Form* was derived from the utterly po-faced seriousness in which the contest was played out, deadpan quality being as common to the presenters as to the team members. The fun of the show emanated from there being no humour in it at all.

*Top of the Form* was at its best when a question was posed that either couldn't be answered or was answered wrongly. A sharp intake of cumulative breath hissed over the airwaves from outrageously partisan school audiences, inclusive of the grimly quailing teachers in the front row who bore the responsibility for putting such dunces on the air. To our great glee we knew that the latter were going to be given stick by the former and we could relate to that only too well.

———

A number of intrepid teachers once organised a quiz evening with *Top of the Form* overtones at Sir James Smith's Grammar School, to which so many parents came that they formed the overwhelming bulk of the audience. The underlying sentiment to the event seemed to be that Sir James's had never got to be wireless material purely because of an oversight by the BBC.

Somehow, and I would have hated to be asked how, I was selected as a member of one of the quiz teams. We arrayed ourselves on a stage, and in the course of the event in front of a packed auditorium, I fielded three questions and considered myself fortunate that it was only three and no more.

The first question to come my way called for me to name the author of *Paradise Lost*. In all my associations with Polly and the marvels of English Literature I had never heard of that one, to the extent that the only thing I was certain of was that the author of the work, whatever it was, didn't come from Port Isaac. If he did, I would have heard of him all right.

As often as not the answer to literary questions on *Top of the Form* was that "Shakespeare wrote it". I had heard of Shakespeare, so I gave his name as an answer. A murmur, rippling on its fringes with poorly suppressed laughter (some of which assuredly emanated from the direction of Polly), almost (but not quite) drowned out the dulcet tones of the quizmaster, Mr Williams, advising me that I was wrong. The question was passed to another team and to my total lack of surprise they got it right.

The next question I got was, "What is Hansard?" That was more like it. I knew the answer, as one of the attributes of the school's library collection was a few copies of that august publication, as tattered and as ancient as they were unread by any pupil that I ever knew of. My answer, to the effect that "Hansard" recorded the "goings on" of Parliament, was repeated by the quizmaster for the delectation of an audience which on that occasion showed little reticence to disguise its amusement.

My third and blessedly final question asked me to define the word "censor". Mr Williams spelt the word out for me, letter by letter. As one who religiously attended the cinema at the Port Isaac Rivoli every Friday night I was nothing if not familiar with the screened certification of the British Board of Film Censors, which was one of the essential precursors to the stupefying succession of listed names that had to be endured before a film could start. I knew what a censor was, although I wasn't sure what he did other than that he was really lucky to be able to see so many films.

I knew what a censer was as well. There was one hanging suspended from the roof directly over the entry to the altar sanctuary in St Peter's Church. I can't say that I ever saw the St Peter's censer used, but it was there, the vicar had explained what it was, and that was good enough for me.

The feeling grew in me that Mr Williams had asked me a catch question, no doubt hoping that my answer would go for the wrong option. I decided not to disappoint him.

There were great precedents for making a deliberate mistake. Mr Ronnie Waldman, the presenter of "Puzzle Corner", during *Henry Hall's Guest Night* on the wireless on Saturday nights was the master of the deliberate mistake technique. Ronnie always put a deliberate mistake in his show and attracted a huge listening audience eager to spot it before, at the end, he told us what it was.

For my answer, I defined what a censer was. The audience delivered a round of appreciative guffaws tempered with a few hoots of derision. The members of my team maintained a discreet silence.

When the show was over, Jonesie came to see me to commiserate, not so much for my one out of three score, but rather to judge my reaction to an audience scoffing at me. Jonesie told me that a few parents had described me as "that poor boy, with so many people laughing at him". She said, "I told them, don't worry about him. He doesn't mind. He likes it! And I'm right, aren't I?"

And she was.

———

I came from the best place in the world. No matter what the audience thought of me, they couldn't take that away. They were the ones who needed to worry, not me.

Port Isaac was going to live for ever as the best place in the world. Just as, in my mind, London was the undisputed capital of Cornwall.

# 2

# The Parish and Divers of its Works

THERE WAS NEVER any argument coming from any of the Port Isaac boys as to where the precise position of the northern boundary of the parish of St Endellion (which contained the Best Place in the World) actually lay.

The location of that northern boundary was very obvious to all of us. It wove a jaggedly scenic course along the coast of Port Isaac Bay all the way from Port Quin in the west to Barrett's Awn in the east, the latter point of reference shoving its toes into the sea a mile or so up above Port Gaverne.

Punctuated by points, headlands, coves, rocks, stretches of foreshore and a multitude of wave worn indentations, the coast-clamped sector of the parish boundary ran, in an average sense, pretty much from east to west.

Mind you, there was a view held by more than a few of our elders (and self-appointed betters), not least among the ranks of whom was an odoriferous complement of opinionated fishermen,

13

that the real northern boundary of St Endellion parish wasn't defined as much by surf-girt cliffs as it was by what they referred to as a "three-mile limit" lying somewhere out at sea. One or two of the fishermen claimed to have reached and breached the three-mile out to sea limit, and I placed as much credence in that assertion as I did in anything else that any fisherman told me.

Looking out to sea, it was deceptively difficult to determine distance. Tintagel Head was all of eight miles away from Port Isaac, lying diagonally across the Bay to the northeast, but it always seemed as if it was a lot closer than that. Out on the impossibly distant horizon, where the sea merged with the sky, and squalls swept along the top of their barely perceptible seam looking like bruised curtains, grey wraiths moved slowly to and fro. These hull-down ships headed to ports of call that we had never heard about and carried cargoes of strange things whose identity we couldn't even hazard a guess at.

The horizon must have been a long way out past the three-mile limit. It could easily have marked the edge of time and existence. A fisherman told me that it did. He said that no Port Isaac fishing boat had managed to reach the horizon yet, and he doubted that one ever would.

Stretching between the coast of the Bay and the horizon was the watery part of the one World we knew. Whether all of that great expanse of sea belonged to St Endellion parish or not was an issue on which most of us were supremely indifferent.

The solid part of the same one World sprawled away inland behind us, dissected by valleys and crowned with fields. The Best Place in the World was at its beating heart. The circuitous boundary enclosing St Endellion parish contained all that we boys knew on earth and all that we needed to know.

In my immediate circle of friends there weren't many who would have been able to pick out the location of the parish boundary on a map, even if their lives depended on it. Port Isaac people in general, including more members of the Council that purported to run the parish affairs than any one of their stick-in-the-mud deferred decisions could be shaken at, didn't tend to have much of a feeling for maps almost as a matter of principle.

The fact of the matter was that, apart from a smattering of bluff and ruddy farmers who owned fields hedging our parish boundary, or perhaps whose land spread over into the contiguous parishes of St Teath or St Kew or St Minver, there was no-one much who dwelled anywhere in the parish of St Endellion who was prepared to tax his or her mind unduly on either where it began or where it ended.

It was enough for us just to know, in the unlikely event that it would ever be necessary to seek it out, that there was a parish boundary hanging around somewhere.

———

The parish of St Endellion derived its appellation from an ancient church of the same name. The church, more formally known as the Collegiate Church of St Endelienta, was situated on a strategic height of land a couple of miles inland from Port Isaac. It was unimaginably old, constructed almost in its entirety from remotely quarried grey granite on which great colonies of orange-yellow lichen had commenced forming a creeping residential crust many centuries ago.

The old church seemed to have served its sphere of influence since time began. It still did, for that matter, in spite of the major diminution in its once captive congregation that occurred when St Peter's church was constructed down in Port Isaac during the 1870s' heyday of Queen Victoria's reign.

Notwithstanding the local sustenance that St Peter's provided for its stalwart if fading flock of churchgoers, most Port Isaac residents, including those with allegiance to the chapel, went "up to St Endellion" eventually, there to rest for ever in the crowded graveyard surrounding the church in the company of departed friends (real and imagined), sworn enemies (always genuine) and family members (whose role as either friends or enemies was open to debate).

The ranks of memorials standing in St Endellion's churchyard, whether they were hewn from granite or formed by slabs of Delabole slate, or (for those who could afford it) erected in marble, or (for those who couldn't afford stone) carved from timber, bore incised gilded or leaded names identifying the subject lying six feet vertically beneath. On certain of the headstones an epitaph and the alleged date of birth and certain date of death of the subject accompanied the name.

The broad rule governing such epitaphs appeared to be that the floweriest of them all were dedicated to the decease of those who had been most despised by their family members in life.

———

From the lip of the cliff up at Barrett's Awn, where the coast-fixed stretch of the parish boundary achieved its eastern limit, the self-same boundary dodged inland on a southeast heading for about a mile. In the course of this inland stretch, the boundary intersected, and possibly even generated, the sole jog in the minor road linking Port Gaverne with China Downs (the title accorded to a crossroads where a desolate-looking collection of small cottages lay scattered about) on the main Delabole to Wadebridge road.

The cited main road was blessed with an official number designation of B3314. The B status implied a road of a rather superior type. Two motorcars proceeding in opposing directions could pass by each other on a B road without the need for the driver of one of the two to be forced to make a grudging show of pulling his vehicle into a gateway to let the other take triumphant precedence.

The run of the parish boundary inland from Barrett's Awn eventually intersected the B3314 about half way between the hamlet of Pendoggett (referred to by far too many who knew of it as "Penny Dog Shit") up at the head of the Port Gaverne valley, and a right-hand turn-off leading to the Best Place in the World via Poltreworgey Hill and Trewetha Lane.

Proximally to its encounter with the B3314, the parish boundary doubled back to the southwest and passed just to the south of a height of land on which Treore farmhouse was prominent. In doing so it denied, much to the sorrow of Port Isaac's devotees of variety in ale, the capture of Pendoggett by St Endellion parish, since such a conquest would have brought along the prize of Pendoggett's famous "free house" pub named the "Cornish Arms".

***

Although Treore farmhouse was also outside the clutches of St Endellion parish, a good deal of the lands of Treore Farm, one of the larger holdings of the district, did not escape so easily. Treore's fields sprawled across to the coastline adjoining Bounds Cliff and Barrett's Awn, and took in a great swathe of the middle and upper Port Gaverne valley.

Down in the Port Gaverne valley below Treore farmhouse, the once extensive workings of a defunct mine named Wheal Treore were located. This undoubted property of St Endellion parish included the standing ruins of a beam engine house, a great (if tottering) spike of a chimney and an associated course of flue.

The flue was in a precarious state. It was built from rough stones and mortar, softly crumbling and held together by no more than a surrounding smother of brambles. It made a secret tunnel sufficiently unblocked for us to crawl through, cosy on a blustery rain-edged day, and cool in the heat of summer.

Wheal Treore was famed as one of only a very few of Cornwall's legion of mines from which gold was alleged to have been won. It was said that it was still possible to pan for grains and flakes of gold on the gravelled bottom of the Port Gaverne valley downstream from Wheal Treore. I never chanced my hand at gold panning, and if anyone else did they weren't giving it a go at any time that I walked up or down the valley.

As in all cases where rumours of gold were rife, the truth was an elusive commodity. According to my Gran Eleanor Creighton there were, amongst the more elderly of Port Isaac residents, "some" who claimed to have seen and even handled Wheal Treore vein specimens featuring visible gold. ("Some" was a word that Gran normally invoked with respect to enumerating people when her vague intention was to convey a count of at least nine or ten.) The identities of the lucky gold handlers were forever shrouded in mystery.

The likelihood of as much as a mote of Wheal Treore gold dust existing in any eye (or brother's eye) in Port Isaac was, I thought, safe to ignore. The genuine gold of the Port Gaverne valley bottoms was seasonally vested in primroses and irises, buttercups, celandines and the daffodils down in Mr Jack Short's withy garden.

Elusive to the touch or not, any gold of Wheal Treore was definitely associated with antimony minerals, the stark grey acicular fans of which blotched undulate veins of otherwise bland white quartz. The dominant antimony mineral of the parish was named jamesonite. I knew because I looked it up in one of Miss Smythe's books at school. Jamesonite was the mineral of interest for a broad scatter of mines (not one of which was active any more) around St Endellion parish.

On the side of the Port Gaverne valley directly across from Wheal Treore I once found several pieces of rock containing jamesonite strewn around on open ground at the edge of a wide brake of gorse bushes. The pieces glinted in gunmetal grey where they were freshly broken, and they felt heavy in my hand. They had been exhumed by no more complicated an expedient than that of the farmer who owned the underlying land (part of Bodannon Farm) having had an unsuccessful crack at digging out a foxes' den.

The then owner of Bodannon Farm was Mr Jack Chapman. Terry ("Tibby") Thomas, one of my friends who knew Jack well, called him "Flacky Jack". Jack's Bodannon farmhouse and adjoining barns stood against the left-hand side of Trewetha Lane on the way up to Colstanton corner and Poltreworgy from Trewetha. The buildings were, on the strength of their appearance, rather less than adequately cared for.

———

In spite of once widespread mining activity, the parish of St Endellion wasn't especially celebrated as a former mining district. The miners from long ago (known as the "old men") were always ready to apply a pick and shovel to any showing of rock that looked interesting – after all, Cornwall and mining activity were inseparably united. The old men missed very little in the way of opportunity, although on overall balance they probably gained very little as well.

In St Endellion parish, testaments to the old men's failed enterprise were vested in a few dark-mouthed adits exposed on the faces of raw cliffs and in a slightly larger number of derelict shafts and mining trials further inland, among which Wheal Treore was by no means the least.

Many defunct works, including adits, trenches, cuttings and shafts, were secreted under cover of trees, bushes and blackthorn thickets that had burgeoned mightily during the many years since the abandonments. Such excavations were so well hidden that it was almost (but fortunately not quite) necessary to fall into them in order to know where they were.

I read (yet again in Miss Smythe's useful book) that a hundred years ago at the Wheal Boys mine near Trewetha, a sharp-eyed mineralogist identified a copper mineral that (according to him) was as yet unknown to science. Of course, the old men of Wheal Boys had undoubtedly known about the copper mineral a long time before the mineralogist arrived on the scene. They called it "wheel glance" in a tribute to the cog-like edges that distinguished its crystalline form. According to the book, the "new" mineral was formally named "bournonite", although alternatively, and much more acceptably, with its crystalline clusters adding lustre to the parish in which it was discovered, it acquired the old men's name of "endellionite".

One of the consequences of our regular cliff-ranging activities along the coast of the Bay was that we located the portals of some abandoned adits. With due care we were able to get into one or two of them. Entering without due care accounted for our gaining access to a couple of others. The best of the adits ("best" being related to the extent to which they could be penetrated), were respectively located high up on the east side of Kellan Head near Port Quin, and way down towards the foot of Crowser cove around from Pine Awn.

On the Shillingstones cliffs that sheered away in between Port Isaac and Port Gaverne down below the bastion occupied by Port Isaac's New Coastguard Station, there was a tiered stack of three accessible adits set one above the other. A column of rudimentary steps hewn into the cliff linked the trio of portals, which faced directly out across the Bay looking towards Tintagel Head.

The Shillingstones adits were driven on the lie of a broad quartz vein. Each was fifty yards or so long. Since they were tacitly held to be the private preserve of the two Vagges boys, Freddie and Michael, sons of the coastguard Mr "Taffy" Vagges, third parties were deterred from visiting the adits on the grounds that it might be detrimental to their well-being if they did.

Freddie and Michael toiled regularly at the three adit faces in the manner of the old men, prising tiny cubes of iron pyrites from the slaty rocks bordering the quartz vein. They stored the cubes in empty matchboxes and were always happy to produce examples from their pockets to display the fruits of their industry to anyone who was interested.

Along the whole line of sea-slivered cliffs that swept up from Port Gaverne to Barrett's Awn and beyond, the one and only cliff adit that we knew of opened to daylight low down on the steep

20

descent to Tartar Cove. The Tartar adit was supposed to be the longest ever driven in St Endellion parish in search of antimony minerals, but unfortunately a roof fall not far inside its portal ensured that its reputation would forever remain an untested quantity as far as we were concerned.

Another tunnel, commencing from an entry high up and well out of the reach of high tide at the inner recess of a long, dark, tight and eternally wet streaming cave located just inside the eastern breakwater of Port Isaac harbour, stretched its subterranean fastness deep down beneath an unsuspecting upper Fore Street. Natural cliff-side caves, of which the coast had no lack, were colloquially known as "gugs". The cited gug-extending tunnel went on to terminate deep down under Mine Pit Corner on Back Hill, where one of the two village water pumps was sited.

It was rumoured that smugglers once used this tunnel. There was reckoned to be a secret passage from its end connecting through to the Old Vicarage in lower Trewetha Lane. The Old Vicarage was no more than a good stone's throw away from Mine Pit Corner.

I once managed to get boosted and bunked up to gain entry to the tunnel together with my very close friends Roger Keat and Michael ("Eyesnot") Bate. Our objective was to investigate the tunnel's secret passage. Assisted by candlelight, we seemed to straggle in a very long way before we were confronted by a blockage which put paid to any more progress. If there was a secret passage anywhere, it must have lain behind the blockage. We found nothing, unless the copious quantity of ochreous slime that transferred itself from the tunnel walls to our clothes was taken into account.

Before its collar was closed off by baulks of timber, a vertical shaft dropping down to that tunnel was open to the sky about half way up on the steep flank of Back Hill directly across from Mine Pit Corner. The shaft collar was thereby incidentally located immediately adjacent to the front pathway leading from Back Hill to St Peter's church.

St Peter's Sunday School pupils were expressly forbidden, by vicar and parents alike, to go anywhere near the timber capping to the collar of the shaft. The grounds for the admonition were no doubt rooted in clerical doubts about the security of the timbering – not that such instructions made any difference to any Sunday School pupil desperate to endow a Sunday afternoon with the kind of excitement that was certain to be denied in the confines of the church. In common with a number of my fellow Sunday School sufferers, I felt that there was no point in the existence of a covered shaft collar if it couldn't be jumped up and down on to test its resistance to collapse.

We gained comfort from knowing that quite a few of the derelict mine shafts of St Endellion parish were fortunately not closed over in the same way. Occasionally a token fence bearing a slack strand of rusty barbed wire might surround one or other of them, but no amount of barbed wire could ever offer an obstacle to those of us who were determined to pass. The open shafts were darkly beckoning pits shrouded in dread, furred around their tops with lank and dripping moss, and embellished on the way down with an occasional fern rooted on a protrusion of rock where a little wind-lifted soil had dropped and accumulated.

Hawthorn trees stretched across some of the open shafts and offered a home for magpies intent on weaving twig-roofed nests into the fabric of the thorn thicket. Such nests were easily spotted, but when it came to getting a hand into them their proximal location above the jaws of doom rendered them inviolate.

Whenever we stood at the edge of an open mine shaft our ritual was to heave into the shaft the biggest and heaviest available stone that we could find in the immediate vicinity. This practice signified much more than a simple attempt to plumb the mysteriously fearful depths. It was as if the tossed stone reassured us that we were safe in the light at the top of a pit of darkness. The trajectories of the falling stones traced lines from the known to the unknown, separating the secure from the potential nightmare.

Legend had it that all manner of things, some mentionable, some not, had been discarded into these shafts at one time or another. The horror we felt about the prospect of actually falling into one of the shafts generated vivid flights of imagination. None of us wanted to think about what might be waiting for us down at the bottom.

Testing the depths of a shaft with a stone gave us a fleeting moment to believe that whatever was down at the bottom of the shaft belonged to the world we knew. At least it did until the stone splashed into water. The water was all right. It was what could be in or under the water that was not.

Sometimes a stone seemed to fall in a shaft for such a long time that we thought it might have been swallowed up. Then a faint splash (or thump) rising from the void signified the end of descent, at the sound of which those of us craning our ears up at the collar could breathe out again. We liked it best of all when a big stone crashed and rebounded against the wall from side to side, the echoes becoming fainter and fainter until yet again the hint of a splash rose from the deep pit.

Now and then a stone thrown into an open shaft might bring up a wing-clattering pair of woodpigeons, disturbed while roosting on either a ledge or the projecting remnants of a rotting chunk of shaft timber. Once, from out of a shaft up at the top of the Colstanton branch of the Port Isaac valley, a tawny owl rose like a ghost and wafted off down the valley in silent flight, suggesting total contempt for our stone-tossing activities.

The portal of the Crowser cove adit drooled a treacly, ochre-stained seep down towards a great jumble of boulders at the head of the coarsely shingled beach below. Ochre and tunnels, we thought, went hand in hand. Gleaming mirrors of fawn-coloured siderite could be cleaved from chunks of rock in the spoil piles that we found littered around at the top of the seep. The mouth of the portal was festooned with a beard of dripping moss. Inside the portal the air was cool, and the floor was occupied by standing water a foot deep, motionless and icily clear. The water was so transparent that it seemed to possess no interface with the air. A short stub of drift forked off to the left of the tunnel not far in from the portal.

On the first occasion that I ventured into the Crowser adit I was with the aforementioned Roger, Sidney ("Sid") Pluckrose, and Tony "Bollicks" Robinson. We illuminated the way with purloined candles. Bollicks, as the only one among us wearing a pair of sea boots, took the lead. Silt-laden clouds billowed around the soles of his sea boots as he edged forward gingerly, hoping against faint hope that the rippling water would not spill over his boot tops.

Sea boots, pronounced as a single unaccented word "seaboots", were made of durable rubber. Although they bore a similar name to the thigh-high wader type of boot that the fishermen favoured for getting into Long Pool down in the harbour where their crab and lobster store pots were kept, the kind of sea boots that boys wore reached only to the knee.

Since I didn't own a pair of sea boots, the consideration of boot height didn't apply to me. My adit entry options, shared as they were with Roger and Sid, were either to forge ahead in hobnailed leather boots and get my feet wet, or take my boots off and go barefoot. We all decided to get our boots and socks wet. Later on, before we went home, we could wash our footwear in the clean water of the Trefreock (known as "Freak") valley stream back at Pine Awn.

Some thirty yards or so into the Crowser adit, the candlelit water ahead of us seemed to take on a dark and menacing glint. The slow billows of displaced silt spreading ahead of Bollicks' feet slumped into a dark patch of water, where the coarser particles drifted in the kind of lazy rocking motion they always took when heading for the deep. We hauled Bollicks back just in time to save him from stepping into a flooded hole (a winze) in the adit floor.

Looking into the water-filled winze we saw the shadowy teeth of broken timbers, furred by rot and ancient sediment but still ripe with the eager ability, untouched by time, to eat us up. Glowering below the timbers were black-browed depths into which Bollicks only just escaped from sinking to meet whatever it was that might be down there waiting for him.

———

Not far inland from Crowser cove as the crow — or, reflecting the cliff-girt location, the more likely resident raven — could fly, an abandoned slate quarry, cut into the upper rim of the Freak valley, had essentially reverted to nature. The quarry, which was neither large enough to repel us nor small enough to be ignored, was flooded up to its outer lip, in common with the Crowser adit winze.

Quantities of slate taken from the quarry by the old men would almost certainly have been used to construct some of the buildings of Roscarrock (known as "Skarrick") Farm. These buildings were huddled together for protection just over the crest of a rolling field stretching above the quarry, from which vantage point they were well within sight of Port Quin. A disused track along a rough cutting, sublimely invaded by bracken and seasonal primroses and bluebells, angled gently up to the quarry from Pine Awn.

The back wall of the quarry rose sheer above the level of floodwater. It was decorated with a palette of dull lichen. Its narrow ledges bristled with spiky grass, an occasional red campion and the odd burst of rogue stinging nettles. Elder and blackthorn thickets, sporadically pierced through by wind-stunted ash trees on the downhill side, formed a tangled canopy hemming the quarry in.

The pond of water in the quarry was roughly circular in shape and had a diameter of about fifty feet. Access to the edge of the pond was obtained by dint of our wriggling along a prickly pathway twisting through the blackthorn. Magpies and pigeons made themselves at home in the thicket. Overall, it offered a sombre prospect to contemplate. When we were in the quarry and beside the pond we spoke in the sort of subdued tones that were generally reserved for attendance at church.

The surface of the pond was covered with a bright green carpet cumulated from a myriad of tiny round scales of waterweed. The green cover hid the underlying water so well that it gave the impression of a smooth flat skin that could be walked on by anyone of us able to summon up the sort of faith that the vicar insisted we had, but about which we were never too sure. We knew that Jesus could have walked across the pond, but we imagined that even He might have had some misgivings about his chances on that surface.

When a stone was thrown into the pond, the green skin split open, generating a crooked starburst of radial cracks from the point of impact. The cracks exposed dark water in which not a single ripple moved. They then closed slowly, silently and insidiously, rendering the weed-sealed surface entire again.

In the spring time so many frogs lived in the pond that it was impossible for us even to guess how many there were, let alone to count them. We were sure there were thousands and thousands of them. Not for nothing had the pond become familiarly known as "Frog Pool". Weed-draped frogs swarmed at the pond's edge, croaking and chiming, many on their own and many more doubled up on piggyback. Glutinous strings and necklaces of frogspawn thickened the watery brew into a tapioca-like mess. It was easy to pluck frogs from Frog Pool at will, wondering all the time not only where they had come from but also where they were planning to go next.

Every year, in common with my friends, I filled a jam jar with frogspawn from Frog Pool and took it home. There, the spawn was poured into a bigger water-filled container, in which it was eagerly examined each day as the little black dots got bigger and bigger and transformed themselves into wriggling tadpoles that seemed to adopt an unfortunate habit of wanting to eat each other up. Tadpoles that managed to survive the cannibalistic rites of passage sprouted legs and began to develop into frogs. For all that, I didn't know of a single homegrown frog that made it all the way to maturity.

Roger told me that he had it on good authority from his Aunt Mary Bate that Frog Pool was bottomless. According to her, anyone who fell into Frog Pool would sink like a stone. The victim would be denied the privilege of surfacing three times before drowning. The menace of the green weed cover was obvious enough. The stillness of the underlying black water through which little light penetrated provided an additional sense of foreboding.

Aunt Mary, who was ideally qualified to stand as a candidate for the office of Port Isaac's doyenne of gossip (should such an office come to be established), was a glorious fund of macabre information. She told Roger as an absolute certainty that the corpse of any luckless person who tumbled into Frog Pool would subsequently be found rolling out in the sea off Pine Awn a few days later. That showed how bottomless Frog Pool was.

Aunt Mary's definitive tale of grisly woe involved a case of premature burial up at St Endellion. She told us that she once witnessed the opening of an exhumed coffin. In the well of the coffin she said, the skeletal fingers of its unfortunate occupant were seen to be hooked around one of the long nails that had once helped to hold the lid down. The underside of the lid was clawed to splinters as the result of a desperate but fruitless attempt of its occupant to break out following a post-interment revival. With such wholesome tales did Aunt Mary regale our all too willing ears.

I imagined that Aunt Mary could easily have enlightened us as to the identity of certain of the items tossed into abandoned shafts. We had a go at pressing her, but it seemed that there were some things that even Aunt Mary seemed to think it was best for us not to know about.

---

Meanwhile, following a failed attempt to capture Pendoggett, not only had the boundary of St Endellion parish met with the B3314 but it also seemed keen to hold on to that association. Consequently, the boundary followed the wispy-grassed crown of the B3314 with the single-minded determination of a steeplechaser marking the strategic landmark of St Endellion church tower as a target.

Having passed the Poltreworgey turnoff, the parish boundary continued along the B3314 (without as much as a murmur) to cover a lengthy downhill stretch prior to reaching a junction with a narrow track on the left known as Gravelin's Lane. That good lane fell away through a stunted avenue of ancient beech trees down towards St Kew and other foreign parts.

To the right of this junction, the Port Isaac valley, the head of which was dominated by the castellated Tresungers farmhouse, commenced its green-folded course towards the harbour and the sea.

Across an open meadow lying to the left of Gravelin's Lane the great woods of Treharrock Manor plumped up like the front of a rolling green tidal wave, alive with rooks. The clamour from the multitudinous residents of the rookery ripped the air to shreds. The rooks lifted in cawing armies to greet the approach of strangers. They dropped into stubbled fields where they formed up in organised mobs, ready for anything.

---

As the B3314 got ready for its final approach to St Endellion, a grey and lonely cottage, accessible only by taking an eternally muddy-footed track half-swamped by overgrowth from its sides, stood sentinel-like on the edge of a field off to the right. The cottage was a distant outbuilding of Pennant Farm. In part it was a living expression of the largesse of Mr Joe Dawe, the Pennant farmer, in providing family shelter for one of his farm labourers.

The outer walls of the cottage were tightly shod in overlapping slates. The cottage possessed two floors. It would have been a safe bet that its interior contained no more than the equivalent number of rooms. In its exposed location, unprotected by any wind-breaking tree, the cottage was a prime target for each and every raging gale that poured in from the ocean through the funnel of the Port Isaac valley.

A numerically significant family named Thomas lived, presumably in the manner of sardines, in the little cottage. The head of the family, Mr Thomas, laboured on the land for his employer Joe. Mr Thomas's wife laboured in the home. Mr and Mrs Thomas were rarely seen in public.

I was never quite certain of precisely how many Thomas children there were. If there weren't enough of them to make a football team, there must have been nearly enough. Those among them who had already attained the statutory age attended the primary school down in Port Isaac.

My own clothes were patched, darned and not infrequently "out to hass and out to helbow" as my mother's saying went, but even so, in comparison with the attire exhibited by the Thomas children, my outfits might have been seen as reasonably princely. The Thomases were an assortment of boys and girls whose current prospects were somewhat blunted by the fell clutch of circumstance.

Of the Thomases who went to school, the eldest was Mabel. In age-declining order after Mabel came Charlie (who was about my age), and then Virginia, Priam and Samuel. Mrs Thomas was occupied in generating several others in an annual sequence. Cast-off clothes passed down the line from top to bottom, gaining in tattiness as they descended.

Virginia, known as Ginny, had a compulsive habit, alarming to anyone who wasn't used to it, of clapping her elbows to her hips and performing a vigorous wriggle as she endeavoured to prevent her knickers, previously worn by Mabel among others, from proceeding in the direction of her ankles.

The favoured colours for girls' knickers were black and navy blue. They were dark colours selected in accordance with a time-honoured tradition that dark coloured clothes didn't need washing so often as they didn't show the dirt in the way that lighter colours did. All three apertures of a pair of knickers featured a sewn-in ring of elastic. Most girls wore knickers that were generally, but not always, more tightly constrained around the waist than were Ginny's.

When they skipped ropes, the girls tucked their frocks up into the elasticised legs of their knickers for ease of movement. As knicker elastic got older, its ability to fight the force of gravity waned. In a uniform edition with the book *The Broken Window* by Eva Brick, it was understood that *Coming Down* by Lucy Lastic was also available on the shelves of the travelling library van that turned up across from Mrs Lynwood Cowling's chemist's shop in Fore Street once a week without fail.

Charlie was as thin as a parish councillor's promise and as light as seeds from a dandelion clock – so much so that he was nicknamed "Shadow". He was likeable and trustworthy, perhaps not desperately bright, but always steady. Shadow's disposition was even. He could be relied on, and was in heavy demand by us for his climbing skills, as much in the autumn when conkers were ripe for dislodging from the ends of perilously high pendant branches as in the spring time when there were crows' nests to be got at up at the top of tall and bendy trees that swayed in the wind.

In the whole compass of St Endellion parish there were only two conker trees that we knew of. One of these spread its boughs over a fair part of the yard in front of Mr Bob May's Archer farmhouse at Trewetha, where its fruits were to all intents and purposes inviolate. Mr Bob May's son Robert (also known as Bob) was a hard-as-nails boy, and we knew that if we even thought about raiding the Archer Farm conker tree, young Bob would be down on us like a ton of bricks. I had had sufficient personal experience of his forceful school playground ministrations in the past not to want any more of the same if it could be avoided.

The second conker tree was located a little way up into the Port Quin valley in the centre of a sloping wood. It was a more straightforward target and, as such, was to be forever blessed.

Regardless of the absolute inevitability that all of the conkers on any conker tree would ultimately fall to the ground for collection by the sharper eyed and more discerning among us (on a first-come first-served basis), custom decreed that acquiring conkers was best assured by picking them directly from the trees. Up in a tree, conkers were alluringly dangling prizes to be won and shared among the group of seekers.

The conker acquisition imperative called for us to move with much more despatch than the opposition. The advantage that freshly picked conkers brought along was vested in promoting the earliest possible start to the conker season. The inherent problem was that most conkers up in the tree swung like the glass balls placed on the extremities of Christmas-tree branches. If a normally weighted boy attempted to reach these prickly appendages, the law of gravity could take hold of him, with precipitate consequences similar to those attending the state of Ginny's knickers.

However, we had the benefit of Shadow, who defied standard weight conventions. Shadow, oblivious to peril, could negotiate his way out along branches that looked as skinny as himself, from where he would either shake off the precious conkers or pick and drop them down to the rest of us waiting below.

Conker season was an annual event of great importance. The earliest conker was figuratively worth its weight in gold. It was a currency exchangeable for a range of marketable items, inclusive of comics, sweets, marbles and, not least, the granting of favours.

Three varieties of conkers featured in the order of play. The most abundant of the three was a rounded or ovoid type, heavy and solid. It grew as the sole filling of a thorny green carapace.

A more delicate variety of conker was the "cheese cutter". Cheese cutters were twinned in a single shell, making two portions (not necessarily identical) of a sphere, each one characterised by a flat face equipped with a sharp outer edge.

The third kind of conker – whether ovoid or of cheese-cutter shape made no difference – was one saved over from the previous year's crop. There were admittedly not very many of those in play.

When it did appear, a last-year's conker, toughened by time, was usually lightly oiled to provide it with an aspect of relative youth. Such conkers gave their owners an unfair (and totally against the rules) edge over their opponents in a contest. Unfortunately for the owner of a last-year's conker, the wrinkles on its skin were generally distinctive enough to alert an opponent to the intended subterfuge.

A venerable conker might also be lightly baked to further improve its impact qualities. On the other hand, age and baking could accentuate brittleness, and too much of the latter quality offered no edge at all in a conker contest.

In order that a conker contest could be staged, a couple of conkers had first of all to be centrally drilled and strung. Care was needed when drilling a conker so as not to split the skin at either the top or the bottom. It was normal to use a meat skewer to make a central hole, always commencing at the fawn coloured, hard-capped top (unless a cheese cutter was involved) and exiting through the glossy brown, softer-skinned bottom. The appearance of a dimple at the bottom of the conker served to provide the driller with an essential warning that the skewer was about to appear. At that juncture the skewer was retracted.

By drilling upwards into the dimple the final part of the hole was completed.

A big boy named John Tamsett had the knack of cupping a conker in the palm of his left hand and skewering a perfect hole through it with a single downward stabbing stroke. It was an awe-inspiring skill. John, who was fitted with a large head and a longish roman-type nose, was graced with the nickname of "Goblin".

One day, fate decreed that Goblin's skewering technique would cause him miss the receptive conker. When this happened, Goblin sat on the school playground wall with his back to the harbour and a look of mild surprise on his face as blood dripped from the point of the three inches or so of meat skewer protruding from the back of his hand.

After a hole was drilled in a conker, a length of string was wormed up through the hole from bottom to top, to be secured at the bottom by a multiple knot that was too big to pull back through the hole. The conker was then ready for play.

Conker contests took place between two players. At arm's length, one player held his conker suspended from a string, while the other player swung his respective conker to deliver a hard strike at the former.

One and one only attempt at striking was permitted before the roles were reversed. A miss was considered to be a valid attempt. The objective was to inflict maximum damage on an opponent's conker. The losing conker was the first to be smashed to pieces. The winning conker, irrespective of its post-battle condition, was then awarded the title of "King over One".

A player's objective was to have a conker achieve King status over as great a number as possible. That was why durability, induced or otherwise, counted for so much. The sharp edge of a cheese cutter could be extremely destructive on a first strike, but the disadvantage was that the shiny flat top of a cheese cutter made a sitting target for a combative blow. Unless a cheese cutter made King over One at a single hit, its mortality was usually of short duration.

Some strikes missed altogether. Other strikes resulted in tangling the pair of strings to such a degree of tightness that unravelling them posed a major challenge. The knuckles of an opponent were by no means inviolate territory. However, the wholesome crack of a swung conker hitting home at the right speed, in the right spot and with the right weight, with the follow through in a smooth arc as the target shattered into a myriad of shards and King over status jumped by One was more than satisfying enough to set aside any prior frustrations.

———

Directly across the B3314 from the entrance to St Endellion churchyard, and no more than fifty yards on from a right-hand minor road junction leading to Port Quin and Port Isaac via Church Hill, the parish boundary turned sharply to the left, eschewing the association with the B3314 in favour of proceeding due south for a mile or so along a narrow little track named Trevathan Lane.

A red post box, framed by neat blocks of trimmed slate as if it were a work of art, was recessed into the hedge at the upper corner of the turn from the B3314 into Trevathan Lane. Above the posting slot the post box bore the embossed letters "V" and "R" set on opposing sides of the royal crown. The post box had borne witness to a long and distinguished postal history. It was not impossible for us to imagine that it might once even have been the recipient of letters stamped with penny blacks.

Between the stones of the hedge into which the framed post box was set, little clusters of succulent pennyworts, thrusting up their flower-trimmed spikelets every spring, had gained footholds. If a large green pennywort was picked and manipulated gently enough to loosen (without breaking) its skin, it was possible to blow into the stem and inflate the pennywort like a small balloon.

Departing from Trevathan Lane, the parish boundary curved broadly away to the west before turning back to the north to intersect the B3314 for the last time, a mile and a half down from St Endellion on the way towards Wadebridge. Thereafter, it continued heading north by writhing along the lower Port Quin valley, where it was overlooked by the conker tree, to ultimately close its traverse for once and for all against the coast at the well-nigh abandoned hamlet of Port Quin.

One day, the Pennant Thomases didn't come in to school. Anyone's absence from school was unusual enough to imply that something serious was afoot. A few days later we were told that they had all gone away. We never saw Shadow again, and with his departure the thrills and benefits of his forays in the high trees were lost to all but fond memory.

It could have been that the number of Thomases resident in the slate-shod Pennant cottage became so great that the cottage was about to burst its seams.

Shadow was missed, but not for very long really. The way it always worked was that fresh tides and changing seasons created new situations for us to cope with. However, Shadow would never be forgotten.

In any case, in the parish of St Endellion it was really only the present day that we had to bother about.

*The Old Mill in the Port Isaac Valley*

# 3

# *Every Valley Shall Be Exalted*

*I come from haunts of coot and hern,*
*I make a sudden sally*
*And sparkle out among the fern,*
*To bicker down a valley.*

Alfred, Lord Tennyson (1809–1892)
"The Brook"

WHENEVER ROGER called at the door for me to go out my mother usually demanded of the pair of us, "And just where do you think you are going?" She never failed to emphasise the second "you" in her question but would probably have done better by stressing, "think".

"Downtown", we replied if we were intending (or even considering intending at the time of our response) to remain within the precincts of Port Isaac. Otherwise our stock answer was, "Out!", which was usually enough to satisfy my mother.

"Out" tended to carry with it an implication that the Port Isaac valley might sooner or later be involved in our itinerary. We might equally end up somewhere else of course, but I for one was never sure when we went "out" quite where that somewhere was going to be.

"Out" could additionally involve, *inter alia*, the Port Gaverne and Port Quin and Freak valleys; all of the stretches of cliffs either up from Port Isaac to Donkey's Hole (located just outside the parish boundary on the far side of Barrett's Awn) or down between Port Isaac and Port Quin; the whole length of Trewetha Lane and onward extensions to Poltreworgey Hill and Pendoggett; St Endellion or Trelights; or even beyond into the St Kew woods where the berried holly grew when it was needed as a Christmas-time imperative.

My grandfather, Granfer Jim Creighton, always referred to the valleys as the "bottoms". Granfer's assertion was made in the context of gardening. Bottom soil, in which his immortal garden was tilled down in the mouth of the Port Gaverne valley, was a generous natural medium in promoting the growth of vegetables and became especially productive when enriched by either storm-tossed seaweed lifted from the beaches or rotten straw marinated in a range of varieties of farm animal shit.

The Port Isaac valley was a wriggling realm of flat marshes, sloping meadows, tight coppices, dense thickets and deep woods that lay cool under leafy trees. Gorse (known as "fuzz") bushes, humped-up brambles and wind-combed drifts of blackthorn filled smooth hollows and overflowed in a commonality of prickliness across the valley sides.

The floors of the woods in spring time shone with primroses prior to their being engulfed in a sea of bluebells. From the mat of winter-brown bracken that crackled underfoot, new growth unfurled green and fresh like a soaring flock of phoenixes as the ferns feathered out.

Here and there in the valleys apple orchards flourished in dis-creet gullies that were fenced around as tightly as they were well sheltered. Each and every apple tree was a target for an autumnal scrump whenever any apple looked as much as passably ripe.

Through it all a vast multitude of scurrying rabbits (each a pie-in-waiting on four feet) were the common prey of owls, buzzards, foxes, stoats, dogs and farmers. There were far more than enough rabbits to go round.

Solitary crows built nests in the swaying tops of towering trees, reckoning not that Shadow could be on the loose. Magpies haunted the forbidding blackthorn; robins and wagtails were at home in stone hedges; swallows constructed half moon nests of down-lined mud under eaves; barn owls resided (unsurprisingly) in barns, water hens in ponds, finches, thrushes, blackbirds, hedge sparrows, wrens and tits in ivy and brambles; and (for their part) rooks, buzzards and tawny owls held high stations in close arrays of beeches and elms.

———

The Port Isaac valley was blessed with greening depths holding deep secrets. Its forks were traced by chinking, slow flowing streams. The valley was smoothly mature all the way from its rambling watershed down to its beach-bound terminus in the harbour.

Over the ultimate couple of hundred yards through the Port Isaac village confines, right alongside Middle Street, the valley stream was familiarly and famously known as "the Lake". The stream water was good for head-down drinking all along its course apart from anywhere related to the Lake.

The Freak valley stream reached its particular beach destination at Pine Awn with considerably more drama than the modest final lifeboat slipway-floored rapid that the Lake could muster. At Pine Awn the stream dropped to the beach over the rim of a waterfall that was at least a score of feet high.

At St Illick's Well to the east of Tartar cove above Port Gaverne, a little valley, short enough and tight enough to be not much more than a glorified cleft, also ended in a tumbling waterfall, this one more than twice twenty feet in height. The St Illick's waterfall was regularly transformed by wind and sun into a glittering bridal veil showering diamonds on the sea.

———

A general panorama of the Port Isaac valley could be taken in from the top of Lobber field. The valley dwindled away into blued distance as spur interlocked over spur back to the source located in the vicinity of Tresungers farmhouse (often referred to as "Zungers" owing to the convention of dispensing with the archetypal Cornish prefix in locality names) by way of lower Pennant.

A tributary joined the main stream coming from Tresungers, a half a mile or so up from Port Isaac. The source of this tributary was below Colstanton corner where Trewetha (or "Wetha") Lane made its second great "S" bend before proceeding to Poltreworgey (even "Polworgey") Hill.

The Port Isaac valley provided us with an exciting feeling that it had originated in strange and far-off places. A walk up to Tresungers or Colstanton starting from down at the Lake was at least two miles long, and even more than that if the usual diversions, deviations and detours were taken.

The springs sourcing the valley rose in quiet dimples from within cloying patches of reedy bog. They generated early trickles chuckling between clay-bound fissures that were never much more than a good hop across. Gathering in volume, the water downstream flowed clear and steady, except when heavy rain fell and the water ran fast, boiling murkily brown. The stream bed rattled over sporadic patches of slippery pebbles, was garlanded with trails of wavering watercress in silent-surfaced pools and was protected all along by drifts of bramble, willow, alder and blackthorn.

---

On the inside elbow of Colstanton corner a broad and well-established rounded pond was located, poised at the very head of the Port Isaac valley as if it were a baptismal font in waiting.

None of us knew how deep the pond was, although it was probably not nearly as profound in depth as was Frog Pool in the abandoned quarry on the side of Freak valley, which on Aunt Mary's impeccable authority we knew to be bottomless.

A key feature of the Colstanton pond was a pair of resident moorhens, which we called "water hens". The water hens threw down a gauntlet each year to those of us who set great store in locating their nesting place in order to get our hand on what, in St Endellion parish, was a much-coveted egg.

Colstanton corner's principal claim to fame was, however, not vested in its hosting a tributary source for the Port Isaac valley, nor in the old men's antimony mining activity that had taken place close by, nor for that matter in the rounded pond and its elusive water hens. Its great celebrity (or more appropriately its notoriety) lay in the dreadful and ever-present likelihood of a traveller meeting up with the "Cheyney Hunt" if perchance the unfortunate traveller should pass by Colstanton corner alone and on foot on a dark night.

According to my mother the Cheyney Hunt was composed of a number of phantom horsemen who, naturally enough I supposed, rode on appropriately phantom horses. I accepted it all without question. What was less easy for me to appreciate was just why the Cheyney Hunt favoured riding around at Colstanton corner and nowhere else. Perhaps there were phantom foxes in the vicinity. The penchant of the Cheyney Hunt was never adequately revealed to me. Since I was assured that anyone who saw the ghostly riders in full cry was certain to drop dead soon afterwards, it seemed that resolving the issue with reference to the living was a lost cause.

Sudden death explained why there were no witnesses alive and thereby able to describe what the Cheyney Hunt actually looked like. On the other hand there were a lot of people who knew of a lot of other people who were related to someone or other who claimed to have seen the Cheyney Hunt and who had consequently come to exemplify the adage that dead men told no tales.

One night, at a very late hour, I was presented with an opportunity to put the legend of Colstanton corner's Cheyney Hunt to the test. This situation arose as a consequence of my having, a few hours earlier, been a willing patron of the "Regal" cinema up at Delabole. The Prout Brothers' bus, on which I had travelled up to Delabole from Port Isaac, managed to depart from Delabole one passenger short for its post-cinema return trip home, the absent passenger being me. Missing the bus was my own fault, the result of procrastination, which, as anyone who listened to Charlie Chester's *Stand Easy* on the wireless knew, was the thief of time. I therefore couldn't complain, and, faced with no alternative other than to tackle the daunting prospect of walking the eight miles back home along the good old B3314, that was just what I did.

On reaching the half-way point at the China Downs crossroads I contemplated turning off to the right to take the narrow side road down to Port Gaverne, but I chose instead to continue onwards through Pendoggett and then down Poltreworgey Hill in the faint hope that the B3314 offered me the best chance of obtaining a lift that I hadn't yet got. In fact I hadn't thus far been passed by any kind of vehicle capable of giving me a lift in any direction.

A lift had yet to materialise as I descended Poltreworgey Hill, wishing that I had made a more sensible decision to turn right when I had had the opportunity to do so back at China Downs.

As I neared Colstanton corner the dull rumble of the Cheyney Hunt pounding on the heavy turf of the field over to my left beat in my ears in concert with the rhythm of my heart. The Cheyney Hunt was on the move. I didn't want to look in its direction, but as far as I knew no one had ever shuffled off this mortal coil from the sound of its passage. I squeezed my eyes shut and raced ahead as hard as I could.

I had an intimate knowledge of every nuance of Trewetha Lane. I sped around Colstanton corner, through the second part of the "S" bend, and was well on the way down to Trewetha before I opened my eyes. Not a single blade of grass on the hedges was disturbed by my passage. My heartbeat slowed, and with it the sounds of the Cheyney Hunt faded. The huntsmen must have observed me, but I hadn't seen them, and that was all that counted.

A footpath faithfully followed the bottom of the Port Isaac valley and held position, as well as it could, just far enough above the flowing stream to avert periodic inundation at times of flood. Mud, as a rule, would have only presented a minor inconvenience to the footpath had it not been for the cloven hooves of itinerant cattle chopping sections of its surface into a quaking morass of rain-filled and dung-spattered potholes.

The heart of the valley was manifest in the so-called mill pool, a watery containment located at the confluence of the streams that came down from Colstanton and Tresungers. The valley footpath bifurcated around the mill pool, the left-hand branch leading towards Trewetha and the right-hand branch continuing on for another half mile prior to diverting into and following a shady brake leading towards St Endellion via Pennant Farm. The valley path to St Endellion sometimes made a pleasant alternative, when the weather was clement and the sun warm, to trudging the road climbing Church Hill.

On the other hand the attitude of the master of Pennant Farm, Mr Joe Dawe, towards the use by pedestrians of the acknowledged public footpath through his farmland could most kindly be described as one comprising apoplectic distaste with an occasional implication of impending mayhem thrown in to enliven the brew. In order to deter anyone approaching his demesne, Joe's stock in trade was to rant, rave and take up arms with whatever implement came immediately to hand. For that very purpose Joe, it was alleged, might easily brandish a stick, or a pitchfork, or a billhook, or a scythe or (maybe) even a shotgun. Whereas Joe might or might not have been what was commonly referred to as "mazed as a brush", little in his effusive manner did very much to nullify the said comparison with that bristle related item.

Joe's person never once came to provide a feast for my eyes. He had that much in common with the Cheyney Hunt as far as I was concerned. The reputation that preceded Joe was in any case enough to deter any wish I might have had to seek him out. However, once again in keeping with my experience versus the Cheyney Hunt, I did once hear Joe at the gallop.

The pretty little brake conducting the footpath up from the Port Isaac valley to Pennant farmyard and beyond to the St Endellion road bore substantial trees and dense thickets both along its edges and up its lateral slopes. It was a prospective locality for pigeons' and magpies' nests. Robins and pied wagtails were known to nest in suitable holes caused by stones falling from its timelessly mossy banks. In spite of our being apprehensive that Joe was in the vicinity, the lure of nests and eggs was always a sufficient counter to draw us to the brake when the right time of the year came along.

I spent the best part of a Good Friday morning in the brake with Roger. We were both dressed in our church-going clothes, and had debated a few times whether or not climbing a tree to look at a pigeon's nest would be consistent with proper Good Friday practice. Prudence won and no tree was climbed.

On the other hand we succeeded in putting off for a while at least the unwelcome mandate of having to sit in St Peter's church through a minimum of one segment – a sermon and hymn – of the ever-arid desert of the three-hour Good Friday service. The vicar demanded our presence in church for three or more segments of the said service (equal to a third of the total ordeal in duration), but even an hour of such sanctity stretched well beyond the limit of my staying power, irrespective of my being assured by the vicar beforehand that shortfalls would merit castigation.

As Roger and I were making our way up to the edge of a thicket on the right-hand side of the brake, a torrent of shouting and screaming came coursing down to us from the direction of Pennant. Seconds later Mr Christopher Piggins, a young man who at that time was no less than the serving curate at St Peter's, came scurrying down the brake as if he was being either pursued by or possessed with demons.

The curate Christopher, clearly not seeking an egg of any kind, quit the footpath to take a shortcut for green pastures new by virtue of leaping over gorse bushes and tearing through rising bracken. The exigencies of imminent Good Friday services might not at that precise moment have been exercising Christopher's mind. The intense stream of not too distantly generated invective that pursued him formed a counterpoint to the headlong rush of his precipitate passage.

With Christopher's exit from the scene, the well-focused frenzy of what could be best described as "hollin' and shoutin'" from the rear dwindled in volume; the associated cursing shrank first to a mumble and then into silence. The quarry had fled. His hunter didn't appear. Roger and I were only too well aware of what Christopher had fled from. Our fearful respect for Joe was racked up a notch or two or even three. We bided our time in the thicket for a long interval before we crept slowly away in the same direction taken with such despatch by Christopher.

After that, the shadowy prospect of an hour in church loomed over us as an even greater anticlimax to the day.

---

Christopher was the son of Mr and Mrs Piggins, proprietors of the Slipway House hotel overlooking Pawlyn's cellars alongside the Port Isaac Town Platt at the top of the harbour. He was as clean-cut and good-looking as any film star we ever saw in a Friday night cinema performance at the Port Isaac Rivoli. Christopher's appearance and personality might easily have incorporated all that was desirable in a truly Wodehousian Church of England curate had he not decided, in what was alleged to have been a road-to-Damascus-styled overnight conversion, to turn himself into a Roman Catholic.

Rumours emanating from the prime gossip centres of Little Hill and the Pentice on Fore Street suggested that the role of vicar's minion at St Peter's church had shaped up, for Christopher, as being a bit too much like hard work. Roman Catholicism was a form of religion so far beyond the pale that the St Peter's faithful would have been much less scandalised if Christopher had switched his allegiance over to Methodism. Chapel was at least the devil they knew.

———

The mill pool was a glorious expanse of murky water, broad, shallow and muddy-bottomed, all contained within a man-made earthen dam reinforced by chunks of slate quarried from the flank of the valley nearby.

The mill pool seemed imbued with an inherent capacity to eventually become a full-blown swamp, although the stream water brought to it from the upper reaches of the valley generally managed to prevail in volume over the sediment. It was home to a battalion of withy trees, which, rooted below the waters, thrust up gnarled and exceptionally well-pruned fists in a powerfully united Excalibur-like seasonal salute, throwing out flaring bursts of withy fronds.

The withy bounty was the fishermen's harvest. Withies were pruned from the trees, piled into bundles secured with hairy twine, and borne on stalwart shoulders down to Pawlyn's cellars to be individually selected and both pleasingly and practically woven into crab pots.

By way of a narrow, removable slate-gated sluice at its

downstream end, the mill pool discharged into a banked millrace along which the full force of the released flow sped slick and smooth for a full two hundred yards towards the agglomeration of buildings and barns that made up the so-called Old Mill. From the Old Mill a wedge of sea could be seen framed in the open "V" of the ever-broadening valley in front.

The millrace at one time had powered a huge overshot water wheel set into a deep recess at the upper flank of the Old Mill complex. The water wheel had been the driving unit for a corn-grinding operation that passed into commercial redundancy sometime before the beginning of the war. The new role for the associated facilities was to provide shelter for a lot of chickens, a few pigs, a couple of cattle and an uncounted multitude of rats.

The diameter of the water wheel was at least thirty feet. Its axle, spokes and rim were all constructed of iron. The arrangement could still be coaxed into hesitant life if the millrace was directed against the array of closely spaced and artfully angled parallel wooden slats set around its circumference. As long as the millrace flowed, so could the water wheel turn, although through lack of gainful employment, the water wheel was fast losing its sense of purpose to rust, creeping green moss and endemic wood rot.

The Old Mill house stood on a terrace cut into a dank wall of raw and weeping slate over to the left of its outbuildings. The house was lived in (for what seemed to us to have been the longest time) by a rather ponderous, and moderately pompous gentlemanly farmer named Mr Porteous.

Mr Porteous was graced with the nickname of "Cowboy Joe". I didn't know exactly how he acquired the nickname – it was enough to know that he had it. Although he made as improbable a cowboy as he did a proper farmer, the sobriquet might have been derived from Mr Porteous' exploits in amateur dramatics involving an association with the popular song "Ragtime Cowboy Joe".

As it was, the Old Mill's Cowboy Joe seemed to be neither rootin' nor tootin', and nor was he from Arizona. He was, however, undoubtedly high-falutin' and a son of a gun to boot. When Mr Porteous eventually moved away from the Old Mill, it was to occupy a cottage high up on Rose Hill in Port Isaac, where he grew lovely flowers in his front garden and showed his true mettle as an exceedingly pious member of the St Peter's congregation.

Fifty yards down the valley from the Old Mill towards Port Isaac and not far from a much loved two-storey barn that we revered as "Top Shed", a pipe gushing with water emerged surreptitiously from the bank of the gurgling stream. Following our discovery of this pipe, Roger and I established that if we obstructed its outlet with clods and weeds so as to build up a head of water in its inner recesses, we could, by pulling the blockage out in one rapid heave, release a gout of water that was well able to strike at the far bank of the stream before it tapered off.

One day it became clear, while we were intent on experimenting as to just how far the blast of water could be made to surge if we plugged up the pipe not with weeds but with sticky clay, that the ensuing head of water had risen sufficiently in behind the plug to have emerged into daylight at the far end of the pipe. Unfortunately, the far end of the pipe was located up in the Old Mill house.

We looked up to see an appropriately furious Cowboy Joe bearing down on us, heavily and at close range. Roger stampeded from the roundup but I didn't have the time. Cowboy Joe grabbed hold of me, lifted me up high and threw me with impressive skill in the direction of Port Isaac. I was airborne downstream for quite a number of yards. I landed on my back in the stream, creating a great splash that surged against both banks. Clay attached itself to me in gobs, compounding the humiliation.

One of Mr Hillson's fields occupied the right-hand side of the valley adjacent to where I fell. It was a field where, after those sadly rare occasions on which sufficient snow fell, we were able to zoom down from top to bottom using a purloined sheet of corrugated metal in lieu of a toboggan.

Reasoning that Cowboy Joe's running capacity would make him reluctant to pursue me up a hill, I took an instant decision to ascend Mr Hillson's field as rapidly as my bedraggled status would permit. Cowboy Joe had by then resolved his pipe blockage problem more effectively than any plumber would ever have done.

———

The bulk of Mr Hillson's farmland lay along the crest of the valley rimming the steeply inclined field up which I fled from Cowboy Joe. His farm was not big in the first place, but it became much diminished a year or two after the war owing to a section of its fields being invaded by a conglomeration of council prefabs. Mr Hillson's farm, sprawling around a clutter of crumbling barns enclosing a muddy farmyard in which chickens, two or three guardian geese and a huge shire horse resided, subsequently consisted of no more than a few small fallow fields, on most of which Mr Hillson's small herd of dairy cattle grazed. A rough track linked the farmyard with Trewetha Lane.

Mr Hillson's shire horse pulled a plough through those of the fields in the spring time of years in which crops of potatoes (best known as "tetties") and cabbages were appointed to supplant the usual cover of grass. With Mr Hillson in control of the reins and handles, horse, man and plough cut the cleanest and straightest of furrows, casting the brown and stony soil aside in long curling billows. To the greater detriment of rudely exposed earthworms, gulls streamed behind Mr Hillson and the plough as if a plume of smoke was being released from the fresh-turned soil.

Mr Hillson didn't live on the farm. His home was down near the edge of the cliff on the Fore Street side entry to the harbour Awn, looking directly across the Awn over the Kenewal rock towards Lobber Point. It was the last house at the end of a cliff track leading off from the outer corner at Fore Street's point of transition into Front Hill. Its association with such a precipitous locality outside of the harbour breakwaters ensured that a portion of the cliff edge on the way out to Mr Hillson's house was, owing to its universal employment for disposing of unwanted household items classified as all things neither bright or no longer beautiful, not to mention dead creatures great and small, known as "Hillson's Dump".

Mr Hillson made the transit up to and down from his farm a number of times each day, and on at least two of those occasions on the farm he milked his cows. In milking he was assisted by his son Horace, a tall, broad and muscular rustic whose ruddy face, unlike the façades of some of the hotels out on the Terrace, required no sign to be hung out to advise observers that there was a vacancy within.

Mr Hillson wore heavily hobnailed boots and clad his lower legs in leather gaiters that appeared to be as inflexible as they were thick. His trousers, jacket, waistcoat, collarless shirt and flat cap were surely as old as he was and reflected the standard residues of farmyard and field in their every thread, fibre, rip and darn.

His chief quality was joviality – he was an entirely benign man to whom a good guffaw was as natural a product of life as was the milk, fresh from the udder, which he purveyed to regular customers. Such good humour served to emphasise Mr Hillson's teeth, which were few, brown and far between. In the words of the celebrated playground rhyme, "My old man's a dustman", it could be correctly said of Mr Hillson's dental remains that, "one lay here, one lay there, one lay round the corner".

My mother obtained her daily supply of domestic milk from Mr Hillson. He walked his milk round carrying a huge and shiny, oval shaped covered bucket slung over one arm, in which milk sloshed freely, as often as not still steaming warm from the cow and embellished with a fleck or two of cud. Mr Hillson employed a half pint dipper to measure and transfer the order of milk from his bucket into my mother's enamel basin. The enamel basin (with the milk in it) was set at once on a hotplate in order to scald out golden clots of cream.

Since I saw him almost every day, Mr Hillson was an approachable figure. Roger and I occasionally took a shortcut to the Port Isaac valley through his farmyard on the strength of our assumed personal relationship with him, although just in case the said relationship wasn't as strong as we surmised it was, we made sure that Mr Hillson wasn't there when we went through.

What we had to watch out for in Mr Hillson's farmyard were his geese, whose objective in life seemed to be to take no prisoners. One of Enid Blyton's "Sunny Stories" dealt with a boy who "wouldn't say 'Boo!' to a goose". If we had ever had the fortune to meet Enid we could have let her know that saying "Boo!" to a goose counted for little in Mr Hillson's farmyard, especially when the goose was a gander. Our association with Mr Hillson's geese was gooseflesh-generating at best.

One day Roger and I noticed a clutch of ten large eggs lying in a depression on a bank of straw in Mr Hillson's farmyard. The layer of the eggs, presumably a goose, was nowhere to be seen. To receive a modicum of our own back we thought it reasonable to "blow" a couple of the eggs. Blowing eggs was a well-practised technique involving the creation of a small hole at each end of the egg, from one of which apertures the contents (yolk and white alike) were induced to be discharged when the other was blown into through pursed lips. Sometimes, in order to rupture the yolk and induce it to flow out freely, it was necessary to probe one of the holes with the pin or the thorn that was used to make it.

The two goose eggs that we selected were blown without difficulty. Then one thing led to another and before we realised it we had blown the lot. An approaching goose honked a warning, so, leaving the clutch of by then empty eggs in place, we determined that discretion was the better part of valour and on that basis it was high time we departed with haste for valley pastures new.

All went well in Mr Hillson's farmyard for the next couple of weeks. The goose continued to sit on the assembled eggshells with the full intention of incubating them. Roger and I put the egg-blowing incident completely out of our minds. Mr Hillson gazed on his sitting bird with equanimity until the date allotted for the eggs to hatch came along and passed by, causing in him a burning need to find out why the arrival of the anticipated goslings was subject to so much delay.

Mr Hillson was not slow in deciding on the identity of the culprits. He made an immediate beeline in our direction to dispense his own special brand of hazel switch-assisted justice, which, as guilty parties, Roger and I accepted without compunction as our due.

—

With Cowboy Joe out of the picture, three spinster ladies entered the frame to assume the occupancy of the Old Mill spread. This trio were probably sisters. Rightly or wrongly, I assumed that was what they were. All three appeared to be quite elderly, although to me the stamp of advanced age could have been applied to all grown ups, including the younger ones.

There was not one among the three who carried any more meat on her respective bones than either of the other two. The jumble sale-styled clothes in which they clad themselves only served to heighten the general similarity.

Two of the ancient sisters were more reclusive than the third. I only ever saw the two former in the act of scuttling away across expanses of muddy ground when I went past the Old Mill on my way into or out of the valley. They were a mysterious pair. I could but speculate on where their cauldron might be located in the Old Mill buildings.

However, the third of the Old Mill ladies was of a much less retiring nature than her siblings. She was named Miss Abbott and could be distinguished as Miss Abbott I, the others being the Misses Abbott II and III.

In the ranks of the three Misses Abbott, Miss Abbott I was the public persona. She sometimes evidenced an amenability to talking to passers by the Old Mill. On the strength of that I got to know her slightly, although never well. As little as I might have had in the way of creature comforts at home, Miss Abbott I always looked as if she had a lot less. I felt both sad and sorry for her – right up to the day, that is, when she gave me cause to review my sense of sympathy.

Miss Abbott I caused a great deal of excitement one day when she told a group of us passing boys that she had seen a widgeon nesting on the mill pool. A widgeon was a new bird in our experience. We looked it up in my *Observer's Book of Birds* and found out that it was a kind of duck that was likely to lay more than enough eggs in one clutch to satisfy the requirements of our egg-collecting circle.

We subjected the mill pool thereafter to the most detailed and intensely sustained scrutiny that it might ever have received in its history. Not a single fringing reed or square inch of its soft bottom was either untouched or untrodden. For all that, Miss Abbott I's widgeon proved to be as elusive as the Scarlet Pimpernel. We sought it here, we sought it there, and we failed to even sense it, let alone see it. So much, we thought, for Miss Abbott I's powers of observation.

At the Old Mill, the Misses Abbott stabled an assortment of horses, no two of which were of a similar size, shape or colour. They (the horses, that is) made a scruffy set of nags, although all of them seemed to be well cared for. So that the horses could earn their keep, they were impressed into forming the key essentials of the Misses Abbott riding school, of which Miss Abbott I was the headmistress.

A revenue-generating summer activity for the Misses Abbott equine establishment, popular with some members of the visiting public, was organised mounted troop plodding around the Port Isaac valley and its vicinity. The Misses Abbott steeds were not inclined to be speedy, either by design or by nature. They formed a line and followed their leader at a pace that a snail would not have been unhappy to acknowledge.

On one afternoon, Roger and I were lying stretched out on top of a haystack (as satisfactory a construction for climbing up on to as it was for sliding down from) located on the other side of a hedge adjacent to the road between Trefreock and St Endellion, not far down from the entrance drive to Pennant farmhouse.

From our vantage point we spotted the file of the Misses Abbott's horses and riders for the day, clopping its slow way along the road. Miss Abbott I was the point rider.

As the last in the line of hacks passed by where we were, its penultimate companion suddenly shook itself and reared up, dumping a tubby female rider flat on her backside on the road. The balance of the horses milled around, if not chaotically, then certainly with much sense of order lost. We watched enthralled as Miss Abbott I did her best to sort it all out.

The spectacle was not without an element of comedy. We burrowed down into the hay to stifle our laughter and thereby avoid being seen. The fallen rider must have remounted, as the procession had formed up again and was proceeding on its deliberate way when we finally looked up.

On the morrow, down in the hallow of the school playground, we recounted the incident to others, and that which we saw from the summit of the haystack lost none of its colour in the telling.

Much to our surprise a day or two later, Roger and I were pulled out of class to be interviewed by Port Isaac's village policeman, who at that time was a promotion-seeking officer for whom firmness and fairness were not always held to have anything in common. He came armed with a complaint from Miss Abbott I, alleging that on the road to St Endellion we had crept up behind her file of horses and stuck a sharp object into the rump of one of the animals, causing it to dump its rider with a consequent injury not only to the rider but also to the horse. It seemed that the quality of Miss Abbott I's powers of observation hadn't changed much since her reported widgeon sighting.

We were informed by the keen bobby that the rump of the horse in question bore a puncture mark from which blood had flowed, although it later emerged that no one involved was sure precisely where the puncture mark was located or for that matter which specific horse had been the victim. Just as clandestinely as we had slipped into the scene to carry out our dastardly deed, so had Roger and I stolen away afterwards, according to the testimony of Miss Abbott I – a testimony which the PC appeared to view as being infallible. Moreover, we were informed, Miss Abbott I's attempts to restore calm to the milling beasts (riders and horses alike) following the incident had resulted in Miss Abbott I pulling certain muscles in her lower back. Roger's Aunt Mary told us later on that we might be required to pay compensation to Miss Abbott I for ever and a day, assuming that either Roger or I would live that long.

Miss Abbott I's story, which we thought of (in Radio Luxemburg two-o-eight metres on the medium wave "it's half past nine, time for Perry Mason" terms) as the "Case of the Horses Ass", seemed to us to be so mendaciously contrived as to carry about as much water as Cowboy Joe's pipe discharge had after we blocked it up with clay.

It quickly became evident that someone had heard the somewhat embellished version of the horse-rearing event that Roger and I had described in the playground and had elaborated on it even further prior to passing it on to Miss Abbott I.

Although Miss Abbott I's threats faded with time, and her charges against us were ultimately dropped, we didn't entirely escape the hand of justice, as we were hauled over the coals for our failure to descend from the haystack to assist in retrieving the situation when the rider was unhorsed. That kind of censure was fair enough for us I thought.

On its way down to Port Isaac below the Old Mill, the valley bottom opened up gradually and surely. There were then subtle hints at a desire by the stream to shoulder at the foundation of incipient meanders. The appearance of Mr Tom Brown's vegetable garden on the right of the footpath a couple of hundred yards below Top Shed offered the first sign of impending civilised order in neat rows of broad beans, peas, cabbages, potatoes, onions, shallots, turnips and runner beans standing in the fine black bottom soil. A couple of distinctive withy trees stood, arms aloft, down at the end of Tom's garden adjacent to the stream.

On a length of driftwood hanging on a frame at a good height above the gate to Tom's garden the legend "Bar 20" was picked out in thick rope, tarred liberally and nailed fast in perpetual loops. The legend reflected Tom's love of western yarns, specifically of the famous series of "Bar 20" novels written by Clarence E. Mulford and featuring Hopalong Cassidy.

Contiguous to the Bar 20 was the "Double Diamond" garden, boasting a more graphic sign, also cast in rope, of its specific brand.

---

At the point at which the first straggle of outlying Port Isaac cottages was reached in the valley, the stream turned into the Lake. There were yet more flanking withies to be seen, interspersed with sporadic apple trees that could easily have benefited from a similar quality of pruning to that lavished by would-be crab pot manufacturers on the withies.

On the foreshore of the harbour the Lake gladly spent itself, braiding a deltaic path towards its merger with the sea, broad and rambling at low tide, tightly content at low tide. The Lake's essential purpose was to ensure the evacuation of household waste discarded into its neatly constrained channel not only by those who lived in its vicinity but also by many who did not.

Among the items deposited in the Lake's cleansing flow were

the solid and liquid contents of chamber pots, vegetable peelings, garden refuse, stale leftovers (there were very few of those), rabbit skins and drowned kittens. The nutritional value of some of this material attracted the occasional presence of long grey eels holding steady against the current in the Lake's lower reaches while they fed.

A wooden flush gate spanned the course of the Lake in front of Mr Tom Saundry's greengrocery shop in Middle Street. The flush gate was hinged on a heavy wooden frame and bobbed freely against the flow of the Lake when it was open.

Mr Ned Cowlyn, officially designated street sweeper, was responsible for the operation of the Lake flush. Old Ned carried out the flushing duty with tremendous zeal. Flushing the Lake by anyone unauthorised to do so constituted the most heinous crime in Ned's book. The perpetrators must needs be tracked down and clipped smartly around the ear. With the curmudgeonly presence of Tom Saundry close by the flush, a double hazard was placed on those among us who genuinely wanted to work the flush at an unscheduled opportunity.

Ned had only one good eye, but he could see well enough with it to know who it was that he had to chase when the occasion demanded it of him. His operation of the flush required him to bear down on the flush gate and brace it shut with an iron bar. This action dammed up the Lake and generated a good head of water upstream. Flushing always took place at a time of low tide and was activated by Ned from a strategic footing on Middle Street. Using a chunk of wood, Ned knocked away the iron bar (to be retrieved later when the ensuing surge was spent).

A great wave of pent-up water then broke from behind the opened flush and foamed down along the Lake to the beach, gathering upon its crest the accumulated mass of all that had been dumped in the Lake in the period since the prior flush had taken place. The boys challenged the flush wave, racing down Middle Street to try and beat it to the harbour.

On the emergence of the flush on the beach its largesse was strewn far and wide in an open display. Vast clouds of screaming gulls homed in on it in an instant, to fight over the choicest of the pickings. The gulls departed only when every last titbit was scavenged, the beach was clean again, the Town Platt was once more the property of the fishermen, and the whole Port Isaac valley was running clean (more or less) from source to mouth.

# 4

# The Paths of the Sea

*And all I ask is a windy day with the white clouds flying,*
*And the flung spray and the blown spume, and the sea gulls crying.*

John Masefield (1878–1967)
"Sea Fever"

PORT ISAAC BAY was the only bay we could lay claim to and, as
such, we knew it simply as "the Bay". The boisterously brave and
soaring coast of the Bay was limited to the west by Rumps Point
and to the east by the squat block of Tintagel Head.
From Rumps Point, the coastline wriggled on an approximately
east–west bearing for a full eight miles to reach Donkey's Hole
on the far side of Port Gaverne.

After Donkey's Hole, the coast of the Bay curved to the north
and continued for a further five miles up to Tintagel Head,
where the fabled ruins of King Arthur's castle were gradually
succumbing to wind, weather and the trials of time.

At Donkey's Hole an old men's slate quarry glowered out of a
cathedral-like wind-scoured recess in the cliff face. On the crown
of the cliff above the quarry entrant, the Tregarget coast watchers'
hut poked up as if it was a concrete boil waiting to be lanced. Way
down below this hut above the shore, an inclined tunnel, open to
daylight at both ends, made a transit of fifty yards or so through
a rocky hump that intervened between the foot of a sharp little

valley and the shingled foreshore of a tiny cove. The lower end of the tunnel, no doubt the original "Donkey's Hole" of yore, emerged into the tiny cove, its footing being only marginally above the level of high tide.

Stacks and racks of long since trimmed roofing slate, lichen crusted and sea pink garlanded, still waited in vain at the tide line on the opposite side of the cove for ships that would never come in. In the meantime, gulls resided in comfort among the ordered slates, happy in the assumption that their homes were eternally safe.

On the rim of the Bay there were three centres of population (and three only) that mattered. Trebarwith was not among their number. Lying just to the south of Tintagel Head, behind a cone-like offshore protuberance named Gull Rock, the settlement of Trebarwith and its big sandy beach counted for less than nothing as far as we were concerned. Of the aforementioned three that did mean something, Port Isaac with a stable (well almost) population of around twelve hundred souls was the biggest by a far cry. At least half of Port Isaac's souls (even more than half) could with the utmost confidence declare blood relationships with one another, cousins at multiple stages of removal being in the majority.

The other two of the three favoured places on the Bay where people gathered to reside were Port Gaverne, located a scant quarter of a mile to the east of Port Isaac (where it might be possible to find as many as a score of people hanging around on a good day in winter); and Port Quin, a sad hamlet of melancholy memory and ghosts set a little over two miles down along the cliffs to the west of Port Isaac.

The harbour inlets for the three Ports (Isaac, Gaverne and Quin) incidentally provided the fishing boats of the Bay with their only supposedly safe anchorages, which characteristic was, it was further assumed, why the trio had been established in the first place.

Mid-way between Port Isaac and Port Quin, a beautiful rock-girt and sandy-floored gem of a cove set in under the lee of the tall cliffs of Varley Head (and thereby known, not unnaturally, as Varley Sands) also made a useful shelter for a fishing boat to pull into in order to wait out a passing squall. The merit of Varley Sands to sustain a longer-term anchorage was depreciated by its being accessible only from the direction of the sea.

With all due respect to the breakwater-deficient harbours of both Port Gaverne and Port Quin (each well able to be entered from both land and sea), it was questionable as to exactly how secure either might be for a moored-up fishing boat facing rolling seas, gale-driven straight in from the Bay with the backing of the mighty Atlantic urging them on. As a consequence the moorings were all in the harbour at Port Isaac.

In addition to the Bay-framing prominences of Rumps Point and Tintagel Head, the generally smooth(ish) overall curve of the coast of the Bay was punctuated by Mouls Island (off the Rumps); by Doyden Point and Kellan Head (enclosing Port Quin's harbour to the west and east respectively); by good old Varley Head; by Lobber Point (entry sentinel to the Port Isaac Awn); by Castle Rock (at the tip of the Port Gaverne Main); and (last and by all means least of course) by Trebarwith's Gull Rock.

The coast exhibited clean lines, crested with wild flowers, coursed by cackling gulls, washed by thundering banks of tide, and slashed about by deep valleys and little gullies, each as sharply defined as a ripsaw tooth. The cold green sea of the Bay, in the depths of which kelp fields waved and swirled, heaved under the manipulative shove of gusty winds. The clasping cliffs were seamed with narrow ledges and yawning voids, splattered with sea pinks, torn apart by dark wet caves, and spiced with flotsam, jetsam and the joy of picking up seasonal gulls' eggs.

On the way up to Donkey's Hole from Port Gaverne the coastal footpath led first of all by way of the Main at Port Gaverne, and then consecutively onwards past Cartway Cove, Welshman's Quarry, Tresungers Point, Tartar Cove, St Illick's Well, Bounds Cliff, Filly Hoss Rock and Barrett's Awn where the parish boundary met the sea. Bounds Cliff, where populous colonies of razorbills, guillemots, shags and cormorants set up nesting sites, was the highest cliff in St Endellion parish, topping out at just over four hundred feet above sea level.

—

A mile or two inland from Donkey's Hole, that bleak town named Delabole stood on the very height of land and frowned down, as was its normal wont, onto the Bay. Delabole's prime claim to fame lay in the gigantic slate quarry that it surrounded, a quarry of vital importance not only to the locality but also to the nation. This almighty pit, in operation over many centuries, had assumed vast dimensions. It was the Delabole slate quarry that supplied Port Isaac with stone to build cottage walls; with roofing slates to keep out the rain (usually with success); with great flags to go underfoot on the kitchen floor; and with the gravestones under which to lay the mortal remains of those who dwelt in those cottages, trod those flags and ate their dinner beneath those (occasionally leaky) roofs. The clustered cottages of downtown Port Isaac constituted a testament in multiple shades of grey to the enduring quality of Delabole slate.

Two hundred year-old Delabole slate gravestones in the St Endellion churchyard bore inscriptions that were still almost as crisp in outline as they had been on the day on which they were chiselled out. Finely milled slate flour marketed under the commercial name "Delafila" had been in great demand by manufacturers of the kind of gramophone records that were played at 78 rpm.

The most famous slab of Delabole slate in Port Isaac was that which, under a cover of green baize, formed the playing surface of the snooker table at the Port Isaac Liberal Club. Joe Davis once played an exhibition match on it. Vestiges of the slab's ultra-smooth upper surface were exposed to the view of Liberal Club members by a few of the more significant cigarette burns that added so much character to the green baize.

---

At school, one of our teachers, the ever-personable Mr Perry, told us that the Delabole slate quarry was no more and certainly no less than the greatest man-made hole in the ground in the whole of the world. I believed implicitly in everything that Mr Perry said, including a side remark that the town of Delabole was an equally big hole in its own right.

Apart from the generation of slate and yet more slate, the most positive aspect of Delabole was its Regal cinema. The Delabole Regal was open on every evening of the week except Sundays and featured two separate big films and full supporting programmes each week. The regular Friday night cinema at the Rivoli in Port Isaac couldn't compete with that kind of frequency. What the Rivoli and the Regal did have in common, however, was that the advertised films were invariably older than many of us who clamoured to see them were.

Twice a week, to ensure that neither of the two said programmes need be missed, a Prout Brothers' bus carried a load of Port Isaac silver screen aficionados up to and then back from (assuming the return bus was not missed by specific patrons) the Delabole Regal.

When Mrs Morman asked my classmate Eileen Byfield at school what Delabole was famous for, Eileen answered, "Please Miss, pictures!" Eileen's sense of priority was commendable. She would surely have accepted that London was the real capital of Cornwall.

My own failure to entertain a huge amount of regard for Delabole was related to my very first visit to that selfsame Regal cinema on a wintry evening shortly after the end of the war. The somewhat later visit incorporating my long walk home and an encounter with the Cheyney Hunt on the way only served to add insult to the injury of that first occasion.

I went up to Delabole in the bus with my mother and my Gran. The big film in prospect was entitled *King Kong*. My eager anticipation of a feature involving wild animals and jungles turned to disillusion when the manager of the Regal refused to admit me to the performance on the grounds that the British Board of Film Censors had certified *King Kong* as an "X" film and I was too young to pass muster. Whatever "X" meant in the context of films, it had far more impact in marking the spot for me than it did for the obdurate manager.

As a result of the BBFC's meanness of spirit my mother and I were condemned to lurk around and about the dismal streets of Delabole (where if anything was happening it was not obvious) until *King Kong* had played itself out and it was time for Prout's to take all of us back to Port Isaac. Human life in the streets of Delabole for my mother and me was made conspicuous only by its absence. Gran, unaffected by the dreaded "X", got in to see *King Kong* but was uncharacteristically close-mouthed as to what it had all been about.

Mrs Emmeline ("Em") Kent, who lived in the so-called "Middle" row of council houses in Hartland Road up at the top of Port Isaac, knew Delabole well as that was where her son-in-law Gerald came from. Em offered me an impeccably rendered truth that as far as the residents of Delabole were concerned, "They d'talk differnt to we in Port Isaac".

When, once blackout restrictions were lifted, I stood in Hartland Road after dark and looked across the Bay towards Tintagel Head, a pinpricked line of lights high up on the right signified where Delabole was. The line of lights comforted me, as I could mark their location in my mind and resolve to try and avoid ever again going where they were.

---

Mr Perry also informed us that the village name, "Port Isaac", was a modernised version of an archaic "Porth Izzyk". Although such information was probably quite interesting and undoubtedly true, it meant not an awful lot to his captive audience.

Mr Perry said that "Izzyk" translated from the old Cornish language as "corn" (or perhaps the products of the same). Since no one that we knew of spoke Cornish (if not "Izzykish"), we had no reason to think, or bother to think, that Mr Perry wasn't right. The curious thing about an association of Port Isaac with corn was that local industry had, for a lot further back in time than anyone could remember, been mainly vested in fishing out in the Bay. On the other hand, the farmers of St Endellion parish still grew rather a lot of corn (a generic name for mixed oats and barley) in quite a lot of their fields.

It was possible that the said farming endeavour had evolved to enshrine the "corn" part of Port Isaac's name prior to the era when fishing in the Bay had taken on a pre-eminent status.

It was much easier for us to accept, once again following Mr Perry's advice, that "Gaverne", as in Port Gaverne, translated as "slate". Whether or not this meant that at Delabole there was a huge gaverne quarry wasn't made clear. There was never any question in our minds, however, that slate was what the former commerce of Port Gaverne had been all about, from the evidence of its flaggy hand-hewn foreshore jetty all the way out along the sheer edge of the Main to the gale-splintered summit of Castle Rock.

Corn and slate thereby took care of two of the three recognised ports on Port Isaac Bay. The burning question then was, what was Port Quin supposed to be about? At face value Port Quin – sometimes written as Portquin, although I preferred the two-word version – didn't have much to recommend it as meaning anything very substantial. "Quin" could have had something to do with "five", although anyone might have been hard pressed to think of as many as five truly positive things to say about Port

Quin. And if there were five people who lived in Port Quin who weren't mazed for doing so, that would have come as a surprise to me.

---

The footpath along the cliffs of the Bay between Port Isaac and Port Quin led, via Roscarrock Hill, along the head of an array of sloping harbourside allotments and then up and over Lobber field, before straggling onwards, following every nuance of the promontories, headlands and sea-bitten cavities of open coves, dark gugs and narrow inlets that lay ahead. Each sea-dashed rock, cliff protuberance, rock face, height and depth that the coast of the Bay possessed was known by us with the utmost familiarity, generally by name. Such names were of the kind that befit friends: a crackling and evocative litany marking off the stages of a walk down to Port Quin, every feature known with affection and cared about with passion.

Port Quin (not least with respect to the conker tree in its valley) marked the generally accepted limit of our expeditions to the west of Port Isaac, much as Donkey's Hole did to the east. Following the haul up to the top of Lobber field, we proceeded to pass by Lobber Point on the right, to take the gently downward angling footpath into Pine Awn and, once there, to hop over the stepping-stones in the Freak valley stream. From the bottom of Pine Awn the path continued on a direct course up the far slope of the steep valley to reach the inner lip of Crowser Cove and proceed onwards to Port Quin by way of Crowser Island, Varley Head, Greengarden, Scarnor Point, Foxhole Rocks and the back of Kellan Head (where a coast watcher's hut once stood, prior to its being accidentally burned down).

If we were keen to go to Port Quin and didn't feel like walking the footpath along the coast with its far too many switchbacks, an alternative was available to us in a cross-country "shortcut". The shortcut diverted inland along a well-defined route commencing at the top of Roscarrock Hill from in between the bamboo-draped fence of Khandalla house on the left and the entry to Captain (retd) Roy May's rat-ridden abandoned quarry on the right.

The main obstacle presented by the shortcut was a great down and up dip in the middle section of the Freak valley. At the bottom of the dip the footpath met up with a sycamore-shrouded stile and a little slate flag bridge over the valley stream. At the top on the far side was Roscarrock (or "Skarrick") Farm, sprawling grey and grim on the divide. Its buildings (probably made from Frog Pool quarried slate) were as weathered as the exposed fields surrounding them. Roscarrock farmhouse was reputed to have a vast kitchen and refectory, once used by monks. It was to my great lack of regret that I never received an invitation to go in and have a look at it.

On passing by the vicinity of Roscarrock farmhouse, the shortcut to Port Quin dropped down along a gentle fall of fields towards the shifting sea in Port Quin harbour. Mouls Island and Rumps Point, both looking in silhouette like a pair of ragged rhinoceros heads snuffling at the Bay, stood out in the far distance as dedicated guardians to the broad sands of Polzeath beach around the corner.

Mouls Island (more concisely known as "Mouls") wasn't very big. Its total circumference was no more than a couple of hundred yards, and it was perhaps only a hundred feet or so high at its peak. Grass, sea pinks and scurvy grass had managed to gain a foothold only on its lee slope. A calm sea was needed to offer any opportunity for making a successful landing on Mouls.

The population of Mouls consisted solely of seabirds. Herring gulls, seasoned with a peppering of great black-backed gulls (or "black annies") took the ascendancy. They were associated with not insignificant numbers of oystercatchers, cormorants, shags, razorbills and guillemots, all in residence on Mouls during the nesting period. It was said that there might have been a few puffins around as well, although I never saw any of those near Mouls or anywhere else on the Bay. I once spotted half a dozen gannets diving for fish around Mouls, but they were unwitting visitors, blown down from south Wales on the wings of a recent storm.

As a birds' egger, I was always beset with a burning ambition to set my feet on Mouls during the egging season. It was an ambition that, sadly, was destined never to be realised. However, when a few Port Isaac fishermen took a boat out to Mouls on a smooth-surfaced day in the early May of one year towards the end of the war and returned to Port Isaac bearing huge withy-made fish mawns loaded to the brim with gulls' eggs, I did receive two of the eggs in the general share-out of the bounty on the Town Platt, and that provided me with a landing on Mouls by proxy at least.

When the air over Port Isaac Bay was as clear and as clean as a breeze-stirred line of sheets on washing day, the ghostly finger of Hartland Point became visible, sticking out behind Tintagel Head. Hartland Point, sighted with wonder, offered us a vision of Devonshire, a county of truly foreign parts, second-rate clotted cream and awful pasties. Even more awe-inspiring than the view of Hartland Point was an occasional glimpse of the translucent sliver of Lundy Island, floating on the horizon not too far to the left of the former.

Lundy Island, known as just "Lundy", was intuitively sensed before it was seen. I always located it by looking just to the side of where it ought to be, and there it was, hanging in the corner of my eye. A more direct glance and Lundy was no more. Sometimes after dark it was possible to look out to sea and catch a suggestion of the faint glimmer of Lundy's lighthouse throbbing like an Atlantic heart. If the horizon was clouded over at night, well, there was sometimes the option of Delabole's trickle of lights away on the side to decorate the darkness.

I knew that Lundy, unlike Mouls, was truly famous for its breeding puffins. Lundy's reclusive human residents used specially minted coins and postage stamps appropriately named for those rainbow-beaked birds. A Lundy penny or half-penny, known respectively as a "puffin" or a "half-puffin", occasionally turned up in Port Isaac in change handed back to an unsuspecting customer across a shop counter.

Some Port Isaac people knew of people who knew of other people who were aware of others who had been to Lundy, yet (just as was the case with the owners of gold out of Wheal Treore and eye-witnesses of the Cheyney Hunt) no one could remember what the names of those venturous travellers were – or, for that matter, what they had actually gone to Lundy for. Lundy was yet another place further away than a Port Isaac fishing boat could reach or would ever be likely to reach even if blown out to sea, and that was far enough off to eliminate any intimations of familiarity with Lundy that we might otherwise have entertained.

The importance of Lundy was derived from what it signified to the more weather-obsessed members of Port Isaac society, which meant most of them. If Lundy could be seen or sensed by the wandering eye then rain was imminent. If Lundy could not be seen, then rain was already falling.

———

Waves hammered at the coast of the Bay as if it were an anvil, pounding forward, sucking back, and chewing at the underbelly of the cliffs without fear or favour. The sea thanked us in fair weather and roared contempt at us in foul. The coastal wear and tear might have been imperceptible over the span of a generation, yet there had been so many generations of such lives moved up from Port Isaac to St Endellion that it didn't need the Brains Trust to look at all the boulders strewn around the base of the cliffs to determine that the destructive power of the sea was inexorable.

The wave-upon-wave-upon-wave-ranked assault of the

sea held the jumbled boulders, some of them of immense proportions, as its testament. Every seventh wave that arrived, we were told, was going to be a big one. I counted off approaching waves many times and I didn't know why seventh waves should be superior, but I always found out that they were. Once in a while an unexpected cascade of rock from a wind-and-weather-weakened cliff provided us with a startling reminder of the proverbial impatience of time and tide.

There was no single day on which the great expanse of ocean that filled the Bay exhibited precisely the same mood or shade as it had done on the day before. The sea's temperament was able to change dramatically even in the course of less than an hour. The sea was easily irritated. Out beyond Lundy, where it was rumoured that to venture was, at its worst, to fall over the edge of the world or, at its best, to meet with sea serpents, the empty sea wasn't about to stop until it reached Labrador.

The sea of the Bay mixed its palette of the day from the sky above and the currents swilling beneath its restless surface. Clear, flat and turquoise in the morning, it could be heaving and fully charged with the churning sand of a ground sea in the afternoon. It sparkled blue beneath a sunny breeze, flecked by the marching chop of white horses and grazed with erratically rushing cats' paws. At other times it lay flat and motionless, shrouded for days in grey clammy fog.

When driven by a deep Atlantic swell, cold green waves up to fifty feet high surged across the Bay in never ending battalions, coming in to crash against the cliffs and rear over the cliff tops, driving a virtual blizzard of seething foam ahead of them.

Great storms piled up mounds of torn kelp and slippery mats of thin and immensely long strands of "oar weed" on the Port Isaac and Port Gaverne beaches and simultaneously threw all manner of driftwood and other items of wreck into rocky coves. There was then a welcome harvest to be gathered. Pitchfork-wielding farmers loaded the marine-donated seaweed largesse into horse-drawn carts, and gardeners armed with forks took away a smaller portion of the slippery bounty in creaking wheelbarrows. The seaweed played an incomparable role in enriching the soil of parish gardens.

"Wreck" was a catchall term used to describe anything floating in from the sea that could be retrieved and made use of. Two notable items of wreck that turned up in the Bay during the war were a wooden case packed with bars of chocolate that tasted only slightly of the sea (at least as far as the more than welcome square of chocolate that I was given was concerned) and the battered and barnacle-ridden hull of a ship's lifeboat. The latter was eventually resurrected to become the fishing boat *Maple Leaf*, owned by the Port Isaac Harbourmaster Mr Anthony Provis.

Most incoming wreck consisted of odd pieces of waterlogged wood; round-pine pit props originally destined for installation in coal mines (making excellent fire-sustaining material in their own right when dried out); and fishing industry debris such as lost lengths of netting and cork or glass floats torn from crab pot lines. The glass floats were grainy green globes as big as my head. They were the most prized finds. Unfortunately, rough sea and great boulders were not especially compatible with the survival of such artefacts of fragile glass, so we didn't find very many of them.

The prospects for getting hold of wreck were usually better in the coves and gugs lying between Port Isaac and Port Quin than they were up along the Bay from Port Gaverne to Donkey's Hole. On the way down to Port Quin there was better access to the high tide line, and the arrangement of boulders, cracks and crannies provided more favourable traps where wreck could lodge pending discovery.

———

The harbour at Port Quin resembled a tight rock-floored box. It was flanked on the west side by a low slate cliff sloping down from Doyden Point and on the east side by a higher and more

71

raggedly crumbling cliff, above which a long, grassy rise drifted up to the summit of Kellan Head. Both Doyden Point and Kellan Head were carpeted by short and spongy turf and studded to seaward by great hassocks of sea pinks.

The smoothness of Doyden Point's humped profile was interrupted by an eerie-looking little castellated folly-like building two storeys tall. The folly was fitted out in front with small gothic-styled lead-mullioned windows and an entry door that appeared as if it probably opened onto a passage descending into the bowels of the earth. The brown grain of many of the folly's facing stones was etched into sharp relief by far more years of abrasive wind than were worth thinking about.

Who built the folly, or why, was neither known nor material to us. Named Doyden Castle, the folly was always kept locked tightly shut at all of its possible points of entry. We tried the door on several occasions, although it was uncertain that any of us would have been able to summon up the nerve to enter if perchance the door had opened.

Offshore, two vicious teeth of black rock guarded the entry to Port Quin harbour. One rock was large and one was small. Together they were known as the "Cow and Calf". The Cow and Calf emerged from the deep only at low tide. Rooted kelp fronds and bladder wrack flopped in the sea surging around them. There was often a cormorant or a shag to be seen paddling at the fringe of the ragged water around the two rocks, anxious for fishy pickings.

Shags and cormorants were common birds of the Bay. The latter looked like the former's poor relations. Both species laid a goodly clutch of slim, chalky surfaced eggs. When the chalky residue was scraped off, taking the greatest of care, the neutral tone of the eggshell was transformed into a beautifully pale translucent blue.

Our elders and betters were not at all thrilled to hear us refer to

72

a shag as a shag. For reasons that were never adequately explained, not one of them seemed to like shags an awful lot. Shags had to be spoken of as "shanks". Cormorants retained their proper names and were therefore left to their own devices.

Whenever we saw either a cormorant or a shank floating out in the sea, we chanted to it, "Shanky, shanky doodle, fish under water!" The bird would then look up, raise its beak in acknowledgement, turn its head around and then flip up and over to make a curling dive down into the depths. We counted off the seconds of time that it remained submerged and tried, invariably unsuccessfully, to guess at where it would pop up onto the surface again.

At high tide in the sunny days of summer, when the Cow and Calf were well under water, Port Quin harbour was visited by many bathers who either walked down from Port Isaac or up from Polzeath, attracted by warm harbourside ledges of sea-lapped slate.

Port Quin had more dwellings than residents, although it had few enough of the former overall and even fewer that were habitable. No facilities designed for the convenience of the public ever came along to fill Port Quin's vacuum. The road from St Endellion via Long Cross entered Port Quin, ran through what there was of the place as rapidly as it could and seemed grateful to rush steeply out again, uphill past Doyden Point and its Castle folly.

A morose atmosphere hung over Port Quin, palpably charged with despair and desolation. A few stark cottages and a couple of larger blunt-stone houses on the Doyden side of the harbour frowned down on the small handful of cottages that clustered around the harbour head and straggled a little way back along the narrow road behind.

On the inner edge of the curve at the foot of the slight hill on the road down from Long Cross, facing directly the point where the entry stile to the Roscarrock shortcut footpath pierced a hedge on the right, stood the Port Quin community pump. On entering (or leaving) Port Quin on foot most of us refreshed ourselves at the pump. The water came up cold, clear and as satisfying to the soul as only water taken at such an optimum juncture of a long walk could be.

Beyond the pump the road led on towards the harbour and passed in front of a recessed terrace of ruined cottages on its right-hand side. The living slate of the slope that the terrace was cut into formed the back wall of the cottages. It was probable that the outer and side walls of the cottages were constructed from chunks of the slate hewn out to make the recess.

The roofs of the cottages had collapsed long ago. Rotting wooden lintels over the gaping doorways sagged alarmingly, but for the most part the outer walls still held firm. The earthy remains of a cloam oven gaped in the corner of one cottage as incredulously as Willie Chadband from Trelights did down at school when the headmaster, Mr C. Victor ("Boss") Richards, asked him to recite the twelve times table.

The crumbling cloam oven spoke of a way of life that must once have made the cottage a happy place to live in. I looked at it and imagined the oven fully charged, the coals raked out, the smell of baking bread, pasties and yeast cake enriching the surrounds, and I mourned for those who once lived there and who were now gone.

Ivy, clumping on wrist-thick vines, snaked across the ruined cottages and hung overhead in a green–black canopy that created a sombre dankness to shut out even the sunniest day. Elder and blackthorn pushed into the ruins from the top of the moss-weeping wall at the back.

When I stepped in through the precarious doorways of the ruined cottages, I felt a chill that emanated from more than the simple shadows, and I lingered only momentarily.

---

A story was told, surely based on fact but perhaps (as was often the case) spiced with myth, that Port Quin fishing families had occupied the cottages in the good old days before the fall. Such an absorbing time of local family life was long past, well out of range of memory. Port Quin was then, it was reputed, a thriving fishing village with a tight fleet of small boats riding out the waves in the box-like harbour protected by the Cow and Calf.

On a certain Sunday, a sighting of a shoal of fish (pilchards maybe) boiling in the water out in the Bay, with clouds of gulls wafting over the shoals, induced the Port Quin fishermen to break a die-hard tradition of not working on the Sabbath. A period of poor fishing may have preceded the appearance of the shoal on that fateful day. The motivation to catch the fish was born of necessity.

The entire fishing fleet put out to sea in what, according to the tale, was good weather. The capricious Bay then threw up a great storm. The fleet foundered under the onslaught of the mighty tempest. There were no survivors. The heart of Port Quin was excised at a stroke by an attributed act of Heavenly Retribution for the breaking of the fourth commandment. God in St Endellion parish was only love to those who toed His line and believed that He moved in mysterious ways His wonders to perform.

As a consequence, the story went on, the families of Port Quin fishermen claimed by Davy Jones' locker left their port of lost hope not long afterwards. They abandoned their cottages to disintegrate under the clutch of the bitter ivy. Some of these self-imposed exiles were reputed to have settled in Port Isaac, where possibly they could have provided an impetus in helping Port Isaac to grow away from being merely Porth Izzyk.

——

"CM", in the year of grace 1699, was someone who tramped the cliffs of the Bay while Port Quin was probably still thriving. Whoever CM was, he (I always thought of him as a he) was real enough to have left his enduring mark on a rock face up above the far side of Lobber Point, where a long slope of slippery, glossy grass stretched down to the cliff edge.

The grass was of the kind that we called "skittery grass", since it offered no resistance to our sliding on it on the seats of our respective trousers. A traditional school playground rhyme honouring the joy of sliding on skittery grass advised: "Up on the mountain, skittery grass, a man fell down and skittered on his ass."

We didn't skitter too far on our asses in the area of Lobber Point of course, since at the foot of the skittery slope the cliff made a sheer drop of more than fifty feet down to the heaving sea. On that rock-girt front the sea always appeared to be angry somehow.

A well sheltered, slate-floored and slate-walled natural alcove lay almost at the edge of this sheer drop. Its front faced onto the Bay. The walls and floor of the alcove were as smooth and as clean-surfaced as if they had been cut by the old quarrymen. It was likely that the alcove was formed by the action of wind and weather on the fortuitous juxtaposition of a set of slaty joints. At the rear of the alcove against the slope there was limited respite to be had from the wind above and the sea surging below.

Chiselled into one smooth face at the back of the alcove was the inscription "CM 1699". Its flamboyance suggested a high quality of personality on the part of its originator, who was presumably none other than CM himself. Both time and care had gone into the realisation of CM's legend. The slant of the numbers and the curl of the initials made a feast for the eye.

On the same rock face, a foot or two beneath CM's masterpiece, a second inscription – this one exquisitely formed in tiny letters and figures – read "Isaac Trevan 1831". Several latter-day enthusiasts, including me, had cut their own names in various other locations around the alcove, but none of us managed to emulate the glorious elegance of either CM or Isaac.

Running my fingers over CM's work allowed me to create a

two-and-a-half-centuries link with a person who, like me, might have skittered on his ass down the grassy slope of Lobber Point. He might even have been one of my ancestors. Stranger things had happened in the Port Isaac community. I thought of CM as a strong, timeless and independent character, not unlike the immortal Wilson from the wonderful stories published in every issue of the *Wizard*.

Whoever CM was, he must have walked along more or less the same footpath that I took from Lobber Point back to the top of Lobber field. From Lobber field CM would have looked down on the Port Isaac (or Porth Izzyk) of his day. He would have seen the clean surrounding hills, the verdant valley in the background and the stony track of Church Hill leading the way up towards the St Endellion church that was ancient even then.

CM would have run, like me, down across the slope of Lobber field and then over the ruts of Roscarrock Hill to reach a downtown Port Isaac, which, give or take a cottage here and an occasional fall of cliff there – and with due allowance made for the absence of breakwaters in the harbour – might not have been radically different from the one I knew so well.

"CM 1699"

# 5

# *A Farewell to Arms*

*A good sword and a trusty hand!*
*A merry heart and true!*
*King James's men shall understand*
*What Cornish lads can do.*

R.S. Hawker (1803–1875)
"And Shall Trelawny Die?"

THE PATHWAY RIPPLED up and over the hump of the hill separating
the Old Coastguard Station adjacent to the foot of Front Hill
from the coast-watcher's hut out on the lip of the flaking cliffs
near Shillingstones. Its uneven footing occupied what was a
virtual gully, narrow, valerian-festooned and bound up by slate
walls. From the coast-watcher's hut a roughish but wider track
took over from the footpath to continue onwards, paralleling the
rim of the cliffs to eventually meet up with the last gasp of New
Road near the top of Port Gaverne Hill.

My Granfer carried out routine duties at the coast-watcher's hut
during the couple of years surrounding the end of the war and
I often walked the pathway with him when he went out to it
to take up station. All in all, the pathway and the track leading
onwards from it made a favoured shortcut used by many boys to
reach cliffs where gulls' eggs were waiting to be gathered up in
late April and early May.

Relatively easy and fairly satisfying climbing was possible
along the cliffs that the course of the said track followed. There

were hideaway hollows set into the grassy slopes that separated the track from the cliff edge. Conveniently located overhanging banks of spongy turf offered shelter from both rain and wind. A retaining wall of slate lining the upper side of the track provided a sound redoubt against which certain gangs of boys constructed rudimentary headquarters-styled camps. Such camps were as keenly attended to by the specific gangs that erected them as they would eventually be by any opposing gang that came along to destroy them.

———

Charm was a quality that the Old Coastguard Station may have possessed but didn't exhibit. The Old Coastguard Station resembled a long and low-slung blockhouse standing at the back of a shingled yard in which all that was lacking to complete the effect was a military parade. The fact that the Old Coastguard Station commanded a prospect of the coast of the Bay that was not only not pleasing but also conspicuous by its absence rendered the visual relevance of the institution to guarding the coast as more than a little redundant.

It was perhaps to ensure an improved conspectus of the coast and all that therein needed guarding that the coastguard unit was relocated to a so-named New Coastguard Station in an elevated position up on the hump of the hill separating the Old Coastguard Station from the coast-watcher's hut.

From its position of superiority the front of the New Coastguard Station could enjoy an impressively strategic overview of much of the Bay, and the officers of its unit could revel in raising the weather cone to signify many more head-on gales than any of them craved. Whatever its inadequacies might have been, the Old Coastguard Station had at least been built in a locality where the worst of the weather passed overhead.

———

Michael Collings, older than me by a year or two, lived in one of the decommissioned former units of the Old Coastguard Station.

He bore the nickname "Cogsy". His bland countenance was round and moon-like to the extent that Cogsy was fortunate to be rather more intelligent than his looks allowed an observer to assume he might be. Among his contemporaries Cogsy seemed to be a sort of young fogey, characterised as having a prematurely old head upon young shoulders.

For a while Cogsy adopted the habit of appearing in a well-frequented location of his choice (examples of which included the school playground, an advantageous part of Fore Street, down on the Town Platt and out on the open beach), whence he was wont to launch into a torrent of pseudo-preaching and sermonising. His braying harangue surged like the Lake emerging in well-flushed debris-charged spate at the head of the harbour.

Since Cogsy's ranting and railing was modulated in tones redolent of the voice of doom, it was as well that the substance of his discourses was less than memorable. In spite of the underlying motives that Cogsy entertained, he was perceived more as a witless curiosity than as a force rivalling either the vicar of St Peter's or any of a readily available army of local chapel preachers. Yet for all that, Cogsy droned strongly enough to acquire, for a time, a second nickname of "Vicar".

The most compelling outpouring of verbal effluent that I heard Cogsy give vent to occurred one afternoon in the vicinity of Varley Head. Cogsy and Gordon "Arker" Keat were my two companions of the day. The glue holding our trio together was manifest in a Webley air pistol, the property of Arker, who, not without a good deal of demonstrable reluctance, sometimes permitted someone other than himself to hold the weapon and fire a pellet from it at a harmless target.

Arker's air pistol was made of black metal. It felt pleasantly heavy in the hand. Its barrel was a tube that needed to be jacked open in order to insert a lead pellet, shaped like a tiny hollow badminton shuttlecock, into the back end. The act of closing the tube by pushing down and clicking it into place compressed a quantity of air capable of ejecting the pellet at high speed when the trigger was pulled. My friend Bollicks once defined the sound that the air pistol made when fired as "a quiet bang".

To augment Arker's arsenal of lead pellets, the supply of which was limited enough to make each one precious, a couple of raw potatoes, liberated from Arker's mother's lower Fore Street fish and chip shop, were carried along to Varley Head by him. By dint of thrusting the back end of the air pistol's loading tube a quarter of an inch or so into a potato, a potato pellet was engendered. Such pellets could be fired, with non-lethal results (contact with eyes excepted), at any suitable target that presented itself.

When my turn to hold Arker's air pistol and charge it from an already well pocked potato arrived at long last, I felt instantly empowered to re-enact a scene from a cowboy film recently shown for our delectation at the Rivoli cinema. Thus inspired, I extended the pistol at arm's length, took aim, and fired a potato pellet high over the top of Cogsy's head.

No actor on the silver screen could have improved on Cogsy's reaction to my shot. Cogsy turned tail well before the quiet bang had an opportunity to reach his ears. He ran, screaming "Help! Help! Murder! Murder!" in his best Vicar voice, haring at full tilt away from the field of fire, back along the cliff path in the direction of Pine Awn.

Entering into the gleeful spirit of the cinematic reprise, which seemed to be improving in quality all the time, I chased after Cogsy, reloading the air gun from the potato on the run and blasting off a sequence of potato pellets in the approximate direction of his by then rapidly dwindling figure.

Arker was left standing on his own. He was not much of a runner, although he was ever a worthy entrant in slow bicycle races, which he won at every Carnival day contest and annual school sports event. There were not always a lot of entrants for the slow bicycle race as the first requirement for a competitor wanting to enter the event was that he had to own a bicycle.

When I reached the top of the hill where the cliff path skirted around the top of Crowser Cove, I spied Cogsy already crossing the Freak valley stream way down below at Pine Awn, still running for all he was worth and persisting in screeching at the top of his voice. It appeared that I was as much out of the game as he was by then out of range.

I stopped and watched Cogsy scuttling up the distant slope towards Lobber field as if his life depended on it, all the time yelling, "He's going to kill me! Help! Help! Murder! Murder! He's shooting at me! He should be in Bodmin!" I wasn't going to kill him – murder was never an issue in my mind – and nor was I shooting directly at him, but Cogsy could have had a point about Bodmin.

Then Cogsy was over the far crest and gone from sight.

What a great afternoon it had been.

———

Roger went one better than his cousin Arker's Webley air pistol when he wangled the gift of a Diana air rifle as a Christmas present. The ultimate fate of Roger's air rifle was its confiscation by Roger's father Les on the grounds of its alleged misuse. However, for the all too short-lived time that Roger retained the air rifle in his possession, it was carried on all our joint forays out along the cliffs and up into the valleys.

We were imbued with a burning desire, with the help of the air rifle, to recreate yet another scene from a cowboy film (where would we have been without this wonderful genre advising us on how life should be lived?), with particular attention to the white-hatted hero advancing unscathed into the face of gunfire with bullets buzzing around him, knocking dusty slivers from rocks, ripping fragments of bark from trees to expose moist white wood beneath and kicking splashes in pooled water around his feet.

In a central area of the Port Gaverne valley woods, the existence and distribution of many great oak and elm trees provided a natural arrangement ideally suited to our artistic needs.

Each of us (taking turns) shouldered Roger's air rifle and climbed with it up to an elevated fork in one of the biggest trees. The other was left below to take refuge behind a tree trunk of his choice in the general vicinity.

On the signal from the rifle-bearer in the tree fork that he was ready, he who was on the ground commenced a stealthy advance towards the position of the former, dodging from cover to cover by making much use of the protection of whatever was available. The rifle-bearer's task was to look for signs of movement and fire hot lead pellets at trees in the immediate neighbourhood of the same, hopefully to induce shards of bark to fly through the air.

Although many pellets were released during such contests it was never clear to us that any bark was dislodged at all, assuming that one or other of the trees was even hit. Nor were either Roger or myself gunned down, irrespective of the fact that our fate in comparison to that of the trees always took on a secondary importance.

A pellet fired by Roger from his air rifle on the Pine Awn foreshore, ostensibly targeting a rock pool alongside which Eyesnot was standing at the time, failed to produce the anticipated result of a salt water splash but was extremely successful in compelling Eyesnot to leap high into the air while venting a high-pitched scream followed by a persistent keening as he collapsed in a heap on the rocks and clawed frantically at his backside with both hands.

The evidence appeared to suggest that Eyesnot had been hit in the ass. Employing a fair degree of haste, we pulled Eyesnot's trousers down to investigate and were greeted by the sight of a small blue circular depression disfiguring the left cheek of what was otherwise a surprisingly pristine behind.

From our encyclopaedic knowledge of cowboy films we knew that when someone was shot, the offending bullet needed to be cut away from the flesh in which it was lodged (unless it had drilled right through) with the aid of a big-bladed knife. Once the bullet was out, and had been dropped with a satisfactory ping onto a waiting tin plate, the residual wound required cauterising by means of applying a white-hot branding iron to it.

We were equipped with a suitable blade, as on my belt I wore a long sheath knife that Granfer had given me. My knife was considered by all present, apart from Eyesnot, as an ideal tool to insert in Eyesnot's left buttock as a means of prospecting for buried lead.

I was very proud of the knife and was devastated when, at a later date, I lost it over the edge of a cliff on the way down to Pine Awn from Lobber. Cutting my initials into a patch of tight turf bordering the cliff edge, as many others had done before me, was a task for which my sheath knife was well suited. However, I should have been much more careful as to where I put the knife down when I stepped back to admire my handiwork.

We didn't have a branding iron with us at Pine Awn, but had push come to shove we could possibly have improvised with one or other of the odd pieces of rusty scrap iron lying around in the shingle. The cauterisation of Eyesnot's wound was rendered unnecessary in any event when a touch of my knife's tip on the little blue mark on Eyesnot's ass made it plain that the skin was unbroken. We deduced that the pellet fired by Roger at the pool must have missed the pool and ricocheted off the rocks to strike Eyesnot's ass a glancing blow. That provided us with as satisfactory an outcome to the shooting as we could ever have wished.

Les's confiscation of Roger's air rifle was not related to parental displeasure regarding any of the near-miss games in which the weapon played a pivotal role; only a close-mouthed circle of players knew about those games in any case. Neither, for that matter, did considerations of the nearest miss of them all, Eyesnot's backside, appear to have featured in Les's decision-making process. It was almost certainly an incident that took place at the very entry to the Port Gaverne valley that occasioned the demise of Roger's air rifle.

The house that stood adjacent to the gate and stile marking the starting-point of the Port Gaverne valley footpath was something of a curiosity – unique in the Port Isaac locality insofar as it was flat-roofed. It was the last house out of Port Gaverne passed by anyone heading up the valley, or alternatively the first house in Port Gaverne encountered by anyone coming down. The house was built in the form of a squat box, the inside of which was sufficiently stuffed to force the walls to bulge slightly outwards towards the top. At the time of the said incident, its residents were Mr and Mrs Tom Honey and their great buzz of children.

On a certain afternoon, Roger (porting the Diana air rifle) and I were walking along the edge of a field bordering the rim of the lower Port Gaverne valley whence we could look directly down on Tom's hive-like residence. The day was grey and drizzly, conditions matched by pegged-out washing on a line crossing the flat roof. Not a single Honey capable of fitting into any of the sodden garments on show was in sight.

In our position high above the desolate array of laundry, we crouched down behind a wind-straggled blackthorn tree in order to spy out the lie of the land. Then, for no better reason than that the circumstances seemed appropriate, we loaded up the air rifle, aimed it at the washing-draped flat roof and fired off a lead pellet.

As if prompted by this attack on his mother's wash-day enter-prise, Colin, Tom's eldest son who was around the same age as Roger and me, appeared at once in view from around a corner of the house. Colin cast his eyes up at the sloping side of the valley above him. He appeared to observe nothing of interest, shrugged his shoulders, and returned to where he had come from.

We waited for a few minutes, fully intending to steal away unobserved when the coast was clear. On the other hand, the opportunity to deliver a second shot from the air rifle in the same direction as the first was too good to be let go, and it was not resisted.

At that, a whole swarm of Honeys, led by the principal drone Tom, emerged to zip around the perimeter of the house more in the manner of blue-assed flies than of purposeful bees. They offered an impression of being entrants in a contest to determine who among them could shout the loudest and gesticulate the most vehemently. Tom shook his fists over his head, looking as if he had just won the competition – or else that he was hopeful of getting into a fight that he might win.

Tom and Colin engaged in a joint charging action, a bracken-crushing beeline straight up the valley slope towards the lone blackthorn concealing Roger and me. I wondered how Tom and Colin knew where we were and concluded that our concealment was not as complete as we would have wished it to be. The quiet bang of the air rifle might also not have been as inaudible as Bollicks once alleged it was.

The entire Italian army could not have legged it with more despatch than we put into our retreat. Whether or not Tom and Colin actually completed the ascent was not known, although we would have been willing to bet that Tom's celebrated partiality to beer and fags ensured that he at least wouldn't have made it. Fury made a wondrous motivator, however, and on the assumption that Colin did get to the top it was certain that by the time he reached the blackthorn tree Roger and I were well out of reach on the far side of Trewetha.

We never learned if Tom knew the identities of those who sniped at his washing. On the other hand, since Les decommissioned Roger's air rifle not long afterwards, we imagined that Tom might have entertained suspicions that were osmotically absorbed by Les.

The crab apple seed from which had grown the burgeoning tree of tart fruit that characterised my association with Cogsy consequent to what he thought of as his attempted assassination by me near Varley Head (and which led to a not unperceptive assertion from him that I should be in Bodmin), was planted at a much earlier date. The roots of it all involved intimations of a failed Christmas feast in the first instance and a bantam cock in the second.

Once upon a time, this was how it all came to pass.

Roast chicken on our table at dinner time was an event so closely linked in my mind with the celebration of Christmas that I could not imagine the one taking place in the absence of the other. Roast chicken was no more or no less than a quintessential Christmas treat. If there was ever a second occasion in the year (there was never a third) when a bit of chicken appeared on a plate put in front of me, it marked an occasion so special and so utterly rare that I believed that Christmas might have come along early.

As a gulf of weeks shrank to a gap of days and Christmas drew ever nigh, the prospect of savouring a portion of roast chicken grew by leaps and bounds in my imagination.

Sometimes my mother, and occasionally Gran, might manage to win a chicken as a prize at one of the many whist drives that the two of them attended both in the parish and beyond it during the autumn of the year. Such awards were as alive and kicking as was the spirit of Christmas when they were handed over. Usually the bird needed to be collected from its donor (as often as not a farmer), assuming that first of all the donor was able to run fast enough to catch it.

Mr Tom Saundry, a man with much relevant chicken–catching practice under his belt, was then summoned by my mother to come along to our back garden, there to despatch the unlucky fowl by applying a thin-bladed knife to its neck. Following the execution, my mother immersed the feathered corpse in a bucket of boiling water to loosen up the attachment to the skin of the said feathers in preparation for plucking.

In the event that my mother's (and Gran's) card-playing ability fell short of being as sharp as the blade of Tom's knife and thereby didn't succeed in bagging a chicken to grace our Christmas table, the disaster was not associated merely with bad luck in the way the cards fell. Whist drives were savage affairs in which every participant knew beyond a shadow of doubt that every other participant was a cheat. The failure of my mother to trump tricks (applicable to Gran as well) was attributed to her being the victim of a collusive clique (in which Cogsy's mother Doris and Gran's sister Eva were alleged to be ringleaders) or to the incidence of marked packs of cards or, as a further alternative, to all of the above at the same time.

I found it exciting to think about the kind of carnage that might have ensued had the ladies of Port Isaac attended whist drives armed with air guns.

At a given point late in a whist drive season, it seemed that no matter what my mother and Gran could do at the whist tables to gain a prize of any kind, let alone the much desired Christmas fowl, the fall of the cards did not favour them. Watching heads being shaken as the unhappy situation was pondered, I took it all very much to heart and resolved to do whatever I could to help.

It so happened that on the grassy stretch bordering the section of cliffs separating Mr Hillson's isolated residence from the coast-watcher's hut below the New Coastguard Station, Mr Leonard Collings (Cogsy's father) had erected a wire-enclosed run to contain a small flock of bantam chickens. It was generally accepted that the run was Leonard's property but the bantams belonged to Cogsy. They were brightly coloured, strutting birds – the bantams that is, not Leonard and Cogsy. No bantam was quite as noisy as Cogsy of course, but all members of the flock were commendable crowers (in the case of the cocks) and cacklers (with reference to the hens) in their own right.

We boys had enjoyed a passing familiarity with Cogsy's bantam flock as a result of our activities on the cliffs nearby. Hence it seemed completely logical to me that Cogsy could be relieved of one of his bantams on the principle that he had many, Christmas was imminent and my mother's prospects of filling the chicken gap were, thanks at least in part to Doris, as substantial as a handful of Atlantic fog.

On a mid-December afternoon, accompanied by two other boys, I entered the field in which Leonard's run was located and approached the construction. We squirmed our way inside the wire and, once there grabbed an unwilling bantam cock (not without difficulty), shoved it into an old sack we had brought along for the purpose, exited the run and retreated from the kidnap scene by climbing over the hedge adjacent to the footpath leading downhill towards the coast-watcher's hut.

The bantam was not particularly happy with being abducted. He made his displeasure at being contained in a sack quite plain, not only to us as his captors but also to an elderly lady and a little dog who were taking a shared constitutional along the footpath at the very moment at which we appeared on top of the hedge.

The sequestered bantam flapped, screeched and imbued the sack with agitated volatility. The elderly lady, forgetting that etiquette required her to remark on the state of the weather before getting down to business, demanded at once to be informed on the nature of the sack's contents.

Our response was, for the most part, scrupulously honest. The sack, we told her, held a small live chicken won at a whist drive, recently collected and destined for the Christmas dinner table. At this she looked much less than convinced. The little dog made an effective partner in disbelief through yipping and yapping in counterpoint to the squawking coming from the sack.

Giving the sack a shake didn't help very much as far as quelling the racket went. It did, however, ensure that the overall clamour became so much worse. With the confrontational attitude of the elderly lady and her dog on the one hand and the violently oscillating sack on the other, a rapid retreat across the footpath, over another hedge and into the field below the New Coastguard Station seemed to provide the best option. Once into the refuge we dropped the bantam-invested sack on the ground and sat on it in an endeavour to conceal the evidence from the elderly lady's eyes, hoping that, for someone of her age, out of sight would soon be out of mind.

Our sitting action had the welcome consequences of initially muffling and then diminishing the bantam's raucous entreaties. At long last there was blessed silence. After a final skin-blistering glare in our direction, the elderly lady proceeded on her way, followed by the now sympathetically silent little dog.

Following the pair's departure we stood up and lifted the sack, which at the time looked rather limp. From its lack of motion, we surmised that the bantam might have gone to sleep, tired out by its vocal exercise. We opened the sack to see the bird lying in a somewhat crumpled condition down at the base.

We removed the bantam from the sack and attempted to revive it. A few small feathers fluttered from the scene, carried on a light breeze. The bantam's neck, ending in a lightly swinging comb-crowned head, dangled like a scrawny pendulum.

It dawned on us that the bantam cock had expired, not necessarily of natural causes. We realised that we had a body on our hands, which rendered an association of the bantam with the pleasures of Christmas just about as appropriate as the thoughts that motivated us to capture the ill-fated bird.

One thing we were sure of beyond any shred of doubt was that, the spirit of Christmas notwithstanding, retribution from one hard-handed quarter or another would already be advancing in our direction. Our minds focused on determining the best means to cover up the deed. A traditional remedy suggested itself at once. All Port Isaac people knew instinctively that, where incriminating evidence was concerned, the way forward was to "Heave it over the cliff!"

Basking in the brilliance of this revelation, we raced down to the far side of the coast-watcher's hut, where we hurled the sack containing the dead bantam cock over the cliff edge, supposedly consigning its body to the forgiving deep. I imagined the bantam making an acceptable Christmas dinner for either gulls or fish. Which of the disparate species got it would depend not only on whether the sack sank or floated but also on the lucky party being able to work out how to get the bantam out of the sack.

The elderly lady who bore witness to the act leading to the bantam's unplanned decease was, unsurprisingly, not at all reluctant to broadcast an account of it. Her story naturally took very little time to reach the ears of both Leonard and Cogsy. The former visited his chicken run to make a roll call of inmates and came up with a count of one bantam cock less than he thought Cogsy owned.

The consequence was that, irrespective of the absence of material evidence and in spite of the fullness of our assurances that what had taken place was nobly intended, the three of us involved were identified as miscreants and were "hammered" in accordance with standard practice.

My mother was required to pay Leonard five shillings that she couldn't afford by way of compensation for the loss of Cogsy's bantam. That should have been the end of the story but wasn't quite, as she proceeded to win a plump fowl at a whist drive held only a few days prior to Christmas. It had to be collected from a farm at Valley Truckle near Camelford, and it wasn't easy to get there – but we managed.

Barry Anderson was the most formidable leader of any of the duly constituted boys' gangs of Port Isaac. His gang established its meeting place cum headquarters camp somewhere in the general area surrounding either side of the track leading towards New Road from the coast-watcher's hut, including Shillingstones and the field in which Cogsy's stolen bantam expired.

Barry was one of the "big boys", being a few years older than me, and tall with it. He had an imposing presence, although as far as I was concerned his was a presence to be avoided rather than to be appreciated. He lived in a house standing on the outer edge of the corner where Front Hill curved around prior to commencing its ascent to the Church Rooms – hence the footpath linking Front Hill with the coast-watcher's hut by way of both Old and New Coastguard Stations commenced right alongside Barry's residence. I received my first ever haircut in the front room of that self-same house thanks to the ministrations of a lovely lady named Josephine.

Barry's gang comprised a dozen or more sycophantic cohorts, the majority of whom were big boys like their leader. A few boys of the smaller variety were co-opted into the gang to perform the function of menials. Bertie Byfield, a rangy, buck-toothed evacuee, whose height rivalled that of Barry, took the role of Barry's second-in-command.

The gang operated on a principle that anyone who was not with it was against it. The quality of neutrality was not recognised. The gang's strength lay in cohesion between its members. They went around *en masse*, and the best option that any small boy who was not a member could expect if he was unlucky enough to meet up with them in a remote place was to be the subject of hot pursuit.

The worst case came from being caught, as Barry's gang was highly accomplished in inflicting punishment on its prisoners.

In spite of its notoriety, membership of Barry's gang was something that many small boys craved. I was no exception to this desire, once upon a time at any rate. When an opportunity to serve under Barry came to me I didn't flinch from seizing it.

In my capacity as novitiate I was brought (or perhaps escorted under constraint would be a more appropriate way of describing the process) to the gang's headquarters camp down in the field below the New Coastguard Station.

The said camp was a rather elaborate affair built against a wall, boasting sides, a roof (of sorts) and a narrow gap for entry that could be closed off with a length of old curtain. Construction relied on chunks of driftwood and other wreck, squares of cut and lifted turf, bits of cardboard, old swatches of carpet, pieces of rusting corrugated metal, and anything else that the gang members, acting individually or together, had been able to scavenge, salvage, liberate, borrow, beg or steal for the purpose.

The initiation ceremonies for new recruits took place at and around this hybrid edifice. In my situation the procedural rules called for me to be thrust into a corner, bound hand and foot with a section of old rope and informed that to ensure my final acceptance into the gang I was required to endure whatever was to follow without uttering any sound or offering any complaint.

A smoky fire was maintained in front of the entry to the camp when the gang was in session. I watched as the ends of a number of long thin sticks were thrust into the depths of the fire, where they were left for a while prior to being drawn out again. The glowing tips of the charred sticks were then touched to a range of exposed locations on my arms and legs. Much to my shame I failed the initiation test dismally at the first hurdle, but since the generation of screams was a factor common to every other prospective small boy recruit that the gang got its hands on, I took comfort in knowing that my shrieks were by no means unique.

In discussions with other failed recruits to Barry's gang, I learned that alternatives to the red-hot stick initiation included being given a cat-o-nine-tails flogging with thin withies, made to run a club-wielding gauntlet of the gang, and being held in very close proximity to the fire while it was stoked into flamboyance.

Barry's gang camp was subject to not infrequent relocation, although without ever involving much in the way of actual distance. The camp's moves took advantage of the vicinity's characteristic features, inclusive of walls, banks and hollows, and thereby helped to keep the external opposition to Barry's gang rule wrong-footed.

Such opposition as there was consisted almost entirely of small boys who had good reason to be aggrieved by their treatment at the hands of the gang, whether or not the treatment was incurred pre-initiation, during initiation or post-initiation. The opposition was intent, through a tried and true practice known as "ragging", on converting Barry's camp into a Lanson jail-like pile of debris.

For obvious reasons it was imperative that camp ragging took place in the total absence of gang members. Would-be raggers skulked around the general area of the camp, as clandestinely as possible, in order to pinpoint the current location. When the main chance presented itself the opposition was then able to pounce at once.

The trick was to get the ragging done and then make haste to get away in order to avoid being caught. Capture guaranteed torture, but even so, a victorious ragging was considered to be almost worth the price of subsequent pain. Roger, Eyesnot and I ragged Barry's camp not once but twice – courageous actions delivering monumental satisfaction to the perpetrators.

—

Our second ragging raid on Barry's camp was so successful that it occurred to us that it would be a good idea to celebrate the event by getting hold of and firing off one of a number of neatly cased rockets that Granfer once showed me when I visited him at the nearby coast-watcher's hut.

We already had experience of precisely how Victory needed to be commemorated and we were by then getting to be so well inured into the annual Guy Fawkes remembrance of gunpowder, treason and plot that we saw no reason why gunpowder treason should ever be forgot at any time of year.

As it was, the door to the coast-watcher's hut was locked when our mission of celebration reached it. Depending on whose opinion was subsequently sought the incidence of a locked door was construed as being either fortunate or unfortunate. With conventional access to the coast-watcher's hut denied us, we attempted to make our way in through a little window at its back. Entry of a kind was achieved when I managed to insert my right hand into the hut by unintentionally shoving it through a pane of the little window's glass.

In the process of shattering, a piece of glass delivered a neat slash to the base of my little finger, carving the finger right down to the bone as if it was the breast of a plucked and dressed whist drive chicken (or even a leg from one of Cogsy's bantams). My blood flowed red, free and copiously. Once the cut was healed its crescent-shaped scar made a bright white reminder of that day thenceforth and for evermore.

The said scar joined two others that I managed to acquire, one of which was a long raised ridge on the side of my right thumb, caused by the scouring action of a chunk of broken pottery that I believed I was throwing away. My other scar of note was (of all places) on my tongue, where a permanently liberated central flap bore testimony to an accidental butt under the chin that I received in the school playground from Maurice, son of the great Revd W. Atterbury Thomas, vicar of St Peter's church. As an aid to concentration, the practice of sticking out the tongue and holding it firmly exposed between the teeth and lips, was an engrained habit of many, including me. Biting into my tongue when Maurice butted me was no more than an accident that had been ready to happen. The worst aspect of a cut tongue, apart from the ordeal of eating, was that it wasn't possible to put a plaster on the damage.

Unusually, no summary punishment fell down on the three of us involved in the coast-watcher's hut window-breaking accident. The evidence against us was much more than circumstantial, but the alarm caused by my gashed little finger and the ensuing streams of blood managed to get us off the hook.

Alternatively, Barry's gang could also have come in for a

portion of the blame. Be that as it may, gang camps migrated well away from the customary area below the New Coastguard Station at what seemed to be a date not a lot later. We didn't hear much about the gang thereafter. They had won battles but must have lost the war.

What we might have done had we actually got into the coast-watcher's hut and laid our hands on a rocket was additionally never an issue, which was just as well really.

———

When Barry's regime was no more, Joey Thomas, Sid Pluckrose and I kept the tradition alive by forming our own gang. Its sworn objective was to do daring things. Aggression was not part of its charter. Damage to private property in the execution of our gang activities was not intended to occur but was a factor by no means ruled out.

At the outset the name that we chose for the gang was "The Little Imps". We soon realised however that such a name not only lacked the redolence of derring-do, but would most likely also be regarded with derision by our contemporaries if it became common knowledge.

We therefore changed the name to the much more satisfactory "Green Triangle", based on a criminal gang we had heard about in a serial on the wireless. That original Green Triangle might have been a force that Dick Barton, Special Agent (not forgetting his pals Snowy and Jock), took an interest in defeating to the strains of the "Devil's Gallop".

The Green Triangle name conferred dignity on a gang boasting, not inappropriately, of three members. Using a penknife we inscribed the gang title onto the flat end of a thick slate course set into a wall in Rose Hill down below where Miss Alice and her brother Mr Wesslick Brown lived. For the sake of economy, this immortalised inscription consisted of a triangular symbol followed by the word "Green". To it we appended our individual initials and surnames.

The exploits of the Green Triangle involved a great deal of climbing and jumping, with particular emphasis on features such as trees, telegraph poles and scaffolding erected on houses undergoing repairs. Trespass in hostile territory was greatly favoured, as on land owned by the likes of Captain (retd) Roy May, or up in Mr John Neal's fig tree, or in Mr Jack Short's withy garden, the proviso being that the cited hostiles, some of whom were even gentlemen, were obliged to read, mark, learn and inwardly digest our trespass and be motivated to give chase. As the quarry of course, we always maintained sufficient distance for fleeing unscathed from their pursuit.

Any boy wishing to join the Green Triangle was required to undertake an initiation test. We borrowed the regulation from our experiences with Barry's gang, the Spanish Inquisition-styled practices of which were, however, consigned to the ragged ruins of its last camp.

On the left hand side of New Road, up above the commercial facilities of J. N. Hicks & Son Family Butchers, stood a grove of five tall fir trees. The trees were dense, feathery, springy and significantly interwoven towards the tops. The Green Triangle's initiation test required new members to ascend a tree at one end of the grove, make their way through the branches from tree to tree, and descend from the fifth tree at the far end.

The three founder members of the Green Triangle made the five-tree passage many times. It was a highly popular activity for us, which for obvious reasons was only tackled after dark. Our gang was bold all right, but not so bold as to take on the fir trees in daylight.

The great pity was that the Green Triangle failed to attract initiates willing to combat the five trees or, for that matter, willing to join the gang under other less exacting circumstances.

The demise of the Green Triangle took place at the top of Dolphin Street on a particularly dark night. Chicago House, the tall sentinel of Dolphin Street, was for once enjoying the attention of builders, and an intricacy of fragile scaffolding was in place all over the Dolphin Street side of the edifice, providing us with precisely what the Green Triangle was inaugurated to assault.

In the absence of Sid, Joey and I scaled up, over and across the maze of scaffolding. We came down by hanging and swinging on one of the scaffold bars and dropping the final few feet to land in Dolphin Street on all fours. We also hit the ground immediately in front of Mrs Ruby Steer, recently emerged from the door of the adjacent Rubena Cottage where she and her husband Will lived.

It was open to debate as to who received the bigger fright – Ruby, confronted by apparitions precipitated from the night, or Joey and myself at the unanticipated sound of Ruby's wild screams coming at us almost before we landed.

Joey and I fled from the scene up to Rose Hill, and from there, hearts hammering, we leapt up the steps to the Little Lane. Ruby hollered her head off behind us. She was a great friend of my Gran, at one with Gran in being addicted to the reading of crime novels. She should therefore have been prepared to encounter and deal with the unexpected, but all too patently hadn't learned as much as she should have done from Peter Cheyney and Agatha Christie.

Thereafter the Green Triangle considered it prudent to fold tents and steal away into graceful retirement, leaving only the Rose Hill inscription to signify to future generations that the gang once knew less ignominious days.

*From Crowser Cove to Lobber Point*

# 6

# Port Gaverne

*Up the still, glistening beaches,*
*Up the creeks we will hie,*
*Over banks of bright seaweed*
*The ebb-tide leaves dry.*

Matthew Arnold (1822–1888)
"The Forsaken Merman"

A CAST-IRON signpost, featuring black-painted embossed lettering set against a contrastingly white background on each of its two arms, stood in the manner of a gallows-in-waiting at the point where the proximate tops of Back and Front Hills united to blend into the lower curve of New Road.

One of the signpost's arms pointed uphill along New Road. The legend on this arm advised those who didn't know, particularly if they could read, that in that direction the metropolis of Wadebridge was separated from the signpost by nine and three quarters miles of road. The second arm served to direct the reader's attention to the fact that a place named Port Gaverne was only a quarter of a mile away. What Port Gaverne consisted of, inclusive of any historical connection with slate, the signpost left undefined.

The part of New Road leading towards Port Gaverne was, however, obvious enough. It gave the impression of a Barry Anderson gang-type gauntlet running between Charlie Lobb's North Cornwall Transport Garage, the Prout Brothers' Trelawney

Garage and Tre-Pol-Pen hotel on the left-hand side, and J. N. Hicks and Son Family Butchers' shop, the Central Garage, and the hotel-girt Terrace on the right.

On the far side of the junction of the cliff track linking the end of New Road to the coast-watcher's hut (and its inviolate store of rockets), New Road bled onwards into a hill leading down to Port Gaverne adjacent to the west flank of a harbour inlet and beach.

The summit of the hill commanded a grand panorama of the eastern reaches of the Bay. Castle Rock was prominent in the foreground and the dark chunkiness of Tintagel Head and Gull Rock occupied the distant background.

The name, Port Gaverne, was considered to incorporate the well-secluded harbour, a shingled beach and a tiny village (or large hamlet) that sprawled around the throat of the valley behind the head of the beach. This low profile (topographically speaking) ensured that for travellers Port Gaverne was a to-be-come-upon-suddenly kind of place. No feature of Port Gaverne could be spotted even with the countywide perspective obtainable by trespassers at the top of the St Endellion church bell tower. On the other hand, from that clandestinely accessed vantage point a visible trace of valley, straggling down to Port Gaverne from its source below Pendoggett, did serve to point the way.

———

"Gaverne" was pronounced "Gay-verne" by those of us who were natives of the locality. Most visitors from up-the-line foreign parts pronounced Gaverne as "Gavverne" – to our great amusement needless to say. We were skilled in prompting foreigners to give voice to this fortunately inimitable pronunciation.

The "Main", a flat-topped elongated promontory terminating seawards in a sheer cliff facing the close-by Castle Rock, formed the east flank of Port Gaverne's harbour. Castle Rock was separated from the end of the Main by a narrow wave-battered chasm that we called the "Gut".

102

The top of the Main was carpeted with wiry turf that gripped the underlying rock using the rooted equivalent of a wing and a prayer. The feet of visiting multitudes had the cumulative effect of a heavy roller compressing the fragile turf into a close-cropped spongy pile open to the sun and sky above and to the sea all around. In the high season of summer, such visitors turned the Main into a daily re-enactment of the feeding of the five thousand. Through much of the autumn and winter the Main was a gale-blasted wilderness on which few set foot willingly.

In fact, from late autumn through winter and into the heady days of very early spring, Port Gaverne, albeit harbour, beach, hamlet or Main, was to all intents and purposes an empty vessel. Life returned during the approach to the summer season and thrived in abundance when the visitors were back and the local hotels and guesthouses were once again yielding at the seams.

The Main was transgressed by several east–west-trending geological faults as widely separated as they were prominent. The ravenous sea had eaten away the Gut along one of the faults and was still chewing away at dark, narrow and mysteriously glistening gugs that it had opened up on three others.

One of the three gugs penetrated all the way through the base of the Main from one side to the other. The sea thrust and boomed into the gug from both entries. Unfortunately the through passage was too tight for us to get into even by crawling. Occasionally, as the tide rose and when the opposing swells were just right, air in the gug was compressed and forced through a tight blowhole creating an almighty blast accompanied by a wildly foaming gout of water. "What a geyser!" as Harold Behrens, on the wireless programme *Ignorance is Bliss* might have observed.

Slate had been quarried in the vicinity of the blowhole. A precipitous flight of steps (offering scant evidence of skill on the part of those who excavated them) tumbled down from the top of the Main to the former quarry floor, which had taken on new life as a tiny, sandy-floored cove called "Teague's (Tagg's)

103

Pit" opening to the harbour. Smoothly sloping rocks adjacent to the blowhole on the north side of Tagg's Pit provided the Main with its sunniest and thereby most popular spot to sit – and it attracted enthusiasts commensurately.

On the other side of Tagg's Pit the main feature was a great triangular-faced cavern, a consequence of quarrying endeavours that were presumably directed by a Mr Teague. The cavern couldn't be accessed when the tide was out but was simple enough for a swimmer to get into when the tide was high (and calm).

Castle Rock was aptly named. It was an invincible mass – high, dry (flying spray notwithstanding) and fortress–like where it walled the Gut; bladderwrack and mussel strewn where it fingered into the sea; and unyielding everywhere to the great gale-driven breakers that regularly smashed over it and turned the Gut into a boiling cauldron.

Cormorants and gulls stood in ranks as low-tide sentinels on the seaward point of Castle Rock, waiting, just like the flaccid seaweed under their feet, for the rising tide to bring bounty to them. Only Castle Rock's inner bluff against the Gut, its flaking cap held in place by a few valiant clumps of sea pinks, stood proudly above the sea at high tide.

Castle Rock's moods were, like Easter, a moveable feast. Mrs Nellie Blake, wife to Mr Wesley Blake, that splendid man, local preacher and quintessential pillar of the Chapel die-hard core establishment, once told me that memories of the well-loved view of Castle Rock from the cliff track near the top of Port Gaverne Hill had provided emotional sustenance to Wesley during his front-line service in the darkest days of the war.

The Gut, in the general manner of Port Isaac's social relationships, was normally alive with twisting undercurrents, even if on the surface all might seem good-tempered. At sea level the Gut was accessible from the outer end of the Main at its harbour opening. The distance between the Main and Castle Rock at that location was too wide to be jumped, and yet at the same time it was almost too narrow to be decently swum across. All that it took for a swimmer to get over was a simple push and glide. More than a few of the smaller boys, including myself, learned to swim in the Gut by the simple expedient of being either pushed or thrown in by bigger boys and left to our own devices to get out.

Once we could swim across the Gut, many of us entertained an ambition to swim through it and make a subsequent circuit of Castle Rock. Despite such intentions being honourable, discretion invariably tended to overrule valour. A circuit of Castle Rock made too daunting a prospect for me, even given an ultra–calm low tide. I could swim well enough to escape drowning if I was close to land, but anything beyond that was outside my limits.

I knew that unexpected things lurked in the depths around Castle Rock. Kelp fronds were down there and all too ready to reach up and snare my feet. Sly currents were plotting to drag me under. Rough rocks were knives wanting to skin me.

Several swimmers not only did the round of Castle Rock but also made the considerably more challenging transit by sea from Port Gaverne to Port Isaac. My mother was among them. Clarence Smith, the cleanest and neatest of three brothers (who made up in size and brawn what they almost assuredly lacked in brains), swam between the two Ports quite regularly up to the time when he was (allegedly) molested by a porpoise in the vicinity of Lobber Point. Porpoises were queer creatures to find in the waters of the Bay, but then, that applied to Clarence as well.

The harbour at Port Gaverne was an elongated V-shaped inlet in plan view, enclosed all about by significantly less imposing cliffs than those that lined the Port Isaac Awn. It was safe for swimming in at all stages of the tide. The top of its beach was characterised by a crunchy shingle bank containing rounded pebbles for throwing at any suitable target (whether stationary or moving) and flat stones for skipping long distances on the surface of the sea.

Rock pools along the harbour edges invited investigation when the ebb tide left them behind. They contained enthralling items of marine life that weren't always findable over at Port Isaac. These included little starfish, tiny cowrie shells (better known as "cuzzie-muzzies") and prickly sea urchins.

Below the bank of shingle, gentle sand formed the harbour floor down to and well out beyond the low-water mark. An ever-popular beach game involved us throwing up a circular sand-walled enclosure in the face of the rising tide. As the sea advanced, we strove ever more frantically from within the construction to build up, strengthen and increase the height of the wall. We called the game "rubber dingy". The sea always beat us in the end, but we made it struggle for a while before it won.

The flowing sea in Port Gaverne's harbour was not entirely devoid of raw sewage, although by Port Isaac harbour standards it was reasonably free of the same. Floating turds of various vintages were a common accessory of the swimming scene at Port Isaac. Aged varieties of the same were seldom encountered in the sea at Port Gaverne. Fresh ones expelled under water by bathers taken short might be quite another matter, however.

The principal pipeline shedding an unrestrained flow of domestic effluent that was destined to influence Port Gaverne harbour emerged at the crest of a sheer cliff a hundred feet high, adjacent to the cliff track linking the coast-watcher's hut to New Road. On the rising ground at the rear, the so-called "new" vicarage and the Castle Rock Hotel were by no means the least distinguished of features.

The pipeline and its outlet probably didn't reside in Mr Wesley Blake's store of Castle Rock memories. The quality of the effluent – on the assumption that not only the vicar of St Peter's (who not unsurprisingly resided at the new vicarage) but also the proprietors, staff and guests of the Castle Rock Hotel were involved in its generation – was, however, clearly beyond reproach. The reverse side of the coin lay in the effluent's odour. It was only necessary to approach the vicinity of the open end of the pipeline to know that any of our betters who thought their shit didn't stink were deluding themselves.

On one sunny afternoon I saw two huge basking sharks, each at least twenty feet long, floating lazily in the sea directly beneath the falling effluent. This pair of discerning marine monsters was presumably feeding on a blend of pre-digested gourmet cuisine of Castle Rock Hotel and clerical origin.

I knew that basking sharks had no appetite for people, although no swimmer (including Clarence) would have wished to meet up face-to-face with an example of the species. A mere hint that a basking shark was about in the Bay would be deep-water deterrent enough.

Mr Frank Rowe, Port Isaac fisherman and incidental proprietor of the newsagent's shop on Fore Street, caught a gigantic basking shark when the creature inadvertently tangled itself up in the nets of his fishing boat *Kate*. The poor shark, which failed to survive the experience, was towed in to the Port Isaac harbour enveloped in a cocoon of netting bristling with herrings. Its carcass was laid out up at the top of the harbour in front of a raised ledge at the base of the lower wall of Granfer Joey Thomas's fish cellar. There, under the robustly destructive attention of weather, gulls and boys, the shark remained until its disintegration was complete.

While the shark ripened, the gulls pecked at it, and the boys ran along its back from tail to head, leaping off at the head and racing around to the tail in transit after transit. A row of fishermen sat on Granfer Joey's ledge at the rear, dispensing wisdom, chewing baccy and spitting tobacco juice at any boy who was foolish enough to stray into their range.

When the pipeline below Castle Rock Hotel and the new vicarage was being installed, individual sections of cement pipe, each about two feet in diameter and six feet long, were spaced out along the line's planned route in a number of triangular stacks. Roger and I, both of us acting in contravention of long-standing, regularly issued and threat-backed orders from our parents, were out hunting for gulls' eggs one day on the nearby cliffs. At the same time, unknown to us, Roger's father Les and elder brother John Tinney were approaching the area, motivated by well-founded suspicions and determined to catch us out and deliver appropriate punishment.

Tactically speaking, Les and John Tinney employed a pincer movement. The latter advanced towards our position from the direction of the coast-watcher's hut and Les came in from New Road and the top of Port Gaverne Hill. We spotted Les, who was less unobtrusive than he probably thought he was, before he had a chance to see us. Dropping to the ground, we squirmed on our bellies up to one of the stacks of cement pipes and wriggled our way into separate sections. The pincer jaws closed very near our hiding places. Coffined in cement, we listened as Les and John Tinney expressed their displeasure at not finding us in terms that for the sake of our ears we were fortunately not all that familiar with.

The frustrated hunters, after a minute or two of vituperative comments, then left the scene. Allowing an interval long enough to ensure that they were really gone, I extricated myself, not without difficulty, from the tight and scratchy confines of the section of pipe that I had selected for refuge. As far as Roger's exit went, however, there was a problem. He was stuck in his section of pipe like a cork in the neck of one of Doctor Sproull's medicine bottles. I pulled at Roger's feet from below and pushed at his head from above, all of which endeavour only seemed to tighten the grip that the pipe had on him. Chasing after Les and John Tinney to get help didn't impress itself upon me as a healthy option. There was only one possible solution: if Roger couldn't leave the pipe, the pipe had to leave Roger.

I looked around for a big piece of hard rock, found one – an easy enough task on that vein-seamed cliff – and hammered at the pipe with it. It was fortunate that the quality of the pipe was well up to the standards of post-war utility, since the pipe broke into pieces at an early stage of the onslaught. Roger was then free of all but the cement shards, and the inventory of pipeline stock was one section short.

—

On the far side of Port Gaverne the road went up through a cutting festooned on either side with white, pink and scarlet valerian flowers shot through with bursts of marguerite daisies. Towards the top of this hill the road made a sharp right-hand bend around a raised bluff on which the stocky, highly visible and not overly attractive Headlands Hotel was sited.

A legend, "Headlands Hotel", daubed large on the whitewashed face of the hotel in contrastingly black block capitals, advised observers among the general public of what it was that they were looking at. My father had a hand in painting (or repainting) it not long after he was demobilised from the navy (on TB-associated medical grounds) at the end of the war. He was not wearing his demob suit at the time, which was just as well, really, as he was struck down while on the job by what my mother told me was an "emerage" and had to be carried away to hospital. Many like him, who were in the submarine service, were TB victims.

Painting at least a part of "Headlands Hotel" was his last job for several subsequent years, during which he was in hospital for most of the time. His right lung and a number of associated ribs were removed. As far as we were aware, this operation was one of the earliest of its kind to have a successful outcome. The surgeon in charge was named Dr Gasby. I never met him, but since his name was a household item for us, I had no difficulty in imagining him, thinking of him in the character of the irascible Dr Gillespie as played by Lionel Barrymore in the "Doctor Kildare" films that came along now and then to the Rivoli cinema.

My father came home for good following a lengthy period of post-operative recuperation at Tehidy Sanatorium down near

Camborne and went on to spend much of the rest of his life bemoaning his fate as a war victim. His Royal Naval background ensured that he took great pains with his heavily Bylcreemed appearance. At a hotel on the Terrace owned by my Uncle Stanley (Gran's placid and long-suffering brother) and Auntie Beattie (the Medusa-like cause of Stanley's long-suffering) in which my father did some light work for a spell, he was known as "Mr Shiny Shoes" and regarded as a look-alike of the "Man in Black", Mr Valentine Dyall.

As a good electrician he never gave up trying to find the sort of employment suited to his skills. In the process he tackled many jobs, none particularly successfully. His most productive role saw him working for a Padstow-based supplier of television sets at the time when television commenced its snowballing assault on the unsuspecting public of north Cornwall. In that capacity he managed a showroom in Bodmin, located on the main street across from the Garland Ox pub.

Aside from the Headlands Hotel, Port Gaverne laid claim to two other such "batter'd caravanserais": respectively, the "Port Gaverne", and (more originally) the "Bide-a-While" hotels. Both of the latter were located down in the open throat of the valley on the right bank of the channelled stream. The bed of the stream between the flat-roofed house and the beach was much more intricately contained between duly constructed walls than was the Lake in Port Isaac, although the stream through Port Gaverne was graced with no Lake-like familiar name that I ever heard mentioned.

The Port Gaverne Hotel had a licensed saloon bar popular with members of the more genteel drinking public, offering them as it did an attractive alternative to the spit and sawdust ambiance of Port Isaac's Golden Lion. Mrs Grew, the proprietress of Port Gaverne Hotel, commissioned Granfer to decorate her saloon bar using a nautical design of his own choice. Granfer's style made much use of coiled ropes and mock portholes set in some of the walls.

I don't know whether or not Granfer ever got paid for the work he did for Mrs Grew in cash terms. To a greater or lesser extent, however, he was paid in kind. The saloon barman was Mr Harry Hackett, who I understood was Mrs Grew's stepson. Harry's pint-pulling generosity was, when directed at people whom he favoured (like Granfer), reputed to be nothing if it was not commendable.

Granfer's seafaring experiences, sometime Royal Navy, sometime Merchant Service, covered half a century and incorporated three wars. They culminated in his spending three days immersed in the sea as a consequence of his ship being torpedoed by a U-boat late in the most recent war. Not long after being rescued he suffered a stroke that left him with hands that shook constantly and one foot that dragged so as to impose wear and tear on the toe of his boot when he walked.

Shaky hands didn't stop Granfer from using tools for gardening or mending and fixing in general, which was counted as a blessing. The handicap did, however, make it difficult for him to lift and convey a glass or cup of liquid to his mouth for drinking. He got around it by sucking up his beverage of the moment through a length of hollow bone inserted into the same. One such bone was kept in readiness behind the bar of the Port Gaverne Hotel, and was brought out by Harry whenever he pulled a pint for Granfer.

———

For those more interested in consuming softer liquid refreshments at Port Gaverne, Strout's café was the haven of choice. An institution of the Port Gaverne scene, Strout's café occupied a long wooden hut located immediately alongside the stream down below the Port Gaverne Hotel. The café was painted all over in creamy green and finished off in a line of darker green marking out its edges.

111

Inside the café Mrs Strout, the genial, ever-smiling proprietress, dispensed in thick china cups filled to the brim both tea of the kind that a spoon could be stood up in and a rather more opaque potion purporting to be coffee that came out of a bottle with "Camp" printed on the label. Her menu listed plates of bread and butter, splitters accompanied by jam and cream (traditional fare – when there was cream), currant buns to order and Künzle cakes on special days. In addition there were bottles of pop on offer (among which Vimto was the best appreciated) for anyone who didn't fancy sampling the tea and the many more who were unwilling to take a risk with the coffee.

A splitter was a soft bread roll torn away from a sheeted batch of the same baked down at Sherratt's in Fore Street. It was manually split in two (not cut and hence its name), yielding easily to the fingers. Jam (commonly strawberry) was spread on the two split faces. Cream was dolloped on top of the jam. It was a source of steady merriment for us to note how many visitors put cream on before the jam. They really didn't know any better.

Strout's café was well patronised. Quite a lot of the visitors who stayed in local hotels came to take afternoon tea under Mrs Strout's benevolent gaze, much to the relief of hotel staff. My mother did seasonal work at St Andrew's Hotel on the Terrace, and her great complaint regarding the St Andrew's guests was reserved for those who had the effrontery to request taking afternoon tea in the hotel as their God-given right, irrespective of the clemency of prevailing weather conditions outside at the time. Having to serve them with afternoon tea was viewed by my mother (in common with all hotel staff) as a major inconvenience. Moreover, their demands provided us with an absolute confirmation that the likes of up-country foreigners had no consideration at all for the sensibilities of the likes of proper Port Isaac people.

My mother sometimes brought home leftover portions of meals served at St Andrew's. I very much liked the exotic remains of curry and rice, but I was for the most part left unimpressed by most of the alternatives, which seemed to me to be lacking in substance, taste and solidity. If such was what visitors had to look forward to for their dinner (which, oddly enough, they ate in the evening and not at the correct time of the middle of the day), it was no wonder that they wanted to fill up on afternoon tea beforehand.

———

The harbour at Port Gaverne, lacking the benefit of either a protective Cow and Calf or a pair of breakwaters at its mouth, wasn't considered a suitable place in which boats (great or small) should be safely moored. In spite of this, however, the harbour was considered to represent an attractive opportunity to Hitler and his cohorts for bringing in their landing craft from which tanks or other machines of war could be run ashore.

As far as Hitler and his immediate circle were concerned, apart from the fact that they should all be in Bodmin, we were advised in song that, "Hitler – he only had one ball. Goering had two, both very small. Himmler was very similar, but Goebbels had no balls at all". In spite of any reluctant sympathy for Hitler's testicular condition, it was deemed essential to ensure that even if his tanks turned up at Port Gaverne none of them would be able to leave the beach. In order to deny them any strategic advantage, tank traps were set up all over the Port Gaverne foreshore. These had the form of staggered ranks and files of concrete pyramids, each around a yard high and spaced about two yards apart. A rusty chunk of iron thrust up like a secret weapon from the peak of each pyramidal installation.

Immobilised by tank traps, the tanks on Port Gaverne's beach would be sitting targets for destruction by a defending arsenal of shotguns (twelve-bore and .410), rabbit rifles (.22) and air guns (both rifles and pistols). The tank traps remained in place during the immediate post-war years. Perhaps it was thought better to be safe than sorry. The scars sustained by the tank traps came from battles with the sea. Wave action moved a couple of them a few feet on from their original sites. Whether or not the tank traps might have frightened the Germans off was never put to the test. What they did serve to do was provide excellent sun traps for beach veterans to lean against in summer for the purpose of consuming watercress, lemon curd, crab apple jelly and marmite sandwiches, all the while swigging stewed tea poured from venerable Thermos flasks.

Shortly before the end of the war it was on the beach at Port Gaverne that I tasted marmite for the first (and last) time. One and only one encounter with marmite was quite enough for me to suit for ever and a day. Although in my well-formed opinion lemon curd was high on the list of the most fearful things ever to be placed on bread, beef dripping notwithstanding, the sandwich filling that eventually placed genuine loathing in my heart was marmite.

I was on the beach with Roger, his Aunt "Queenie" Welch, and Queenie's two tiny children. The rare treat of a picnic was in prospect for us. Anything related to food ranked high in my estimation. Queenie handed me a quarter-round of a sandwich, which I seized with alacrity. When I put my teeth into it, however, I sensed that my eagerness was misplaced. The quarter-round of bread shut in an excruciatingly vile-tasting brown paste. Had I been of a less tender age, I might well have screamed out "Shit!" and have hit the nail smack on the head.

Subsequent enquiries led to the identification of the brown paste as marmite. At the time, what it was called seemed to be less important than what it was doing to me. The impact of my first bite at it was only equalled by a jolt I got when I pushed a forefinger into a light bulb socket and received in return a surge of energy that threw me from one wall of my bedroom to another. The electric shock affected only the arm attached to my questing finger. By contrast the taste of marmite shook my whole body. I could feel it shivering in my hair and toes.

114

I held the bite of Queenie's marmite sandwich in my mouth for what must have been at least half an hour until an opportunity arrived for me to crawl away and surreptitiously spit it out. Death would have shaped up as a preferable option to swallowing it.

Against the backdrop of the array of tank traps it was one thing for me to disgorge a single bite of a quarter round of marmite sandwich but quite another to eliminate the balance of the quarter round, which I had managed to squash into a brownish oozing ball in one of my hands. "Don'tcha know there's a war on?" (a meal-time declaration regularly made by Granfer even when there wasn't a war on any more) meant that all food needed to be eaten up, irrespective of the eater's distaste.

Taking great pains not to be observed, with my free hand I scraped a hole in the sandy shingle against one side of the tank trap in front of which Queenie's picnic was taking place. When I believed the hole to be deep enough, I proceeded to inter the balled-up remains of the quarter round of marmite sandwich in it without the rites of funeral.

This disposal certified that during the war at least one dangerous item fetched up against Port Gaverne's array of tank traps. I supposed that a compliant ground sea took the item away eventually, at a time when peace reigned and the spectre of a rejected quarter round of marmite sandwich invading the beach was no more to be feared.

The road down the hill leading to Port Gaverne from Port Isaac occupied the floor of a cutting, the average gradient of which was not particularly steep. The road was secured from the cliff edge on the left by a rocky berm a yard or two high and a couple of yards wide, the precinct of pedestrians. On the right side of the road, a high and grassy bank, spangled with primroses in season, rose towards the Terrace above. Reputedly, convicts brought down at His Majesty's pleasure from Dartmoor Prison had excavated the cutting. Those same rock-breaking experts in arrow-marked uniforms were additionally supposed to have dug out Port Isaac's Back Hill and to have sculpted the slate jetty down on the inner Main.

Adjacent to the upper section of the Port Gaverne hill, where the cliffs were sheer and at least a hundred feet high, those who walked along the berm were prevented from falling over the edge of the cliff by virtue of a tall and solid wooden picket fence. A fine view of Castle Rock and the Main could be made out through the narrow gaps separating the individual pickets.

The cliff topped by the fence edged a wave-cut platform of sea-polished purple and grey slate that was known as "Moon's Grave". Roger's Aunt Mary told us that in pre-picket fence days a boy, the son of an altogether appealingly named Dr Christmas, peered over the edge and fell to his death, mesmerised by the wavering reflection of the moon in the calm sea below. Another tale of how Moon's Grave came to get its name was equally exciting, involving a smuggler, pursued by excise men, who went over the cliff in a moonlit chase. Whatever the truth might or might not have been, the erection of the picket fence was its consequence.

Along the left-hand side of the lower section of the hill a stone-built wall performed the identical function to that of the wooden fence up above, albeit that the cliff capped by the wall was no more than twenty feet high at best. On the other hand, that twenty feet looked to be still a long way down.

The wall was about four feet high and peaked on top. Many of us liked to walk (or preferably run) along the top, planting one foot on one flank of the peak and the other foot on the other flank. Walls of that kind in our experience were built for walking on, not alongside. Avoiding a fall to the Port Gaverne beach was the best part of the wall-walking exercise.

The Main's jetty was a quarried-out bench about ten feet wide that stood at a height of twenty feet above the beach. It could be accessed from the beach via a flight of cut and concreted steps at

116

its upper end. The lowest of these steps were under water at times of high tide.

The jetty, fitted with a pair of installed granite capstans, was constructed for the express purpose of shipping out finished building and roofing slates produced at a number of quarries of the district, most of them small, a few a bit bigger, and one (at Delabole) absolutely gigantic. Productive quarrying activity, as with the jetty's *raison d'être*, had for the most part faded into the murk of memory.

Access to the far end of the jetty was obtained along a rude track, down which the slate formerly destined for export must have been brought. The track commenced in the shadow of Headlands Hotel at the outer curve in the road to China Downs out of Port Gaverne. It wandered through a shallow cutting leading into the heart of the Main, took a sudden reverse hairpin bend close to the top of the steps down to Tagg's Pit and, having done that, slipped down to the jetty through a gully equally as deep as it was narrow.

Within the gully, the track crossed the void of an open (geological fault-related) gug. A few baulks of timber, two of which were still in place, appeared to have provided the essential means of spanning the gug prior to the construction of a wooden footbridge complete with side rails. Notwithstanding the availability of the wondrous bridge, we greatly preferred crossing the gug by crawling on the rotting baulks.

———

A row of cob-walled fisherman's cellars occupying the right-hand side of the road at the foot of Port Gaverne hill offered convincing evidence that cob, a mud-like blend of earth, stones and chopped straw, was not an especially weather-resistant material. The wall required no more than a hard glance in its direction for its cob to start crumbling. Sparrows nested in holes eroded adjacent to the decaying ends of timber beams jutting through the cob. Swallows flitted under the eaves inside the cellars.

In behind this row of fisherman's cellars the "White House" squatted in relative seclusion at the back edge of a narrow courtyard. The White House was large, solid and extensively whitewashed. Whether the name was a consequence of the whitewashing or the whitewashing a consequence of the name wasn't known. The name might have been regarded as being a little less than imaginative had it not been for the fact that across the way, close by the Port Gaverne Hotel, was a house painted pink (with what we thought of as pink whitewash), which was known as the "Pink House". We assumed that the house names were devised to benefit colour-blind postmen.

The road flattened out in front of the row of cob-walled fishermen's cellars and curved sharply to the left to pass by the head of the beach and rise again towards the Headlands Hotel. An adjoining track ran up into the valley from the outer rim of this curve, flanked on its left-hand side by a line of straggling tamarisk trees surmounting a low hedge that provided an insubstantial shield to a small cottage. Only a little further up on the right-hand side, looking almost dwarfed against the valley slope above it, a derelict flat-topped limekiln and a defunct kipper house squared up to one other on opposite sides of a patch of greensward. What remained of the limekiln resembled a redoubt of the kind that we saw the French Foreign Legion defending against hordes of Arab fanatics on the screen at the Rivoli. The vacant maw of the limekiln gaped at us from under a heavy stone arch.

There was no more appropriate name than "the Fort" for us to assign to the old limekiln. It was an ideal setting for our attacking games, not the least of which substituted Red Indians for Arabs. However, the greatest challenge to occupiers of the Fort came from a foe in the person of Commander (retd) Llewellyn Davis RN. The worthy Commander resided in a picture-postcard cottage sandwiched in between the Fort's bulk and the cob-walled row of fishermen's cellars. He was lean and imperious, a man born to don a duffel coat, face up to a North Atlantic storm

118

on the bridge of a plunging destroyer and sip strong cocoa from a thick and most likely chipped china mug. When he appeared in sight, we evacuated the Fort, beating a hasty retreat to the hills.

The Commander was incidentally the chairman of the Port Isaac Conservative Association. Conservatism was a straggling political weed in north Cornwall's lawn of die-hard Liberalism. For a while my father served as a less than proficient treasurer of the PICA, which placed him too close to the Commander for my Fort-related comfort. My father hero-worshipped the Commander, to an extent that made it certain the Commander's naval credentials rather than his political association made the more powerful drawing card.

A succession of lovingly tended vegetable gardens covered the valley bottom on both sides of the track for a full hundred yards stretching between the top end of the defunct kipper house and Mr Tom Honey's flat-roofed (and one-time sniper-targeted) house. The largest of the gardens was the furthest one up on the left. It was looked over by the flat-roofed house and (perhaps not inconsequentially) was well protected by a hedge enhanced with a few strands of barbed wire. The owner of the garden was the Commander's wife. She was an almost skeletally thin, exceedingly tall and outwardly leathery lady with an impeccably brittle and refined accent, who defied convention by regularly wearing slacks.

Mrs Commander poured her soul into tending the garden, which was famed for its crops of strawberries and raspberries. Desirable though such soft fruits were to the vigilant eyes of scrumpers like me, the combination of the barbed wire and the tireless vigilance of Mrs Commander ensured that the fruit was kept more or less secure from the ministrations of predators.

Granfer's garden, which he tended almost every day, was the first one on the right in the sequence of valley-bottom gardens. He had a wonderfully productive row of blackcurrant bushes growing along one side of his garden, and he raised his tobacco crop, in which pursuit he maintained an intense rivalry with Mr Joe Honey (known as Old Joe), in the shade of the blackcurrants. Old Joe's garden was located directly across the valley track from Granfer's, so comparative studies were not difficult to make. Each competed with the other to produce the best smoke. The valley stream truckled in its gully adjacent to the far edge of Old Joe's garden, providing Old Joe with an edge combining irrigation with Granfer's irritation in times of drought.

Granfer nurtured his tobacco plants using mulch prepared from a secret formula in which sheep shit played a leading part. I was delegated by Granfer to be his official collector of sheep shit, in which capacity I was despatched to Lobber field (not only a fount of sheep shit at its most prolific but unfortunately also rather too far away from the location of the tobacco plants for my liking) when the occasion demanded it. I set out for Lobber with a large hessian sack over my shoulder, under strict orders to bring home as much of the essential commodity as the sack would take or as I could carry, whichever was the greater. In principle my compensation was fixed at sixpence per sack of sheep shit. Sometimes I got paid and sometimes I didn't.

Sheep shit, unless it was so recently dropped by a sheep that its constituents were wet enough to hold together, normally defied a simple gathering up in bulk. As it dried, sheep shit fell to pieces. I might just as easily have tried to fill up the sack with rabbit shit.

My occasional attempts to cut corners by bulking the sheep shit out with pats of cow dung were never well received by Granfer. His mulch recipe and cow shit were incompatible.

I hated having to carry a loaded sack of shit up through Fore Street. Someone was bound to ask me what the sack contained and wouldn't welcome being told. On the other hand, it was only necessary for any observer to have a quick look at the sack to know what was in it, as brown drops of moisture from the freshest pieces within were apt to weep their way out through its weave.

A hundred yards or so up into the valley past the flat-roofed house, a stile, overhung by blackthorn trees, interrupted the track. In the shadow of the blackthorns on the far side of the stile, the track became a pathway, crossed the thin stream of water (no more than a muddy trickle for most of the year) draining the little brake that pointed to a shortcut towards Trewetha on the right, and proceeded along the upper edge of a withy garden belonging to the eternally sanctimonious and archetypal miserable old bugger Mr Jack Short.

We couldn't imagine that Jack had ever been a young man, let alone a boy. Jack, a retired fisherman, exhibited a marked intolerance for all boys whose ages were measured by a single figure. It was not for nothing that we thought of him now and then as Jack Shite.

Jack's withy garden was marshy underfoot. Snowdrops grew there in great profusion in the early months of the year and were always replaced by clumps of fanfare-trumpeting daffodils when spring arrived. In that season of the year (and in Jack's absence) we picked bunches of the daffodils to hand over to our respective mothers on Mothering Sunday. Mothers weren't supposed to enquire where the daffodils came from. It was the thought behind the gift that counted.

Jack and his wife Phoebe lived in a cottage on the left-hand side of upper Dolphin Street, not far down from Rubena Cottage and Chicago House. From his residence he wended his way down Dolphin Street, along Middle Street to the Town Platt and into Pawlyn's with unctuous self-righteousness oozing from every pore of his tautly pink skin.

Phoebe, with her hair customarily bound in a tight grey bun, clacking false teeth and an aquiline glare framed by thick-lensed spectacles, was exactly the kind of person who lived up to everything that might be expected from someone with a Christian name like that – and who moreover was married to Jack Shite.

Jack's fisherman's cellar was located up towards the top of Middle Street facing the high outer wall to the garden of Trevan House. The sliding door at the front of the cellar was no more than a few paces away from the old downtown village pump. One day when Jack was inside his cellar someone slid the door shut, clapped its padlock to and threw away the key. I was suspected of having done the deed, although I wasn't formally accused.

I had a faint memory of standing at or near at the door of Jack's cellar on a few occasions, but as to whether I was guilty of incarcerating him, I genuinely couldn't remember. However, I found it gratifying to have it thought that I was the culprit. If it wasn't me who locked Jack in the cellar, I could but wish that it was.

The incident enhanced Jack's detestation for me. He probably took his feelings up to St Endellion with him when his time came. It was regrettable if that was so, but in my book Jack and forgiving qualities never went hand in hand.

# 7

# *Nature's Bounty*

*Blossoms and dewdrops — at the bent spray's edge —*
*That's the wise thrush; he sings each song twice over,*
*Lest you think he never could recapture*
*The first fine careless rapture!*

Robert Browning (1812–89)
"Home Thoughts, From Abroad"

ONCE THE HARBINGERS of spring had fulfilled the more essential tasks in their list of harbinging duties entirely to their own satisfaction, the devastated tangle of last autumn's dead and decaying bracken on the slopes of the valleys could yield to the testing touch of the fresh, green-hooked fiddle heads thrusting up from the dank soil below.

Nature was on the move.

Early primroses, making subtle splashes of colour displayed in fan-like spreads of crinkly veined leaves, blinked through gaps in the protective mesh of spent bracken.

As spring really picked up its pace, seemingly limitless swathes of primroses were not only strewn about in the valleys, they also lined the borders of fields under the shelter of ancient stone hedges and burst out of soil-dribbling cracks and crannies on the hedges themselves.

Primroses made a highly saleable commodity for us. The earlier we got them, the more valuable they were. Competition for the earliest primroses was intense.

A bunch of primroses, comprising enough cumulated stalks to fit within a circle made by a touching thumb and forefinger, tied up with a piece of either cotton or wool and with a ruff of leaves surrounding it for effect, could be sold for as much as sixpence when spring made its first hop, skip and jump. Unfortunately, it came to pass that all too soon a time of scarcity gave way to a time of plenty (three pence per bunch) and ultimately a time of absolute glut (when primroses could barely be given away).

We picked primroses by the basketful and seemed to not even dimple, let alone dent, their profusion. Completed bunches were laid in what was known as a "chip basket", fashioned out of interwoven paper-thin laths of crude and splintery veneer. A chip basket had an oblong shape and was held together by a stapled and mildly reinforced rim. Its handle was a curved strip of thin metal slotted and riveted at both ends. Normally a residual ear of metal stuck out alongside each slot and rivet in order to ensure that a slice would be excised from at least one of the basket carrier's fingers.

Chip baskets came in two sizes, one big and the other small. It took much effort, high optimism and sterling resolve to fill up a big one, but there were lots of people who managed it regularly, not only at primrose time but also in the season of bluebells, of mushrooms, blackberries and sloes. Lined with fresh bracken ferns and topped up with either flowers or berries, chip baskets combined duty with honour.

Primroses were my favourite wild flowers, delicate and delightful, light in appearance, scent and taste. The taste of a primrose was characterised by a modest sweetness and a subtle hint of cool fragrance to match the scent. We relieved afternoons spent picking primroses by consuming a portion of the floral surplus. The nutritional value of primroses might well have been a subject for debate, but eating them did no harm to any one that I knew of.

Cowslips, the absolute royalty among wild flowers, were found growing wild only in the vicinity of Welshman's Quarry out to the east of Port Gaverne. They occurred nowhere else in the parish. At Welshman's Quarry a great drift of cowslips, in close relative company with primroses, bloomed right at the edge of the soaring cliff. The multiple deep yellow flowers hung like defiant fairy bells, proud on sturdy pink stalks. The wind keened over the top of the cliff, bending the stalks but never forcing them to yield. A bunch of cowslips was a rare prize, worth as much as nine pence to anyone who picked it.

On the steep slope of the Freak valley rising to the rim of Crowser Cove from Pine Awn, a carpet of primroses presented an annual spectacle attracting many visitors to look, ponder and marvel at. A pale yellow blush seeped across the slope as primroses woke up. In the sunlight the slope was a golden glow that might have defined the end of a rainbow.

When I stood in the midst of that primrose wash my eye was drawn to the wink of violets, tiny, understated, and yet utterly intense. Pine Awn was also alive with violets flourishing under the spell of the primroses. Unfortunately, gathering a posy of violets was a tortuous task. A violet posy, fresh and mesmeric, was sold with reluctance, even when a shilling was proffered for it.

As the primroses faded, the miracle of Pine Awn in spring moved into second gear. Great seeps of blue bled across the slope in the shake of a day, merging to form a thick flood of bluebells in an array rivalling the sweeping sky.

Walking in bluebell-floored woods on a warm evening, the sun close to setting but still gracing the calm air with its touch, brought deep contentment. The cool green leaves overhead were fresher than daisies. Birds sang, and moss lay like velvet on tree trunks. The sound of a peal of St Endellion bells (the bell-ringers practising under the direction of Mr Coppin from Trefreock Farm) sometimes sifted across the still fields. Twilight closed in like a benediction.

We revelled in the utter reliability of wild flowers. Each species claimed its rightful place in the relevant season of the year. The presence of wild flowers was a life-inspiring constant. They flickered through the race of days and the run of months in an eagerly anticipated spectrum of colours beating a gentle rhythm of consolation for the hard-paid dues of winter.

The last throw of winter's dice was pushed from the table of play by the clean white-on-green of snowdrops. Out in Mr Jack Short's soggy withy garden the snowdrops (with little or nothing to expect from Jack) clumped their heads together as if they were willing the daffodils to come and take charge. The snowdrops probably knew that further up in the deep woods and mossy banks of the Port Gaverne valley, where a mighty host of little white bluebell bulbs were considering putting up shoots, tiny stars of three-leaved wood sorrel were making an equally white and glittering display.

At the same time, on distantly seen cliff ledges and sub-vertical faces, pungent bursts of succulent white-flowered scurvy grass resembled patches of hoar frost. The big daisies that we knew as "marguerites" filled conveniently sheltered cliff hollows as effectively as if they were imitating driven snow.

Employing their formidable beaks, all through the month of April gulls were out tugging away lengths of scurvy grass to use for building nests. On the nineteenth of April in one year I found a gull's egg in a nest constructed entirely from scurvy grass. The nesting material had been available in the right place at the right time for the gull, but its egg was laid unusually early, not at all in keeping with our well-known couplet, "'Tis in the first week of May, that the gulls begin to lay".

As spring marched and aprilled onwards, along the verges of many lanes and roads and topping hedges around fields, tall snowy thickets of lacy-headed cow parsley sprang to attention on stalks that were as hollow on the inside as they were fluted on the outside. Cow parsley overwhelmed lesser plants for the duration

126

of its season of growth. When ripe, cow parsley stalks were both rigid and tough. A length of cut and trimmed stalk made a potent peashooter. It was fortuitous that the elder trees were concurrently sporting inverted umbrellas of hard green berries to provide an ever-ready charge of peashooter ammunition.

The fragrant white-clustered flowers of the elder needed to fade and die in order to release the green berries. Later on these berries were destined to redden, soften and proceed to turn glossy black. Ripe elderberries were the fundamental ingredients that went into preparing homemade elderberry wine. Some makers of elderberry wine also dabbled in elderflower wine; however, since too much of the latter meant there would be less of the preferred former, harvesting the same was a finely judged process. Such beverages, which were widely available as domestic staples imbibed (for medicinal purposes) even by chapel people, ranged in taste from being merely nauseous to absolutely dreadful. As with many Port Isaac people, age did not always treat such wines with kindness, and nor did they travel well.

To load a cow parsley stalk peashooter, all that was required was that the mouth should be filled with green elderberries taken fresh from the tree. To activate the weapon, one end of it was placed firmly between the lips, the cheeks were inflated and pressurised to the extent that the charge of green elderberries would allow, and the pressure was released along the stalk with all the force that the lungs could muster. Thereupon, the green ammo was directed in an explosive stream towards its designated target.

To discourage pea shooting, many of our elders and betters, legitimate targets all, instigated a rumour that placing a cow parsley stalk between the lips was certain to cause an appalling disease. In the process of offering this advice more than a few of the advisors would be in the process of either lighting up or contemplating their sixteenth or seventeenth fag of the day.

No amount of dire warnings could deter the pea shooting brotherhood. We all believed we were immortal in any case.

What a forecast of severe incapacitation implied to us was the prospect of accepting a few days of discomfort on the way to several more days of recuperation on which we wouldn't have to attend school.

A much more pressing concern related to cow parsley was its perverse tendency to grow hand in glove with the benignly white-flowered yet altogether deadly-leaved plant appropriately named stinging nettle (a name telescoped to "stinginetle" in popular parlance).

Stinging nettle leaves were powerful foes of legs that, grazed and grimed, lay open to the world betwixt stocking top and short trouser bottom. To some extent long trousers helped to counter the menace of stinging nettles, but such protective garments wouldn't be available to any of us boys until either we became fourteen years old or grew tall enough to nullify the handicap of limited age.

Stinging nettles were tricky. When a stinging nettle was unhesitatingly and firmly grabbed hold of, its poison was at once neutralised. Sometimes it was even possible for us to walk boldly into dense masses of stinging nettles and emerge on the far side as unstung heroes. But that was only sometimes. Normally the faintest brush of the skin against the hairy venom of nettle leaves and stalks immediately raised a violently itching rash which demanded to be scratched (the more frenziedly the better) until blood flowed.

Lush stinging nettle growth barring our path called for unrelentingly ruthless measures to be taken. Armed with long sticks cut from a convenient hazel thicket, we felt duty bound to lay about ourselves in order to flail the offensive stinging nettles to the ground so as to proceed on our way.

Chance stings were soothed by means of rubbing a freshly plucked dock leaf over the infected area of skin as vigorously as the circumstances required. Dock leaves were prolific and were never hard to find when they weren't urgently needed.

As if the blitz of primroses was not enough for us, spring cemented its arrival by covering the tangled thorniness of winter-gaunt blackthorn thickets with a veritable blizzard of may blossom. The delicate may blossom petals sifted in the breeze and lay on the ground like the fine confetti did on Back Hill after a wedding in St Peter's church. All up, down and through the valleys the blackthorn sang the song of the may.

Curiously enough, it was during the month of April when may blossom reached the peak of perfection at which its crusted-branch fragrance begged to be gathered in. However, custom decreed that to pick may blossom prior to the first day of the month of May would bring bad luck to the picker. The inherent risk was considered not worth taking under any circumstances.

Ignoring the custom would ensure that misfortune fell immediately upon the household unfortunate enough to have the errant may blossom picker as a member. Once the may blossom appeared, I was repeatedly warned by my mother as to precisely what dreadful fate awaited me if I succumbed to temptation and plucked the least sprig of it

As a consequence, may blossom was always left to be admired in its natural condition. It rested securely on the blackthorn until the month of May came in, although by then the petals had become decidedly brown at the fringes and had thereby lost the desirability that characterised them when they were fresh yet sadly unavailable.

It was probable that may blossom was named by someone with a sense of humour. The use of "may" (rather than march or april) as the qualifier for the blossom was redolent of a convivial atmosphere, of warmer days and an opportunity to be joyful. There was no doubt that "may blossom" had the kind of easy, tongue rolling resonance about it that a blossom named for bleaker preceding months could never really offer.

For all that, what was important was that blackthorn branches were wont to hang heavy with may blossom in late April, creating a mighty garland that genuinely glowed. Waves of may blossom rolled surf-like amongst blooming ponds of yellow gorse, splashing sufficient colour in the valleys to herald the visit of a pope.

———

May blossom had to die so that sloes could live. Young, hard, small and green sloes formed highly appropriate charges for peashooters. Sloes were tiny plum-like fruits, ultimately bending the blackthorn branches under their cumulative weight.

A ripe sloe exhibited a perfectly translucent purple grape-like bloom on its skin. Beneath the skin there was far more stone than flesh, although with a bit of luck a tree of the larger and meatier variety of sloes known as "bullums" – heading for but falling somewhere short of damson dimensions – might be encountered. The only bullum tree that I knew about overhung the lower side of the roof of Mr Jestinian (Jess) Steer's fish cellar on the edge of Trewetha Lane just above the top of Rose Hill.

Sloes and bullums were nominally edible. At optimum ripeness their taste was almost pleasantly tart. Unfortunately, a state of optimum ripeness was all but impossible to assess. The normal consequence of biting into a sloe was that the inside of the biter's mouth seemed to dry out as effectively as if it had been stuffed with blotting paper.

Dedicated makers of elderberry wine were ever ready to harvest sloes and use them to infuse gin and give rise to a powerful beverage that was not unnaturally known as "sloe gin". The liquid consistency of sloe gin sat somewhere between that of a fortified wine and Lyle's Golden Syrup. The kick that sloe gin delivered was not intended to be enjoyed for itself alone, although those who took pleasure in downing the stuff in quantity (yet again for medicinal purposes) could well have disagreed.

Somewhat more palatable than sloes were young blackthorn and hawthorn buds pinched off just as they were ready to burst into leaf. The taste of such buds was described as "bread and

130

cheese" and wasn't far removed from the savour of that classic sandwich, on the assumption that the bread was a little stale and the cheese not too mature. It was possible that the allusion to the bread and cheese taste was derived from the preference of yellowhammers to flit around and peck at burgeoning buds. Everyone knew that the yellowhammer's song went, "A little bit of bread and no *cheese*!"

The month of May would have been incomplete for me without advice from my mother that, no matter how pleasantly warm the weather outside seemed to be, it could be confidently relied upon that the temperature was going to drop like a stone before the day was out. Therefore she (in keeping with most other mothers of the village) decreed that the apparel that had acceptably clad me since before last Christmas would remain in place during May. The policy was summed up in the adage, "Cast ne'er a clout, till May be out". In the mid-spring sunshine I was condemned to swelter in a woolly jumper, a vest, gloves, and a jacket, waiting for the merciful onset of June to provide relief. Fortunately I didn't have to don a balaclava helmet – not all boys were so lucky.

Taken at face value, the prospect that no clout would be cast till May was out was not displeasing. I knew a bit about clouts of the kind that raised the power of a customary clip around the ear by a degree or two. Clips around the ear were regular, all-purpose reactions by our elders and betters to just about any activity we undertook. Clouts came along with less frequency than clips around the ear but weren't strangers when they did.

Whether or not we gave offence deliberately or inadvertently to our elders and betters was immaterial. In the absence of offence, elders and betters were experts at manufacturing excuses for delivering a clip around the ear, if for no other reason than to "encourage the others". Any anticipation that May might be a month in which a moratorium was to be placed on ear clipping (or clouting) practice was always doomed to be disappointed.

As it was, May sunshine was deterred from benefiting our winter-toned fish-belly pallid skin by several layers of clouts of the non-ear-clipping kind. Rents and rips in the outer clout were usually sealed off by the underlying layer, and if not, then by the third beneath the second. And so on. Many such holes were either darned or patched, but some were left as they were for ventilation purposes.

When I was clad in well-perforated garments my mother described me as being "more holey than righteous". Our ragged-assed fraternity of boys was, in almost complimentary terms, told that it was "out to hass and out to helbow", which appraisal clearly specified the more common locations of clout wear and tear.

Irrespective of whether or not our clouts were cast off or kept on during May, we knew that the year was changing for the better. The weather might step two paces forward on one day only to take a pace back on the following day, but the balance of change was what counted, and it was nothing if not positive.

An annual May Day celebration enjoyed a short yet memorable career at the Temperance Hall in lower Trewetha Lane. The organisers were no doubt motivated to set up an event with potential to grow into a long-term tradition, but what they omitted to do was to devise a strategy to combat the strong currents of deep apathy that ran beneath the still waters of the Port Isaac public. There was no shortage of people ready to shoot a good idea down on sight.

The leading light of the doomed May Day enterprise was Mrs Soady, wife to the gung-ho St Peter's vicar of the same name (successor to the much-missed Rev W. Atterbury Thomas) to whom Miss Jessie Pidler, pre-eminent among his congregation, referred with unintentional perception as the Rev Soddy.

The focal point of the May Day celebration was a tall, thick pole of telegraphic proportions, erected in the centre of the Temperance Hall auditorium. It was identified as the maypole.

A host of long coloured ribbons were attached to the top of the maypole at a point just beneath the roof, whence they dropped to the floor in a rainbow cascade. The white-clad celebrants of May Day, among whom I was (once only) numbered, formed up in a broad circle centred on the maypole, each holding on to the end of a ribbon as if his or her life depended on not letting go. The tautly extended ribbons pointed at the top of the maypole in the manner of a skeletal cone.

To the accompanying strains of, "Come lasses and lads, take leave of your dads and away to the maypole hie" (providing new meaning to Charlie Chester's "Stand Easy" assertion that "once again a popular tune is murdered at the piano"), the celebrants tripped (mostly figuratively but sometimes literally) and danced in and out and around one another, weaving and unravelling patterns with the ribbons, while endeavouring to defer the inevitability of at least one tangle.

The wild flower plants, grasses, creepers, bushes and trees of hedge-rows bordering the lanes and roads of the parish (as well as the verges of the public footpaths) needed no incentive to flourish and did so, up, down and sideways. The job of maintaining the hedgerows and verges in trim in order to keep the lanes, roads and pathways open to the unimpeded passage of infrequent vehicular traffic and the much more frequent strolling public was carried out by Mr Frank Gilbert. Frank lived with his wife Lena, a model of bustling kindness, in the very last of the so-called "middle" row of council houses up on the right at the top end of Hartland Road.

Frank was tall and burly. He wore coarsely woven trousers, on which grass and mud stains fought a battle for precedence. As protection against the sun, Frank sported on his head a flat cap drawn from the good stable of long and arduous service. If inclement weather caught Frank when he was out on the job, he draped an empty sack over his shoulders to soak up the rain.

133

Frank's tools of the trade were few in number. The tally consisted of a clasp knife and a whetstone (both in a pocket); a hard bristled broom; a Father Time styled scythe; a wickedly curved billhook and a hazel stick about a yard long with a fork at one end that under different circumstances would have made an excellent catapult. He travelled around on an old pushbike. The scythe went over his shoulder, and the broom, the billhook and the hazel stick were tied onto the crossbar of his bike with hairy twine. Frank used the hazel stick to hold in place the more rank and trailing species of vegetation that he wished to trim off. He was a familiar figure in Trewetha Lane, holding his scythe on end and stroking its already sharp blade to an ever-increasing keenness with the whetstone.

Armed with his formidable kit Frank covered the length and breadth of the parish, attending to the order of the hedgerows and verges without disturbing by one iota their natural function as havens for fauna and flora. On Frank's beat, birds nested, vipers and lizards sunned themselves on exposed stones, mice and rabbits crept, and flowers bloomed as and how nature intended.

Frank was an unheralded master of conservation, as reliable as was the arrival of day following night. He never defaulted and never displeased. The greatest tribute to the quality of Frank's expertise was that it came to be taken for granted. He was an institution benefiting everyone who trod the highways and byways of the parish of St Endellion during his tenure.

The cold white of late winter flowers and the cooler white of early spring-time blooms merged into a variety of warmer yellow shades when the daffodils opened, the mighty host of primroses spread out, and the dry-crackling gorse bushes exploded into sun-lit billows as bright as the yolk of a fresh gull's egg. In glutinous valley-bottom marshes, yellow irises leapt like banners of victory above an army of sword-like green fronds.

We made music by blowing through pursed lips against

the edge of an iris frond secured tightly between our thumbs. Whatever the notes may have lacked in harmony, they made up for by carrying over long distances. By loosening the grip on the iris frond the pitch of a note could be altered. It was possible to create notes ranging from the screech of a badly tuned violin to the raspberry-rattle of a well-placed fart. Using a blade of coarse grass as a substitute for an iris frond generated a shrillness of tone that only a dog could appreciate. Care was needed in blowing at the edge of a blade of grass as it was all too easy to acquire a cut – and such cuts, small though they might be, could be exceedingly painful.

There were a few of the fishermen who were able (and, more importantly, ready and willing when faced with no alternative but to yield to our persistence as a means of getting rid of our unwanted presence in Pawlyn's cellars) to make excellent whistles for us from short lengths of withy.

The practice of whistle making required the selection of an appropriately straight and unflawed withy. A section a few inches long was cut from the withy, trimmed square at its top and bottom, and then slowly rotated by the fisherman, all the while being tapped at gently with the bone haft of his clasp knife. The tapping loosened the thin bark. A notch was cut close to one end of the length of withy, following which the bark was pulled off in one cylindrical piece to expose the clean white wood. The end of the withy section in behind the notch was shaved down a little to form a mouthpiece. The cylinder of bark was then replaced, and the whistle could be activated until it was lost, broken or confiscated. Its ultimate fate depended on how piercing was its note.

When the soil of the close-cropped grassy meadows began to draw sustenance from spring sunshine, little daisies, golden centred and pink tipped, woke up with a jolt. Daisies opened their eyes one by one, and then score by score, and went on to eventually outnumber the blades of grass and leaves of clover around them.

Lobber field was spangled over with daisies. It shimmered with spring-scented warmth and was spiced in summer by droning bees and chirping grasshoppers. We could sit down in Lobber field and, without getting up, reach around and pick more than enough daisies for fashioning, stem run through stem, into long necklaces and crowning garlands.

Shining buttercups enriched the corners of fields and damper stretches of hedge bottoms. A freshly plucked buttercup, held face up beneath the point of someone's chin, provided a definitive reading of the subject's liking for butter, measured by the intensity of the reflected glow of the flower on the skin.

We heard at school that buttercups were not only the little children's dower (whatever that was) but were also far brighter than a melon cauliflower (which sounded fair enough).

Since butter was rationed, we assumed that a positive outcome to the buttercup test contained an element of wishful thinking. Yet, although the test might not have found favour in scientific circles, it was an established fact that if it was applied to determining the extent of a liking for margarine, the result was always negative.

My mother was totally unwilling to spread margarine on bread. If she couldn't get butter, our bread and butter became bread alone. We learned at Sunday School that man couldn't live by bread alone, but all that that meant to us was that we didn't have to worry much as far as women and children were concerned when there was no butter for them. My father spread dripping (the fatty rendering of roasted beef) on his bread and seemed to enjoy it. There were many things that I had to either eat up or go without, and dripping was one of them. I rated dripping as a commodity to which bread alone was to be preferred.

———

Yellow dandelions were equally as widespread in distribution as were daisies. Dandelions grew everywhere. Their flower heads were glorious but were ruled out for picking. Anyone unwise enough to pick a dandelion flower would be destined to wet his (or her) bed at some stage during the night which followed. If seen, the unfortunate holder of a plucked dandelion flower was subjected to less than sympathetic taunts of "Piss the bed! Piss the bed!" from the delighted observers.

Once a dandelion flower matured into seed, however, it lost the capacity to induce bedwetting. Picking the heads was then not only acceptable but essential. The number of puffs that it took to clear away the round cottony clump of feather light seeds on a dandelion head provided an accurate measure of the hour of the day according to the twelve-hour clock. This property of the dandelion might have found a more universal application had the time of day mattered more to us than it actually did.

Considerations regarding the gathering of dandelion leaves, known as "dashels", were also more lenient than those related to the flower. Where dashels were concerned, urinary incontinence was not an issue. Dashels could be picked with impunity at any time. Their milk-seeping stems, accompanied by groundsel or chickweed, were relished at mealtimes by pet rabbits. Although slightly bitter to the taste, dashels were a substitute for lettuce and were eaten with either bread and butter or, to the great regret of some who passed the buttercup test and whose weekly ration of butter had run out, with bread alone.

As the year progressed the palette of wild flower colour moved on from the white and off-white of winter and through the ever deepening shades of spring-time yellow into summer red and blue and autumn brown. In late spring and early summer Frank's hedgerows were daubed with campions, and down in the valleys armies of foxgloves leapt up to tower over pale blue-eyed cornflowers. Garden walls were swamped by waves of valerian, and the cliff tops were scattered with hassocks of immortal sea pinks.

Cornflower blooms looked as if they had recently escaped from a bag of Liquorice Allsorts, so closely did they resemble in their overall shape and size the crusted blue disc-like members of that celebrated Bassett's family of sweets. Apart from the little cylinders of black liquorice that none of us liked, not least for their unfortunate resemblance to a chaw of baccy, the blue-coated specimens were invariably the last of the breed left at the bottom of the paper bag when the ration was about to run out. By that time, however, next week's ration was pending and any kind of sweet would be reckoned as better than none at all.

Although campions (more positively known as "red" campions) were not unattractive when viewed from a distance, they were very much less pleasing to encounter at ultimately close quarters owing to their intimate association with ants. Red campion stems and flowers were frequently rife with such fluid and industrious insects, for which reason red campion flowers were seldom picked for inclusion in wild flower bouquets.

The red campion was not an especially gregarious species of flower. Although red campions were found all over the place, they normally gathered only in small aggregated clumps. However, once in a while an extensive swathe of red campions might appear on one or other of the less precipitous cliff slopes. One such location was on Bounds Cliff, where, looked down on from above, a full flood of red campions spread out like a great battle flag.

Those red campions chose to break into flower at more or less the same time as the sea birds commenced laying their eggs. A scramble down the red campion clad slope so as to approach, from the west side, the jumbled rocks and high, tight ledges on which gulls, guillemots, razorbills, shags and cormorants were nesting involved us in ploughing through the whole blooming assemblage.

The experience was not pleasant. The crushed flowers smelt moist and meaty. The red campion stems were woven through dead bracken and so tangled up our feet that we fell down frequently. Battalions of ants transferred themselves from the flowers to our arms and legs.

We fought our way down through the floral obstacle to visit some nesting sites that were accessible and others that were not so readily accessible. Afterwards, it was unfortunate that we were faced with tackling the more onerous uphill return trip through the red campion barrier.

---

The delicate maroon and green tracery of ragged robin provided a subtle foil to the red campions on Frank's hedges. The wispy-red flowers of the ragged robin were so understated that they might have been tagged on to their stems as an afterthought.

Ragged robin was known as the "cuckoo flower". To justify this sobriquet, at least in part, ragged robin stems were something of a storehouse for the deposition of frothy wet balls of "cuckoo spit". The more likely justification, however, was that ragged robin hit its prime of growth when the distinctive double call of the cuckoo was not only in the air but often filling the land with as many as a dozen of the parasitic birds calling one other from far and wide. I struggled to understand why a cuckoo only ever seemed to let me know where it was when it was a long way away from me and therefore impossible to track down. Cuckoos were much heard but never seen – they didn't ever call me from close by, or for that matter from anywhere in my line of sight.

---

Diminutive wild flower blooms (irrespective of colour, odour, appearance, and capacity for attracting ants) were called "Jesus" flowers by many of the very young residents of Port Isaac. In their minds the proprietorship of Jesus ran additionally to tiny crabs, little fish, baby rabbits, kittens and fledgling birds.

Regular attendances at Sunday School, in which consideration for all God's creatures was given unremitting (and totally unrelenting) attention by the teacher via frequent harmonium-accompanied renditions of "All Things Bright and Beautiful", "Jesus Wants me for a Sunbeam" and "I'm H-A-P-P-Y!" among other hymns of note, had more than something to do with creating a link between the small and defenceless and the ownership of the Son of God.

All of us who went to Sunday School (church or chapel, the willing and the compelled alike) knew that Jesus once said, "Suffer the little children to come unto Me, and forbid them not, for theirs is the kingdom of heaven". This was one indisputable reference for us to hold onto in which "little children" counted for something. There weren't many others, apart from the one involving a buttercup dower.

In the harsher light of weekdays, down in the school playground where the big boys ruled, the comfortable words of Jesus rearranged themselves to, "Let the little children suffer when they come unto me". Sometimes in the playground ours was not the kingdom of heaven.

Once St Peter's Sunday School was (thankfully) over and the weather permitted it, Jesus' little children went for afternoon walks along the valleys and up the lanes. They all marched in Sunday best-clad groups, singing familiar hymns (A&M) as they strolled along. "Yes, Jesus loves me!" Such songs of praise brought them all with one accord into one place and linked the lot in a common purpose – which was quite enough for Sunday since tomorrow would be another day.

―――

At foxglove time, those pagoda-like floral tributes appeared to stand up to be saluted wherever I went. They threw out tapered tiers of lightly mottled pink trumpet-like flowers in multiple flights rising as long and lazy arcs to peaks leaning over in the manner of the church spire at St Minver.

The little, and as often as not the less-than-little children, liked to pluck out the biggest of the florets towards the bottom of the foxglove column and place the florets over fingers and thumbs one by one until both hands were fully gloved. The first hand was easy to dress, whereas the second always needed some third-party assistance.

Hands decorated with foxglove florets, held with fingers upright and spread out to stop the florets falling off, offered an impression of the vicar bestowing a benediction on one of his infrequently large congregations. Nothing could actually be done with foxgloved hands, but wearing the florets created a good feeling, which was all that mattered. The ends of the florets on the finger tips tasted sweet on the tongue, and although they were reputed to be toxic, no one that I knew, including myself, was ever the worse for the experience of sucking at a few of them.

In the event that anyone might have been poisoned by the inadvertent consumption of one too many foxglove florets, it was authoritatively declared by some of those in the know that the foxglove root would provide a life-saving antidote. Others, who claimed to know better, were adamant that it was the other way around, the florets forming the antidote to the poisonous root. In the face of such dilemma-creating opinions it was as well that neither expert theory ever had the occasion to be put to the test.

Among all the red wild flowers signposting the way ahead to summer, the valerian was most welcome. Valerian asked little but gave much. Its roots took purchase and drew life from little more than a crack in a wall or a cleft on a stony hedge. In its tenacity to flourish against the odds, valerian mirrored the courage and resilience with which fishermen, farm labourers and old mining men once scraped a scant living in the rough and stormy parish of St Endellion and put up with the rapacious depredations of the landed gentry.

Hanging on to a mere toehold, valerian threw out great cascading heads of airy blooms. There were white and deep

141

scarlet varieties as well as the more common pink. Valerian was a steadfast companion and, in the time-honoured tradition of loyal friends, was ignored more often than not.

---

Although the characteristic gales of autumn and winter sooner or later gave way to the drying winds and light zephyrs of spring time, the westerly component of the blows remained pretty constant. Sea breezes were deceptive sources of false comfort. Force eight might not be far behind them. Sudden gales shivered and shredded mature wild flowers as easily as their precursors had ripped dead leaves from the trees last autumn. No matter how forcefully the wind gusted however, exposed trees had learned to adapt to it, yielding and resisting simultaneously.

Such trees flowed along the path of the wind rather than bending to it. They set their twisted and arthritic backs against the wind, bowed but undefeated. They shrugged their gnarled shoulders and stretched inland, pointing tattered branched fingers along the palm of the wind's hand.

---

As fruiting blossoms came and went we took careful note of the prospects for the wild fruit harvest. The richest bunches of elderberries that had survived the peashooter season were marked for future attention, as were the plumpest sloes, the sharpest crab apples, the most lustrous clusters of hazel nuts, and (last but never least) any holly trees considered likely to bear berries.

Berried holly, an absolute essential for Christmas decoration, was so rare as to be remarkable to us when we found it. There was no shortage of holly trees, but unfortunately none of them growing in the Port Isaac and Port Gaverne valleys appeared able to develop berries. We had to cross over the parish boundary and head out into the woods around St Kew and the Port Isaac Road railway station if we were to have any chance of finding holly berries. The exclusivity of the crop ensured that the stolid farmers who owned it would guard the prize against theft with more than their usual predatory zeal.

Those of us who were dedicated to gathering in the woodland fruits of the autumn each had our specific harvesting locations identified and subjected to a heavy blanket of secrecy. Keeping a secret in Port Isaac, however, was a process imbued with the survival characteristics of a snowball placed in the grate of a copper on washing day.

I monitored the progress of the selected wild fruit that I "bagged" as my own with a kind of anxiety-driven frequency that only served to broadcast to others where the fruit was. The monitoring was designed to ensure not so much that the harvest would be reaped at its point of optimum ripeness as that it would be gathered in, ripe or not, by me before the avid pack of other would-be gatherers could get to it.

Hazelnuts, a staple of our Christmas fare, were normally scarce. The eagerness with which they were sought guaranteed that they were under-ripe when picked. To obtain any reasonable quantity of hazelnuts out in the muddy brakes of the valley bottoms was to make an achievement of great substance. The hazelnuts were taken home, squirreled away at the back of a dark cupboard and left there to await the arrival of Christmas.

We knew the locations of quite a number of apple and crab apple trees growing in places where they were supposedly unencumbered by obvious ownership. They had the advantage of being easily got at. Any eventual pursuit of us by an irate farmer was then made on the grounds of our trespassing and not scrumping. The disadvantage of apples on such trees was that they were as sour as the expression on Mrs Phoebe Short's face on a bad day at chapel. The apples were not even very good for baking, although certain varieties of crab apple were boiled up and rendered down into a jelly favoured by some for spreading on bread.

———

Of course, not all the apple trees of the parish were of the wild variety. There were several apple trees prominent in domestic circumstances, and more standing in company in a number of little orchards. These trees, when the fruit hung ripe on their branches, merited visits by apple scrumpers wishing to relieve the tree of the burden of at least some of its load. A similar consideration applied to gardens containing strawberries, raspberries and black-currants – not forgetting small and juicy white turnips (Mrs Commander's barbed wire fence notwithstanding).

Many of us were assiduous scrumpers. A major disadvantage of apple scrumping from gardens lay in the likelihood that we could be seen, recognised and subjected to the certainty of retribution.

Discretion dictated that apple scrumping was best practised in one or another of the established orchards that we knew. We crawled around and inspected the orchards in detail out of season in order to determine the optimum means of clandestine entry at harvest time, locate the places where we needed to place lookouts, and establish the means of making an exit rapidly and safely in the event that the owner should put in an unscheduled appearance.

Mr Tom Saundry's apple orchard in the Port Isaac valley was considered to be holy ground, not to be trodden on. No one among us was prepared to risk an encounter with Tom and his hobnail boots by scrumping from him. In any case, the sour grapes side of the tale was that Tom's apples were reckoned by us to be not especially choice.

Mr Button's orchard near his Tregaverne farmhouse, located on the east rim of the Port Gaverne valley about half a mile up from Port Gaverne, also carried a high degree of risk for apple scrumpers, but we felt that that risk was reasonably manageable.

If Tom was a fierce ogre, then Mr Button was judged to be a friendly giant. Mr Button was close to seven feet tall, a mountain of a man peering down over the top of a pair of rimless spectacles on all beings of lesser stature, which meant everyone. His remaining hair was white and wispy, streaming out in the wind like clouds coming off a snow-clad peak.

Although toughened by the agricultural profession, Mr Button possessed an innate kindness, making him a princely gentleman among farmers. This didn't imply, however, that Mr Button would turn a blind eye to anyone seeking to relieve his orchard, which lay in a sheltered crinkle in the valley slope below his farmhouse, of a few of its crop of apples. Mr Button was always ready to go "Fee, fie, fo, fum!" when the occasion demanded it.

A single running stride by Mr Button was equivalent to three or four of our paces, but his ability to cover ground was limited by his staying power. Mr Button could be outrun when we had a sufficient lead over him to start with. What gave Mr Button an edge was his nimble son John, himself several inches in excess of six feet tall.

John was the man for us to beat. He mirrored his father's qualities, but although he smiled a lot, there was a wild gleam in his eyes that made it clear that he would take no prisoners. I was only thankful that he never took me.

The best apples that we scrumped came from a one-of-a-kind tree in an apple orchard in the Port Quin valley. The apples in question were big, round and yellow-fleshed, sweet and succulent. Their skin was streaked with all the bright colours that made autumn leaves a delight to roll around in and kick in the air. We didn't know which variety of apple they were and didn't care. Whatever they were, they were wonderful.

Fate decreed that one of the boundary fences of this orchard stood no more than a couple of dozen yards away from the famous Port Quin valley conker tree. Since apples and conkers both ripened at about the same time of year, it seemed natural enough that conker collectors would diversify laterally into grabbing some apples – a seamless move from the conker tree over the fence to the orchard.

Curiously, given the well-known intensity of the attention we paid to the conker tree, the adjacent orchard never appeared to be guarded. The identity of whoever it was that owned it was a mystery that we put little or no thought into solving. It was enough that the owner didn't chase after us.

Loaded with conkers and apples, we abandoned the conker tree and orchard, crossed the Port Quin valley and climbed up the far slope to reach the road back to Port Isaac. Our pockets and jerkins bulged with the bounty. We ate every bit of every apple (core and pips included) on the way home.

In the late summer and early autumn, picking blackberries was, scratches apart, a much less hazardous way to spend time gathering fruit than apple scrumping. Bramble bushes grew just about anywhere that we cared to look, and they all bore blackberries in season. However, as with most things in life, some bramble bushes in some places cropped more prolifically than did some others in some other places. The secret of ensuring a successful afternoon of blackberry picking was to know precisely where the biggest and plumpest fruits were to be found.

Most hedgerows along the roads and lanes were hung with blackberries of sorts. They were easy to pick. However, the golden rule governing blackberry picking, that the easier the blackberries were to get at the poorer would be their quality, always applied. Roadside blackberries all too frequently tended to be small and hard even when they were ripe. They lacked flavour and their fruit was noted more for pips than pulp.

The best blackberries grew on the open slopes of the valleys, usually dangling in glossy clumps in the middle of broad, tangled mounds of brambles. The section of Port Isaac valley known as "Fuzzy Hill" (in between Tom Saundry's tangled orchard and the lane up to Pennant Farm down which Christopher the curate ran) was particularly good blackberry hunting ground.

On the west flank of the Port Gaverne valley a lengthy, bracken-invested stretch called "Seven Acres" (owned by the

Blake brothers of Trewetha Farm) was also excellent blackberry territory. Down below Seven Acres at the valley bottom, a spongy marsh seeped oily iridescence into the sunken hoof prints of passing cattle, and sparkled with yellow irises in the spring.

Picked blackberries were accumulated in the ever-reliable chip baskets. A day's picking ended when a personal chip basket was full up. To reduce the picking side of the equation, we padded the inside of the chip basket with green bracken ferns. In the event that we were taxed to find sufficient blackberries that were both big and ripe at the same time, the time-honoured technique (borrowed from both of Port Isaac's greengrocer Mr Jim May and fruiterer Mr Altair ("Old Tair") Bunt) of secreting less ripe fruit under a ripe layer of the same was invoked without a twinge of conscience.

The time required to fill a small chip basket was directly proportional to the quantity of blackberries eaten by the picker along the way. The amount of blackberries consumed could be estimated by referring to the evidence of the blue-black stains tattooing the picker's hands from fingertips to wrist and the picker's lips from corner to corner. Blackberry juice on a picker's hands blended with dotted lines of blood oozing from multiple scratches inflicted by over-protective brambles.

A small chip basket filled with blackberries (and bracken fronds) was sold for sixpence on the open market. The price covered the contents only – the chip basket remained the property of the picker. Most of us picked blackberries on commission for a pre-agreed COD price. A full big chip basket could be worth up to two shillings if the client was in a jam-making frame of mind.

Port Isaac's champion of blackberry pickers was Miss Sybil Couch. On the face of it, Sybil appeared to be an unlikely candidate to acquire such an accolade. As a result of contracting the much-feared infantile paralysis when she was small, Sybil had limited control over the articulation of her arms and legs. Her frame was twisted and her shoulders were permanently hunched.

She was painfully thin but heart-warmingly cheerful in the face of adversity. In all weathers and through all seasons of the year, when Sybil was out she wore a shabby black beret pulled tightly down over her ears and a very long dark, faded red coat that fell well below her bent knees.

Sybil was the elder daughter of Mr and Mrs Charlie Couch, who resided in one half of the semi-detached middle row council house standing on the inner corner of Hartland Road's dogleg. Sybil's sister was named Pamela, or Pam. A familiar figure all around Port Isaac, Pam was as plump as Sybil was thin. Pam was what was known as a Mongolian idiot, which was why her parents cherished her so specially.

Sybil went up into the valleys, always alone and invariably porting a large chip basket over the crook of one arm, intent on gathering the prime of whatever was in season at the time. She always returned with her chip basket brimming, whether the harvest was of primroses, bluebells, blackberries or mushrooms – it made no difference to Sybil's industry. Sybil, unlike prophecies, never failed. She walked awkwardly, slowly and carefully so as to make no mistake as to where she placed her feet. Sybil could weave and worm her way through the tightest of thickets and insinuate her contorted frame into the very heart of the bramble mounds where the finest blackberries were waiting for her. The brambles accepted Sybil as a kindred spirit. Their thorns didn't harm her.

We found out where Sybil was picking only if she let us find her. Sybil couldn't be followed. In her expert knowledge of the terrain, she knew and used every evasive trick in the book to shake off trackers.

The practice of tailing someone like Sybil to profitable hunting grounds in order to gain an advantage was known as "corking". It enjoyed its most overt manifestation out at sea in instances where an out-of-luck fishing boat would blatantly take up station in close vicinity to another fishing boat that was enjoying better fortune. This would very much evoke the *ennui* of the skipper of the latter craft. Corking was frowned on, and its persistent practitioners sowed the seeds of family feuds.

———

Blackberry picking was motivated by two noble nutritional objectives. The first of these was directed at the preparation of a goodly supply of blackberry jam. Making jam was a major household exercise involving saucepans boiling and overflowing with foaming blackberry magma and arrays of empty jars of various dimensions into which the jam would be poured. Whether or not the jam set would depend on who made it. I hated the kind of jam that flowed or (even worse) was liquid enough to soak into the piece of bread on which it was spread.

The second objective was the royal destiny of blackberries, namely their inclusion in a blackberry and apple pie. Blackberries and apples ripened at the same time – definitely a heaven-sponsored coincidence. The respective flavours of the two fruits in a pie were totally complementary. They were made for each other.

With a slab of pastry crust on a plate, crisp and golden on top, white, moist and peeling underneath, a mound of succulent blackberry and apple sitting in a pool of its own juice, and a dab of cream to set on top when we had it, no better "afters" at dinner time could be imagined in the whole world.

Blackberry and apple pie scaled the true peak of nature's bounty.

*Canadian Terrace, front and back*

# 8

# Canadian Terrace

I remember, I remember
The house where I was born,
The little window where the sun
Came peeping in at morn.

Thomas Hood (1799–1845)
"Past and Present"

A TERRACED ROW of nine tiny yet stout cottages united to fill in what would otherwise have been an open space between the respective bottoms of Front and Back Hills up at the top end of Fore Street. The row was named Canadian Terrace.

The Fore Street front of Canadian Terrace gazed as if from on high across the roof of the school towards the head of Lobber field on the far side of the harbour. The back of the terrace was frowned down on from even greater heights by the grey bulk of St Peter's church.

Reputedly, Canadian Terrace was almost a hundred years older than I was. Both the construction work and the materials that went into it were reported as having been paid for by a Port Isaac man returned from voluntary exile in Canada and loaded down with more money than sense. Not that that worried anyone very much. Since most Port Isaac people lived principally for the present day and weren't exactly enamoured to do so, they had better things to do than to dwell for long on something that had taken place a long time ago. The residents of Canadian

151

Terrace believed that their row of cottages was much more than equal to the sum of its not especially big individual parts. The parts were in fact decidedly small, each of the nine constituent cottages consisting in principle of two rooms (one upstairs and one downstairs) measuring approximately twenty feet by fifteen feet in plan view.

The walls of Canadian Terrace, front and back, were capable of withstanding a siege. They were between three and four feet thick, built using that famously variegated mixture of earth, clay, straw and stones known as cob. The breadth of the walls ensured that the modest external cottage plan dimensions enclosed even more unassumingly sized interiors. Little multi-paned sash windows, front and back, pierced the redoubtable walls like glass-fronted embrasures.

---

I was born in Number Six Canadian Terrace on the eighth of August 1939, and resided there for the next nine years with my mother and (post-war) my father, my younger (by three years) brother and my much younger (by six years) sister. Gran and Granfer Creighton lived next door to us in Number Seven. It was a satisfying situation. I spent more of my time in Number Seven than in Number Six and on that basis at least I could be said to have had a "good war".

Space in Number Six was limited, but as limited space was all we were familiar with, we neither sought nor missed anything more commodious. In any case we were able to treat Numbers Six and Seven as natural extensions of one another, in which happy circumstances we were enabled to spread ourselves around as much as we wished.

In 1949 we moved from Number Six Canadian Terrace to Number Nine Hartland Road, one of several newly constructed council houses right up at the top of Port Isaac. Our more spacious Hartland Road accommodation (not forgetting the novelty of internal plumbing and the availability of electricity) brought us certain advantages but didn't always provide the type of congeniality that characterised Numbers Six and Seven Canadian Terrace.

---

The one up and one down rooms in each of Numbers Six and Seven were subdivided by skilfully installed thin wooden partitions at least a couple of generations old. Crafty painting and papering created the impression that the partitions were enduring walls.

Downstairs, common to both cottages, a partition near the back door enclosed a pantry adjacent to the kitchen in which the food was cooked and eaten. In its turn the kitchen was segregated by another partition from an area designated as the sitting room.

Upstairs, a judicious arrangement of partitions was used to establish two bedrooms (front and back) and a landing linked to the staircase. Any additional subdivisions, whether up or down, would have required us to sip from a bottle of Alice's shrinking potion marked "Drink Me" for the purpose of getting around.

The back bedroom in Number Seven, in addition to its role as sleeping chamber, was employed as a repository for household items that had seen better days but weren't yet ready to be heaved over the cliff at Hillson's Dump. Nothing was thrown away deliberately as no one ever knew that it might not be useful in the future.

I shared the back bedroom in Number Six with my brother. As there was space in the room for our one bed and not much more, the practice of shoving residua beneath the bed, where out of sight was equivalent to out of mind, was the order of the day.

It was in the back bedroom that, a year or two after the end of the war when Canadian Terrace was connected up to the mains, I encountered the miracle that was electric power.

As if by magic one day, a Bakelite socket into which a light bulb could be fixed appeared above the head of the bed. In the absence of the said bulb I pushed two of my fingers into the open socket and instantly took to the air, flung across the bed to hit the back wall with a cob-shaking crunch. A masterpiece of modern technology had finally arrived. It was fortunate that I missed contact with the bedroom window.

It was with the greatest of ingenuity that Granfer designed a narrow partitioned-off entry hall leading to the staircase from the front door of Number Seven. The hallway added greatly to the tone of the residence. When I came into Number Seven through the front door and stretched my arms, my hands simultaneously brushed against both sides of the hall, one side marking off the sitting room on the left, and the other formed by the wall held in common with Mr and Mrs Dick "Trapper" Morman's abode in Number Eight on the right.

Hanging on the right-hand side of Granfer's hallway a matched pair of bison horns were individually mounted on small slabs of crude hardwood cut into the shape of shields. They were marvellous things to look at, but as they were never taken down, even for dusting, they were forever out of my reach.

Two little carved ebony elephants lived in the sitting-room sideboard of Number Seven. They were much more tangible artefacts than the horns, fitting as perfectly into the curves and folds of my hands as if the carver had made them with me in mind. Although the elephants might have seemed identical in appearance to the untutored eye, I had only to touch them once to know them apart. The two black jumbos were my steady playmates in Number Seven until, regrettably, I outgrew them.

In the back of the same sideboard a Japanese porcelain tea set of the most exquisite delicacy (another of Granfer's trophies from far away places with strange-sounding names) was securely stacked. The teacups were eggshell thin, almost transparent. I thought that if a charge of tea was to be poured into any one of the fragile cups, the handle would fall off when anyone tried to pick the cup up. Those cups were not designed with the soaking of slices of bread and jam in mind.

154

Every piece of the tea set — teapot, plates, saucers, cups, sugar bowl and milk jug — was decorated with a hand-painted motif in blue, green, yellow, white and gold, showing two Japanese ladies standing in a flower garden. Each was a unique work of art, far too precious to be handled by the likes of me.

As it was, I never knew the Japanese tea set to ever come within sniffing distance of liquid tea. It gathered up dust within the sideboard, and since there was no glass fronting that item of furniture, God's good daylight rarely cast its bright eye therein. I was told that the one occasion on which the tea set did emerge was when my mother married my father. Wedding guests both couth and uncouth drank tea from the cups, all of them watched over with great trepidation by Gran.

"God's good daylight" was a commodity invoked by Gran and Granfer and milked to the full by them during the approach to dusk. Gran lit no lamp until it was almost too dark to find the lamp. Both she and Granfer carried on reading for as long as a scrap of that good daylight of God permitted a page to be turned and the writing on it deciphered. "But I can't see!" I said to them. "In that case you'll have to feel!" came their reply.

Ebony elephants notwithstanding, the best ornament in Gran and Granfer's sitting room was a brass moneybox, made by Granfer. Once a week the exterior of this item was polished to a mirror-like intensity with the aid of a lot of "Brasso" and much more elbow grease. The brass moneybox rested on one end of the mantelpiece above the fireplace. It was the heaviest member of a brassbound quartet that also comprised a lidded tea urn and two small hinge-fronted boxes bearing the embossed effigy of a younger Queen Mary. The pair of boxes, Gran said, originally contained chocolate and cigarettes. Granfer was given them in connection with a general handout of conscience-salving Christmas largesse by Buckingham Palace to people like him in the front line of action during the Great War.

The allure of Granfer's moneybox was in its manufacture from a 7.5-centimetre diameter German shell, type M.15, presumably handed out in the Great War more in anger than in sorrowful charity. The lid and the body of the moneybox were formed from a cut section of a shell maybe six inches high. At the centre of the lid was a firing cap, clearly impacted. Above the cap was the stamped inscription "Berndorf", with "1915" set immediately below. The serial number of the shell, inscribed beneath the year, was "508".

The fitted base of the moneybox was made from the end of another Berndorf shell of the same calibre, this one carrying the serial number "341". I could imagine the carnage and suffering spread by the inventory of the one hundred and sixty-six shells linking those two serial numbers.

Granfer had cut a horizontal slot through the moneybox about an inch below its rim. The aperture of the slot was sufficient to more or less permit the passage of half a crown. It was not likely of course that half a crown would ever be pushed through the slot. There were better things to do with half a crown than to put it in a moneybox. Farthings, pennies and halfpennies were fair enough fodder for the slot, but I really had to think twice about depositing even any of those, since the base of the moneybox was soldered on so tightly that once a coin went through the slot it was as good as lost.

A true and much tried coin retrieval procedure called for upending the moneybox and inserting a knife through the slot in the anticipation of catching and withdrawing a coin on the blade. It was, sadly enough, a proposition that was only practical in the hands of an expert knife manipulator, which I most definitely was not.

On the front of the moneybox, under the slot, a round silver badge – once the property of a Turkish soldier – was soldered in place. The badge, Granfer said, was a souvenir of a Great War visit he had made to a place called Gallipoli. The contrast in colour between the silver and brass was almost regal. Years of polishing had caused the badge to wear smooth, yet the star and crescent remained in clear recall of that ill-fated campaign.

———

Away from the confines of their cob walls, Canadian Terrace's cottage properties were liberally endowed in terms of garden space. Each cottage had a good long garden at the front stretching down to a bank along the edge of Fore Street, and a similarly extensive strip of back garden occupying the stepped up terrace at the rear below St Peter's. Most of the front gardens tended to feature a patch of mixed grass and weeds designated as a lawn plus a border of flowers (not the least species of which was the wallflower) in season. The back gardens were entirely dedicated to the cultivation of vegetables.

Granfer, acknowledged as an expert gardener, tended the back gardens of both Numbers Six and Seven. His vegetable produce was seasonally as straightforward as it was conventional, comprising (*inter alia*) savoy cabbages, turnips (swede and white), radishes, potatoes, lettuces, cauliflowers, broccoli, curly greens, onions and shallots. In his half of a stone-walled and slate-roofed shed standing hard against the retaining wall of St Peter's at the top end of Number Seven's back garden, Granfer stored the accoutrements of the gardening trade; his tobacco-making paraphernalia; and (not least) a cobbler's last. The other half of the shed, separated from Granfer's side by a wall as thick as it was crude (attributes shared by a few farmers I had fled from) was the precinct of the aforementioned Mr Dick Trapper.

Granfer worked the two Canadian Terrace vegetable gardens only during the mornings, as in the afternoons he walked out to look after his garden in the Port Gaverne bottoms where the all important tobacco plants were nurtured.

Tobacco leaves were brought back to Canadian Terrace to be hung in annual festoons from the low eaves of the back garden shed for drying and curing. As the tobacco harvest eliminated any more need for sheep shit-inspired mulch, my new assignment was to tread the local highways and byways to collect coltsfoot leaves for Granfer to blend into his final product. He marinated the lot in molasses and compressed it all into a solid block, which he shaved down into fine shreds of authentic-looking baccy with the help of a homemade guillotine.

Unbeknown to Granfer, groundsel, which often thrived in association with coltsfoot, was another additive used to augment the tobacco leaves. It was much easier for me to include groundsel than to struggle to exclude it from the coltsfoot gather.

The benefit of the coltsfoot association with tobacco leaves was derived not only from the size and the appropriateness of shape of the coltsfoot leaf but also perhaps from the traditional use of coltsfoot as a remedy for chest complaints. Whether or not groundsel carried equal medicinal benefits I didn't know. Probably the best that could be said was that exotic elements in the homemade tobacco that he smoked did no obvious damage to Granfer.

The back doors of the Canadian Terrace cottages opened onto a deep and narrow alley from which a couple of steep (and perilously slippery when wet) right-of-way flights of slate-shod steps led to the back gardens. Directly across the alley from the back doors, a distance of no more than a couple of paces, a row of washhouses, one per each cottage, lined up along the facing wall.

The principal features of a typical washhouse were a quite recently installed lavatory bowl; a fearsome-looking clothes mangle; a small copper in a corner for boiling up things; a hundredweight (or more if it could be afforded) of coal dumped alongside the copper by Mr Harold Spry, the coalman; a jumble of variegated firewood adjoining the coal; a gallon can of paraffin to boot; and a small galvanised metal bath tub hanging from a hook on a wall. The lavatory bowl flushed with a pull chain system that showed considerable resistance to functioning in freezing weather.

Such space as was still available around these items was used for the storage of odds and ends considered inappropriate by virtue of their size, shape and relative condition of decay for depositing up in the back bedroom. No piece of wood was too worm-ridden, no scrap of metal too rusty or corroded, no piece of rope or wire too short that it was not worth holding on to. A place could always be found to fit in anything of that sort. In some washhouses the accumulation of junk was so monumental as to almost preclude human entry, even on washing days.

The copper was a square-sectioned, hollow, chunky, stone-built construction that stood between three and four feet high. A cauldron that belied the red metal title by virtue of being made of cast iron was mortared into the top of the arrangement. In the area below the concave base of the cauldron was the fireplace, complete with grate and riddle and ready to consume either coal or wood or both commodities at the same time. In essence, the copper formed a simple device for heating up a goodly amount of water fairly quickly.

The copper endowed a washhouse with a sense of purpose. Various items of clothes, sheets and pillowcases (and sometimes even tablecloths) were boiled up in the copper on the designated day (usually Monday) for doing the weekly washing. A yellow cake of "Sunlight" soap was an element critical to the success of the operation, and to augment the whitening power of that famous detergent a cube of "Reckitt's Blue", securely bound in a muslin cloth, was added to the soapy infusion.

The mangle was located strategically close to the copper on the right-hand wall of Gran's washhouse. The dripping, steamy mass of boiled and blued washing was lifted from the copper by means of a thick wooden stick. Once untangled, the washed items, within a prevailing envelope of damp heat, were laboriously fed one by one between the twin rollers of the mangle. Hot soapy water sloshed away from the near side of the mangle as the opposing rollers squished it out of the laundered items to render them ready for hanging on the line come rain come sunshine. Steam writhed around in clean and fragrant billows.

The rollers were massive, made of wood and mounted in a heavy iron frame. The pressure with which they contacted one another was adjusted by turning a two-handed wing nut on the top of the frame. The nut tightened (or alternatively loosened) a leaved spring that looked as if it might have been stolen from an Austin Seven car. It took a powerfully muscled lady, of which brand there was fortunately no shortage in Port Isaac, to operate a mangle effectively.

Gran's copper was sometimes impressed into service for cooking crabs in bulk, although such circumstances were rare as there was some reluctance to fire the copper up for anything other than the weekly wash. It wasn't even used, quite unaccountably I thought, as there never seemed to be enough hot water to go round, to provide us with hot water on bath days.

For cooking crabs, Gran generally employed a huge blue-enamelled saucepan standing on the coal-fired grate of the kitchen stove at Number Seven. She and my mother boiled, picked and dressed crabs to order for a few of the hotels up on the Terrace. Otherwise crab meat, destined to please the palates of foreigners sometimes regarded as our betters, was far too expensive a commodity to appear on the table of Number Seven – or for that matter of Number Six.

Our supply of hot water for bath day was also derived from the infallible expedient of the great blue-enamelled saucepan. As a rule, we all took a bath once a week, Sunday being the day of designation and Sunday afternoon the assigned time of day. For that momentous purpose the zinc bath was taken down from where it hung on the washhouse wall and brought from the washhouse into the kitchen. In the kitchen, the bath was set down in front of the fire, which was still exuding an afterglow from its Sunday dinner exertions.

The sequence of bathing was pre-ordained. It related entirely to the seniority of the participants, the willing and the unwilling alike. The dimensions of the bath were such that fitting the person into the tight confines demanded the skill of a circus contortionist. All the same, it took at least two or three boil-ups of the blue-enamelled saucepan to provide sufficient hot water to charge the bath once. A supply of clean hot water was therefore not unsurprisingly dedicated only to the first in line for the ablutions.

As a consequence, all of us involved in the bath-day ritual made use of a single complete charge of hot water. Once my turn to bath arrived, and if I was lucky, it was sometimes possible to lift the sinking temperature with a little water quickly boiled in a kettle for me by my mother.

When the sequence of baths was concluded, the water that had by then served five or six people was well on its way to being worn out. It had acquired the consistency of a thin, grey gruel thanks to gleanings from the multiple neck, feet and wrist tidemarks built up by the said bathers throughout the preceding week, and a certain amount of pee generated more recently.

It was good (post-bath) for me to be a little bit cleaner than I had been (pre-bath); but for all that, having to have a bath was a weekly chore that was best when it was over and out of the way for another week. There weren't many among my school playground contemporaries who were anxious to take a bath more frequently than once a week. Life was reckoned to be too short for any of us to weaken ourselves by too much washing.

On the outside wall of the washhouses for each of Numbers Six and Seven, a box-like frame covered by fine aperture wire screening was prominent. The front of the box was loose, hinged on one side for opening, and fitted on the other side with a hook to drop into an eye for closing. Inside the box were a couple of wooden shelves. The box was known as the "meat safe". Items of perishable food (not necessarily restricted to meat) were placed on its shelves in an attempt to prolong freshness in (relatively) cool conditions. The screening kept the flies out. It all worked well as long as the duration of storage of any item was not more than a few days.

Every cottage in Canadian Terrace was equipped with one mains-supplied tap (cold) from which the domestic water supply emerged. The tap was located out in the alley at the top of a length of a rising pipe attached to the cottage wall adjacent to the back door. The water supply froze in the winter and often trickled and occasionally failed altogether in the summer.

There was no plumbing inside any of the cottages. Adequate cover for this shortfall, not least in the days prior to the installation of lavatory bowls in the washhouses, was furnished by china chamber pots lying in wait beneath the beds. A chamber pot was affectionately known as a "po" or a "jerry". A trip to the washhouse lavatory bowl in the night by anyone taken short never got to assume the status of a popular activity.

---

Mr Dick Trapper from Number Eight was a tubby little man whose face carried a permanently harried expression. He walked with a subtle forward-leaning stoop as if he was demonstrating an intention to get somewhere quickly, although without being quite sure where that somewhere was.

Mrs Dick Trapper was at least twice the size of her spouse. She was grey haired, whiskery featured and invariably turned out in a wrap-around apron. It was said that in all her life she had never set foot outside the accepted limits of Port Isaac village. Mrs Dick Trapper owned a couple of brown teeth that were definitely hers and was devoted to exposing them frequently when she laughed in a shrill treble capable of making flesh creep.

I knew her screeching laugh only too well from visits to the Rivoli cinema, at which august establishment Mrs Dick Trapper was such an unfailingly regular patron that she had a personal seat reserved for her use by divine decree of Mr Charlie Lobb,

162

the cinema proprietor. Woe would betide any poor soul who unwittingly sat in Mrs Dick Trapper's place.

The kind of things that Mrs Dick Trapper and her ilk appeared to find funny in some films were mystifyingly obscure to those of us who sat on the sixpenny wooden benches down at the front wondering what the film was all about.

Kitty and Anita (or "Nita"), Mr and Mrs Dick Trapper's daughters, respectively married to Mr Roderick ("Roddy") Thomas and Mr Jestinian ("Jess") Steer, lived in Numbers Three and Four Canadian Terrace, no more than a short walk along the alley, close at hand to their mother's abode. A walk up to see Kitty and/or Nita was probably not too taxing an activity for Mrs Dick Trapper to undertake in venturing abroad, although I never saw her do it. The traffic appeared to move almost entirely from Numbers Three and Four down to Number Eight.

Kitty was a little plumper than Nita, although in the mould of their father, neither of the two was gifted with enough height to carry the weight with ease. Both Jess, who was an itinerant fishmonger (locally known as a "fish jouder"), and Roddy, whose actual profession escaped my memory but who was closely connected with some facet of seafaring, were also of similar construction to Dick Trapper.

Roddy's figure was spherical to the extent of reaching near geometric perfection. His son David offered every indication of becoming yet another roly-poly chip off the old Trapper block.

Roddy seemed to be forever ambling in and out of the back alley to Canadian Terrace, his flat cap square on his head, a hand-rolled fag pasted firmly in his mouth and hands pocketed away in the black trousers that stretched across his not inconsiderably sized ass. It was impossible not to like Roddy. Of the two Mr and Mrs Dick Trapper daughters, Kitty obtained by far the better bargain in the marriage stakes.

The problem with Roddy was that, unlike with Jess, it was less than easy to understand anything he said. Roddy had a voice which was so seriously guttural that when he spoke it sounded as if it had been reluctantly exhumed from great depths of fine gravel. The advertisers' announcement, "Hoarse? Go suck a Zube!" was wasted on Roddy.

Jess had the reputation of being something of a comedian. He greeted his customers, as often as not, with a salesman's patter and a rustic joke. He possessed undoubted comic talent. The pity was that his repartee moved in intentionally ribald directions. Jess cloaked suggestive innuendoes with a homely veneer that was cleverly designed to circumvent giving offence.

The bouncing joviality affected by Jess enveloped one-liners of a quite explicit nature that he was adept in addressing to men and women of all ages. Shrieks of forced merriment from females at the receiving end only served to mask their unease. Subsequently they might have contemplated why they had laughed at what Jess said to them and (maybe) why they hadn't reacted more contentiously.

They were then inclined to say, "Ah well, 'tis only Jess!" as if that made an excuse sufficient unto the day. It was only Jess, and only Jess genuinely knew what he was about. When Jess joked, tendrils of cold weed flickered below the Lake-like stream of his monologues.

———

For a time, Mr and Mrs Clifford Sloggett were our neighbours in Number Five. There were two Sloggett children, David (the younger) and Pauline. David, known as "Sloggy", held the record for the most rapid descent from the school playground to the beach, via a slip on the cliff and a bounce off the rocks. It was only by great good fortune that he survived. David was about the same age as me, although we were not close friends.

Mr and Mrs Sloggett almost certainly merited one another's company along life's road. Mrs Sloggett was an expert minder of other people's business. She was reputed to be not unhappy to learn of the misfortunes of others, especially if she had had a hand, directly or indirectly, in bringing the tribulations about.

Clifford was a dyed-in-the-wool curmudgeon whose arche-typal credentials for the same were consistent with the best of Port Isaac's "miserable old bugger" breed. He was known as "Digger". It was a nickname that I assumed he had earned during the period of the war that I understood he had spent in the Far East. "Digger" could equally have been derived from his penchant for excavating virtual night soil to throw at and over anyone within easy reach.

He was small and thin, as aggressive as one of Cogsy's bristling bantam cocks. In his work Digger drove a delivery truck for a Wadebridge hardware and building supplier. Whether on or off the job Digger appeared to have a low tolerance for pleasure – both for his own and for everybody else's.

Much to my mother's dismay, fate contrived to bring us back into close proximity to the Sloggetts not long after our departure from Number Six Canadian Terrace, since they also subsequently moved up to Hartland Road. There, they took up residence in the council house (recently vacated by Mr and Mrs Robert Smith and their three strapping sons Charlie, Clarence and Stanley) directly opposite to ours at Number Nine.

From his Hartland Road point of vantage Digger could expand his horizons and indulge himself in incurring the displeasure of far more people than was feasible in the narrow world of Canadian Terrace. Only the brave of heart chose to approach the limits of Digger's property too closely. In his bombast, Digger was more than ably supported by Mrs Sloggett.

Although she was not often seen on open parade, Mrs Sloggett's ever-vigilant indoor presence was signalled by the twitch of her front-room curtains. Behind that lacy shield her consuming eyes recorded all movements in the field of vision. Whether such movements were great or small, Mrs. Sloggett applied rancour to them with an even touch.

Following the exodus of the Sloggetts, Mr and Mrs Tom May moved into Number Five Canadian Terrace. They were stalwart church people, each one elderly, reduced of stature, modest in nature and sober of living. The extent of Tom's tenure at Number Five was sadly short lived.

A week or two after Tom's final journey up to St Endellion, the vicar of the day (the bustling Reverend Soady), having made a visit of ministering compassion to the bereaved Mrs May, came up to Hartland Road to call on my mother who warranted his attention by virtue of being on the sick list.

The good old Reverend Soady described to my mother, within the full hearing of my sister who was aged then about five, how Tom's body was "opened up" by surgeons and was "found to be riddled through with tentacles of cancer". (It was interesting to consider that in Port Isaac no one ever "had" cancer or "suffered from" cancer, or was even "stricken by" it. The afflicted were always spoken of as being "riddled" with the scourge).

This exchange between my mother and the Reverend Soady took place during the week following an attendance by my sister at the Rivoli to see a film entitled *Meet the Ghosts* starring Bud Abbott and Lou Costello. In the film the antics of Bud and Lou took place in the company of Count Dracula, Frankenstein's Monster and the Wolf Man, respectively played by Messrs Bela Lugosi, Glenn Strange and Lon Chaney Jr.

No patron of any age at the Rivoli cinema in his or her right mind (and there were many of both persuasions) would have anticipated being terrified by the likes of Abbott and Costello. My sister's reaction to Bela, Glenn and Lon Jr, however, was contrary to such an expectation, and became compounded in her mind by the Reverend Soady's colourful vision of Mr Tom May being consumed from within by a tentacled creature. My sister thereupon adopted a clerically inspired phobia of the dark, which took well over a year to fade away.

166

The sitting rooms of Numbers Six and Seven Canadian Terrace were focused on their fireplaces. The cheer-dispensing characteristics of glowing coals and blazing hearth notwithstanding, the radius of warmth cast by the fires in those fireplaces was generally quite narrow. It was necessary to get almost within licking distance of the flames for any calefactory effect of the fire to be felt. Even in close proximity the fire warmed only those body parts that were directly exposed to it. The front of the body roasted while the rear fought against residual chill.

Lighting the fire was a seriously taken ritual, either performed by those who believed themselves to be experts in the art and genuinely were, or botched by those who considered themselves to be experts and actually were not. The latter easily outnumbered the former.

Once the morning ashes of the previous night's conflagration had been shovelled out of the grate, a tightly crumpled sheet taken from yesterday's newspaper was put in their place. A few pieces of split kindling were then artfully arranged around and on top of the newspaper. Small knobs of coal were placed on the assembly in convenient locations. A match was struck, and the ensuing flame was applied to the newspaper on the principle that a thereby engendered flare would transfer from the paper to the kindling to the coal in that order, permitting additional coal to be then added to build the fire up to its ideal state of glory.

In practice, the fire lighting process rarely worked precisely as it ought to have done at the first time of asking. The sheet of crumpled newspaper sometimes caught alight only to subside into a mess of impotently smouldering blackened flakes. The kindling (brought in from the washhouse) might be over-damp or otherwise too thickly chopped to ignite readily. Zeal in the initial placement of pieces of coal might be either too prolific or too miserly to suit the transfer of flame.

The coal delivered by Mr Harold Spry was reputed to be associated with more than enough of its fair share of fragments of slate (blamed on those who mined it), or water-bound slack (Harold's doing) to jeopardise efficient fire lighting. When a blaze was up and running, bits of slate crackled off like small arms and frequently shot glowing fragments out into the sitting room. That was not always good news for those huddled around the fireplace at the time. The counter-placement of a fireguard failed to provide a satisfactory solution. A fireguard did offer protection from slate shrapnel to those sitting in front of it, but at the same time it absorbed and nullified far too much radiant warmth.

A modified process for streamlining, accelerating and generally adding more efficiency to fire lighting was sought, and surely enough an ingenious panacea to fix the ill was devised.

It required, when the crumpled piece of newspaper at the base of the stack of kindling and coal was alight, that a second sheet of newspaper taken from one of the Sunday broadsheets must be spread over the front of the fireplace to enclose that feature in its entirety from chimney breast to floor of grate. The broadsheet was held in place by the fire maker's hands, one hand at the top and one at the bottom. The closure induced the chimney to "draw" at the embryonic fire and suck it into active life.

Although this method of drawing the fire worked as often as not, there were side effects from time to time. As well as livening up the flames, the chimney draw inhaled the broadsheet, with the result that the broadsheet might suddenly burst into flames to the detriment of whoever was holding it. Scraps of burning newspaper then whirled up high into the chimney where great accumulations of soot, long deferred from receiving the attentions of a sweep, delivered the basis for creating a roaring chimney fire.

When all else failed, the last full fire-lighting measure taken was to pour paraffin onto the recalcitrant kindling and coal and throw down a lighted match. The timing was crucial to the technique, since kindling, coal and volatile paraffin in the presence of an updraft tended to form an explosive combination. It was not unknown, especially when my father was in charge, for paraffin-induced detonations to distribute kindling, coal and charred scraps of newspaper over most parts of the sitting room in the blink of an eye capped by a singed eyebrow.

The principal fireplace in each of Numbers Six and Seven was not, however, the one in the respective sitting rooms. The critical fireplace in both cottages was located out in the partitioned-off kitchen area behind a shiny, black-leaded, closed-over grate adjacent to a ponderous cast-iron oven. Lighting the fire in the kitchen was not so much a daily task, as the kitchen fire was kept going and stoked steadily, particularly when the weather turned colder.

Black-leading the fire grate, the oven door and any connected or linked metal strip, flange or appendage was an early morning ritual undertaken prior to building up the fire for the day. The essential tools were a bottle of black lead liquid, a hard brush and a great deal of effort. The black leaded metalwork was polished until it took on a shine with gleaming depths that looked as if they could be reached into.

———

Within the kitchen, the consequences of the regular baking, roasting and boiling activities generated an atmosphere not entirely dissimilar to the one that people I once saw frequenting a Turkish bath (courtesy of the good old Rivoli) appeared to enjoy.

The kitchen ambience was soporific, made for relaxation and contentment, happy indeed when the emergence of currant-studded yeast buns from the oven was imminent, and well nigh ecstatic when the dish for afters was a rice pudding with a spotty brown skin on top. Eagerness to grab a bun resulted in my fingertips getting burned. Gran put butter on the seared digits. "The bun was too hot!" I complained. "Well," said Granfer, "it came from a hot place!"

It was alleged that there were people in Port Isaac who "couldn't knock the skin off a rice pudding"; if such people existed I didn't want to know them. In close proximity to a rice pudding, any boy worth his salt was prepared to fight for the privilege of knocking off the skin and to gobble up and savour every sweet morsel that lay beneath.

The enamel dish in which a rice pudding was baked was the ultimate prize to win because it provided the opportunity for getting stuck into scraping away and revelling in the luxury of the melt-in-the-mouth curling remnants of the rice pudding skin fused to the edge of the dish. Those bits were so delicious that I would have scraped the enamel from the dish to make sure I didn't miss a single speck of the bounty.

I ate more dinners seated at the heavy wooden kitchen table in Number Seven than I did in Number Six. A tablecloth to spread on the table was something that Gran thought would be nice to have but was not essential to the conduct of an ordered life. Yesterday's dismembered newspaper placed on the table deputised for a tablecloth quite acceptably and additionally allowed me to read while I was eating without being rebuked for bad manners. Although I was banned from perusing the *News of the World* on Sundays, I found that at dinner time on Mondays I could extract from its pages a whole load of information about various and altogether curious intimacies that had occurred.

Pasties always took pride of place for dinner. Boys told one another that, "No one makes a pasty like my mother." For good or ill, that assertion was the absolute truth as far as my experience went, and there was no one who could "tell me different".

A pasty was the staff of life in a convenient shape and size that could be eaten from a plate or taken down to the beach to be eaten in the hand. In spite of the fact that they all incorporated a set of basic ingredients – namely a standard mix of potatoes, onions and beef (preferably skirt), respective "mothers' pasties" were imbued with the individuality of their maker's fingerprints. Sometimes turnip was added to the recipe – turnip for me was a taste detraction to be avoided at all costs.

If a dozen pasties from a dozen cottage ovens were lined up

and sampled one by one it would be easily possible to identify precisely who had made them. The definition lay in the texture of the pastry, the pattern of the crimp, the relative moistness (or dryness) of the contents, and the accumulation of gravy in the corners. The quantity and quality of gravy in the corner of a pasty stamped the hallmark recording the pasty maker's innate skill.

The ability to make a good pasty was a God-given talent. Some had it and some didn't. My mother was one who did, but in Gran's case, although she headed in the right direction, her style of crimping produced hard ropes of pastry that could have been used to caulk ships' timbers.

On the underside of Number Seven's kitchen tabletop I discovered a recess where a drawer had rested in the days before it was lost, stolen, strayed or chopped up for firewood. In the recess I managed to place some of the more tooth-resistant pasty crimps, hiding them one by one for a long while. The number of concealed crimps eventually became a crusty hoard, clandestine until it was discovered. It was only fortunate that I wasn't required to dispose of the durable stockpile by eating it all up.

Granfer told me that when he was a boy, food that he left on his plate was brought back to him at each subsequent meal time until he finally had to give in and eat it. He said that a particular serving of steadily rejected porridge appeared so many times in front of him that hair began to grow on it.

In the kitchen of Number Seven a narrow cupboard closed by a tall door was recessed deeply into the wall on the left-hand side of the oven. The cupboard's innermost sanctum had in all likelihood been untouched either by God's good daylight in any of its many shades of dimness or by the diffused light of the paraffin lamp that hung from the ceiling in the centre of the kitchen. I knew that if I crawled too far back into that cupboard I would never come out again.

Looking through the cupboard's open door, I saw only black

depths in which something was lying in wait and undoubtedly sizing me up. I sometimes tried to catch a glint from the eyes (or eye) of what was in there, but whatever it was, it was too clever by half to give itself away.

The so-called "Cornish Litany", which was manifest on just one of a range of several postcards sold by Mrs Cowling at the Old Drug Store down at the bottom of the front steps, offered a plea directed at the ears of the Good Lord that he should deliver us from "ghoulies and ghosties and long-leggedy beasties and things that go bump in the night".

Just like Syd in Sunday school who, when he was asked by the vicar if he believed in Holy Communion, told the vicar yes, of course he did because he had seen it done, I knew that the creatures of the Cornish Litany were real because I had read the postcard down at Mrs Cowling's.

I concluded that one or other of the Litany's quoted quartet of Cornish horrors, probably a long-leggedy beastie, the appearance of which would have been unimaginable had it not been for its representation on the postcard, was in residence at the back of Gran's cupboard.

However, since its undoubted presence there didn't worry Granfer, I decided to try not to let it bother me, although when the cupboard door was even as much as slightly ajar I gave it as wide a berth as was feasible – which, given the constraints of the kitchen, was never quite wide enough for my liking.

# 9

# *Talking Shops*

PORT ISAAC was endowed with sufficient shops to furnish all that the everyday household ought to ask in order to satisfy its trivial round and common task. Most of these vending establishments were located in Fore Street, which thoroughfare ensured that shoppers were given no room to deny themselves a road (although whether or not Fore Street was a road to bring them daily nearer God might be open to debate).

In descending order from top to bottom, the Fore Street litany of illustrious sellers of goods vital to the sustenance to the general public included the Old Drug Store (proprietors Mr and Mrs Lynwood – "Lightning Lyn" – Cowling); the grocer (Messrs L. Chapman and Sons); the fruiterer (Mr Altair – "Old Tair" – Bunt); the bakery (Mr and Mrs Sherratt); the greengrocer (Mr Jim May, and, subsequently, Mr and Mrs Stan – "Clokie" – Cloke); the newsagents (Mr and Mrs Frank Rowe); and the chip shop (Mrs Keat).

As if that list didn't incorporate more than enough creature comforts for shoppers to attend to (or not attend to as the case might be), and in sure and certain proof that the Best Place in the World was alive and well, Fore Street was also graced by:

the Liberal Club (custodian Mr Freddie Honey); the county primary school (Headmaster Mr C. Victor "Boss" Richards); the barber's shop (Mr William John Honey in attendance); the Post Office (Mrs Olive Bate in nominal control and Miss Jinny Hills in absolute domination); the Golden Lion pub (mine host Mr Harry Irons); the Wheelhouse (the café run by Mr and Mrs Tommy Atkins); the Harbour Café (presided over by that prince of verbal flannel Mr Ted Robinson); and Pawlyn's fish cellars (managed by the charismatically laconic Mr Tom Brown).

On the strength of a glorious catalogue like that it could be surmised that no one could or would have wanted to ask for more, but Port Isaac wouldn't have been what it was if that had been the case. To satisfy the significant Oliver Twist element in local society the slack was reeled in by: the Co-op up at the head of New Road (operating under the captaincy of Mr William Auger and his recalcitrant adjutant Miss Cassie Saundry); the Family Butcher (J. N. Hicks & Son) plus a shoe cum gift shop (proprietor Mr H. G. Lansdowne), both located on the lower part of New Road where they were separated only by the grove of fir trees that so inspired the Green Triangle; a second butcher's shop (Mr Worden) adjacent to the Lake flush gate in Middle Street; and a cobbling emporium (with the stone deaf Mr Harry Morman always first at the last) in behind Worden's on lower Church Hill.

Taken as a whole, Port Isaac's inventory of mercantile luminaries demonstrated not only the compelling claim of Fore Street to be the paramount commercial artery but also that the blood of trade flowed from that stellar conduit to vending parts beyond without causing any heartache.

As a consequence of its status as the focal point for the daily domestic shopping routine, Fore Street was a channel of crucial importance in the dissemination of items of gossip both choice and mundane and of rumour uncontaminated by the need for substantiation.

Vindictive grains of tittle-tattle dropped into the Fore Street pool by gossipmongers threw ripples out to the far reaches of the parish at lightning speed. Sour berries of suggestion were held up as premium fruits for sucking dry. The smallest spat-out pip was a stone for casting by those who were not without sin. Facts didn't matter. The embellishment of well-tested imaginations made up for the absence of anything as immaterial to the cause of gossip as truth.

Fore Street's first law of mudslinging declared that once an opening shot was fired it would progress in the manner of a snowball coursing downhill, gathering pace and weight as it went, changing size and shape with each revolution and taking on ever more inspirational tints at every bounce. (QED).

On any morning when the weather was clement and the temperature equable, Fore Street was studded with stationary knots of would-be shoppers whose pressing intent was to demonstrate an expertise in the art of dishing out the dirt. Time was not of the essence to any of them. They gave of their time most willingly when scandal was in the air, leaving no tapestry of shame unfolded in order to make sure that every detail was embroidered in vivid primary colours.

The gossip blossomed and fruited in its telling and retelling. It was rapidly swallowed and immediately regurgitated. A tale originating at the bottom of Front Hill was transformed into something very different by the time it arrived at Little Hill. Once it got down as far as the vicinity of the Pentice, the fictional content of the yarn reigned supreme, erstwhile saints had evolved into current sinners, and dedicated public servants were being defined in the guttural accents of Mr Jim Honey as bweddy buggos down to the last man among them.

Among the inveterate gossips who made Fore Street their daily beat, one of the best (if not the finest) in terms of persistence, nosiness and an instinctive ability to plant and cultivate the least vestige of rumour in the rockiest of soil, was Roger's Aunt Mary, queen of the gruesome parable.

She was a long-term spinster of this parish. Aunt Mary lived with her brother Mr Sam Bate, a bachelor of the same locality, in one of a short terrace of tallish houses down at the bottom of Front Hill alongside where the cliff footpath leading out to Mr Hillson's house commenced. Unlike the nearby Canadian Terrace, Aunt Mary's terrace of residence didn't have a proper name, although for reasons that I could hazard a pretty fearful guess at, it had managed to acquire the popular title of "Rat's Terrace".

Sam was a florid and exceedingly jovial man-about-town who appeared to have learned the hard way, via a long association with Aunt Mary, to keep his own counsel. In common with many members of Port Isaac's more venerable male population Sam was a former seafarer. Eschewing the kind of flat cap that was (almost) definitive of the breed, Sam sported a rather rakish trilby-styled hat redolent of lively days spent by him well beyond the parish boundary.

In his past Sam must have been (and possibly still was) a man with a penchant for lifting a pint. I wondered therefore how he managed to satisfy his thirst, as the imbibing of ale would have been anathema to Aunt Mary's blinkered sensitivities. Whatever Sam did, he carried it off with a panache that was his trademark.

The general area on either side of lower Front Hill was territory dedicated to the accommodation of the enjoined Bate and Keat family. Roger's father, Mr Les Keat, a man as solid in virtue as the day was long when he wasn't out on the warpath actively tracking Roger and me down, had married Sam and Aunt Mary's sister Alice. Les and Alice had four children who in descending order of age were John Tinney, Marguerite, Roger (of course) and Nora. They all lived in the left-hand part of a big semi-detached house, optimistically named "Bay View", on the St. Peter's side of Front Hill, looking towards Rats Terrace. Queenie, sometime maker of marmite sandwiches and younger sister (or maybe cousin) to Alice and Aunt Mary and Sam, occupied the right-hand half of Bay View with her husband CPO Arthur Welch RN, the well-loved maestro of the St Peter's PT Club.

To cap the tribal aspect off there was Les's mother Gran Keat, kindlier and statelier by far than Arker's grandmother, her Dolphin Street namesake. Gran Keat was the matriarchal resident of "Atlantic Cottage" located on the side of Front Hill just down from Bay View.

My mother told me that the Bate family tree had true blue sap flowing through its branches and twigs. Back in the realms of history a Spanish aristocrat, shipwrecked on the Cornish coast following the defeat of his country's Armada by a fleet of ships commanded by Sir Francis Drake, was reckoned to have introduced his bloodstock into a line of descendants among whom the Bates ranked high.

For our delectation at school we were taught that the Sir Francis Drake in question, for once not in his hammock and a thousand miles away, was participating in a "rubber of bowls" on Plymouth Hoe when the great Armada came. It was interesting to speculate on just how much the rubbing of his bowls had contributed to Drake's success.

It took a Drake-styled Herculean effort to reconcile ancient aristocracy with the current demeanour of Sam and Aunt Mary; however, where Alice and Queenie were concerned, it seemed that no stone was left unturned in an endeavour to demonstrate that their self-assessed social status was well above that of the Port Isaac rank and file.

John Tinney, Marguerite, Roger and Nora were all endowed with the jet-black hair and warm complexional characteristics of what, from a familiarity with Mexican bandits on the screen at the Rivoli, I assumed might be typically Spanish traits. Had any of the four been fitted with a wafer thin moustache, a giant sombrero and a tendency to say *"Caramba!"* there would have been no doubt at all in my mind about where some of their ancestors had come from. (Port Isaac wasn't entirely bereft of genuinely continental foreigners of more recent vintage, as a French seller of presumably French onions made a visit to the village once annually. He wasn't Spanish of course. He rode into town on a bicycle festooned all over with long strings of onions, every onion as plump as he was himself. There were so many onion strings hanging from his shoulders that his characteristic jersey of thinly alternating horizontal black and white stripes could barely be made out. A black beret floated on his head, neatly angled towards his right shoulder.)

Roger's resemblance to Scrapper Smith, a close pal of Lord Snooty, who appeared regularly on page three of the *Beano*, only served to ally Roger even more closely with the ascendant classes. Roger was marked with a small but very distinctive black streak on his forehead directly over one eye. Iberian ancestry could not be blamed for the blemish, as its presence was the consequence of someone slinging a lump of coal at Roger in the school playground. That sudden impact with fuel on the move provided him with a permanent tattoo.

Nora was brought up to be a young lady destined to eschew the common manner of speech and the even commoner habits of her school contemporaries. She undertook lessons in proper speaking (referred to by someone who knew about those things as "elocution"). Given that she exhibited grace in her movement, it seemed likely that there had also been some instruction on the side regarding the improvement of her personal deportment.

The first time I was struck by the imponderability of the word "deportment" was when it appeared on one of my Sir James Smith's Grammar School end-of-term reports. My form mistress was none other than Jonesie, who recorded on the report that although I was "academically sound", my "manner and deportment need improving". (So too did my elocution, although Jonesie was kinder than Polly would have been in alluding to that particular shortcoming.)

178

Prior to Jonesie's discerning observation I thought that deportment referred to someone walking around with a tottering pile of books on top of his or her head. I had to look up what the word really meant before I could accept that Jonesie had judged me not harshly.

The money spent on Nora's elocution lessons was not handed over in vain. The sounded "R" was expelled from her speech totally, absorbed in a mouthful of marbles, alleys and bottle washers, never to return. She spoke in imperious tones, always managing to rise a grand cut above the rest of us. At so-called "talent" contests put on for the entertainment of the public, sometimes at the Temperance Hall and at other times in the Church Rooms, Nora appeared on stage to regale the audience by reciting poems that no one had heard of, written by authors whose name rang few bells either. At the end of her turn Nora received a ripple of relieved applause and responded with a deep curtsey.

Nora seemed to favour reciting from the work of one Eleanor Farjeon. I suspected that her choice of poetical gems was not so much intended to transmit any enduring quality of Eleanor's lines as it was to place Nora's rolling delivery on an evocation of Eleanor's surname.

Aunt Mary spoke with clarity, even if elocution lessons had clearly not come her way. No doubt her advanced age precluded her association with such things.

She was of moderate height but was compelled to appear rather shorter than that owing to an uneven posture. Aunt Mary hunched her thin frame forward while leaning slightly to one side, favouring the right leg and dragging the left. Her left arm was stiff and twisted to effect a palm-up position, the hand held claw-like, tight against her side as a consequence of having been afflicted in her younger days by infantile paralysis.

The common ailments of childhood were measles, German

measles, whooping cough, mumps and chicken pox. Most of us got them, weren't bothered, made our way through, and moved on with impunity. Although the much more feared diphtheria and scarlet fever were contracted by more of our number than seemed reasonable, it was seldom that anyone succumbed entirely to such risky diseases either.

The incidence of infantile paralysis was fortunately rare in Port Isaac. It was, however, by no means unknown and was usually regarded as a black-cap (or at least an iron lung) sentence passed on those who got it. Aunt Mary, just like Sybil Couch, defeated infantile paralysis, and although the victory came at a price, it was a price that in all fairness handed her the absolute right to become a dyed-in-the-wool *quidnunc* in the ebb tide of her years.

Aunt Mary's encounter with infantile paralysis could have played a part in generating her celebrated love of all things morbid. She delivered cautionary tales and dire warnings in rich and hair-raising detail. However, the management of rumours was her meat and drink, and the elaboration of gossip was hers to prize.

A morning patrol for Aunt Mary generally covered the section of Fore Street in between Rat's Terrace and Little Hill. Occasionally she might proceed onwards from Little Hill to go as far down as the Post Office or Sherratt's, although the frequency of her passer-by buttonholing manoeuvres *en route* served to preclude her covering quite that much distance before the imminence of dinner time called her home.

The free movement of whomsoever Aunt Mary met up with was destined for arrest. It was well nigh impossible for selected victims to evade her clutch. Ducking away from her into an open shop was not always the best option for one of Aunt Mary's intended targets to take, since no matter how many essential purchases needed making within, there were limits to how long it was possible to skulk inside a shop, and Aunt Mary was not only liable to take up pursuit by entering the shop as well, she was also a patient waiter.

Aunt Mary moved down Fore Street with the snail-like deliberation of one to who time was not a commodity related to a ration book. She was filled with an enormous resolve to corner the unwary, solicit items of gossip, and to pass the same on to captives she was going to grab later on.

I was familiar with Aunt Mary's hostage-taking technique only too well from the many occasions on which she placed herself squarely in my path so as to block off my opportunity for escape as I approached her. She bonded herself to me in the first instance by seizing one of my arms with her good hand. With my arm in that vice-like grip, her clawed fingers entered the state of play as tenaciously as if they were the talons of a winged raptor. Their touch was misleadingly light, as was at once evident to me when I made the mistake of trying to pull away from her.

One of the most exciting of the weekly serial films that we saw at the Rivoli was entitled *The Clutching Hand*. In that *magnum opus* of cliff-hanging entertainment, a disembodied hand moved hither and thither and did an effective job of strangling people at the rate of one or more per episode. We loved it. The singular hand often appeared on the screen both in dreadful silhouette and as a sinister shadow slipping across a wall. Aunt Mary could well have taught the Clutching Hand its technique.

A ten or fifteen minute exchange with Aunt Mary constituted the minimum penance for those she adhered to. The inconvenience of taking a lengthy detour was seen as a small hurdle to surmount in order to avoid meeting her. I adopted the habit, when I descended the front steps to Fore Street from either Numbers Six or Seven Canadian Terrace, of peering out and reconnoitring from the foot of the steps so as to determine if Aunt Mary was anywhere in sight before I dared to enter the street. It was not that the precautions made all that much difference, as Aunt Mary was able to materialise with eerie suddenness and set her version of the Clutching Hand in motion. All that would then be lacking was the accompaniment of blood-curdling atmospheric music.

Phil Harris, the American entertainer whose coarsely sanded voice of experience sounded as if it had been cured in cigarette smoke, was frequently featured on gramophone records played on the wireless in *Two-Way Family Favourites* at dinner time on Sundays. One of his most popular numbers was "Never Trust a Woman" containing the line "She'll Paul Revere the gossip round the town". Aunt Mary, assuredly pre-eminent among her peers, could have been seen as the Pauline Revere of Fore Street, true to both the letter and intent of Phil Harris's immortal ditty.

———

Clearly, Aunt Mary showed little reticence in following candidates for her attentions across the thresholds of shops. In contrast, however, the placement of as much as one of her toes across the doorstep of an establishment such as the Liberal Club, William John's barber's shop, and the Golden Lion would have been unthinkable, countered by an aversion to these facilities that was as heartfelt as it was supreme. In all fairness, Aunt Mary would not have wished to be seen dead within any of that triumphant trio of (more or less) exclusively male domains, notwithstanding that the barber's and the Golden Lion were well beyond the lower reach of her normal range of surveillance.

The Liberal Club, located on the lower corner that Back Hill made with Fore Street, was a bastion of banter, badinage, billiards and bullshit, permeated by the combative odours of sweat and rank tobacco. Dodging into its precincts was a refuge-seeking option I used, not infrequently, when I spotted Aunt Mary coming and believed that she hadn't yet seen me.

The custodian of the Liberal Club was Mr Freddie Honey, a creakingly elderly gentleman in whose company it was impossible not to revel. Freddie told me that when he was a boy (so long ago) he ascended and descended Lobber cliff many times.He would take advantage of the long and grassy transverse ledge that sliced across the cliff's otherwise sheer top quadrant and take the ledge at a run. I revered him for his courage to the extent that I set out several times to follow in his footsteps along the ledge, but whether going up or coming down, my nerve failed me at the half-way stage on every occasion. It wasn't always easy to imagine the gaunt and fragile tower that Freddie had grown into as a stripling boy. He was proud to tell us that he was a founder pupil at the Port Isaac county primary school when it first opened its doors to the thick and the thin of the village in 1877.

Freddie observed that Lobber's green ledge had been a more substantial feature when he ran along it than it was in the post-war here and now. The decay of time had taken its toll of the ledge in much the same way as it had done with Freddie. He went on to add that the ledge was regularly used by workmen keen to make a rapid passage between the cliff top and harbour floor while the breakwaters were being constructed in the 1920s. Loaded into wet sacks, the raw concrete for the breakwaters was transported from the top of Church Hill to the head of Lobber cliff by way of Washing Pool Lane. Once arrived at Lobber, the concrete was lowered down to the construction site on strung cables with what I could only assume was a fair amount of difficulty.

Not all of the concrete reached Lobber in a fluid state – some of it set prematurely in the sacks in which it was contained to form unmanageably great solid blocks. These were set into the hedges along the way into Lobber. The sacking eventually rotted away, gone but not forgotten as its warp and weft remained in effigy on the surface of the blocks, cast in concrete as it were.

Freddie held court as a fireside king in the billiard room of the Liberal Club. He could perhaps be more accurately described as a stove margin philosopher, since a paraffin-fuelled portable stove, looking as evil as it smelt, provided the only source of artificially generated warmth in the Liberal Club that anyone knew about. There was a fireplace of course, located behind the spot where the paraffin heating unit was usually placed, but it was used only as a convenient repository for spent matches, pipe dottle and spit.

Freddie's spirit was as great as his age. In the noble tradition of Mr Andy Oaten on his regal seat down at Little Hill, Freddie provided an inexhaustible fund of anecdote and cracking repartee to anyone who dropped in at the Liberal Club by either impulse or design.

He governed the Liberal Club all the year through, a well smoked pipe gurgling away between his dentures, a battered trilby hat on his head and a khaki greatcoat that might have been no stranger to trench warfare covering his bony shoulders. The Liberal Club was Freddie's life, and for so many of us Freddie was the manifestation of the Liberal Club, the one being the perfect complement of the other.

———

According to the deeply incised figures beneath the peak of the Liberal Club's roof on its front wall alongside Fore Street, the building was opened in the year of grace 1911. The original objective behind the institution would have been to further the arguably admirable aims of the Liberal Party of the immediately post-Edwardian day by providing a focus in which members of that illustrious political party could assemble and plot ways and means of doing their rivals down.

The passage of time and a couple of wars had, however, acted to ensure that an exclusive association of the Liberal Club with the Liberal Party was as tenuous as that of the Temperance Hall with the devoutly teetotal.

Subsequent to its founding, the Liberal Club had evolved principally along lines favouring the pursuit of billiards and snooker. Age was no bar to qualification for playing a game. Skill was important, but it was ownership of a cue that really counted. The elegant tournament-sized billiard table was topped with a single perfect slab of the best quality Delabole slate covered with cool green baize.

Meter-operated electric floodlights hung above the table. Joe Davis came along once to play an exhibition match. Tobacco-darkened, highly uncomfortable wooden benches ready for spectators lined the walls on three sides of the table, the only empty space being beneath the memorial scoreboard. In the fourth wall was set the defunct fireplace, in front of which, adjacent to the noisome paraffin stove, a rickety card table doubling as Freddie's office desk stood in position for those who either favoured cards or draughts or dominoes or didn't own cues.

Yet the Liberal Club remained a venue into which a few of Port Isaac's shrinking band of traditional Liberal voters were drawn to meet their parliamentary candidate on the occasions when he deigned to show up. His name was Mr Dingle Foot, but he was better known as "Dangle Boot". The presence of Dangle at the Liberal Club provided a sure sign that a general election was coming, as his overbearing persona was otherwise seen so rarely that it was considered to be the result of pure accident when it happened. Secure from unwelcome brickbats within Freddie's demesne, Dangle made promises to his followers that were as hollow and as significant in content as was the well-missed brass spittoon standing at one corner of the billiard table. Even Aunt Mary's rumours contained more substance.

In spite of the Liberal Club's shortcomings as a cauldron of political intrigue, the Chairman of its administrative committee was nevertheless an inveterate Liberal in whom the party could delight. His name, resonating leadership, was Mr L. E. V. Castle. He lived near the top of Front Hill in a big house adjacent to the grounds of the Church Rooms in which the war memorial stood. Outside the front door the house was fitted with a glass porch, festooned with tomato plants cultivated by Mrs Castle. Rich red tomatoes hung seasonally from the plants.

Mr Castle was short and rotund in the Pickwickian sense. His trademark affectation was a bow tie, which did nothing to diminish the status of well-respected local gentleman that he enjoyed. His triple initials stood for Lionel Edgar Victor. All three Christian names were redolent of greatness, and Mr Castle was indeed a man born to have greatness thrust upon him. He gravitated almost automatically to positions of ultimate local authority, assuming a paramount role in the affairs of the Liberal Club, the parish council, and other well-meaning committees that in the best political traditions promised much, talked more and organised something or other even if no one was too sure what it was.

Mr Castle was the target for unconcealed contumely from third parties only with respect to his cutting-edge command on stage at public meetings of the parish council. Such meetings always gave an impression of being set up more for the entertainment of the general populace than for demonstrating that the management of parish affairs was meaningful. A parish council meeting open to the public filled the Church Rooms with an audience eager to experience pithy exchanges between the floor and the chair on issues of otherwise stultifying triviality.

Parish council meetings were games characterised by impotent and ineffectual debate under rules set by the council, all played out in the full understanding that whatever the council wanted to do, it would do, irrespective of the volume of protest. The council's guiding mandate was that all decisions needed to be deferred, on which basis taking action could be obviated for as long as possible.

It was therefore less than kind, in the light of Mr Castle's wholehearted dedication to public service, that he became known from the style of his parish council meetings performances as "Mr Putting-it-forward". In an even deeper delve into lack of charity Mr Castle then became "Mr Eh?" after the celebrated character of the same name from Tommy Handley's peerless wireless programme *ITMA*.

The Port Isaac harbourmaster, Mr Anthony Provis, additionally dubbed Mr Castle "Levi" at a public meeting, and Levi was thereafter enshrined as Mr Castle's nickname in the popular consciousness.

Following Mr Castle's final departure up to St Endellion, a beautifully polished hardwood scoreboard was set up in the billiard room of the Liberal Club as a tribute to his everlasting memory. The scoreboard was fastened to the wall on the left-hand side of the billiard table. The numbers were etched onto it in gold leaf. Sliding indicators drew attention to the score of a game in progress. A plaque beneath the scoreboard commemorated Mr Castle's transcendent life.

Freddie merited a plaque to be erected in the Liberal Club in his memory just as much as Mr Castle did, but the uniqueness of Freddie's faithful tenure to the yellow and red was destined to go unsung. The Liberal Club committee might have hung its collective head in shame at their failure to recognise Freddie's pillar-like loyalty, but it would be too much to suspect that it did.

Freddie's life, from cliff-running boy to ancient man of character, enveloped an impressive span of Port Isaac history. When he was gone from us, I felt his worthy spirit scurrying in Fore Street between the Liberal Club and the primary school, ever sure of foot and always bright of eye.

*The fishermen's cellars beneath the Pentice wall*

# 10

# *Where Fore Street Bends*

FROM WHERE IT BEGAN at the bottom of Front Hill, Fore Street slipped downhill to Sherratt's on a course that deviated neither to the right nor to the left. Those who walked the route were on the straight and narrow. For some of them it was a unique experience.

Fore Street's inclination was gentle. The same could not be said of all of its denizens. All the same, any dedicated forty fags a day man was able to gasp his way up from the Golden Lion to the Liberal Club in a single pass without needing to stop and take a breather, assuming he didn't meet up with Aunt Mary on the way.

Nor was the way down to Sherratt's in any way undulate underfoot. The opportunity for aiming and firing a gun along Fore Street on a deep winter's day with no risk of hitting any man or beast was denied to no one. It was an opportunity much considered but never executed.

Fore Street's only bend was an almost acute angle to the right opposite Sherratt's. From there the balance of Fore Street made a fifty-yard descent to the Town Platt through a darkly somnolent house and cottage-bound canyon, the confines of which were relieved only by the blessed intervention of Mrs Keat's chip shop on the left. Across to the right, the flank of the Wheelhouse rose like a cliff to hold the afternoon sun at bay.

In those former days when the Port Isaac lifeboat was kept in the Old Lifeboat House up beside Little Hill and the school playground, that life-saving craft needed to be negotiated, no doubt with an impressive mixture of care and fortitude on behalf of its manipulators, around the Fore Street bend on its way down to be launched from the Town Platt slipway beside the Lake. I could only assume that urgency was treated as a secondary consideration of the rather odd practice.

On and around Fore Street's bend the prospect was pleasing. Rowe's newsagent's shop anchored the inner curve of the bend, facing across Fore Street to the greengrocer's shop on the ground floor of the sharply peaked Victoria House. A cobbled alleyway, a direct extension of the descent of Fore Street, gave a through passage to Dolphin Street via the straits of Temple Bar and led past the upper wall of Victoria House.

The entry to Sherratt's bake house lay at the back of a small slate-flagged yard on the other side of the mouth of the alley. Joined to the bake house in more ways than one and fronting the outer bend of Fore Street, Sherratt's bakery shop dispensed bread, pasties and saffron cakes made at the bake house. Sherratt's shop window commanded an excellent view of the door that provided access to the public bar of the Golden Lion, which was held separate from Rowe's by another cobbled alley, this one as tight as it was steep. From this public portal of constant ingress and egress during opening hours, the rest of the Golden Lion occupied the flank of Fore Street all the way up to the Pentice.

The Post Office was located on Fore Street not far above Sherratt's. It occupied a goodly part of the Fore Street façade between the junction with Rose Hill and a tight and mysteriously wriggling ope that was seemingly hewn through a jumble of cottages to meet with Rose Hill across from the foot of Margaret's Lane.

---

The Golden Lion was a tall, awkward, and chunkily rambling building that at its back glowered over and attempted to dominate the beach at the top of the harbour. As a pub, the Golden Lion was tied to St Austell Breweries and was consequently mandated for the exclusive dispensation of St Austell ales to its many patrons. The licensee in charge of pulling pints was Mr Harry Irons. Harry was Welsh by origin. He was a great stretch of a man, although not quite as tall as Tregaverne Farm's Mr Button. However, the way in which Harry loomed over me whenever I met him still endowed him with what I felt to be the presence of a giant recently descended from a beanstalk.

Harry appeared to favour appearing in all seasons in his shirtsleeves under an unbuttoned waistcoat. For all I knew, he might not have owned a coat. His shirt was visibly equipped with a collar stud but rarely adorned with a collar. Harry ran the Golden Lion by sticking to certain of the criteria that once made Sparta great, although to be fair, the times were austere enough to call for austere measures. Harry's regulars could do none other than accept the status quo.

The entry door to the exalted public facilities of the Golden Lion on Fore Street was fitted with an aggressively noisy latch. As a consequence the door was normally left standing ever so slightly ajar during opening hours. Both habitués and the sons of habitués were enabled to slip through the doorway under cover of as much unobtrusive silence as they desired. The more furtive of them did their reticent best to avoid the cold eye cast on their intentions by any chapel-going worthy in the act of purchasing this day his or her daily bread at Sherratt's.

With an hour or two of imbibing pints of St Austell ales both mild and bitter under their straining belts and pendulous braces, the said regulars emerged, one by one, out through the unlatched pub door with the kind of overt alacrity that signified nature's call. In the open, each one took a right–angled turn to the right and clattered off down the alley between the Golden Lion and the newsagent's. The cobbles underfoot were honed to a such a high gloss thanks to the long–term ministrations of generations of footwear (leather soled and hobnailed alike) and the runoff of rain, that they could on occasion be lethally slippery. The alley led down to the "Bloody Bones" courtyard, undeniably cobbled as well, where the Golden Lion's urinal welcomed them, holding its odour fast on the harbour front.

Access to the business area of the urinal was achieved via an opening that had never known the presence of a door. The walls within were devoid of vitreous china, owing their stability to the properties of slate, on the flat surfaces of which an algal bloom had not only taken up permanent residence but was also showing every sign of continuing to thrive for ever under the sustenance of regular torrents of pee directed at and over it.

A water cistern was attached to the target wall of the urinal. From the cistern, a vertical flush pipe descended to a T-junction from which it extended horizontally along the full length of the wall, perforated every few inches. The cistern could sometimes be flushed. A shallow trough of minimum gradient occupied the base of the wall, slowly conducting rank effluent to a drain that discharged directly onto the harbour beach. The drain was generally clogged with ooze cumulated from the passage of countless pints of St Austell Breweries' celebrated products through equally countless sets of kidneys and thickened with gobs of spit.

Although the boys knew the interior of the Golden Lion's urinal quite intimately, none of us, myself included, had ever been inside the pub. What went on in there was a mystery to be devoutly pondered over. All the same, we were able to sniff the fragrance of blended sweat, fag smoke and stale beer that thrust its tendrils out into Fore Street each time the pub door swung to and fro on its hinges. We received frequent admonitions, both at home and at Sunday School, to pass by the Golden Lion on the Sherratt's side of Fore Street, as if by doing so any threat of contamination could be avoided.

When Harry gave up his landlordship of the Golden Lion, moving to join up with all those fishermen and other deceased regulars up at St Endellion, a younger man, a certain Mr James Pallister, came along to take his place as landlord. The revolution that James brought to Harry's former demesne involved the erection of class boundaries rather than the institution of eternal joy.

James comported himself as a being who, by his own cognisance, was considerably superior to the Port Isaac rank and file. He spoke in a plumstone-littered accent that even Nora Keat might have admired. The patronising approach that James applied to the regulars of the public bar suggested that he had most assuredly received his education at a teaching establishment that was not a County Primary school.

One of James's initial actions on assuming Harry's mantle, as recounted to me by Mr William (Gaggy) Hosking, was to segregate the bar into public and saloon-styled areas. A new door was installed as a barrier (said the admirable Gaggy) to prevent public-bar riff-raff from obtaining access to the saloon bar in which the cream of Port Isaac society, plus Captain (retd) Roy May, were seated on comfortable stools, sipping exclusive beverages from small glasses.

Although the deterrent door could be opened by no greater expedient than the lift of a latch, according to Gaggy it was clear that two-way traffic through the door was not in accord with James's intentions. As an issue-settling measure to prevent intrusion from the public-bar side, James decided that the door should be kept locked. As if to cement the arrangement, James raised the price of beverages in the saloon bar above the prices that he charged regulars in the public bar.

A war of nerves broke out. Bar custom dwindled on the public side. Regulars deserted in droves. Tempers rose. Gaggy said that James was sent to a place named Coventry. It was left to St Austell Breweries to do the honourable thing, on the assumed strength of which James departed suddenly, to the eternal regret of few if any.

Mr Frank Ellis, the landlord succeeding James, had the offensive door removed on his first day as landlord. My father (another regular) told me that Frank planned to exhibit the dismantled door, with a sign painted on it to the effect that "This is THAT door!", in a place where it could do no harm.

In his great and sadly unfinished work, *Weir of Hermiston*, Mr Robert Louis Stephenson wrote, "He who goes fishing among the Scots peasantry with condescension for bait, will have an empty basket by evening." James appeared to have found this out to his cost in his piscatorial conflict with the great unwashed of Port Isaac.

———

It would not be unfair to allege that the respective ambiances of the Post Office and the Golden Lion were akin to chalk and cheese. The disparity was all too clearly manifest in the *raison d'être* of those who lived to serve in these two institutions. The physical separation of the one from the other, by no more than the width of Fore Street, created a narrow no-man's land bordered by polarities held in abeyance as if they were the sort of pushy magnets that caused a tiny King Tut to arise from a Bakelite sarcophagus.

Its customers regarded the exterior aspect of the Post Office as being both cold and daunting. In this their judgement may have been less than fair, but they were well acquainted with the forbidding regime that lay within those walls, and so it was a question of condemnation by association.

Inside the Post Office, the fixtures and fittings were best described as basic. On entering the precincts, the customer was confronted by a tall transverse counter made from wood stained to approximate a mahogany hue and surmounted by a metal grille. A similarly decorated wooden bench was set against the wall over on one side for the benefit of the footsore, and that was that as far as furnishings went. A pervasive odour of recently mixed ink filled the air as effectively as if it had been distributed from a swinging censer. The said counter split the Post Office in two, separating an outer public area (directly in from the street) from an inner sanctum that formed the inviolable nerve centre of the business empire run by the postmistress Miss Jinny Hills and her associate Mrs Olive Bate.

Jinny was a sister of the Port Isaac undertaker (and also master carpenter and boat builder) Mr Harry Hills. She lived in a solidly built cottage located about half way up Front Hill. Her cottage, which she shared with a second Hills brother named Wilfred, adjoined the dank Bellevue Terrace and cast its front face down across a small meadow of tangled grass, at the bottom of which loomed St Peter's church. Looking over to the left of St Peter's, Jinny and Wilfred's cottage commanded a broad panorama of much of downtown Port Isaac, with the blued valley spurs and Church Hill in the background.

Brother Harry's residence stood, in a location that seemed wholly appropriate to his surname, up at the point of junction of Front Hill and Back Hill. Harry's cottage was constructed of slate, on which the rough had been made smooth by the regular application of coats of whitewash. A low wall surrounded the property, enclosing a pretty flower garden rife with roses, wallflowers, marigolds and nasturtiums. A riot of red valerian covered the outer wall on the Back Hill side.

I wasn't sure if Harry was or was not a nice man to know. He owned Canadian Terrace, a man of means and incidental landlord towards whom his tenants needed to maintain a respectful reserve and to whom they had to pay up the rent of twelve and six a month on demand.

In his capacity of undertaker, Harry was as familiar with the dead of Port Isaac as he was with the quick. I didn't want Harry to look me over, let alone touch me. If that happened, Granfer said, Harry might be sizing me up for fitting with a wooden overcoat.

During the one and only year that I spent in Boss Richards' class at the primary school (a year that commenced with Richard ("Rich") Couch — one of the big boys of the class — staring at me and heading off at once to say to his even bigger friend Brian ("Otch") Orchard, "Have you seen what we've got coming in with us?"), the class was required by Boss to read passages from *A Tale of Two Cities* by Charles Dickens out loud. In the paragraph or two with which I was called on to regale the class, the words "officiating undertaker" came up. I struggled a bit over how I should pronounce "officiating".

Boss stopped me. "Do you know the name of any undertaker?" he asked. I gave him the only name that came into my mind. "Please sir, Sir Stafford Cripps, sir". There was a roar of derisive laughter from the assembled class. Boss held up a hand to still the commotion. "You may be right," he said thoughtfully.

The jobs that Sir Stafford and Harry did for a living both ended in "ker" or something like that. Even with Boss's generosity, I was well on the way to being half right.

As one who was brought up with allegiance to the Church and all that that implied, I took it for granted that Harry's outlook on life, as a devoted member of the chapel persuasion (Roscarrock variety), had to be more or less narrow minded, devoid of a sense of humour and not very tolerant of even the simple vices (whatever they were). Everyone knew that that was the way of all chapel people. I heard it described at St Peter's Sunday School so it had to be true.

What was in no way open to question about Harry, however, was that his word was his bond and his probity was absolute. Harry's handshake placed an enduring seal on any agreement he made. He might have been less than generous towards Canadian Terrace tenants who owed him rent, but he was scrupulously fair in all his dealings aimed at recovering the same.

———

Wilfred was permanently bedridden and thereby never seen. He was allegedly confined to a room on the upper floor of the cottage he shared with Jinny. The wooden frame around his bedroom window bristled with a complicated array of expertly oriented hexagonal and circular mirrors, attached to adjustable arms of various lengths. With this arrangement of mirrors, so it was said, Wilfred in his sickbed could observe pretty much anyone transient in the streets of Port Isaac during the hours of daylight. If through slumber Wilfred missed anything of importance, there was no doubt that some of the fruits of Jinny's daily interaction with the public in the Post Office would be fed to him in the evening to bring him up to date.

Jinny was an archetypal spinster-postmistress model. She was tall and statuesque, with a ramrod straight back and the piercing eyes of an eagle. She looked like a middle-aged version of the *Dandy*'s Keyhole Kate. Her greying hair was drawn into a tight and severe Victorian-styled bun. Her dresses were darkly Edwardian. A chapel lady (Roscarrock of course) to the core, Jinny's mind, body and soul were moulded into a set as tight as Temple Bar.

Jinny's personality, in the mould of her brother Harry, was characterised by total rectitude. She was fastidious in her duties, scrupulous to a fault, correct in her accounting to the absolute farthing, and conducted her every transaction according to the Post Office book of rules. The duties that Jinny carried out in the ascetic halls of the Fore Street Post Office were guaranteed to be totally worthy of the customer's trust. Jinny had no sense of class discrimination – she intimidated both the highborn and the low, and suffered no fools gladly in the discharge of her sacred duties.

My mother came home one day and told me that Jinny had

sacked the then Port Isaac postman "with a minute's notice" for irregularities allegedly involving the unauthorised extraction of the contents of items of registered mail. It was a mark of the awe with which Jinny's authority was regarded that the time constraints of the postman's dismissal provided far more grist for the Fore Street gossip mill than did the eventual departure of the by then ex-postman to spend a year or so at His Majesty's pleasure somewhere up the line.

The mettle of Olive, Jinny's sidekick, was cast from a kindlier forge than that which produced the steely Jinny. Olive's face was round and rosy, her clothes demonstrated marginally more colour than those of Jinny, and her style of hair was often moderately modish. Many Post Office customers went to great pains to ensure that it was Olive and not Jinny who was on counter duty before they elected to enter the Post Office to conduct their errands. Jinny's presence behind the counter was not a prospect that anyone contemplated lightly. She fixed her eyes on customers as if she possessed certain knowledge that their objectives were nefarious. She instilled in them the guarantee that in her view they were guilty until they proved themselves innocent.

—

A thick bed of loose gravel covered the surface of the L-shaped yard that flanked the back of Jinny and Wilfred's cottage. The finely tuned gravel could emit a resonant crunch under the weight of no more than a heavy sigh. It was impossible for even a cat to creep silently into Jinny's yard, let alone for the feline to crap and creep out again.

A small bay tree, which as far as I knew was the only such example of the species growing in or around Port Isaac, flourished in a sheltered corner of the gravelled yard. When Jinny's beady eye was not directly monitoring the wellbeing of the bay tree and its leaves, it was quite certain that a reflection of the little tree in one of Wilfred's external mirrors guaranteed that it was under constant surveillance.

The fragrant leaves of the bay tree were much in demand in domestic kitchens as one of the essential ingredients used for preparing "marinated mackerel", a popular dish of freshly caught mackerel steeped in malt vinegar flavoured with bay leaves and peppercorns.

To prepare marinated mackerel a few of the so-named fish, in classic Mrs Beeton tradition, had first of all to be caught. In the bountiful waters of the Bay, that was a task easily completed. Subsequently (and more problematically since Jinny was less than willing to release leaves from her one-of-a-kind bay tree to the many who were anxious to possess a few of them), the bay leaves also had to be acquired.

Sprigs of bay leaves fresh for the purpose were generally liberated in the dark of night from Jinny's bay tree, preferably with a rough gale blowing and booming to provide adequate soundproofing cover to the scrunch of larcenous footsteps on the gravelled yard.

In spite of (or perhaps because of) a host of pruning assaults on Jinny's bay tree, the tree not only survived but also thrived. Its leaves flavoured the incremental marinating of what must have been many shoals of mackerel.

---

To help a shopper recover from the rigours of a visit to the Post Office when Jinny was on duty, Sherratt's bakery shop was ideal as a nearby port in a storm.

Mr and Mrs Sherratt, supported by their sons John (the elder) and Tommy (the younger), baked their own brand of bread, splitters and currant-starred cakes and buns of saffron and yeast specification in the bake house adjacent to the shop. A yeast cake (or bun) was a saffron cake (or bun) without any saffron.

No crust was crustier, no bread was ever fresher or sweeter-smelling than bread sliced from a loaf baked by Sherratt's. Sawn in thick slabs with a bread knife, and subsequently buttered (or not as the case might be) and spread with jam or treacle, Sherratt's bread and splitters were regal fare, made even better – to the extent that anything better was possible – when topped by strawberry jam and a layer of oozingly thick yellow cream.

Once a week Sherratt's made a big batch of pasties. It was a measure of the popularity of those pasties that they were sold out before any one of them had time to cool on the rack. The pasties came along in rich pastry flaking at the touch. Customers could have their pasties prepared to order, in compliance with preferences such as the amount of turnip or onion that should be added to the staple beef and potatoes. Now and then there were also jam or apple pasties, keenly anticipated as treats for "afters".

Although I never refused or criticised a Sherratt's pasty (I wouldn't have dared to), I had to confess that the potatoes they contained were perhaps a little bit too mushy for me. I couldn't really see the point in my mother going out to buy pasties when at home she was able to make bigger and better ones.

My mother's pasties were in the order of a foot long and four inches broad. For consumption they were cut into three pieces. The middle piece was eaten first, and then the two end pieces (known as the "corners") were tackled. The ideal flavour was found in the corners where the gravy resided. The assurance of gravy was an art, and to their everlasting credit, a Sherratt's pasty matched up to the art as a rule. A hot pasty begged for no condiment to contaminate its majesty. A cold pasty always accepted a puddle of HP sauce on the side as a complimentary complement.

Mrs Sherratt was a powerhouse, constantly in motion. She was tiny and wiry; with thin, sucked in cheeks due in no small way to her adamant refusal to wear false teeth. She told my mother that she had put her teeth in once when she first got them and the discomfort she then felt was not something that she wanted to repeat. My mother told me that Mrs Sherratt's gums were hard enough to cut through one of Mr Tom Saundry's greenest apples. Mrs Sherratt's liveliness of character contrasted sharply with the dourness of Mr Sherratt, who took great pride in successfully exhibiting an air of unearned misery.

When he was serving behind the shop counter and was proffered either a pound or a ten-bob note by a customer ready but not necessarily willing to settle the account for goods purchased, Mr Sherratt's practice was to hold the note up to the light filtering in from Fore Street and subject it to an inspection that did not stop far short of being forensic. His face bore an expression of extreme suspicion blended with a hint that he was anticipating the worst. On the admittedly rare occasions when a five-pound note was presented to him, Mr. Sherratt's face turned whiter than the note itself as he refused with absolute finality to as much as touch, let alone accept, the flimsy item. The spirit of Miss Jinny Hills was perhaps not entirely absent from Sherratt's after all.

—

My first-hand association with monetary notes of the realm, whether they were brown, green or white, was to all intents and purposes non-existent. I knew what they looked like of course, but was more aware of what they meant to people like us who didn't have many of them. So it was that on one particular early summer evening when a trio of such notes came my way as a *de facto* coup, I had no thought of emulating Mr Sherratt by looking a gift horse in the mouth.

On the evening in question I chanced to be taking a shortcut in the direction of the Rivoli cinema and the New Coastguard Station through the area behind the Prout Brothers' Trelawney Garage. The sight of a pound note wafting by on a breeze halted my progress. I arrested the flight of the note by plucking it from the air. Then, lo and behold, I spotted another pound note resting on open ground nearby, and yet another lying on a weed-straggled verge. Suddenly I was in profit to the tune of three quid.

In the absence of any banking facilities in Port Isaac, a bank used a little hut, located in the general vicinity of where I found the three notes, to offer a weekly service for the convenience of those few local people who had an account at its Wadebridge branch. As that very same day had been bank day, it was not improbable that the three one-pound notes were inadvertently liberated either by the bank representative on duty or by one of his customers.

I scouted around in a quest for additional treasure, but it was to no avail as the three finds were the only members of the pound (or any other) note species that I was destined to come across. All the same, three pounds was for me much more than a small fortune. I took the notes home (Number Nine Hartland Road at the time) and gave them to my mother, who immediately assumed that I must have stolen them. It required a lengthy period of explanation for me to convince her that the largesse was quite literally a breeze-borne windfall.

My mother placed the three one-pound notes in a small flat tin with a reverence that suggested the laying out of a deceased relative. The little tin was interred at the back of the top shelf of our airing cupboard where it made an unwitting companion to a leather-bound copy of *The Pilgrim's Progress*, each of the two resting in warmed up peace.

Much soul searching was then carried out in an attempt to decide what could be done with the instant riches. My mother's conscience called for the three pounds to be turned in to the policeman at his official station (which was also his house) on Tintagel Terrace. This noble view struggled against my father's opinion that possession was nine points of the law. I didn't know what the tenth point of the law was. My father's position won the day. Three pounds was just too much money to be given up, no matter where it came from.

My mother wrote down the serial numbers of the three notes for quick reference. She perused subsequent issues of the *Cornish Guardian* (as well as the *Daily Sketch*) from cover to cover with the assiduity of the fine-tooth comb that was used to scour my hair for fleas whenever I scratched my head too hard in front of her. She was anxious to discover any reference in print to the loss of three pounds being reported and a list of their serial numbers being made known to all establishments in north Cornwall where money changed hands.

Any thought of us spending the three quid in Port Isaac was never considered. It was only necessary for my mother to imagine Mr Sherratt holding one of the three notes up to the light and looking sceptically at its serial number for her knees to be set trembling with fear.

I didn't know for sure whether any of the three one-pound notes were ever spent. They might well have remained fast in the small flat tin at the top of the airing cupboard as a permanently dark secret that my mother could never summon up the nerve to break.

It was perhaps just as well for transactions involving money in note form at Sherratt's that Mr. Sherratt was usually kept out of sight toiling away back in the bakery rather than serving in the shop. The running of the shop, in which as well as bakery produce a small line in groceries was also available, was normally in the hands of Mrs Sherratt and her elder son John.

John was endowed with a gift for delivering sarcastic observations and studied insults to his customers, all of which had the effect of endearing him to relatively few. He both dominated and overshadowed his brother Tommy, an effete character who was destined to stay out of the shop in order to conduct the bakery delivery van on its rounds, since the output of Sherratt's bakery was celebrated in parts of north Cornwall that lay well out beyond the boundary of St Endellion parish.

John introduced the concept of ready-sliced bread to Port Isaac. Most of his domestic customers believed in tradition, however, and, unimpressed by this modern phenomenon, preferred to continue cutting their own doorstep slices from whole loaves.

Nevertheless, quite a few hotel and guesthouse proprietors snapped up all the sliced bread that John could provide them with while presumably exercising their minds over what ought to be the next greatest thing to it.

I worked for John in the bakery shop for a few weeks of one school summer holiday. My wages were thirty bob a week, not bad at all. Each morning in the hour or two before the shop opened, my first task was to transform loaves of bread into slices in accordance with the previous day's orders received for the same. Day-old loaves were used, mounted on a bacon machine for manual slicing.

The bacon slicer was equipped with a disc blade as keenly edged as one of William John's freshly stropped razors. I discovered the quality of the edge of the blade on the day when I turned to one side to pick up a loaf and accidentally offered my right elbow to its attentions. The thin sliver of flesh that the blade took out of my elbow went from skin down to bone. Unfortunately, when the copious flow of blood was staunched and mopped up from the general surroundings, the sliver of flesh was never found. I wondered if it ended up in a hotel guest's sandwich lunch.

—

The Victoria House greengrocery shop, formerly the property of Mr Jim "the Ice Cream Man" May, subsequently passed into the capable hands of Mr Stanley and Mrs Lillian (Stan and Lil) Cloke. Stan was known as "Clokie". To judge by their spoken accents, both Clokie and Lil hailed originally from a place well within a radius covered by the sound of Bow Bells.

Lil was thin featured but heavy ended. Her shape was not unlike one of the pears she sold when pears were available. She had a high-pitched voice that could reasonably be described as plaintive. Her hair was cut in a forehead-hugging and eyesight-jeopardising fringe, from which it fell like rain on either side to almost, but not quite, touch her shoulders. Lil was constantly in the shop, shuffling around in front of the counter or behind it as the mood took her, with arms folded protectively high up on her chest.

Clokie was a man who was small in both stature and bonhomie. He was normally out on the road delivering fruit and vegetable produce to customers from a supposedly well-stocked van. He looked like a ferocious version of the comedian Arthur Askey. I knew implicitly, however, that, unlike Arthur, Clokie would not contemplate greeting me as one of his playmates, nor would he be especially likely to say "Ay theng yow!" At the same time, everyone knew that Clokie was the epitome of a healthy, grown-up busy little bee.

Victoria House was a prime target for "knock down dolly", a popular pastime followed by some of us during the darker evenings. In principle, knock down dolly required us to knock at a door, ring on a doorbell if there was one (or knock and ring simultaneously), and run away at great speed before the signal was answered. The knocking and/or ringing process was perpetrated by preference on doors behind which resided individuals (Clokie among them) that we categorised as miserable old buggers. Clokie could be counted on to produce a wild reaction.

Great fun though it was, the enjoyment of knock down dolly was substantially enhanced if it was possible to observe the discomfiture of whichever miserable old bugger opened the door to respond to the knock and found no caller on the doorstep. It was critical that the observation should be carried out from a vantage point associated with safe retreat.

The entry to the cobbled alley leading down to the Bloody Bones yard adjacent to the Golden Lion – or better yet, on top of the flight of steps leading to Mr and Mrs Rowe's back door on the downhill side of the cobbled alley – was an excellent point of concealment offering a clear view of the front of Victoria House when knock down dolly was fostered on Clokie and Lil.

One evening, Joey Thomas and I set out to determine just how close to the limits of apoplexy we might be able to drive Clokie, using knock down dolly as the tool and the security of Rowe's steps for concealment. Following our initial knock, Clokie, framed and backlit in his open doorway, appeared to demonstrate subtle indications of anger. With the second knock, Clokie was seething, his shoulders heaving like a basin of milk about to boil over and ruin the cream. The third knock had Clokie out in Fore Street screaming blue murder, illuminating the bend in Fore Street with his incandescence.

At that point enough was judged to have been enough. Joey and I decided that it would be unwise to test Clokie's boundary limits any further. We remained under cover at the top of Rowe's steps until, reckoning that the coast was clear, we descended and tiptoed across Fore Street in order to go up the alley leading to Temple Bar. We had already entered the alley before we remembered that Victoria House had a side door opening onto it. Our oversight was made evident when the side door was flung open and the enraged figure of Clokie, primed to commit an act of violence, leapt into the alleyway.

We took to our heels in flight as if our lives depended on it, which at that galvanic moment they probably did. Joey, although smaller than me, was a lot faster on his feet than I was. The pounding of Clokie's pursuing feet formed a counterpoint to the tumbling fugue of curses that he hurled like knives in the direction of our backs.

The three of us, hares and hound, raced in a close-order file through Temple Bar and took lower Dolphin Street in a charge that Alfred, Lord Tennyson, would have recognised. I could see distance opening between Joey and me. From the sound of his pursuit, Clokie seemed to be much less than half a league behind and closing fast. I leapt despairingly into a deep doorway on the left-hand corner at the bottom of Dolphin Street near Mr and Mrs Jimmy Baker's house on Middle Street. Joey forged onwards along Middle Street in the direction of the Town Platt.

I was a rat in a trap, and I prepared myself for the worst, only to see Clokie flit by. He was close enough for me to touch him, although given the exigency of the moment I was rather more concerned about me being touched by him. He was brandishing a walking stick, held high in his right hand, ripe for exacting vengeance. He hadn't spotted my disappearing act. Perhaps he was blinded by rage.

Joey told me later on that he ran down to the beach with Clokie still on his tracks. The tide was out, making it simple enough for Joey to lose Clokie in the darkness among the rocks and boats and gugs, thanks to Joey's superior knowledge of the harbour layout.

I lost no time in heading up to the top of Dolphin Street with mercurial wings on my heels. We never discovered what Clokie did with the rest of his interrupted evening.

The newsagent's shop was the property of Mr and Mrs Frank Rowe. Frank, in the pursuit of his alternative profession of fisherman, was more of a casual than a regular presence inside the shop. It was Mrs Rowe, a tiny, slightly hunched, bird-like lady of gentle manner, who ran the shop. She was graced with a bell-like tinkle of a voice and spoke in eloquent clarity. For all of her diminutive stature, however, Mrs Rowe was more than able to maintain the establishment in working order.

From Monday to Saturday, Frank and his sons Jack and Peter delivered daily newspapers from door to door around Port Isaac with regularity and precision, not to mention the utmost reliability. Rowe's didn't handle Sunday newspapers, and on Sundays, like God, the Rowe family rested.

The Sunday newspapers were available from Mr Bill Meluish, who hailed from Trelights. Bill came to Port Isaac every Sunday afternoon in a car loaded with the supply. He parked in specified locations at specified times, and his customers came to him. Bill was a morose individual who failed to offer any evidence that he enjoyed what he was doing.

Peter was a lively boy a few years older than me. He was a splendid footballer and sportsman in general, and he was my contemporary at Camelford Grammar School for a while, although we were never close to one another.

Jack was several years older than Peter. It could have been said of Jack, like Cogsy in his Vicar guise, that he was old before his time. He appeared to have about him an air of unremitting misery and to show the part of the world that he inhabited a sour mouth from which a good grumble emerged as second nature. Comics flowed across his mother's counter, but it was difficult to link Jack and the fun-filled *Beano* in a single thought.

The internal dimensions of Rowe's shop were not great. Inside the narrow, small-paned door where the customers entered, the confines could easily have been described as claustrophobic, had any of us known what claustrophobic meant. A perpetual twilight reigned, adding to the sense of interment. In the pervading gloom a small counter could be made out, lurking at the far end of the shop. Behind the counter, a row of big wide-mouthed jars containing assortments of boiled sweets glinted faintly as they caught such light as was able to penetrate that far.

Gran's adherence to God's good daylight found another great champion in Mrs Rowe, who, in the manner of Gran, had long ago conquered and suppressed any urge she might ever have had to put a light on prematurely.

As a customer entered Rowe's shop, a bell at the end of a rusty curled spring fastened to the inside top of the door was induced to jangle a few times. At the seconds-out sounds of the bell Mrs Rowe emerged like a wraith from the recesses of the secret depths behind the counter. She insinuated her presence into the dim surrounds, a soundless manifestation, materialising without a whisper.

Mrs Rowe's customers were always happy to grope for their regular magazines and comics on the counter, where the latest issues received were laid out in neatly overlapping rows. The surname of the subscriber was written in blue-black ink at the top right-hand corner of each copy by Mrs Rowe's own firm and attractive hand with the help of a broad-nibbed pen. It was personalisation of the first water.

No periodical graced by Mrs Rowe's handwriting, untainted by either blot or erasure, was ever destined to belong to anyone other than the bearer of the registered name.

Collecting the latest issue of my weekly comics from Mrs Rowe was always a thrill. There were exciting stories to be read. Good laughs were in store.

Emerging from Rowe's into the contrastingly blinding light of Fore Street's bend, with a copy of *Adventure* securely in my hand, I took a short, hard run downhill to the right, and skated the last stretch on my hobnails, alongside Mrs Keat's chip shop and past the corner of the Wheelhouse to reach the Town Platt in the very best of heart.

*The Browns' enclave on upper Fore Street*

# 11

# The Salt of Upper Fore Street

*It is an ancient Mariner,*
*And he stoppeth one of three.*
*"By thy long grey beard and glittering eye,*
*Now wherefore stopp'st thou me?"*

Samuel Taylor Coleridge (1772–1834)
"The Rime of the Ancient Mariner"

ON THE OPPOSITE SIDE of Fore Street to Numbers Six and Seven Canadian Terrace stood a row of three adjoined, individually distinctive, yet disparately constructed cottages. Concealed behind this array, secret strips of garden backed on to the edge of the harbour cliff.

Each of the three cottages was united with its two respective fellow dwellings under an umbrella of happy serendipity providing domestic shelter for various members of the family Brown. The bearded patriarch of this cosy familial assembly, whose Christian name was obscured by the fact that he was revered by all and sundry under the title of "Pa", resided in the lower cottage of the row.

The bottom wall of Pa's cottage was pierced by a couple of small windows and clad in an artful arrangement of split Delabole slates that could be admired by anyone undertaking an ascent of Fore Street. The cottage wall surmounted the deep-cut hollow of the primary school infants' class playground in the manner of a castle redoubt. It cast its long shadows over the infants at playtime,

211

and helped turn the playground into a virtual cockpit. Against the side of the playground, immediately below Pa's kitchen window, the school's matched pair of coal and coke bunkers tried as hard as they could to look like a buttress, but all to no avail.

In contrast, the wall capping the playground on its Fore Street flank downhill from Pa's cottage was supported at its base by a buttressing feature far more capable of preventing precipitate collapse than a mere bunker was. This feature was constructed entirely of concrete. A smoothly surfaced slope angled up from the playground floor to the bottom of the wall at a gradient steep enough to ensure that no infant could ascend the slope from a standing start. Even when I had the backing of a good run at the slope it was usually only possible for me to scramble part of the way up prior to reversing my course in a gravity-inspired backwards slide.

The common goal of all of us who tackled the formidable obstacle of the slope was its summit. If we reached it, we hung on by virtue of fingers hooked into one or other of a number of gaps where the concrete did not fit quite as tightly against the foot of the wall above as was originally planned. Since the ensuing descent invariably meant skinned knees it was just as well that the summit was conquered by relatively few.

The other residents of Pa's cottage were Ma Brown and Pa and Ma's four (so far but wait for it) unmarried offspring. The latter were named Winifred (otherwise "Winnie"), Frank (known as "Nibs"), Edwin ("Tinker") and George (who surprisingly had no nickname).

It would be fair to say that the Browns, like us in Canadian Terrace across from them, were as poor as church mice. That begged the question as to why a church mouse was any poorer than any other kind of mouse. It was not impossible that a church mouse's poverty was the fault of the churchwardens, as everyone knew that they were among the thriftiest of men. The comparative expression, to be "as mean as a churchwarden", was supposed to say it all.

On the other hand as far as I was concerned, the churchwardens at St Peter's, Mr John Neal (for the vicar) and Mr Westlake Brown (for the people), could never have been described as mean. John was certainly prudent, but such prudence befitted a man who combined his duty as churchwarden with that of St Peter's honorary treasurer – even if the takings when the bag was passed around at Sunday services represented the opposite of a fortune. Westlake, a great man of the church, didn't have a mean bone in his body.

Cogsy once informed me that I was as mean as a churchwarden, as a consequence of which I took the opportunity to enquire of him as to why a churchwarden was mean. Cogsy said, "A churchwarden sweeps the church with the hairs of his ass and gives the gleanings to the poor". Visions of John and Westlake thus engaged haunted my dreams for some time afterwards.

In addition to Nibs, Tinker and George, three more Brown brothers remained to be counted, but they were all married (to extremely worthy ladies) and lived in places other than at Pa's. This trio of espoused Brown siblings consisted of Tom, occupying the cottage at the far end of the three-cottage row; Carveth ("Veth") who resided in a house in lower Trewetha Lane near its junction with the summit of Rose Hill, and Bill ("Bill Pink") who hailed from a dwelling about half way up Rose Hill where he was a near neighbour of the aforementioned Mr John Neal.

Tom and his good wife were blessed with three children, consisting of two boys (Leonard and Harold) and a daughter named Noreen. Leonard, very sadly, lost his life on active service during the war. Mrs Tom was a genteel lady of taste, possessing impeccable manners, Brown by association. She and Tom named their cottage (which was actually more of a house) "Lenhareen" in honour of their offspring.

Veth and his wife Ellen had an only son named Maurice. Ellen, it was alleged, had wished for a girl but was not disappointed in making do with the boy that fate delivered into her hands. She endeavoured to redress her failed preference by ensuring that she brought Maurice up to be a mother's boy. It said much for Maurice, a rose-like intellect set in the midst of a tangle of thorns, that he soared above his limiting influences.

With only Maurice's name for insertion into an offspring-generated title for their own house, and equally to keep up with the Browns and not be outdone by Mr and Mrs Tom, Veth and Ellen sandwiched fragments of their own appellations alongside a slice of Maurice, and named their residence "Carlenice".

Bill Pink was married to the former Sue Oaten, generally known as Aunt Sue, sister to the charismatically garrulous Andy and the taciturnly gloom-laden Harry, better known as 'Arr. Andy and 'Arr, a pair of die-hard bachelors, lived with Bill Pink and Aunt Sue in their Rose Hill Cottage, which (perhaps fortunately as "Arsubian" sprang to mind), boasted no characteristically aggregated name. Bill Pink and Aunt Sue had no children, which was considered a great pity. Her many admirers regarded Aunt Sue as having been placed on earth for the purpose of mothering a large brood. Perhaps for that reason the bachelor brothers Andy and 'Arr tended to play her surrogate children.

Nibs was also a lifelong bachelor, completely dedicated (as were George and Tinker in the great tradition of Andy and 'Arr) to being waited on hand and foot by his apparently willingly slavish spinster sister Winnie.

He was gifted with highly articulate hands, which he used with expertise in the pursuit of his profession as second-string fisherman on the fishing boat *Winifred*. He could talk nineteen to the dozen without ever managing to say anything memorable or express any coherent train of thought that a listener could take away, recall and be able to repeat to someone else.

I found that no matter how long I spent in Nibs' ever-enjoyable company, I was unsure afterwards as to exactly what it was that he had told me, if indeed he had told me anything at all. Although it always seemed that there were golden nuggets begging to be panned out of Nibs' rambling discourse, they were totally obscured by the barren gravel that contained them.

"Well boy," Nibs would say, in tones couched with the broadest of Port Isaac accents, "'Tis a matter hov, ed'n it?" and off he would be at an endless collection of tangents, beating not only about the bushes but under and over and through them as well.

Nibs was at best of no more than average height. He was heavier than he ought to have been, tubby for sure, although not exactly fat. He had a soft, pink impish face, usually clenched like a fist around the stem of an old curved pipe. The pipe was a fixture in a corner of his mouth, out of which a seeping brown dribble oozed regularly.

Apart from wearing an off-colour flat cap, Nibs dressed himself entirely in black – trousers, jacket and jersey alike. The flat cap could have been of any imaginable hue when it was new, but that was a long time ago, since when even its stains were stained. Nibs wore the flat cap at a rakish droop, the peak at half-mast over his left eye.

His vestments were decorated with spots of Winnie's gravy, pasty crumbs, fish scales and tobacco ash. Immediately beneath the moist brown line exuding down his chin from the pipe stem, the darkness of Nibs' jersey took on drip-sponsored highlights.

The catch phrase larding Nibs' conversation, "'Tis a matter hov," was as good as any heard on the wireless. It was invoked to achieve its ultimate advantage during the summer, when Nibs took on a starring role in the public bar at the Golden Lion in front of an audience of attentive holidaymaking visitors. Since the visitors changed over at least by the week, or at most by the fortnight, their custom never came to stale Nibs' limited variety.

Nibs established himself as an archetypal stage Cornishman. The visitors took pleasure in his company, standing him so many free pints of St Austell ale that Nibs might have said "'Tis a matter

215

hov bein' too much for me!" but if he ever did say that, no one ever reported hearing him do so. His rustic charms, both natural and contrived, allowed him to turn opacity into a lustrous work of art as he wove to and fro through the green pastures of close-cropped vocabulary while his cup ran over.

In their everyday lives the Browns were all, to a greater or lesser extent, involved in matters related to the fruits of the sea. Pa was an old sea dog in the you–mought–call–him–captain tradition of Billy Bones. Tinker was another of the same, although in his case the cast of the mould was more relevant to Black Dog, if not to Blind Pew. Nibs and Bill Pink, salt-water veined to the deep heart's core, trod in Pa's piscatorial footsteps on the respective decks of the Port Isaac fishing boats *Winifred* and *Lilla*. The *Lilla* was a smaller craft than the *Winifred*, but in its yellow and red painted trim it somehow appeared to be the more distinctive of the two, and was certainly the more liberal in inclination.

George was a yachting type; a crew member serving on a succession of high-class craft calling at exclusive ports located far away from the coast of Cornwall. His badge of office was manifest in the creamy white of the yachting jersey he habitually wore.

George travelled up the line to embark on craft from the harbours of fabled cities of the likes of Southampton, Liverpool and London. He was reckoned as being very much a Man of the World, although the acquisition of that status seemed to have done little to improve his restrained ability to carry a sensible conversation. In Fore Street George comported himself as a true Brown, slight of body, hunched of shoulders, hands in pockets, a self-rolled fag pasted between the lips, and a phlegm-rattling emphysematic cough heaving away in his chest.

One of George's most significant attributes was artistic talent. He produced a number of fine paintings in what might have been described as a primitive style by anybody who knew a lot more about art than I did. It was no surprise that his preferred subjects were seascapes heaped with tossing waves and vessels heeling over at improbably wild angles. George's paintings constituted as close a brush with genius as any Brown boy ever achieved – other than Tom's droll and desert-dry wit, that is.

I never knew what Veth either did or had once done, if indeed Ellen had ever let him do anything at all once she got hold of him. On the other hand, Veth invariably clad his torso in a conventionally black seaman's Guernsey, which spoke in volumes of a history of seafaring.

Winnie quoted her age to me as being "one less than the year", which allowed me to calculate the year in which she was born. She was exceedingly thin and stringy. Her manner was bird-like. She peered through thick-lens spectacles at the immediate surrounds of the small part of the world with which she was only too familiar. Her glasses, considered in conjunction with the tightly drawn bun of her hair and a prominence of front teeth that could have made a male rabbit jump for joy, accented a face that barely stopped short of being hatchet-like.

Winnie's function was to care for the daily needs of Pa and Ma and the "boys" at home. If Winnie was a martyr to domestic drudgery she never complained about it. She seemed to have come to terms with drawing a short-straw lot in life.

Winnie had become so immured in her daily routine that she appeared to be unaware of the extent of the advantage taken of her by those whom she served. At the same time it was also true that they, whose individual routines had taken on the easy familiarity of the venerable clothes each clambered into every day, were equally lacking in any appreciation of the extent to which they were imposing upon Winnie.

Winnie was acknowledged as an expert in assembling jigsaw puzzles. The more complex the subject of the jigsaw, the greater the number of its constituent pieces, and the more varied the interplay of the overall tone and colour, the more capable Winnie was in rapidly putting them all together in the proper order.

She owned a large collection of jigsaw puzzles, which she kept stacked one on top of the other inside a cupboard in Pa's cottage. The puzzles were available for lending to other jigsaw aficionados. My mother regularly borrowed jigsaws from Winnie during the winter months and worked on them in the evenings.

I was adept at helping my mother to find the straight-edged pieces that formed the puzzle boundary, but my patience was as thin as Winnie's shoulders where the odd-shaped inside pieces were concerned. Dashing a shower of them from the table in frustration was a feature of my standard order of play.

We usually dissembled completed jigsaw puzzles into their individual pieces before returning them to Winnie, although sometimes a completed puzzle of particular aesthetic merit was left intact in case Winnie wanted to put it in a frame to hang on a wall.

Winnie was of course long on patience. Her hard-pressed life would not have been sustainable without the inner quality she seemed to possess for calmly taking each day as it came. Winnie's time slipped by in an unending sequence of making pasties and yeast buns, preparing cups of tea, slicing bread, stoking fires and tending to Pa, Ma and the "boys" Brown.

For all her practice at the stove, Winnie was a plain cook. Her pastry was devoid of the lightness of being, and her yeast buns were instant jawbreakers. It needed at least two days of sitting in a tin for most people's yeast buns to achieve such a status. Among the few relatively strong opinions that I ever heard Gran express, one was that she would neither eat nor touch anything that had its origin in Pa's kitchen at Winnie's hands.

That kitchen occupied a small slate-flagged area accessed at the bottom of a flight of steps leading from a downstairs sitting room in which the family lounged around the fireplace in overstuffed chairs glossed with a patina of aged grease. The fireplace grate paid tribute to the poor aim of those who spat and those who threw dead matches and fag ends at it. To support the charming scene, a worn deal table lurked on one side and waited on dinner time to liven it up.

Two or three semi-tame resident rats appeared out of the kitchen shadows from time to time to snatch an opportunistic nibble at the results of Winnie's culinary endeavours placed on the counter. Pa, when bedridden in the long days before he went up to St Endellion, spent his waking hours yelling at rats both real and imagined in the confines of his upstairs room. His declamations reached us across Canadian Terrace and raked the length of upper Fore Street.

Tom managed the Pawlyn brothers' fish cellars. His gift for the dispensation of sharp wit, wry humour and lightning repartee in the hallowed court of Pawlyn's, where he was king, honed up his proficiency for holding conversations of an entirely sensible kind on the rare occasions when the need arose.

We boys were enthralled by Tom's clasp knife, the edge of which was known to be of legendary keenness. Tom showed his knife to us when he was asked, and opening it up, he read out an inscription that he swore was etched on the main blade and which none of us disbelieved. "This knife," recited Tom, "of the best Sheffield steel, is guaranteed to make a figgy duff tremble, and a leg of mutton jump off the table!" We reckoned that a leg of mutton down in Pawlyn's cellars would not only have jumped from the table but would have fled away up Church Hill when Tom and his knife were around.

The antithesis of Tom's knife was the kind of knife we used at home in combination with a fork at dinner time. My mother described a blunt knife as "one that you could ride all the way to London on". I assumed that a very blunt knife would let me ride it even beyond London without any problems, maybe as far on as Scotland.

When the knife grinder made his regular visits to Port Isaac, all of the knives (bone-handled to a fault) in my mother's meagre holdings of household cutlery were checked for lack of keenness

219

of edge, and an appropriate selection of the implements was handed over to the knife grinder for sharpening.

According to my mother, pretty much any pointed object borne in my hands, inclusive of a blunt knife, was something that would easily "put my eye out". In order for the warning to have substance, it must have happened at least once that someone, somewhere, had put out one of his eyes through careless manipulation of an otherwise innocent pointed item, but whoever he was, he didn't to my knowledge live in Port Isaac.

Another opportunity to meet a distressing fate was regularly advised to me when I placed a foreign object in my mouth while I was in motion. The admonition in that instance was that, "that will go through the roof of your mouth!" It gave me a pitiful vision of running down Fore Street with the roof of my mouth firmly penetrated by a stick (or a blunt knife) and a put out eye lying behind me outside the entry to the Liberal Club. There were so many hazards of that kind afoot that it seemed best not to bother about them.

On occasions when the boys' behaviour and manual coordination were both more irrational than usual, people like Tom were wont to characterise us as being "as mazed as a brush", to compare us to "a cow handling a musket" or to declare that we "didn't know if it was Christmas or Easter".

I particularly appreciated having myself likened to "a fart in a colander". That was an expression governing circumstances when a decision as to what I should do when confronted with a surfeit of uninteresting options became impossible to make. "You don't know which hole to go out through first!" Tom said.

All of which may (or may not), to borrow from the Pawlyn's cellars' immortal vernacular, have been as "far fetched as a bucket of shit from China". Having collected numerous sacks of shit for Granfer up on top of Lobber Field I could easily envisage what a bucket of shit looked like. What puzzled me was why anyone would want to bring a bucket of it all the way from China.

Even Tom couldn't give me an answer to that particular question; sometimes it wasn't possible to count on anything.

One of the mysteries that Tom did solve for us involved the rationale behind the packing of lobsters under a layer of sawdust in wooden boxes at Pawlyn's. Tom told us that during transportation out of Port Isaac the crustaceans ate the sawdust and shit planks. At their destination the shit-out planks were collected and sawn up and used to make new boxes. The ensuing sawdust formed the packing for the subsequent despatch of lobsters. All that was lacking in order to render the process self-perpetuating was to get the lobsters to shit nails as well, and Tom said he was working on it.

The skilled articulation of such profound matters by Tom was not an art that was practised by Winnie and the brothers, whose combined attention spans would have had trouble in bridging the Lake.

It was therefore a matter for amazement how Nibs and Tinker, not to mention a host of other local residents of their ilk for whom the two times table was what they and their next door neighbours ate their dinner on, were instantly on their toes if they were short-changed in a financial transaction.

By a similarly astounding token they could accurately maintain the progression of a darts score (inclusive of accounting for doubles and trebles) even as the arrows thudded into and around the worn board in the public bar at the Golden Lion. In their hands scores were calculated and chalked up well before the third dart thrown had ceased quivering where it struck.

———

Tinker, a consumptively thin-bodied grouser, took a daily delight in stepping out into Fore Street, lighting up a fag and conducting an exercise in rank pessimism by moaning at and about whatever and whoever he saw to anyone whose attention he could latch on to. Since Tinker on the rant was often facing numbers Six and Seven Canadian Terrace, Granfer needed to take great pains not to defile Fore Street with as much as a single leaf fallen from a tended garden bush, as Tinker would pounce on the offence like a gasping tiger.

Tinker appeared to me to have no good word to say for anyone or anything. Little that met his eyes was viewed in a positive light. He knew a thousand and one ways not to be constructive. His thoughts could be as dark as his guernsey and trousers were when new – whenever that was.

I always imagined that Tinker could have been inserted seamlessly into the *Al Read Show* on the wireless in the event that Al had wanted a rural substitute for his "'Ow d'ye do?" Johnny-know-all ("You've met 'em!") character.

One day, to the surprise of many, Tinker got married to a strapping wife of ample proportions. It was only a shame that by then Pa and Ma weren't around any more to be amazed as well. From the way the new Mrs Brown spoke, with little trace of the accent common to the rest of us, she was an educated lady who had lowered her sights in an unguarded moment.

Tinker and Mrs Tinker were probably linked by the kind of attraction that characterised opposite poles. Mrs Tinker was a Peggy Mount type, which similarity was made flesh in her volume of voice. She and Tinker took up residence in the cottage sitting in between those of Tom and of Winnie and the boys.

We called Mrs Tinker (not to her face of course) the "Sergeant Major". Her parade ground was Fore Street. Her military title was reduced to "Sarge" when, having got to know and appreciate her, we perceived a kindly light lying beneath her bushel of superficial severity.

Sarge's orders kept Tinker, Winnie, Nibs and George well on their mettle. Veth and Bill Pink were not involved, however, as Ellen and Aunt Sue not only knew their own minds but also knew the respective minds of Veth and Bill Pink as well.

Sarge was an active member of the St Peter's church congregation, in which capacity I got to know her. She saw something golden in Tinker, but heaven, where Sarge was destined to end up, only knew what it was that she saw, as whatever it was, it was buried too deep down for anyone other than Sarge to ferret out in this world.

I often wondered if the brothers (and sister) Brown were shaped into being what they were by virtue of their birth in Port Isaac, or if the Port Isaac of their (and my) day was what it was because it was lucky enough to have them as essential ingredients contributing to the recipe for its essence. The answer, I suspected, lay somewhere in the middle – the Browns were of Port Isaac, and Port Isaac was of them, a blessing for all concerned.

Tom, that inveterate reader of western novels who conducted his life in accordance with the code of the range, told me how much he had enjoyed a yarn written by Luke Short (*Dead Freight for Piute* – the title said it all) that I once passed on to him. "Whatever page you choose to look at," he said, "you're either on your hoss, or your gun is in your hand, or you're involved in a fight!" It wasn't, he said, like some other books he had read in which the author took pages and pages just to describe what the characters were eating. "Where is the action in that?" Tom asked.

I could imagine the Browns on John Ford's "Stagecoach", heading west into a glorious sunset, their destination that ever-happy valley over the hills and far away. Tom, the tall man in the saddle, would be the marshal at the reins in the box up in front, with Bill riding shotgun at his side. Seated within the stage would be Veth the timid whisky drummer; Nibs the garrulously burned out doctor whose full powers of invention were directed at bumming bottled stock from Veth's valise; Tinker the dour and overly-suspicious riverboat gambler; and Winnie the misunderstood and unappreciated saloon-keeping lady with a heart of gold.

As for George, he would be out there somewhere in the distance, down the track, holding onto his gear and waiting for a lift that he would be sure to get.

*The Lake flush gate in Middle Street*

# 12

# *Rats' Tales*

*"Take thy beak from out my heart, and take thy form from off my door!"*
*Quoth the Raven, "Nevermore."*

Edgar Allan Poe (1809–1849)
"The Raven"

IT WASN'T HARD for anyone to locate a rat in Port Isaac, even if they didn't want to. Rats hung around in places (kitchens included) where they knew they could surreptitiously grab a bite to eat, in which respect they had a lot in common with us boys. When one rat moved in, more followed, as if the first had paved the way like John the Baptist.

I regularly saw a rat or two scavenging from domestic discards that were stuck, pending the activation of the flush by old Ned Cowlyn, in the channel of the Lake alongside Middle Street. Filled with the spirit of clearing up fallen or otherwise abandoned fragments of fish, rats made a darting presence as much in the recesses of Pawlyn's cellars as around the rubbish bins of fish-joudering establishments. When all was safely gathered in ere the winter storms began, rats scurried to and fro in ricks of corn shocks in an endless quest for sustaining grains of oats and barley.

On one morning when I was standing in Gran's weakly illumin-ated kitchen at Number Seven Canadian Terrace, I looked through the window at the washhouse roof on the far side of the alley behind, and exclaimed delightedly to Gran that there was a kitten walking on the roofing slates.

I quickly changed my mind when I realized that the perceived kitten was in fact not a small feline but a large rodent, a rat in fact. My sudden reappraisal was accompanied by a shocked sensation that I had fallen into icy water and was drowning in its biting clutches. I felt as if the top of my head was being peeled back by a rusty tin opener, and a stiff and sharply pointed wire was being drawn across the top of whatever lay beneath (it wasn't a brain as I had been told many times that I didn't have one of those) in the manner of a thin needle scratching across the surface of a bent India rubber, almost, but not quite, inducing the rubber to split asunder.

The feeling went away after a moment, although it returned from time to time in the course of a few subsequent years, always triggered by visual proximity to a rat. The horror of seeing the big rat on Gran's washhouse roof never left me. George Orwell's Winston Smith in Room 101 had no greater phobia for such rodents than I did.

Pigsties were localities much favoured by the rats of St Endellion parish. The tendency for them to gather in large numbers in pigsties was greatly assisted by owners of pigs who were not only careless in their placement of swill, but were also an awful lot less than industrious in mucking out pig shit invested straw.

In his field adjoining the back garden of Number Nine Hartland Road, Mr Tom Saundry kept quite a lot of chickens and several pigs. The chickens ran free, whereas the pigs were incarcerated inside a large sty. A multitude of rats were camp followers to Tom's pigs. A professional rat catcher was a not infrequent visitor to the sty, about which it could be said that the person who coined the phrase "It looks like a pigsty!" may well have had Tom's version in mind. It was fortunate (for me at least) that Tom's rats didn't favour spilling over too much in the direction of Hartland Road.

Tom's attention to cleaning out the living accommodation of his pigs was characterised by its relative absence. The pigs' quarters were mucked out only when the pigs' backs were beginning to wear transverse grooves in the sty's corrugated sheet metal roof. The odour that arose when the by then monumental accumulation of rotten straw, ripe pig shit, dead rats, remains of farrows that didn't get out of the way of a rolling sow in time, and festering swill was finally removed by Tom so as to permit his pigs to move relatively freely again on temporarily clean straw, was solid enough to have been cut into blocks and shipped in buckets to a far-fetched China without any threat of deterioration on the way. The noisome air could well have manured virtually every garden in Hartland Road free of charge.

The rat catcher was a vital associate of the shit-shovelling exercise and always lived up to his professional title with ease. He took many more, and markedly bigger, rats than those legendary creatures that lived in the quartermaster's store. When it was all over, Tom was out of pocket, the pigs were happier, the rat catcher was delighted, and the residents of Hartland Road gained relief as the smell of pig shit diminished, or when they got used to the smell, whichever came sooner.

If Tom's particular rats were the rodent equivalent of the Biblical five thousand and were fed in accordance with the said miracle, the rats residing in a pigsty owned by Captain (retd) Roy May, located in what we referred to as "May's quarry" at the top of Roscarrock Hill, could have been called Legion, for they were many.

Roy was a sworn adversary of all of us boys. He knew it and we knew it. He lived in a gaunt mansion-like house that stood on the dank left-hand side of Roscarrock Hill, just downhill from the hollow of May's quarry. Generally shunned by the sun, Roy's house threw an implacable gaze over the harbour and stared threateningly across at the primary school.

His house was one of the biggest of its kind in Port Isaac. Although it was big enough to be imagined as either a hotel of substance or a guesthouse of note, its stark and unforgiving appearance made it plain that there was nothing conducive to a welcome within.

Robert Louis Stephenson could have used Roy's house as a model for the "House of Shaws". In nightmares I visualised it as a place of blank windows and locked doors behind which unimagined horrors might lie, threaded by dark and perilous staircases that Roy pursued me up and down.

Those who knew, or at least reckoned they knew, said that Roy occupied only one room of the house at a time. When sufficient dirt, debris and rot had accumulated in the current room of choice to become intolerable even for Roy, or when the floor of the room simply gave up the ghost, Roy (they said) simply closed and locked the door, threw away the key and moved on to reside in another room.

Roy, on the strength of the amount of time that he appeared to spend in her company, was rumoured to be a suitor of a certain Mrs Wiffin, who lived in the south wing of the great house called Khandalla adjacent to May's quarry in under the sloping curve of Lobber field.

At one side of her large front garden Mrs Wiffin nurtured a small brake of bamboos. Left to her own devices, Mrs Wiffin would probably have posed no appreciable threat to any boy anxious to take possession of one or two of her bamboo canes. However, through her association with Roy, Mrs Wiffin was imbued with a formidable intolerance of trespassers, which tilted the balance against us.

She was a burly lady. Her hair was dark with grey highlights. She strode manfully around her property dressed in stiff tweeds, baggy cardigans and heavy shoes. She spoke with a brittle, cut glass accent. It was obvious that Mrs Wiffin was (or had been) a lady of means and elevated class. Mr Wiffin, for reasons unknown to me, was absent from the picture. Hence the field of conquest was open to Roy. It was not difficult to appreciate why the eternally seedy Roy had set his cap of decaying gentry in pursuit of Mrs Wiffin, but Mrs Wiffin's interest in the likes of Roy defied rational explanation.

In fairness, Roy cut a dapper figure when seen from a distance. He moved with a military-honed strut and swagger. In close proximity, however, an odour redolent of the Great Unwashed (disagreeable even to those of us with native claims to membership of the same company) reached out from Roy with such substance that we felt we could actually see its tendrils drifting in the air. In a society in which washing of the person was undertaken as a once weekly event at best, Roy stood head and shoulders (and the kind of dirt-creased neck in which it was claimed that "tetties could be grown") above us in his disdain for the application of soap and water to the more exposed parts of his person.

Suffice it to say that we liked to give Roy a wide berth. He knew how desirable Mrs Wiffin's bamboos were to us, especially during the pea-shooting season, and he was ever vigilant to prevent the theft from the brake of as much as a single cane.

Mrs Wiffin's bamboo canes were beautifully flexible. They were multifunctional items. Peashooters aside, they also made excellent arrows for shooting from a bow made from a hazel stick and a length of string, swords for the fencing which was always in vogue during the week following a Friday night showing of a Douglas Fairbanks Jr film up at the Rivoli cinema, or simple whippy sticks for cleanly slicing heads from valerian, nettles, bracken or any other innocent wayside growth.

Mrs Wiffin's bamboo brake, protected by a rusting iron fence, grew immediately alongside the shortcut footpath to Port Quin, just up above the entry path to May's quarry. The fence was so

229

swamped by tall weeds and bamboo fronds that the authorities must have missed it when they commandeered iron scrap metal during the war. They didn't miss taking the school railings and most of our saucepans, however.

With a little bit of contortion it was possible for us to lie down on the shortcut footpath, wiggle a knife-wielding arm through Mrs Wiffin's iron fence and cut a bamboo loose at ground level. The task was achievable but didn't meet with success very often. Roy could smell the act of bamboo theft in progress, which was no mean feat given the impedance of his body odour. He was out on the warpath immediately, armed with a stout stick or some alternative implement that he wouldn't hesitate to use to belabour anyone of us that he caught up with.

In between the front gate to Mrs Wiffin's wing of Khandallah and the top of Roscarrock Hill stood a grove of ancient poplar trees, thick and bent inland in accordance with the wind-ridden location. The closest poplar tree to Roy's gloomy mansion leaned at a very shallow angle, pointing across the shortcut footpath at May's quarry. In front of the grove the concave sweep of the Lobber allotments dipped away in all its glory.

The poplars were ideal trees for climbing in. They were rife with boughs and hollows and were cool and leafy in the summer. Their gnarled backs were all the more agreeable to climb along. In our minds they were ships or canoes on one day, horses on another, or space rockets on a third, especially when a "Flash Gordon" serial was current at the Rivoli. We scaled from tree to tree, swinging on branches in the definitive manner of Johnny Weissmuller as Tarzan, or if an alternative was called for, in the style of Cheetah.

Roy provided the element of the unexpected that turned our games in the poplar trees into adventures. The assumed accumulation of wax in Roy's ears over the years had done little to impair his quality of hearing. At the first unnatural rustle of a poplar leaf, Roy reacted. He and Mrs Wiffin hunted us like lions, he prowling from his side, she from hers, aiming to trap us in a flanking movement of the kind that Roy might have remembered from his military days.

When we climbed the poplar trees we kept a lookout for Roy but weren't always successful in spotting his stealthy arrival. However, the advantage we held up in the poplars was that we could move hither and thither along branches. Roy and Mrs Wiffin couldn't simultaneously cover every point of descent. Once we were in the tree at the bottom end of the grove it was easy to jump to one side or another to evade their clutches.

The options for the direction of escape comprised: ascending the shortcut footpath; running into and up the side of May's quarry; heading down Roscarrock Hill into Port Isaac; and darting up to Lobber field along the coastal footpath at the head of the allotments. A history of cadging drinks and fags in the saloon bar of the Golden Lion had left Roy with an impaired ability to take up hot pursuit. Both he and Mrs Wiffin had ceased to be nimble long before Roy bought his most recent bar of soap.

Tibby Thomas told me that he was once up in one of the poplar trees when Roy showed up with a shotgun apparently loaded for action. Roy had previously brandished a billhook at me from the foot of the poplar tree that I was in at the time, and so I didn't doubt that Tibby's allegation was true. The shotgun ploy may have been designed more for effect than for intended discharge, but where Roy was concerned one never knew.

Once when escaping from Roy I went up into the quarry, knowing that I could scramble around on the right flank and seek refuge in the depths of tangled thickets of low blackthorn that spread in such profusion across the hill slope behind. My route took me between Roy's pigsty and the quarry wall. The pigsty showed every sign of having been cleaned out with all the regularity and enthusiasm that Roy was known to put into his schedule of personal hygiene. The floor of the sty seemed to be rippling. It gave me such an eerie sensation that I stopped to

231

shake my head and blink. My eyes focused, and I saw that I was looking at an army of rats, seething around the pigs' trough. I didn't stay to enumerate the vast array. Real fear, of Roy and rats in concert, placed wings on my heels.

———

One of the legendary penchants for which Mr Norman Short (known to his friends and admirers as "Ningy") was recognised, was close-quarter familiarisation with rats. At a pinch, Ningy was ready to settle for mice as well. His family abode was a cottage standing on a sharp corner at the bottom of Back Alley near the Wesley chapel and the top of Middle Street.

Ningy was a tall, loose-bodied, sharply angular man, all skin and bones. As he walked, the upper part of his body appeared to shift about in peculiar directions beneath the oversized brown jacket that he normally wore. He was totally toothless. If Ningy owned a set of false teeth, he never inserted them in the face that he showed to the public. It was a face that incorporated the characteristics of a failed sponge cake, collapsing inwards at the core.

Pawlyn's and the Town Platt were able to count on Ningy as one of their most ardent and inveterate *habitués*. In the cosy circles of fishermen's chat Ningy could always be relied on to add a touch of humour to the proceedings in a style favouring the foolishly facetious manner of a court jester. Wit was not his forte. Ningy didn't know a great deal about being clever, but like Ted Ray he did know how to raise a laugh.

If words failed him, and they often did, Ningy invoked his talent to gurn. He was a master gurner who could effortlessly contort his rubbery face into a state of abandon that would have been impossible for me to imagine if I hadn't seen it with my own eyes. Ningy could suck his cheeks halfway down his throat and bury his nose in its entirety between ferociously pouting lips and a set of eyebrows heading for an appointment with his chin.

In the autumn of the year Ningy often assisted the crew of a steam-driven threshing machine which moved between various farms of the parish charged with the task of separating grain from the corn shock harvest that was ricked under tarpaulin covers for drying. The itinerant threshing machine was popularly known as the "thrasher" – it was a complex of spinning flywheels, huge meshing cogs and a consummately dangerous cat's cradle of flapping and snapping drive belts. Fatal accidents, like the one that occurred to poor young Fred Hawkey, were occasional events. Injuries of lesser or greater degrees or seriousness were commonplace.

Both rats and mice took up residence in the ricks, eagerly homing in even as the ricks were under construction. Enormous numbers of rodents built up within ricks of long standing. The rustle and scurry of their movement, and the shrill squeaking of their communication made a well-populated rick seem to be alive and ready to consume anyone who got too close. During the thrashing process the resident rats and mice were, to say the least, rudely disturbed in the comfort of their ricked-up habitats. They leapt from the straw in profusion as a rick was dismantled, flitting all over the place like drops of spilled quicksilver.

Ningy was an acknowledged expert in the art of grabbing fleeing rats with his bare hands and despatching them by biting off their heads through the power of his gums alone. The blood of the so-decapitated creatures dribbled through the bristles of Ningy's gurning chin.

I didn't know what Ningy did with any of the rodent heads inside his mouth. Perhaps it was as well that no one told me about it. I did, however, hear that with a bit of encouragement Ningy was prepared to swallow a live mouse in a single gulp and rub his stomach contentedly afterwards. Subject to verification, I had no reason to doubt my informant. On the other hand, as Andy Oaten observed when he drew conviction from the jaws of uncertainty, "Well missus, ef t'wudden true, 'twus false".

Miss Maud Lark, popularly known as "Maudie", lived in a stone-built cottage up at the top end of Tintagel Terrace near Hartland Road's inner dogleg corner. It was two storeys high. Its woodwork always gave an impression of having been freshly painted, cream and green being the hues of choice. The front windows of the cottage commanded a grand view of the stretch of the Bay between Port Gaverne and Tintagel Head.

As the crow flew, Mr Tom Saundry's rat-ridden pigsty was located not much more than a hundred yards from Maudie's back door. She could only have failed to appreciate the existence of Tom's pigsty if she had had no sense of smell. As to Tom's rats and whether or not Maudie was aware of them, that didn't matter, as Maudie had her own rat obsession to occupy her mind.

Maudie's back door was set in the front of a half-glassed porch. To get to it from Tintagel Terrace it was necessary to open a little gate set in a low cement-block wall, descend a short flight of steps to a sunken geranium-bright flower garden and cross the garden over a pathway of crazy slate flags.

Maudie was of an uncertain age. She was not yet ancient but must have moved quite a bit beyond the borderline of middle age. Severely cut hair, false teeth and glasses did little to dispel the notion of Maudie as a long-term spinster intent on achieving old maid status in the not too distant future. She was diminutive and bustling, an aproned presence dedicated to the maintenance of all things pristine.

Her garden was a delight, bursting with blooms and clearly tended with devotion. In our eyes Maudie was inextricably linked with her garden in a bond forged for us by Alfred, Lord Tennyson, whose poem "Maud" contained a request that a heroine of the same name should "come into the garden". Tennyson didn't know when he wrote "Maud" that his efforts would gain recognition at Port Isaac County Primary school and go on to disadvantage not only Maudie but also anyone else in the parish who had the misfortune to be christened Maud by insensitive parents.

When we passed Maudie's cottage and Maudie was not in evidence in her garden, some of us were motivated to call out, "Come into the garden Maud!" Should Maudie be in her garden, and therefore unavailable to be thereby called upon to make an entrance, all was not lost as our fallback position was to let her know first of all that the black bat, Night, had flown, and (depending on the circumstances) that "I (or we) am (or are) here at the gate alone". Following such pleasantries, Maudie, forever a good old soul, was ready to talk of other things.

My mother, who was very friendly with Maudie, told me one day that Maudie believed that her house had been invaded by rats. What exactly it was that triggered Maudie's concern wasn't clear. Possibly it was related to the light sound of rasping or scratching at her back door during the black bat of night. I knew of boys who weren't averse to doing such things as a variation on a theme of knock down dolly. Under certain circumstances I might well have counted myself among them, but I didn't approve of such visitations at Maudie's door.

Maudie might easily have spotted a rat wandering either in her garden or up on Tintagel Terrace and have gone on to imagine that it was an advance scout for an approaching horde. I knew that at the best of times and in the best of places in Port Isaac rats might well be out of sight but would still be looking at me with some kind of plan in mind. Lots of rats didn't even bother to conceal themselves. If there was an advantage to be taken, a rat could be relied on to take it.

Maudie's worry about sharing her cottage with a company of rats eventually grew into an obsession. When I stood at Maudie's gate subsequently, alone or not, the subject of her conversation with me took the form of an anti-rat diatribe. It wasn't that she actually saw any rats as much as that she claimed to be hearing them regularly. When she couldn't hear rats she listened out for them because she knew that they were just biding their time prior to piping up again.

A range of experts was called upon in an attempt to provide the final solution to the alleged rat infestation of Maudie's cottage. Builders ripped up floorboards and hacked holes in her walls. Nothing untoward was found. The rat catcher put in an appearance, drawing a complete blank for once in his lethal career. A representative of the council showed up and, to the surprise of no one, provided Maudie with nothing of either comfort or consequence.

Maudie was dissatisfied. She was certain that there were rats in her house and if they couldn't be found she was adamant that it was only because they were hiding away from those who sought them. In the light of my enduring phobia for rats and any aspect of their society, Maudie had my sincerest sympathies.

One day as I was passing Maudie's garden gate she trotted over to the foot of the steps and, in a reversal of roles, invited me to come into her garden. I obeyed her command, albeit with reluctance. She led me to her cottage, filling me with a similar level of joy to that which would have attended an order to throw myself over the edge of Moon's Grave. Maudie explained that there was something in her sitting room that she wanted to show me.

It was inevitable that a rat would be playing a leading role in the occasion, and the anticipation of it was enough to turn my boots to dull lead and my heart to Lake water. However, I owed Maudie some consideration, having shown her little enough by quoting Tennyson's immortal lines at her, and so I went along, ready to flee in an instant, deep-sea diver boots notwithstanding.

Much to my dismay, Maudie closed the back door behind us. She took me into a small sitting room. Attempts by God's good daylight to penetrate the room were successfully countered by a pair of thick, velvet-like curtains that were almost, but not quite, drawn shut. The room smelt mustier than the interior of St Endellion church. A round table covered with a coarse greenish cloth occupied the centre ground, looking like a perfect setting for a séance. We stood alongside the table.

"Listen!" squawked Maudie, in a tone implying that any refusal by me to obey would not be tolerated. I listened, and heard nothing but the hiss of silence. The passage of time seemed to have been suspended.

Suddenly, interrupting a pressing desire to be elsewhere that was threatening to overwhelm me, Maudie grabbed hold of my left arm with one rapacious hand. "There!" she whispered through tightly clenched false teeth, gesturing dramatically at the ceiling with the index finger of the other hand.

Whether or not my hair stood on end was a sensation obscured by my jumping at least a foot into the air at the instant when Maudie seized me. My feet came back to the floor on legs paralysed with terror. Maudie's fingers sank like a set of barbed conger hooks into the flesh of my arm and held on so invasively that if I had tried to pull away I was sure that part of my arm would have been left behind in her clutch.

Maudie's eyes were as big and as bulging as gulls' eggs. The twilight of wild and uncharted country fogged their depths. Her mouth was open. Her finger pointed upwards as if it was cast in iron. For an interval I trembled on the edge of thinking that I was dying of fright, absolutely convinced that I was trapped in the presence of someone who (since it took one to know one) ought to have been in Bodmin.

The long run of ground sea–like anguish flowed back down the beach of fear, leaving both Maudie and me high and dry again. Her grip relaxed. She let go of my arm. Although I couldn't remember leaving her I was well aware afterwards that I was never going to come into the garden with Maudie again. Five blue bruises made by her four fingers (plus one thumb) on my arm took two weeks to turn yellow.

It would have been better if Maudie's inability to declare a truce with her elusive rat companions at home had faded as well, but I don't believe that it ever did.

*Granny Spry's chip shop ope on the right*

# 13

# *Black Doors*

*I will arise and go now, for always night and day*
*I hear lake water lapping with low sounds by the shore;*

William Butler Yeats (1865–1939)
"The Lake Isle of Innisfree"

THE SLIPWAY HOUSE hotel stood in all its tall, grey hulking austerity at the rear of a fairly large yard that was clad underfoot with big slate flags individually outlined by interstitial weeds. The front wall of the yard was fitted to the curve around which the last of Fore Street merged into the foot of Church Hill. Pawlyn's cellars were directly across the way from the wall. Weather permitting, Slipway House hotel guests were able to take their morning coffee or their afternoon tea (although not both at the same time) *al fresco* in the yard.

The towering right-hand flank of the Slipway House hotel made a virtual canyon of the bottom of Church Hill, through which the road glided as if it were competing with the Lake for precedence. The Lake gurgled in a dark and deep channel to the immediate left of the hotel and proceeded onwards through a tunnel beneath Fore Street to make a last hurrah before gaining freedom in the harbour.

The name of the hotel was derived from consideration of the lifeboat slipway that angled down to the harbour in between the outer wall of the far from fragrant Pawlyn's and the Lake on one side and the Town Platt on the other, where tight knots of

239

venerable fishermen hung around waiting for something that not one of them ever expected to happen.

The Lake's tunnel under Fore Street was required to cope with surges of water as substantial as they were sudden, some of which originated from cloudbursts over the Port Isaac valley, and others of which were let go as a result of Mr Ned Cowlyn's skilled attention to the flush gate in the Lake alongside Middle Street.

A few of us were not averse to crawling up through the tunnel once the flush had run and cleaned it out. I went up the tunnel on a number of occasions and splashed onwards in the Lake's channel to reach the nearest point of egress beside the cottage named "Cor Anglais" where Mr and Mrs Jimmy Baker lived. It was only when Tibby Thomas reported on an encounter he claimed he had had with rats inside the tunnel that I placed a permanent moratorium on my Lake tunnel forays.

Bounded by lower Middle Street and the Lake's channel adjacent to the Slipway House hotel yard, a barn-like building of substantial size was utilised as a garage facility for the benefit of any Slipway House hotel guests who possessed motorcars.

Prior to becoming a garage, the building was used to house the Port Isaac lifeboat, in which context it was a rather more practically located successor to the Old Lifeboat House up at Little Hill. It had been the final home for the Port Isaac lifeboat before the latter was decommissioned and sent to a new domicile at Padstow. The front face of the Slipway House garage, poised on the edge of lower Fore Street, would have presented the lifeboat with an ultra-short and absolutely clear run at the slipway.

A huge wooden portal, which lifted upwards and pivoted inwards when it was opened, covered the building's face from the roof gutters down to ground level. For the convenience of the visiting public, a conventionally sized hinged door was set in the centre of the base of the portal. The portal was painted black – it might even have been tarred. As a consequence both the building and the portal had come to be known as "Black Doors" by the boys. The Black Doors portal was a recognised rallying point for us. We tended to assemble at the Middle Street side of Black Doors, so as to be as far away as possible from where the Slipway House yard wall made a pointed corner against the Lake. It was alleged that the ashes of a certain Mr Piggins (a former Slipway House hotel proprietor and father of Christopher the erstwhile C of E curate) had been scattered on a rather ropey-looking little flower bed in that corner. None of us wanted to run the risk of making an inadvertent contact with a speck of the late Mr Piggins.

The Black Doors portal was the starting location for an enduring game that we called "Chasers". Commencing at that focal point, a game of Chasers spread out to involve every thread of the familiar network of streets, alleys, passages, opes, beaches, gardens, quarries and gugs of Port Isaac, Port Gaverne and, at a pinch, perhaps even Trewetha, St Endellion and points in between.

The name "Chasers" was definitive. At the outset, a boy whose key attribute was fleetness of foot was picked out to be the "chaser". He then took up position at the Middle Street corner of the Black Doors portal, facing into the corner in the (perhaps not inappropriate) manner of a dunce. From this set piece, he was required to count up to one hundred, or possibly, in order to give slower participants an extended lead-time, beyond one hundred.

Irrespective of the ability to run fast, the need to count up to as many as that disqualified more than a few of us from consideration for the chaser role. It took some of us (shades of Jack Dempsey versus Gene Tunney) far too much time to count as high as a hundred even if we knew how to do it. All was not lost, however, since as a fallback position the rules allowed the chaser in the corner of the Black Doors portal to count ten times up to ten, using fingers for the units and toes to mark off the lapsed number of tens.

The other Chasers participants made a pack for the chaser to pursue. Sometimes there were as many as twenty or thirty of us in the pack. As the chaser's century count commenced, the pack departed from the vicinity of Black Doors with great despatch. All of us didn't necessarily run in the same direction. On completion of the count, the chaser set out after the pack to try and catch up with them so as to "tig" (or touch) them one by one.

In one sense Chasers had a lot in common with the school playground game that was named "Tig". Tig involved dodging about to avoid being "tigged" within a restricted field by whoever was "it" at the time. Chasers, with no such constraint placed on the field of play, was more wide-ranging and adventurous in concept than tig could be.

Once the chaser tigged a member of the pack, that member had to join the chaser and become a pursuer – poacher to gamekeeper in an instant. A game of Chasers could last for hours, finishing only when the last of the running pack was tigged. Some of us dropped away when we ran out of steam or came upon more interesting things to do. There were never any outright winners in Chasers, but equally there were no losers.

Chasers was vested in us running around as haphazardly as we liked, and getting away with whatever we could get away with. No form of escape from the chaser and his ever-burgeoning team of tigged allies across private property was considered (by the pack) to be off limits, whether it led us through flowering gardens, over walls, up and down drainpipes and telegraph poles, under motorcars and lorries, in at someone's back door and out through their front door and vice versa, or through the Lake's tunnel where only a rat or two kept watch.

One of the pack's favoured detours was to leap onto a low wall on the left side of Church Hill just uphill from the telephone box and directly across from Mr Harry Morman's cobbler's shop. We dropped from the wall to the roof of a shed in the garden of Leat House where the butcher lived. From the shed roof we jumped and scrambled down into the butcher's garden and fled across it to hurdle the entry gate and dash across the Lake on the small bridge upstream from the flush gate. Our main concern was to avoid being tigged (in more ways than one) by the butcher. Getting the flow of a score or more of boys safely through the butcher's garden was no mean feat.

We were additionally addicted to being chased up a ramp that was more accustomed to guiding the genuinely self-righteous towards the Roscarrock chapel entry door in lower Roscarrock Hill. From the top of the ramp we made a rapid exit by sliding down an adjacent (and detrimentally splintery) telegraph pole.

One evening, believing ourselves to be under pursuit by a big chaser team, three of us stretched a cord at ankle level across the Dolphin Street end of the narrow Temple Bar opening in order to impede the team's passage. Unfortunately for us, old Granfer Glover chose to come up through Temple Bar from the Fore Street side in advance of the arrival of the chasers. Granfer Glover looked like a biblical patriarch, complete with fiery eyes, an irascible disposition, and a grey and flowing beard that could have bowled Dr W. G. Grace's version of the same for a duck at any time of the day or night.

The unexpected encounter of Granfer Glover's feet with our Temple Bar trip line resulted in him measuring his prophetic length on the hard ground in an instant, although it was for the blink of an eye only, as he rose on the rebound and laid into the three of us with his walking stick almost before our jaws finished dropping open. With Granfer Glover in Clokie-styled flailing pursuit we ran all the way down Dolphin Street to Middle Street, at which point he gave up, no doubt prepared to bide his time and get us again, sooner rather than later.

Granfer Glover's instantaneous reaction offered us a clear demonstration – not that we needed it – that many of our elders failed to share our enthusiasm for Chasers. As we hared on our chosen way, censoriously shouted comments from various of the said elders informed us of what we already knew only too well, "You little buggers! I didn't fight a war so that you could behave like this!"

<hr />

As far as the hundred count for chasers was concerned, a fair few of us were able to count up to at least ten without causing ourselves too much bother. We learned it down at the primary school. Counting to ten was why we were all equipped with four fingers and one thumb on each of our hands. That made eight fingers and two thumbs in total, exactly the number that I had, other than when I was informed on good authority that I was "all thumbs".

Extending the counting ability from ten to twenty required a little more ingenuity than simply looking at my hands. I needed to take off my boots and socks to expose ten toes that had possibly, but not probably, been recently washed. Well defined tidemarks around my ankles didn't often enter into a count, but when they were available, which was on every day other than bath day, they could at a pinch raise the countable quota to twenty-two. And my wrist and neck tidemarks were still held in reserve to bring the count up to twenty-five.

For all that, numerical precision was not normally something that we worried too much about. Estimates were more the order of the day. Anything that was near enough was good enough for the likes of us. We weren't just experts in the science of rounding numbers off, we rounded off as intuitively as if we had been to the manner born.

It was much less easy for us to estimate the lower numbers than it was for us to judge those that were seemingly without limit. If there were lots involved there were lots involved and that was that. It was when there weren't lots involved that the situation called for more careful assessment.

A problem that I always had was that the fewer there were in any gathering that I was asked about by my mother, the greater were her demands for the accompaniment of specific details. Estimating had to rely on accuracy as well as intuition. This principle was stretched to its ultimate limit in reports in the sober pages of the *Cornish Guardian* newspaper dealing with social get-togethers, outings, births, christenings, weddings, deaths, funerals and what have you. The reporter's wellbeing would be placed in some jeopardy through the displeasure of anyone whose presence at an event was inadvertently (or not as the case might be) overlooked. It was all grist to the mill, food for the imagination.

Port Isaac convention eschewed directness to the extent that the very word "directly" (pronounced "dreckly") defined a circuitous route unlikely to be completed very soon, if ever. In that capacity, dreckly needed to be distinguished from the slightly more urgent "just now", which implied that whatever was going to happen, it wouldn't happen before tomorrow (or next week) at the earliest.

An estimate of zero was simple enough to make. It was expressed as "nought" (or "nart" as the pronunciation went), although the good old village standard of "bugger all" offered a much more satisfactory means of expressing the concept of nothing.

After bugger all came the count of one, which we estimated in terms of "hardly any". An estimate of two was "not many", for three it was "one or two", and by the same token four was something like "two or three".

"Pretty few" was a means not only of appraising five but also of introducing the supremely important word "few". On the strength of such progress six could be communicated as "a fair few", seven as "a brave few", and eight as "more than a few".

"Some" implied that a figure of around nine was involved; ten was "a handful" and eleven "several". "Some" and "several" were words as critical to the articulation of our ideas as was "few". Without the "some" who hid behind their cloaks of anonymity there would have been bugger all opportunity to convey gossip to the "several".

245

Twelve was "a dozen", an easy one to recall. Thirteen as "a baker's dozen" was a little less easy to appreciate, however; I wasn't sure that Mr Sherratt ever handed thirteen of anything over to any individual among some or several who paid him for only a dozen of the same. Fourteen as "a dozen or more" was straightforward enough to understand of course.

By the time a number as big as fifteen was reached there were "lots" to reckon with. Sixteen, seventeen and eighteen were even more that that and respectively referred to as "piles", "heaps" and "loads". Nineteen reckoned to be "heaps and heaps". Twenty couldn't be anything other than "a score".

Any count ranging from twenty-one to twenty-four avoided niceties in being "a score or more". Twenty-five was "pretty many", thirty was "dozens", thirty-five manifest itself as "great crowds", forty as "some many", forty-five as "scores", and the good old stand-by for fifty was "tons".

Sixty qualified itself as "a bugger of a lot"; seventy came along as "great whacks" and eighty as "thousands". A hundred of anything, whether animal, vegetable or mineral, was so big that we described it as "millions" – on the far side of a hundred we entered uncharted territory and called them legion, for they were many.

———

Two games less controversial than Chasers, at least as far as our elders were concerned, were also associated with the Black Doors portal. One game was named "podge" and the other was "weasel". The derivation of the names was anyone's guess. In the manner of Topsy from "Uncle Tom's Cabin" they probably just growed.

The rules of podge required that a ball, which could be of any type or size, should be kicked against the closed portal of Black Doors. That was all there was to it. The players, with no limitation placed on whether their numbers were one or two, or a few, or some, or several, or even heaps and heaps, lined up in the part of Fore Street that separated Black Doors from the step up to the

Town Platt and took it in turn to boot the ball against the portal on the rebound. Those who broke the sequence were out.

Weasel also involved a ball, but the rules of play were a little more complicated than those of podge. The weasel ball was thrown at a rudimentary wicket propped against the Black Doors portal. The objective was to hit the wicket and knock it down. The wicket was an assembly of three short lengths of driftwood, two being uprights and one spanning the top in the manner of a bail. If we had known what the mathematical symbol "pi" looked like, then "pi-shaped" would have described the wicket to a tee. All players were given one throw at the wicket. Anyone managing to fell the wicket then had to make a racing circuit of the Town Platt and avoid being hit by the ball that the other participants threw at him, some of them throwing with impressive degrees of force. If (or when) the ball hit him his game was over. If he completed the circuit unscathed he could have another go at dissembling the wicket.

Neither of these two games, podge in particular, excited my imagination much. I wasn't an enthusiast of ball games that called for coordination between my eye and a ball, since I didn't possess any. On that basis podge left me cold.

It was highly probable that the war also hadn't been fought so that, when the dust cleared, weasel and podge could be played down at the Black Doors portal. However, the men who claimed to have done so much recent fighting were, much though they might have tried, unable to dredge up a sound reason why the little buggers of Port Isaac shouldn't play at either game.

During the winter months, when the fair weather visitors were long gone and that mythical gun was limbered up ready to be fired down Fore Street from top to bottom without hitting a living soul, the portal of Black Doors enclosed a Slipway House hotel garage that was as empty as a local chapel preacher's sincerity. It was then that a regular series of weekly "Fishermen's

Classes" took place in the echoing confines fronted by the portal.

Fishermen's Classes were an institution for dark evenings and were generally extremely well patronised. They were oriented to instructing attendees on practical aspects of local commercial fishing. Piscatorial lore was taught to the willing, and some of it was certainly absorbed by them. I attended Fishermen's Classes regularly, and reckoned that a majority of my fellow pupils were, like me, there for purely social reasons.

At Fishermen's Classes we were shown, *inter alia*, how to handle, store and maintain ropes in good order; how to tie a whole range of knots; how to weave and mend herring nets; how to catch mackerel with feathered hooks and white fish with baited long lines (which really were long); how to rig up a breeches buoy; and how to make crab pots from cut withies. Perhaps the best thing that Fishermen's Classes brought to its fellowship, however, was an appreciation of the variety and natural history of the marine life that frequented the Bay.

The protagonist sponsors of Fishermen's Classes were the ever worthy and greatly revered gentlemen Mr Anthony Provis (the harbourmaster) and Mr Tom Brown. Class instructors were drawn from the cadre of Port Isaac Fishermen, not the least among whom was Tom's brother Nibs ("'Tis a matter hov!").

Class sessions nominally commenced at seven o'clock in the evening and ended at around nine o'clock. The observance of punctuality was not a feature of the proceedings. The minds of attendees were rarely exercised by a perceived need to be there at exactly the right time for the start.

The high tide surge of waves rolling and grinding shingle down on the beach at the head of the harbour; the wind slamming gusts against the Black Doors portal prior to making a whooping escape up along Middle Street; the clean scent of new rope and bruised withies lightly layered over with hints of tar and tannin; a cup of strong tea turning up at an appropriate juncture – all blended to produce a level of comfort akin to that which a well-loved cushion provided to a worn out backside.

As a consequence, when the appointed moment to wind up the evening's entertainment came and Nibs was wont to tell us, "'Tis a matter hov goin' 'ome!" it demanded quite an effort for us to step out and brave the hasty elements.

———

At Fishermen's Classes, crab pots were manufactured using a basic timbered template assembly consisting of a thick and heavy round table about a yard in diameter and two or three inches thick sitting on top of a central support about five feet high. It resembled a device for feeding birds. The diameter of the table was equal to that of the pot to be eventually created. The assembly was completed with an iron hoop, having a similarly equivalent diameter, installed and centred on the base of the central support.

The table was perforated by a number of closely concentric circles of drilled holes. These provided the positions for the insertion of uniformly quarter to half-inch thick butt ends of selected Mill Pool withies that would surround the aperture of the throat of the crab pot.

The withies were inserted one by one into these holes. Once they were all in place and standing proud, they were ready to be transformed into the skeleton of a crab pot. The throat was made rigid by virtue of weaving very thin and whippy withies in and out through the circle of thick standing withies to a height of about six inches above the table.

The standing withies were then bent in sequence over a block of wood with a specially curved profile to form the crab pot's ribs. The block was stepped at the base so that it could be fitted to and moved around the outer circumference of the table. The technique, involving maintenance of the integrity of the withies so as to avoid their cracking or splitting while ensuring retention of the crab pot's fundamental shape, demanded considerable expertise. As each withy was bent downwards over the block, its free end was fastened with a piece of twine to the iron hoop. In order to stabilise the final framework, a rope-like rib of flexible withies was woven around the structure, commencing at the throat and spiralling gently down to the base.

To finish it off, the incipient crab pot was lifted away from the template. A flat base was prepared by twisting and weaving the free ends of the ribs together, with additional withies inserted to close up gaps at the discretion of the pot maker. Untidy wisps of withy were trimmed off with a sharp clasp knife.

An active crab pot was usually baited with a couple of dead gurnards (or "gurnets") pinned to the inside base with carved wooden pegs known as "skivvers". Securely linked by well-tarred rope into individual lines with a marker buoy at one end, great numbers of crab pots were taken out by the fishing boats to be dropped (or "shet") in the waters of the Bay. The most prized catches when the pots were hauled up again were brown waiter crabs. Spider crabs were rather less desirable. Lobsters were of course very much more than acceptable, and a russet red crayfish was reckoned to be even better. Occasionally a long conger eel, hungry for ripe gurnet, might come to surface in a crab pot and engender an unwelcome surge of excitement in the breast of the fisherman.

—

The opportunity for Fishermen's Classes attendees to construct crab pots was limited by the paucity of the template assemblies available. Practice in knot tying, however, was subject to no such constraint. Knotting was among the most popular of the activities on offer, since it gave results that could be immediately appreciated.

Of all the knots demonstrated by Nibs *et al* for our delectation, our perennial favourites were the monkey's paw and the hangman's noose. The former was greatly admired for its weight and heft. A monkey's paw was a round, fist-sized knot out at the end of a length of thin rope. It made an ideal club with which

250

its maker could whack his friends. The application of a monkey's paw to this enjoyable function was responsible for many evictions from Fishermen's Classes on the grounds of conduct unbecoming a student of the fishing profession.

If a monkey's paw loomed in our imaginations as a tale yet to be told (by anyone other than Mr W.W. Jacobs, that is), a hangman's noose formed the stuff of legend, exercising a morbid fascination on our minds. We thrilled and shuddered as we placed the finished product around our necks and slid the geometrically neat (more or less) running knot to its tightest grip.

We all knew a lot about hangings. For a couple of weeks prior to one taking place in one prison or another somewhere up the line, the elapsing days were counted off one by one, almost too eagerly, in newsprint. During the week preceding the so-called drop, the newspapers recorded the movements of Mr Albert Pierrepoint, the national hangman. We followed Albert's preparations and trembled when his departure for the place of execution from a public house that he owned (curiously named "Help the Poor Struggler") was announced. We studied the menu for the last meal to be taken by the condemned man, anticipated the grim toll of a bell before his eight o'clock walk to the gallows, and saw a grainy photo of his execution notice being pinned on the gates of the prison under the scrutiny of a small cluster of onlookers who seemed to be doing their best not to appear to be too keen to be there.

It was no wonder that we all delighted in getting our hands on a genuine hangman's noose at Fishermen's Classes. A noose was an essential accessory benefiting any good game of "Cowboys and Indians" or, for that matter, "Cops and Robbers".

One excellent hangman's noose prepared by a boy (who much to my regret was not me) was used to ideal effect in a certain game of Cowboys and Indians that took place one day up in the middle of the Port Gaverne valley. Sid Pluckrose was the Bad Man designated for stringing up from a convenient elm tree bough.

Sid was the second youngest of a large family of evacuees that came along to Port Isaac from the East End of London early in the war. Unlike most evacuees, who went back home when wartime hostilities ceased, the Pluckroses took up permanent residence in Port Isaac where they lived on one floor of a tall house out towards the far end of the Terrace.

In accordance with protocol, the hangman's rope was slung over the bough of the tree, and the noose was placed around Sid's neck. The symbolic hanging should have ended there and then, but somehow Sid was pushed off the bank he was standing on. Suspended by his neck, Sid floated in a graceful arc over a depression thickly bottomed with dead leaves. It was fortunate that at the end of his trajectory Sid drifted back in the manner of a pendulum to regain his footing on the bank once again. He appeared to us, in the wash of a wave of relief capped with slight disappointment, to be not much the worse for wear.

—

Herring nets, perhaps including some that were inexpertly darned at Fishermen's Classes, were taken to a building known as the "Bark House" in Dolphin Street for an annual outing. The Bark House was a good-sized fisherman's cellar located across from Dolphin House, not far downhill from the Temple Bar exit. It was faced with a tall pair of sliding wooden doors. Within the Bark House there was nothing to be seen above the floor but stark eaves supporting the underside of a slated roof.

A prominent feature of the interior of the Bark House was a huge cast-iron copper, bricked in and set atop a solid stone fireplace. The Bark House copper celebrated its day of glory in the autumn, when it was filled up with a "bark" (strong tannin) solution, and the fire was stoked and drawn up to the roaring proportions that were necessary to boil up the bark solution.

It felt to us as if weeks of preparation leading to countdown days of eager anticipation led to the unique event at the Bark House. On the allotted day the fishermen brought along their nets, checked, mended and precisely arranged in neat folds, to be barked. Younger devotees of Fishermen's Classes followed hard on the fishermen's heels.

The process of barking was not dissimilar to that of washing clothes, other than that no mangle was involved. Nets were dipped and steeped one by one in the bubbling copper and agitated with heavy wooden poles for effect until it was judged that their each and every fibre was pervaded by bark solution. They were then lifted out and hung over wooden frames to drip and dry.

Once barked, nets were protected for a season against the worst ravages of the destructive qualities of salt water and were ready to drop in the paths of the herring shoals that would stream into Port Isaac Bay in the not too distant future.

Barking Day was an extra-special social event. There was a sense of bustle to it, a happy certainty that herrings were coming, and a mellowness of outlook that although summer was over, winter was yet some way off. The great leaf-kicking season of bright autumn was nigh. Guy Fawkes' day was drawing near. The harvest was as safely gathered in as it was ever going to be, and beyond that, God our maker was (hopefully) providing for all our wants to be supplied. God often fell a bit short on making provision for some of our expectations, but we forgave him his trespasses against us and presumably vice versa might have applied as well, although I wouldn't have bet on it.

Cheerful conversation took place in the Bark House, illuminated by the reflected heat and glow emanating from beneath the copper. We brought along potatoes and thrust them into the incandescent coals that dribbled from the grate. Charred on the outside and almost raw at the core, too hot to hold as they were tossed from hand to hand and from person to person, no potatoes ever tasted better or were enjoyed more than those baked under the copper at the Bark House.

The burden of wending the dark road home from Fishermen's Classes was greatly eased when the Port Isaac chip shops were open. Anyone willing to part with threepence could purchase a bag of chips charged from a batch of the same recently hoisted hot from a deep fryer and then eat them on the way so as to keep the chill at bay. With a little more money available to hand over it was possible to obtain a piece of fried fish coated in crisp batter to accompany the chips; however, such a level of funds normally eluded my pocket.

The bags in which chips were served were prepared by inducing a square of newspaper to become a cone through what seemed to me to be *Rupert* Annual styled origami. The publication date of the newspaper in question was normally by no means current. The cone of newspaper, with the chips in it, was secured for consumption in a socket formed by making a circle of the fingers and thumb of the left hand. The chips were extracted from the cone by means of the right hand.

Salt out of a large cellar of battered metal, and dark pungent vinegar from a bottle that might once have contained a stronger brew (that was naturally designed to be taken for medicinal purposes), were consecutively shaken over an order of chips as a routine behind-the-counter measure, whether the customer wanted the condiments or not.

As a consequence my chips down at the point of the cone were apt to be more than a little soggy and sour of flavour by the time I had mined all the way down to them. Sometimes there was a bonus, however, as small conglomerations of rogue batter might have been lifted out of the fryer with the chips. Batter, when present, always seemed to reside at the very tip of the cone.

Port Isaac was blessed with two chip shops, both located (almost) within the radius of a good baccy chaw spit from the Black Doors portal. The first of these, situated a couple of doors up from Ted Robinson's Harbour Café near the bottom of Fore Street was the one owned by Mrs Keat, Arker's mother.

Mrs Keat's chip shop was quite well lit, and when blackout restrictions ended it stood exposed in its entirety to Fore Street passers-by behind tall and broad windows. Chip fat bubbled in the troughs of Mrs Keat's big shiny fryer on the right at the rear of a high, narrow and marble-topped counter. A neat pile of meticulously torn squares of newspaper, destined to become cones, were in attendance at one side of the counter adjacent to the salt and vinegar dispensers.

Mrs Keat's chips were long and uniformly square in cross section. They were extruded as the white and glistening subdivided products of big peeled potatoes forced through a cutter grid by depressing a manual plunger. When fried, the chips were golden brown and crisp on the outside and soft and dry on the inside. Mrs Keat made a consistent product to the extent that, apart from the ever-welcome surprise of a stray batter piece deep in the cone, her customers always knew what they were about to get. At one juncture Mrs Keat diversified her endeavours into making crisp chips, which became exceedingly popular. They were paper thin, crunchy and full of flavour. No vinegar was ever permitted to touch them. Their quality was far superior to the "Smith's Crisps" we could get up in Chapman's grocery shop. All that a bag of Mrs Keat's crisp chips lacked was the inclusion of a pinch or two of salt contained in a tiny twist of blue waxed paper.

Port Isaac's second chip-vending establishment was owned and run by a certain Mrs Spry, who, owing to her success in having reached an advanced stage of life, was known by her younger patrons as Granny Spry. By the same logic, her chip shop was referred to as "Granny Spry's". Granny Spry was the matriarch of a long-established local family. Her surname described her character. She might have been stooped with grey age and heavy enough to have to shuffle rather than walk, but her eyes were bright and her mind was sharper than the blades of her chip cutter.

To get to Granny Spry's from the Black Doors portal required a right turn to be taken into Middle Street, a wind-assisted walk for ten yards or so and a subsequent sharp left-hand diversion into a sheltered "ope".

The opes of Port Isaac were almost all located within the jumble of downtown. Opes were sometimes tunnel-like and otherwise tight, open gully-like features that wormed their way into and through otherwise impenetrable clutters of cottages so as to provide access to hidden back doors, fishermen's cellars, and storage vaults contained behind battered wooden doors in secret courtyards. Most of the opes permitted the easy passage of tubby persons, although a few were wide enough and tall enough to allow the entry of a vehicle as large as a horse drawn cart with the horse attached to it.

The ope within which Granny Spry's chip shop was located was one of the wider variety. A wooden beam, quite as heavy as it was ancient, formed the lintel across its entry. I could put up my hand and trail my fingers along the bottom of the beam provided that I jumped up in the air when I did it. As a result of very many generations of similar finger-trailing the beam had acquired a smooth patina, not a little of which was sustained by the greasy attribute of Granny Spry's chips.

A narrow door, for several years unacquainted with the administrations of a paintbrush, opened directly into Granny Spry's on the right-hand side of the ope. The interior of the chip shop was characterised by the sort of muted illumination that in Port Isaac was so normal as to be considered unremarkable. Customers were, on entering, reasonably able to perceive the broad outlines of what Granny Spry might be about to serve them, but the dimness ensured that there was less clarity concerning the finer details, which was probably just as well.

It wasn't exactly necessary to feel the way through Granny Spry's, yet for all that there was a sense of having to grope towards the counter made flesh beneath a shroud of steam mixed with the smoke of overheated fat. Tom Brown's clasp knife could have sliced the charged atmosphere into cubes.

The spongy heat within Granny Spry's was an ideal antidote to the cold winds of the waning year without. It was a more intimate venue than was Mrs Keat's. The opportunity to warm up at Granny Spry's countered the inherent risk of the inconsistency of her chips, which formed the obverse side of the coin in comparison to Mrs Keat's version.

Granny Spry's chip fat bubbled and spattered away in a hulking two-pan fryer, only incidentally blessed with the facility of a curved sliding hood to close off its active section. Jammed as the hood was by a venerable deposit of accumulated chip residue cemented by spilled fat, it was never shut, or at least never was on those occasions when I went in for my three penn'orth.

The quality of Granny Spry's chips varied from the not too bad to the downright awful. It was possible to determine in advance how the chips were likely to taste on a given night by the smell emanating from the fat of the day. As was the case with Granny Spry, some of the fat in the fryer had been around for a long time. The fat was topped up to maintain a steady level rather than being periodically changed in its entirety. Like the famous curate's egg, some parts of the load of fat were better than others. There was a rumour, never substantiated, that Granny Spry's ration of chip fat was eked out by additions of axle grease.

The chips that were lifted from the boiling oil were limp, soggy, tightly matted and running slick with grease. As a newspaper cone-filled serving was eaten, the spectral flavour of yesterday's recycled chips fought with the taste of today's augmentation and often won. The chips congealed like a soft wad of dead men's fingers, from which pieces were peeled away for consumption.

Yet, to give credit where credit was due, Granny Spry's chips never failed to banish the rough edge of a dark night downtown when the wind howled and the rain spat around corners as if it had taken a lesson in the art from Granny Spry's fryer.

———

Now and then, to add a touch of variety to the standard bill of net mending, knot tying, hook baiting and crab pot making, a breeches buoy put in an appearance at Fishermen's Classes and some advice (rather than instruction) on its function was offered to those in attendance.

The breeches buoy (pronounced "britches boy") was an essential device – looking like a set of gawky, baggy canvas underpants suspended from a firmly wooden hooped waistline – for rescuing shipwrecked mariners. Permission to step into and try the breeches buoy on for fit was a privilege highly sought after by us. It was only unfortunate that none of us were ever destined to ride in the arrangement along a rope. The breeches buoy experience offered us yet another object lesson in our never quite getting what we wanted.

The use of the term "britches" in conversation never failed to generate a ripple of sniggers. We all knew that it was an impolite word used to describe knickers, the fit of which on a lot of the girls in the playground at school was reckoned to be not so much better than that of the breeches buoy on us at Fishermen's Classes; there was supposed to be a book on the subject, entitled *Britches Away* by the author Nick Erless.

If ever an innocent girl enquired what time it was by asking a boy who was in on the joke, the boy was apt to reply (with total impunity for a change), "What's the time? Half past nine. Hang your britches on the line!" Great satisfaction was obtained from unrestrained usage of the word britches on breeches buoy evenings at Fishermen's Classes.

The breeches buoy and its accessories were maintained and secured in good order in a small building set in the middle of a slate-walled enclosure behind the telephone box up at the top of Back Hill, where it was sandwiched between the Church Rooms and the North Cornwall Transport garage. Although the edifice was not far away from the New Coastguard Station, the distance was sufficient to preclude intruding on the coastguard's field of view. The coastguards all showed every sign of having better things to do with their time than waste it in keeping an eye on the small building, not excluding battling with their better halves and, in one special case, running a clandestine book on the horses for furtive followers of form.

The breeches buoy-related inventory of stored equipment included a rocket launcher; a number of rockets; seemingly unlimited coils of ropes of various thickness; a mountain of blocks, pulleys and other tackle; and, naturally enough, the breeches buoy itself. It was a matter of huge regret to us that neither the rocket launcher nor any of the related rockets managed to accompany the breeches buoy on its periodic excursions down to Fishermen's Classes. However, all was not lost, since once in a while the entire assembly and the technique of using it was subjected to testing by means of a full-scale manned practice.

The harbour's eastern breakwater was cast in the role of a sinking ship for the purpose of the exercise. When the tide was about half way in (or out) and the sea was calm, the fishermen designated to form the crew of the sinking ship were rowed out to the eastern breakwater in a punt, there to be marooned like a pack of Ben Gunns and left to ponder on their eventual fate.

The rocket launcher was set up on the beach clear of the edge of the tide, charged with a rocket attached to a line of very thin rope, aimed in the general direction of the eastern breakwater, adjusted for trajectory, and activated.

The firing of the rocket was the moment that we had all longed for. We cheered in unison with the whoosh and roar of the rocket as it soared away, leading a whipping trail of line. The rocket achieved the crest of its trajectory, stalled, and dropped like a stone into the waiting sea out in the middle Awn.

The crew of the sinking ship grabbed hold of the rocket-borne line, by then draped conveniently over the eastern breakwater. The rocket was never (well, hardly ever) off target. A thick rope was attached to the shore end of the initial line to be drawn to the sinking ship by the crew pulling it in, hand over hand.

On the top of its seaward end the eastern breakwater was fitted with a tall pole braced at its base by four stout stanchions and capped by an open-hooped globe-like device. The whole array was fashioned from iron that the sea was slowly but surely eating away. The rope line and tackle were firmly anchored at both the stanchions and the shoreline end. The breeches buoy was attached to the line on shore and was then pulled out in its turn to the sinking ship.

All that then separated the set-up from a satisfactory conclusion to the exercise was that a volunteer should step into the breeches buoy and make a safe passage from sinking ship to shore. The task was not aided by a tendency of many Port Isaac fishermen to be of a girth, bulk and unwillingness to sorely test the strength of the set-up.

The crew of the sinking ship could easily have formed a circle so as to proceed through an "Eenie, meenie, minie, mo" or an "Ickle, uckle, black buckle, ickle, uckle, out" routine in order to select a crew member who would be "it" for the journey in the breeches buoy. However, as random selection was probably too objective an approach for fishermen to ever take, it was normally pre-agreed that the fag-consuming consumptive, Mr Sammy Dyer Thomas, who lacked weight, bulk and even, as it seemed at times, the ability to draw breath, would be "it" every time.

It was never certain that Sammy Dyer was additionally lacking in willingness, but he could at least rest easy in the illusion that in a genuine rescue he might be the first one to be saved, always assuming that the fishermen's priorities held steady under such circumstances.

It was an established tradition of breeches buoy exercises that Sammy Dyer in the breeches buoy should be dropped into the sea at least once, straight down into the water as if he were a piece of bread and jam being dipped in a cup of tea. Practice made that popular feature of the breeches buoy routine perfect.

Large crowds turned out to watch breeches buoy performances. When wave conditions in the harbour were too rough to permit a scheduled practice to be undertaken, alternative locations were available either up in the field adjoining Lobber field, which was crossed by the shortcut footpath to Port Quin, or on the edge of the Port Gaverne Main above the slate jetty. The former option generally took precedence over the latter.

Up in that field next to Lobber, from where it was possible to look down into Freak valley and see Pine Awn away to the right, a wooden mast, at least twenty feet tall, painted yellow and much too broad in diameter for me to wrap my arms around it at the base, was a permanent feature. A set of diametrically opposed triangular blocks nailed to the sides of the mast allowed it to be climbed from bottom to top. Launching a rocket alongside the mast sent the rope line flipping all the way over to the Roscarrock Farm side of Freak valley. The breeches buoy was rigged for action from the top of the mast.

It would have been an absolute treat for us to watch Sammy Dyer being hauled across Freak valley in the breeches buoy. In that event, improbable though it would have been for Sammy Dyer to be plunged into water, we were sure that something appropriate could have been arranged.

Sad to recount, the journey of Sammy Dyer in the breeches buoy from the top of the mast was only a short one, amounting to not a lot more than an angled descent to the surface field. Sammy Dyer was worth more than that kind of anticlimax.

*Port Gaverne*

# 14

# The Bill of Fare

*Fair fa' your honest, sonsie face,*
*Great chieftain o' the puddin-race!*

Robert Burns (1759–96)
"Address to a Haggis"

MOST OF THE ingredients of the food that appeared on my plate at dinner times were intended to be filling rather than satisfying. There was never so much food placed before me that more wouldn't have been welcome, but the feeling of a full belly when it was eaten and gone was what counted.

Whether or not the food on offer was "good for me" was not a subject deemed worthy of polite debate. What I was given to eat might be beneficial to my state of health or it might not. No matter, there was food on the plate, it had to be eaten up by me, and I had no alternative but to get on with it. That was the mandate governing every one of my strictly scheduled meal times.

When Granfer's oft-repeated admonition, "Eat up – don'tcha know there's a war on?" had, by virtue of there no longer being a war on, been worn thinner than the soles of my father's one and only pair of shoes, Granfer switched tactics to tell me to, "Eat it all – you don't know where your next meal is coming from!"

"Leftovers" therefore weren't allowed to exist. I couldn't leave anything on my plate – well, not much anyway. On those occasions when the unpalatability of the culinary offering of the day defeated all entreaties involving the currency of the war and the uncertainty of the immediate future, I was admonished for ingratitude and told in no uncertain terms that there was a child somewhere else in the world who would be very glad to eat what sat in front of me. "Then why don't we send it to him?" was a suggestion I made that went down with those to whom it was addressed in a manner that was as acceptable to them as their inevitable follow-up clip to my ear was to me.

As a consequence, I perfected a sensory art that went on to establish itself as a committed habit, involving first sniffing at food and then, if the odour was displeasing, rapidly shovelling up and swallowing the despised comestibles without permitting any portion of them to make contact with my tongue.

Once in a while I was forced to forsake food that I genuinely liked because I got too much of it at the first helping. That didn't happen very often, as the judgement of quantities was subject to forces beyond my control. If I didn't seize what I could of what was available when I had the chance then I might lose out to my brother later on. I was accused of having "eyes bigger than my belly", but I didn't mind that when the dinner was a good one.

My brother and I watched each other's plates from the corners of eagle-keen eyes. Both of us were ready to rise and take up arms in an instant if we felt that we were not being apportioned our due share. Although it always seemed to me that my brother managed to get the "biggest half", no doubt vice versa was equally applicable. Complaints from either of us always fell on deaf ears, apart from our own ears, that is.

When Gran prepared a batch of pea soup in her all-purpose blue enamel saucepan, cleaning up my first serving was not only not difficult, it was accomplished with speed and vigour, permitting me to act like Oliver Twist and ask for more – provided I hadn't been beaten to the mark by someone able to eat even faster than me. Once I knew for sure that there was no more pea soup in the offing, my ultimate act was to lick the plate shiny clean.

264

The licking process was carried out so industriously that Granfer told me he was worried that I was going to remove the pattern from the plate. However, he also said that licking saved on the washing up, so that was good enough for me.

Most residents of Port Isaac cottages took all their meals – breakfast, dinner, tea and supper (where applicable) – at a family gathering seated around the home kitchen table. When a family assembled thus, the atmosphere surrounding the occasion was often rather more cloudy than sunny, especially when the edge of competition for the last few morsels was acute.

Going out to eat, apart from visits to the chip-dispensing outlets of Mrs Keat and Granny Spry, was an activity as unsought after as it was generally unknown where most of us were concerned. Restaurants were by implication places patronised by a higher (but not necessarily better) class of people than most of us either believed we were or wished to emulate. On the other hand there were some of us who might be spotted every now and then in the act of partaking of fare in a pop or tea-vending establishment that was classified as a "café", such as Mrs Strout's out at Port Gaverne. That was just about as daring a move for us as any externally oriented dining excursion could ever be.

Restaurants in the local hotels catered in principle only to paying guests, although a few hotel proprietors advertised that their restaurants were equally "open to non-residents". It seemed, however, to be well understood (if not directly stated) that in order to be acceptable as diners, the non-residents were not to be drawn from the ranks of the village's great unwashed.

Such considerations were applied in full measure at a restaurant established by Brigadier (retd) Reed in his home at Trevan House adjacent to the Bark House in Dolphin Street. In the august dining room of Trevan House the Brigadier played host to refined patrons, who were all chosen and admitted with the utmost discretion. The Brigadier's pioneering endeavour, offering a dining experience on what was rumoured to be very fancy food sold at even fancier prices (table bookings in advance only), in a location that was neither at home nor set in a residential hotel (open to non-residents), was an object of wonder for those of us whose lot it was to only stand and stare.

The concept of "dining" (and perish the thought "dining out") was as foreign to us as was the practice of eating dinner in the evening, as we all knew that dinner time came along at the start of the afternoon.

The Brigadier was a diminutive bouncy ball of pure gentry capped with Brylcreem. Towards the privileged diners who stepped through his Trevan House portal, the likes of us, being at least as half-baked as the potatoes we scoffed nearby on Bark House day, bore not a single jot or tittle of envy.

It was fitting that the Brigadier's back door, which he no doubt referred to as the "tradesman's entrance", opened on the Bark House side of Trevan House. His front entrance, through which his eager patrons arrived and later departed, was located up in Middle Street across from the old pump and the front of Mr Jack Short's cellar. The door was set in a high wall behind which lay a garden that few had seen and even fewer would ever be permitted to see unless they were prepared to climb over the wall first.

The good old potato, occasionally known as a "spud" but more normally as a "tetty", was the quintessential back garden-grown centrepiece around which the majority of our dinners were constructed. We would not have survived long in the absence of a pile of tetties on the table.

Chopped up tetty formed the core of the pasties that we ate at least once a week. On the strength of that attribute alone a noble tetty needed to look at no greater claim to fame.

During the not infrequent scarcity of meat, tetties were influential enough to stand alone on the plate, sometimes mashed up, but generally boiled. Favoured tetty-flavouring additives were, (when we had them) butter or grated cheese or chopped parsley. The three Smith brothers, Charley, Clarence and Stanley, all of them big strapping chaps and (apart from Clarence) almost as rough as the Gut in a ground sea, were reputed to enjoy great individual batches of boiled tetties piled high in a basin with the product of a dissolved Oxo cube (what Granfer called "a cow in a cube") poured over the lot.

The basic pasty ingredients were additionally combined to prepare the ever popular "tetty and turnip pie" in a deep dish beneath a pastry crust. The piecrust was prevented from sagging by means of a strategically placed hollow china implement of support within which the bulk of the pie's gravy had the habit of rising and collecting.

Yet another recipe involving onions and tetties (minus turnip) rendered down to a watery pulp in a frying pan and (hopefully) augmented by a couple of slivers of fatty bacon, was named "tetty uddle". It was served in a bowl and eaten with a spoon. The last smears of tetty uddle in the bowl were mopped up with a chunk of Sherratt's new bread.

Cottage pie, sometimes referred to as shepherd's pie, featured onions, tetties and meat, although in that particular case the meat was minced up with the onions and the tetties were layered in a mashed condition on top of the concoction. Cottage pie came along as an inevitable third-day attribute of a Sunday joint of meat, when there was one.

A Sunday joint lasted us for a full three days of dinners. It was roasted and eaten hot on Sunday, served as leftover cold meat with boiled potatoes on the side on Monday, and (whatever of it then remained) laboriously minced up as the basis for either cottage pie or (maybe) generic sausage-like "rissoles" on Tuesday.

Every Tuesday morning my mother took the remnants of our Sunday joint, inclusive of any cold vegetables (roasted or boiled) left from the two previous days, and ran the whole lot through a hand-cranked mincing machine. Gristle snapped like a volley of gunfire as she laboriously wound the collation through the mincer's revolving cutters.

Since the nature of the meaty remnants was never identical from week to week, dishes made from the product of the Tuesday mincing varied greatly in taste and texture, and were generally all the more acceptable for carrying an element of the unexpected.

The value of rissoles as sausage substitutes could not be overstated, much though we craved "real" sausages. The latter were so difficult to come by that they were reckoned to be worth their weight in gold when we got them. The first task of any family group participating in the annual St Peter's Church Sunday school outing to the pantomime at the Palace Theatre in Plymouth was to traipse around any commercial sectors of the city that had not been entirely flattened by German bombs in a quest for half a pound of sausages. When (or if) located, the prize was snapped up with alacrity, as indeed was the equal glory of a short length of the related and euphemistically named hog's pudding.

At Christmas the Sunday joint gave way to a chicken, as often as not (as has already been established) thanks to the run of the cards at a whist drive. A chicken, in the Sunday joint tradition, also provided us with three days of dinners. On Christmas Day it was roasted and eaten hot, on Boxing Day cold slices were served, and on the third day the fowl rose again to have its bones, with such attached shreds and traces of adhering meat or skin as were (improbably) overlooked on Boxing Day, boiled up to make a thick and luxurious stew in the company of tetties, turnips and suet dumplings.

Had there been an option for a fourth-day chicken dinner it could have involved sucking at the ends of the chicken bones softened by the preceding day's stew, had it not been for the fact that that sucking process had already taken place on the third day.

When Christmas past was but a fond memory and Christmas yet to come was still well out of sight in the unimaginable distance, Granfer told me all about "chicken point" and "Russian duck", both of them useful as dishes for bridging the great poultry gap. They were available at any time. Granfer said that if I pointed at my empty plate and imagined a roast chicken leg (or better yet a parson's nose, my personal favourite) sitting on it, the conditions of chicken point would be satisfied. Russian duck demanded a more energetic preparation, and called for me to leave the kitchen for a moment, rush back in, and duck under the table.

Our supply of meat was rationed. The ration was what it was, we got what we got, and in the over-the-counter sense nothing could be done about it. So that was that. Some under-the-counter meat was available to those who were adept at exploiting the system, thereby excluding far too many from contention, unless special favours entered the equation. It was only on rare occasions at the butcher's shop that it would be possible to inspect a Sunday joint ration sitting on the sheet of newspaper that was shortly to enfold it and truly believe that the animal providing it did not perish in vain.

However, feelings of exaltation arose when a side of either lamb or of pork was seen hanging on one of the butcher's hooks. The subsequent Sunday dinner time then shaped up as an event worth anticipating. I always knew that when (and if) I bit at a slice of pork or lamb there was a good chance that my top and bottom teeth would make contact without too much trouble. Where the customary beef was concerned I never knew for sure whether my teeth would be up to the job.

The customary durability of the beef may have been attributable to the way in which my mother roasted it, but the more likely reason was that it was taken from the carcass of a venerable cow. Beggars, my mother told me, couldn't be choosers. In my mouth, beef all too often refused to dissemble, even following an assault

269

of prolonged chewing. I cut away the fat part (which I loathed to the core of my being) and swallowed the remaining bits in mangled strings that I could feel sliding all the way down to my stomach.

The shortcomings of a Sunday joint were made up for by a substantial array of accompanying tetties, sometimes crisped golden brown by dripping, and sometimes merely puffed brown around the edges when water entered the roasting scheme. I didn't care for the latter variety of roast tetties at all, but was forced to eat them by being informed that they were roasted "the Cornish way". If the advice was meant to appeal to a sense of patriotism it was doomed in my mind to be more representative of the last refuge of a scoundrel.

Additional seasonal vegetables enhancing the Sunday joint were "greens", mainly derived from various fresh species of the cabbage family, and members of the rooted gang of turnip, parsnip and carrot. Dried peas were available all through the year, normally extracted from a packet. Even after being soaked over Saturday night in the company of a big tablet of soda and boiled to death on Sunday morning, such peas were bullet hard on the plate and tasted like something that Tom Brown's boxed lobsters would have appreciated.

The butcher patronised by both my mother and Gran was Mr John Hicks, the J. N. of the firm of J. N. Hicks & Son Family Butchers in the lower New Road. John quite often provided us with alternatives to beef, which he loosely categorised as cow "offal". I tended to think of those options as cow "awful".

Pork offal was not quite so awful, however, and when we got hold of some it was normally reserved for the preparation of brawn, a chunky conglomeration of well-boiled pig parts held in anonymous suspension in a matrix of yellow-brown jelly. Gran's homemade brawn was wonderful and usually remained uneaten for a lot less time than it took Gran to make.

270

Prominent varieties of cow offal were a much-dreaded trio comprising liver, lights and tripe. Kidney might also have been a member of this awful inventory, but in its particular case it was so infrequently available that anyone of us could be forgiven for forgetting about it. A handful of kidney did come along now and then to serve as a minor ingredient in a steak and kidney pudding, sometimes known as a suet pudding when the concoction was enclosed in a thick suet casing. The distribution of pieces of kidney in a suet pudding was similar to that of silver threepenny bits in a Christmas pudding, neither the meat nor the metal being easy to locate. The advantage held by the kidney over the coin was that a tooth couldn't be broken on the kidney.

A suet pudding was constructed in a basin and then tied up for boiling in a muslin shroud. Inside the suet carapace the pudding contents were rich in gravy. When the pie was opened, the gravy began to sing, not very daintily, but fit for a king all the same.

My mother came home one morning with a tinned suet pudding, the first of such that I had ever seen. As dinner time approached she placed the tin in a saucepan of boiling water, left it for a while, and removed it for opening when she judged the heating-up process had gone on for long enough. It would have been prudent if my mother had punched a pressure-releasing hole in the lid at the outset, since at the first touch of a tin opener on it, the lid blossomed and exploded in the manner of an oil gusher that I once saw head for the sky in a film starring Clark Gable up at the Rivoli.

The soaring burst of suet pudding was halted only by impact with our kitchen ceiling where it spread and clung in its entirety like a mat of streaky brown glue – apart from the few clots and drips that succumbed to the law of gravity. By the time the bulk of the errant suet pudding was safely scraped off the ceiling and gathered in it was well past our dinner time, but we ate the pudding all the same and, considering its adventures, it didn't taste too bad at all.

Roast heart of the cow-offal variety appeared on our Sunday dinner-time table much too frequently for my liking. In fairness, there may have been a point reached during the process of roasting such hearts when the organs achieved their peak of edible perfection. That being so, it was unfortunate that my mother never seemed able to hit it on the head. An underdone heart was an object that I wanted to flee away from with great urgency, as a consequence of which my mother tended to overcook it well beyond the far limit of prudence. Her roasted hearts emerged from the oven bomb-like in shape, rock-like in texture, and knife bending in durability.

That was the problem with roast heart. For every roast heart that was more or less edible there were at least half a dozen others that weren't. Those of us who ate heart (or were rather compelled to eat it) were, when age should finally equip us with the power of choice, determined that no morsel of such would ever again pass our lips.

Where liver was concerned, it was interesting to me that the words "liver" and "leather" sounded very similar, especially when spoken with a Port Isaac accent. No matter what was done to cook those shivering slabs of dense purple tissue, the invariable outcome was a product that offered a much greater benefit to the soles of boots than to the inside of a stomach.

The preparation of liver for consumption was a lottery that was lost more often than it was won. On the other hand, winning could bring good times. Fried liver and onions (the latter being liver's chief associate as we knew it) was one of my favourites, always provided that the liver had been extracted from a younger than usual bovine. The pity was that all too often the cows supplying the livers that we obtained from Mr John Hicks were, like John, antiquated members of their species.

John sold the very aptly named tripe cut up into pale rubbery sheets, flat and shiny on one side, and coarsely furred with minute tentacles on the other. Tripe was the worst penance visited by cow offal on an unwilling palate. When tripe was cooked it turned oleaginous, deathly white, slick and slimy. At the least contact with a fork, a piece of tripe slid ominously on the plate as if it were intent on taking evasive action. The touch of tripe on the inside of my mouth was an abomination. I swallowed tripe without tasting it. It was the only way.

Cow's lights were unpleasantly spongy pieces of lung. I didn't know of anyone who ever sat down to eat lights on Sunday, or on any other day for that matter, although that didn't necessarily mean that there weren't some people somewhere in Port Isaac who were so inclined.

Cats ate lights with relish. The non-feline Mr Ernie Brown might have shared his own cat's taste for lights. Ernie, a sometime resident of the middle section of Khandalla, was reputed to enjoy sandwiches spread with the contents of tins of newfangled proprietary cat food.

———

The suet that enclosed bits of steak and sporadic pieces of kidney so as to successfully turn the ingredients into a steak and kidney pudding also provided substance for the wonderfully formed dumplings that sat on top of so many stews. Sticky on the outside and firm at the centre, dumplings were a chewy, stomach-filling dream.

Shaped like a loaf of Sherratt's bread and studded with raisins or sultanas or currants (depending on availability), a dumpling mix was transformed into a legendary "figgy duff". In spite of fearing Mr Tom Brown's clasp knife, a figgy duff was the ideal sweet/savoury sliced-up accompaniment to the delectable concoction of lentils flavoured by a bony knuckle of ham that was known as pea soup. Although there was a lot more bone than ham on any knuckle that went into Gran's pea soup, Gran boiled the knuckle until the meat fell off the bone, so not a shred of ham was lost.

A steamed pudding with a suet base made a memorable treat, especially when it was capped with treacle. It wasn't quite as good as rice pudding, but we were happy to live with the difference. The treacle (Lyle's Golden Syrup with its unforgettable motto OUT OF THE STRONG CAME FORTH SWEETNESS) soaked into the summit of the pudding, and when the pudding was turned out ran down the basin-conjured side slopes like lava coming out of a volcano.

Jam was a reasonably adequate alternative to treacle in a steamed pudding. Lemon curd wasn't. Not for nothing was lemon curd known by us as "phlegm and turd".

---

When it came to us augmenting the stodgy delights of rice, tetties, macaroni and their ilk, bread featured high on the list. As far as I was concerned, a crusty white loaf of new bread or batch of freshly baked splitters from Sherratt's bakery was no more or no less than an unequalled miracle of the baker's art.

A new loaf was placed on a wooden board on our kitchen table to be cut into slices with a long, wooden-handled, serrated-edged bread knife. The crust crackled and splintered as the knife bit into it. The benefit of new bread was that it was so soft that it was only possible to cut it into thick slices.

A cut slice was spread with butter if any of our butter ration was still available, and then jam or treacle (which we always had a pot or a tin of) was slathered on top of the butter. Lack of butter didn't matter at all when we had the alternative of cream for scooping away from the scalded surface of the morning's delivery of milk.

We weren't very inventive in making sandwiches with Sherratt's bread. Variety in sandwich filling was not the spice of that aspect of life. Paste for spreading on bread was bought from Chapman's or from the Co-op in little jars labelled with generic titles as anonymous as they were ominous. There was "fish paste", and "meat paste" and "sandwich spread". The actual ingredients making up the contents of the jars were anyone's guess. Fish paste tasted fishy, but meat paste didn't taste all that meaty.

Lettuce and tomatoes were fresh seasonal entries in the sandwich stakes. Peppery tasting watercress could be gathered from the streams in the valleys for those who liked that sort of thing on their bread. Cucumber was thinly sliced and soaked in vinegar before it was eaten and was also sometimes included in sandwiches – although in that respect we considered cucumber sandwiches to be the property of our betters, and not fit for consumption by lowly people like us.

I liked egg sandwiches but could only indulge that penchant to its full over a limited period in spring time when the gulls were laying eggs.

As Sherratt's new bread aged and headed for staleness, cut slices became ever-thinner possibilities. Fried bread smothered with the all-purpose treacle could form the essence of breakfast. Treacle was also used as a sugar substitute to be dribbled in spirals on top of porridge.

Fried bread at breakfast tended to alternate from day to day with the classic dish of bread and milk (sometimes known as "milky sue"). Stale (or at best approaching stale) slices of bread cut into small squares and covered with hot milk and a little sugar (or treacle) formed the ingredients of milky sue. The great virtue of hot milk was that it softened up the by then mightily tough crusts.

The crusts (waste not, want not) were never trimmed off – even from the bread slices that were used to make layered bread puddings for "afters". With a scattering of currants sown between the slices, such puddings featuring Sherratt's bread were always worth waiting for.

Toasted bread was usually restricted to being an evening treat in front of the fire once the staleness of the remaining portion of a loaf reached a point at which little green spots were starting to appear on its surface. We scraped the mould away, mounted a slice of bread on a dinner fork and extended its face towards the glowing coals for crisping. All too often the hand of whoever held the fork got toasted along with the bread, but no one ever complained about it.

We didn't normally get our yeast or saffron buns from Sherratt's as my mother and Gran regularly made batches of them at home. Such buns were usually left to mature in a big tin, from which they were offered up as an accompaniment to a cup of tea for anyone happening to drop in. The buns didn't always age quite as well as the visitors who partook of them. Some buns could easily blunt teeth. I quickly learned from whose home it was wise not to accept a bun, although for me to refuse food took a lot of effort.

For all that, even a rock hard yeast bun was preferable to Gran's "seed cake", named for its association with caraway seeds. Once tasted, seed cake was another thing – like marmite, heart, tripe and lemon curd – to be thereafter forever avoided.

In the midst of this modest cornucopia, a piece of fish other than mackerel on the table did not come to pass as frequently as it ought to have done in what was first and foremost a village with its own fishing fleet.

Mackerel were not uncommon, although I would have liked a mackerel a lot better if it had offered me a few less bones to have to watch out for in case they choked me to death. In fairness to the silvered mackerel, the means of preparing it for eating by marinating it in malt vinegar with accompanying peppercorns and (thanks to Miss Jinny Hills) a couple of bay leaves, did have the effect of softening up the bones to the point of near acceptability.

Herrings were plentiful in the autumn, and if a mackerel was bony, a herring was supremely much more so. To drive a herring safely down my throat I needed to chew it up with a lot of Sherratt's new bread. The best part of a herring was a hard roe when the herring had one. The hard roe was known as the "pea roe", a delight to the taste buds when fried.

Shellfish in the form of crabs and lobsters were available only to those who could afford to buy them, and there simply weren't many who had that kind of money. However, down in the harbour when the tide went out we collected other shellfish – specifically winkles – by the bucket load and carried them home for preparation by boiling. Mussels, limpets and whelks were prolific almost to a fault, but for reasons that were lost in history probably, we instinctively avoided collecting them. It took a lot of effort to extract the meat from a winkle, but an accumulation of winkle innards soaked in malt vinegar always made a rewarding snack, even if the curly bits were somewhat rubbery.

Number Six Canadian Terrace was located so close to the school that while I lived in that cottage I was able to go home every dinner time. When we moved to Number Nine Hartland Road my heading all the way home for dinner was a less practical proposition. Still, since Gran and Granfer remained at Number Seven Canadian Terrace I could go to them at dinner time so the problem was solved. It meant that during my days as a pupil at the Port Isaac County Primary school I didn't have to partake of school dinners in the way that other pupils whose homes were located further away than Canadian Terrace had to do. The best of it was the assurance that I didn't have to eat things cooked by people with whom I wasn't familiar.

My luck ran out in 1950 when, as a result of passing the so-called "eleven-plus" examination I began attending the Sir James Smith's Grammar School at Camelford. It was then that my ability to go home for dinner expired totally, and I was condemned, for the first time ever, to take school dinners. To add insult to injury, at Camelford Grammar School we were required to refer to dinner as "lunch".

As was the case back at home, so (and yea even more so) stood the CGS mandate that servings of lunch must be all eaten up, right down to the very last scrap. The practice of plate licking was frowned on, although in the light of the prevailing fare, the motivation for me to set tongue to plate was rarely pronounced.

To ensure that the order for total consumption was obeyed without question at all times, an invigilating teacher paced up and down the aisle that separated the twin rows of school canteen tables in the manner of a prison camp guard. The return of uneaten food to the kitchen was not an option that the invigilators, and more importantly the headmaster Mr K.A. ("Kayay") Sprayson, were prepared to countenance.

The nature and origin of the dinner-time food that we had at home generally carried little of mystery about it, but the dishes that emerged from the CGS kitchen at lunch time appeared as often as not to be bounded in a fog of doubt not only as to what ingredients they contained but also as to who had managed to make such a mess of them.

The way the lunch system worked was that there were two assigned sittings of half an hour each in duration, one for the girls and one for the boys. The canteen, the kitchen and, incidentally, the adjoining fourth-form classroom, were set apart from, and at a lower level than, the main body of the school. These directly linked facilities for cooking, dining and either learning or wasting time were installed in a long single-floored prefabricated building. The tables were lined up in two rows in the canteen, their ends abutting against the two sidewalls with an open aisle in between. Nine pupils sat at a table, four on each flank and one at the head. Tables were assigned to and held by those who sat at them in what seemed to be perpetuity or until a pupil left school, whichever came sooner.

A sixth-former, normally a prefect, sat at the head of each table in nominal charge and bearing responsibility for keeping the flankers in order. If ever the table head's commission appeared to be failing, the invigilating teacher stepped in to lend a hand in enforcing the cause.

Every dispute that occurred at the table at which I sat related

278

to food and the fair apportionment of the same.

Prior to food being served, all of those present in the canteen were required to stand and simulate an attitude of reverence while someone, generally the invigilator of the day, said grace. "For what we are about to receive, may the Lord make us truly thankful." Even the Lord couldn't manage to make me thankful for some of the things we were about to receive, I thought.

The meal on offer was delivered to the tables from the kitchen, contained in as many or as few receptacles as were necessary to respectively satisfy the variety of the fare or more likely the dearth of the same. A stack of nine empty plates accompanied the largesse. All that seemed to be lacking was an appearance by Mr Wackford Squeers to exclaim, "Here's richness!"

It was the task of the table heads and the pairs of acolytes appointed as servers, who were seated to the immediate left and right of the head at the top of the table, to dish the food out in equal shares onto the nine plates and to pass the first six of these down to those occupying their table's nether echelons. The servers were, not to put too fine a point on it, pupils whose expertise in the art of what we called asshole creeping had won the table head's favour in a way that all the others at the table had not. Table heads and servers formed an Orwellian Big Brother triumvirate capable of wielding tyrannical power over the remaining six. When the lunch was not nice, these three collaborators sent the largest portions of it down the table, and when it was good they served the greater part of it to themselves.

In the regions of the six, strength and seniority counted for everything. The process of the strong seizing desirable morsels of food from the plates of the weak, and forcibly transferring the more repulsive items from their own plates back in return, was well established. The brunt of the action was borne by the pair who sat with shoulders up to the wall right down at the table bottoms. They were always the runts of the bunch and least able to retaliate.

There were times when lunch offerings were so vile that even I was not able to bolt them down my open throat for fear that I would gag them back up again. It was then that I was in trouble with the invigilator for returning food that incorporated not only my own serving, but also the additions to it that at least a couple others had dumped on my plate. The solution to the problem came along just as accidentally and definitively as many brilliant solutions tended to do.

It so happened on that fateful day that lunch, the ever-popular sausage roll with boiled potatoes, was good for once, thereby opening the opportunity for bigger boys to take as much as possible of it away from the plates of smaller boys.

I was then a humble first-former seated down at the bottom of the table against one wall. Directly across the table from me was a second-former named Bob Pethick, a little red-haired boy who hailed from Camelford. In the next seat up on Bob's side was David Callaway from St Teath. David, known as "Joe", was also a second-former, but was a lot bigger than Bob. As might be expected from someone who came from St Teath, Joe's table manners lacked refinement. His relative size set no bar on his grabbing at anything that he liked from either Bob's plate or mine or both, which was what he did on the day in question.

Bob was obviously miffed by Joe's predatory tactics and attempted to retrieve his stolen sausage roll. Joe caught hold of Bob's questing right arm with both of his hands. Bob pulled back with as much strength as he could muster to get his arm free. Joe suddenly let go. Bob's arm flipped back like a released piece of stretched knicker elastic. His elbow struck the canteen wall at high speed. Fortunately for Bob's elbow, prefabrication standards ensured that the canteen wall was not made of stern stuff. His elbow penetrated what was no more than fibreboard sheeting, creating a hole about four inches across and pushing a flap of the fibreboard, as if it was hinged at the top, into the hollow that lay between it and the rather more solid outer wall of the canteen.

To begin with, Bob, Joe and I were appropriately horrified, not so much by the damage that was caused as by the thoughts of the formal retribution by Kayay that might follow. However, Bob discovered that if he inserted a couple of fingers under the flap that he had created it was possible to pull the flap back so as to close the hole effectively enough to make the break lines almost invisible.

As neither the invigilator nor the table head and his serving cronies appeared to have witnessed the damage-causing incident, all engrossed as they were in working their way through disproportionately large heaps of boiled tetties and sausage rolls, we decided that there was no need to let them know about it.

It was not certain who among those of us at the bottom of the table first had the idea of employing the cavity behind the hole in the wall to dispose of food that we didn't like. When it arrived, the idea was reckoned to have sprung from no more or no less than a stroke of genius, justifying a shining light bulb to appear above our collective heads.

For a while, we were decorous about reopening the hole in the wall. The flap was eased back and a few spoonfuls of offensive grub were clandestinely put through the hole for consignment to the dark oblivion below. The flap was then fingered shut again, and all was well with the world.

Following a period of using the hole in the wall to get rid of the worst elements of lunches, all caution was thrown to the wind. The great leap forward was taken during what felt like an endless sequence of lunches consisting of wafer thin, ultra-fat beef served with lumpy mashed tetties swimming in a kind of gravy redolent of the scientific truth that oil and water did not mix. That menu was delivered to us day after day after day, and day after day after day the condemned ingredients went wholesale into the hole in the wall.

There appeared to be no limit to the space available in the wall's cavity to hold the rejected commodities. We were inclined to believe that sides of beef, buckets of gravy, hundredweights of tetties, and fields of over-boiled greens went in through the hole that Bob made.

I liked to think that there was a co-operative rat down in the cavity that was more truly thankful than we were for what he was about to receive. He received what we provided, ate it up, and did us a favour in being the critical factor to guarantee that the hole-in-the-wall disposal scheme went undiscovered by the invigilators.

# 15

# Messing About in Boats

O hear us when we cry to Thee
For those in peril on the sea.

William Whiting (1825–1878)
"Eternal Father Strong to Save"

A FEW BOYS were proud owners of model yachts. One or two of these miniature craft were so well designed that anyone could be forgiven for thinking that the only thing separating them from true perfection was the absence of a tiny effigy of Mr George Brown to place on their respective foredecks.

Sometimes model yachts were brought down by their owners to the harbour for sailing to and fro across the barely ruffled Long Pool, provided the keels didn't get fouled on one or another of the reef-like summits of crab and lobster store pots standing in the way.

Such vessels weren't sailed out in the open waters of the harbour where the ever-present possibility of a loss aided by a stray breeze posed much too great a risk for their owners to envisage taking.

As far as craft of any size whatsoever in the harbour were concerned, the harbour was the precinct of Port Isaac's fishing fleet and homemade models commemorating the same. Quite a lot of us possessed at least one model fishing boat constructed out of either old tin cans or chunks of cork

A tin boat was made from one or more flattened-out cans,

carefully seamed together and beat into the requisite shape via the skilful application of a hammer. Stable buoyancy of a tin boat was a function of the owners' expertise in distributing shingle or lead ballast along the inner keel.

A cork boat was sculpted by clasp knife from a single piece of stray cork that, as often as not, was jetsam picked up by a beachcomber following a storm. Lengths of straight withy shoved into the deck of a cork boat made as fine a set of masts as could be imagined.

—

The fishing boats that inspired the artisanal tin and cork flotilla lay at their familiar tracery of moorings in the harbour. I never actually counted how many fishing boats there were altogether – there must have been at least a dozen and perhaps as many as a score.

A fishing boat was formally identified by a unique registration, issued over in Padstow and consisting of three consecutive numbers preceded by the letters "PW". The registration was grandly painted on one flank of the top front of the bow and again on the stern below the boat's proper name.

Some fishing boats took their proper names from members of the distaff side of the owner's family – as in the case of the *Winifred* (better known as the *Winnie*), the *Kate*, and the *Amanda*. Other names favoured more esoteric (not to say exoteric) predilections from the mind of the owner, such as the *Willing Boys*, the *Bluenose*, the *Why Not* and the *Maple Leaf*. Still others, like the *Hope*, the *Dawn* and the *Gleaner*, appeared to embody names searching for unrequited dreams.

—

The *Maple Leaf* was the property of Mr Anthony Provis, Port Isaac's harbourmaster. Originally a deep-sea merchant vessel's lifeboat, possibly Canadian, she had had a difficult history.

One day during the waning stages of the war she appeared drifting and bobbing around out in the Bay as a barnacle-infested

284

half-sunk waterlogged hulk. She was picked up and towed into the harbour as salvage. Anthony must have recognised quality lying beneath the superficial manifestations of disaster-wrought damage. He rebuilt and refurbished the wreck, gave her a healthy green and black painted trim, christened her *Maple Leaf* and took her back to sea as a fishing boat.

Naturally enough there was no shortage of local Jeremiahs ready by force of habit to declare at either the drop of a sweat-stained flat cap or the wave of a hand-rolled fag that the *Maple Leaf* was certain to bring bad luck down on Anthony. Dismal prophecies had the merit of often being self-fulfilling, although in the case of the *Maple Leaf* the alarmists were proved wrong.

The transformation of the *Maple Leaf* was carried out by applying design criteria consistent with the standard appearance of the members of the fleet of fishing boats that she joined. The fundamental elements featured an open-planked deck; an inbuilt auxiliary engine housed beneath a hatch in the decking; a heavy, iron-shod wooden tiller at the stern, manipulated by a long and impressively stout handle slotted through the tiller's head; and a single mast and outrigger at the back on which a triangular canvas sail could be raised.

In order to guarantee that forward momentum could be maintained at sea under the rare conditions of a lack of wind or of either the absence of an engine or a breakdown of the same, all fishing boats carried a pair of heavy wooden oars on board. If use of the oars was required, they were set in place amidships, each oar mounted on a swivelling metal rowlock. A protective sleeve of hard leather covered the section of oar nestling in a rowlock.

By virtue of muscle and a touch of sheer willpower, an engineless fishing boat could be rowed (or "pulled") out through the Awn to pick up the wind beyond Lobber Point. Later on, or if the Aeolian zephyrs failed to oblige, she could be pulled back into the harbour again in the same way.

The fishing boat *Bluenose* was owned and worked by a Mr William Brown, who was distinguished from his namesake Mr Bill Pink Brown by being known to all and sundry as Billy Pompom. Billy Pompom was short, rotund and jolly, a comfortable and singularly good-humoured man in a true Pickwickian sense.

Billy Pompom lived in a neatly maintained, white trimmed bungalow located near the top of Dolphin Street, almost (but not quite) under the shadow of Chicago House above, and itself overshadowing the residence of Jack and Phoebe Short below.

In carol-singing season we knew that Billy Pompom was usually good for handing over a silver coin of the realm when we knocked at his door and gave him one of our faltering renditions of alleged Christmas cheer. Holding our recompense in his hand, Billy Pompom stood on his doorstep facing us and recited, "I had a little donkey, I fed it on grass, and if he wouldn't eat it, I'd stick it up his____". This ritual demanded that we should provide the final missing word before we could be paid. We did it in tones that were much more eager and harmonic than those that characterised the recently massacred carol.

If Billy Pompom was truly a man apart, so too was the *Bluenose* a boat apart. She incorporated a mould-breaking innovation of a box-like wheelhouse cum bridge on her superstructure – a feature implying a degree of comfort on the high seas that no other boat of the fishing fleet possessed. As if extreme exposure to all winds and weathers was what fishing was about, many fishermen were not backward in coming forward to deride the soft conditions within Billy Pompom's wheelhouse on the *Bluenose*, which they nicknamed the "Nobby Clark".

Within the fleet the *Bluenose* was second in size only to the *Winnie*. That alone offered good reason for the skippers of smaller boats to try and undermine Billy Pompom.

The skipper of the *Winnie* was Mr Tom Brown's son Harold. Nibs ('tis a matter hov) Brown was the *Winnie*'s first mate. The great size of the *Winnie* determined that she required three men to crew her (the third being yet another of Harold's uncles drawn from the prolific ranks of the Brown family) rather than the two-man crew that was customary in the remainder of the fleet.

—

Excluding the *Winnie* and the *Bluenose*, the average dimensions of a Port Isaac fishing boat were in the order of twenty feet long and six feet broad, with six feet of draught separating the keel from the gunwales. Although such boats were normally heavily tarred from the keel up to a level where a plimsoll line might have been painted but wasn't, they tended to be more colourfully adorned on their respective superstructures.

The ballast consisted of sea-rounded boulders and rust-flaking pigs of iron. A hand-pump was used to evacuate the bilge water, if the term "water" could genuinely be used to characterise the thin gruel of discoloured oily liquid that the leather-washer bilge pumps discharged with a satisfied slurp each time the pump handle was raised. The ensuing effluent spread like a halo around the hulls when the tide raised them on their moorings, bleeding outwards in an iridescent film sequin-spangled with fish scales and streaked with filaments of viscous slime, the origin of which was best not thought about.

Every fishing boat was figuratively joined at the hip to a small dingy or "punt" employed by the crew either for facilitating water-borne access around the harbour or for ferrying gear and the day's catch between boat and shoreline when the tide was in. A punt was traditionally painted in colours that matched its parent boat. When the parent boat was out at sea, its punt was generally left tied by a painter to the boat's mooring buoy. Some of the fishermen were, however, not unwilling, as an alternative to mooring, to hand their punts over to the control of groups of boys, who then "kept" the punt within the confines of the harbour for the duration of the time when the fishing boat was out in the Bay.

The rules for keeping a punt were simple enough and always

followed in spirit if not in substance. Appointed keepers of punts were honour-bound to stay clear of the rocky edges of the harbour; to remain well inside the breakwaters; and, when on board, to behave with due decorum.

A punt was equipped with at least one oar, although occasionally there were two oars available with a pair of removable metal rowlocks for pulling. The oars were by no means sleek and varnished specimens of the carpenter's art but tended to be solid, heavy-bladed (and even slightly waterlogged) chunks of worn timber. They were rounded, rough and splintery, planed or whittled down at one end to give the semblance of a moderately flat blade, and tapered to provide a manageable handle at the other end. The handle was as shiny as were the callouses on the hands that frequently used it. The section of punt oar fitting the rowlocks was again girt about with a sturdy flap of leather, riveted to the body of the oar with copper studs.

Punts were rarely pulled around inside the harbour. By preference they were propelled by "sculling", a technique employing a single oar set out over the mid-point of the stern in a half moon-shaped, brass-rimmed rowlock-like groove. A figure-of-eight motion was manually applied at the handle of the oar for transfer down to the blade, by virtue of which action the punt was impelled to make way.

Sculling could be carried out either using two hands with the sculler facing backwards or with one hand (requiring much more skill) with the sculler looking forward and, rather importantly, able to see where he was going. Most fishermen were very expert scullers, able to execute all kinds of rapid manoeuvres, using a single wrist action so finely precise as to be almost imperceptible to the eye.

An inherent disadvantage for us in keeping a punt in the harbour was that we were subject to steady observation by lounging habitués (and sons of the same) on the Town Platt as well as on the steps leading up to the harbourmaster's office on top of

Pawlyn's cellars. Transgression of punt-keeping rules of conduct was almost certain to be spotted and reported without delay to the punt's owner by one or other of the shore-bound characters who paced the Town Platt beat with metronomic intensity.

Mr Jack Short, yet again failing to disguise his distaste for me, employed his characteristically sanctimonious ire to dress me down for committing the offence of standing on what he called the "thot" of a punt that I was helping to keep. Jack, for whom the quality of mercy was not unstrained, heaved the word "thot" at me so many times in the course of his tirade that it branded itself on my mind.

It was my brother, who was far better versed than me in the technicalities of keeping a punt, who told me that a "thot" was the plank crossing the punt amidships on which a keeper could seat himself if he wanted to pull with two oars. Perhaps Jack intended to say "thwart" to me. On the other hand I knew that Jack was a man who thought himself incapable of being thwarted.

However, had he been directing his customarily miserable old bugger's evil eye towards the harbour on one particular day, Jack would have discovered sounder grounds for bringing me to task. These grounds related to an incident that took place when I was the assigned keeper for the punt belonging to the *Maple Leaf*.

A spell of highly energetic sculling followed by an acutely sharp turn for which I used the *Maple Leaf* punt's oar as a tiller resulted in the oar sundering in two at the outer rim of the stern rowlock. The crack, as the top and bottom halves of the oar parted company with each other at the lower limit of the leather sleeve, echoed off the face of Lobber cliff. Such satisfaction as was generated by the reverberating echo was tempered by the realisation that on the return of the *Maple Leaf* to the harbour Mr Anthony Provis would be chasing after me, seeking his pound of flesh.

The portion of the oar bearing the rudimentary blade floated away from the punt, well out of reach. The punt was adrift. It suddenly dawned on me that an expression I heard mentioned by a customer in William John's barber's shop about his being up shit creek without a paddle suited my existing circumstances very well.

I seized up a little grapnel-like anchor lying on the floor of the punt (underneath the thot) and cast it onto the waters with the intention of arresting the slow and yet inexorable movement of the powerless craft on an ebbing tide in the direction of the gap between the breakwaters. Unfortunately the anchor was not fastened to a painter. The anchor made a nice splash before it headed unconstrained into the depths.

The punt floated on. I was lucky in managing to grab hold of the outer mooring rope of one of the few fishing boats remaining in the harbour, from which point of comparative security I dragged the punt back to the beach, hand over hand along the outer mooring, the gunwale of the moored fishing boat and then the inner mooring. At the end there were enough ha'porths of tar on my hands with which to spoil several ships.

I recovered the discarded anchor from where it lay on the harbour floor once the tide went out and exposed it. The piece of broken oar headed out into the Bay and was never seen again. Anthony's reaction was exactly as predicted. He chased me with a stick in his hand out of the harbour, up Fore Street as far as the Pentice and then onwards into Rose Hill to reach a point adjacent to Mr John Neal's great fig tree.

There, when it dawned on him that he wasn't going to catch me, Anthony hurled his stick over a gate and cast his final imprecations at my retreating back. I was not permitted to either keep or set foot in the *Maple Leaf*'s punt again.

---

The fishing boat moorings were, as I knew only too well, thickly tarred, heavy-duty ropes running from the foot of the Town Platt to a position just short of the eastern breakwater. Seen from the top of Lobber cliff when the tide was out, the mooring ropes looked like lines drawn on the page of a school exercise book by a pupil with a shaky hand.

Each end of a mooring rope was expertly spliced onto a majestically heavy, impeccably secured and solidly anchored chain traversing the harbour from side to side. On entering the harbour when the tide was in, a crew member of a fishing boat picked up the mooring rope with the help of a "gaff", a sturdy stick with a wicked-looking shark or conger hook bound to one end of it. The gaff hooked the cork or hollow metal sphere marker buoy that was attached to the mooring rope by a thin line. By hand-over-hand retrieval of the thin line the mooring rope was raised up. A ragged square of rotting sail or tarpaulin tacked onto the top of a withy stick mounted on the buoy performed the function of a flag drawing attention to the buoy's location.

———

The full might of the Port Isaac fishing fleet bobbed prettily at the moorings. In deference to their relative size, the *Winnie* and the *Bluenose* were moored out at the head of the fleet. The *Winnie*, as suited the status of an undeclared flagship, was the vanguard. As the newcomer to the fleet, the *Maple Leaf* was assigned to the rear.

The rank and file of the fleet were moored in between the *Winnie* and the *Maple Leaf*. Prominent among these, all in black and white trim, were Mr Frank Rowe's *Kate*, Mr John Glover's *Amanda*, and Mr Sammy Dyer Thomas's *Boy Terry*.

A welcome splash of colour blossomed from the *Lilla*, painted yellow and red. These were the incidental colours of the Liberal Party, although it was likely that the colourfully named Mr Bill "Pink" Brown, the skipper of the *Lilla*, never intended to impose any politically inspired theme on his boat.

Bill Pink's crewman on the *Lilla* was his brother-in-law Mr Harry ("'Arr") Oaten. 'Arr's mission in life was reckoned by observers to be vested in saying nothing about any one alive that could be misconstrued as complimentary. However, 'Arr was not afflicted with the sour edge of causticity personified by a man like Mr Jack Short, nor did 'Arr carry in his heart any shred of the overt paranoia that typified Mr Jim Honey's inimical assault on what Jim referred to as the "bweddy buggos" of the village, parish and world at large.

'Arr was certainly well able to summon up fits of rage, but he was not of a violent disposition and it was rare, as far as I could judge, to see him even get particularly excited when angry. What was seen with 'Arr was what was got. He was a master curmudgeon and supremely content in his ability to harmlessly denounce or declaim at will at the world around him.

It was 'Arr, in answer to an enquiry by a questing visitor on the empty Town Platt as to where the fishermen were to be found, who advised the said visitor that the fishermen were all "Up to St Endellion". Only the dear departed who were up to St Endellion, whether once benign or malign, were able to rest easy in the certain knowledge that no one, including 'Arr, was likely to speak ill of them. Thinking ill of them was not ruled out of course.

The daily veneer of salutations and meteorological observations passed between regular acquaintances like 'Arr and Jack and Jim and Nibs and so on and so forth covered an understanding that for far less than a ten bob note (even a half a crown would be considered) each would be more than happy to do the other a disservice. The dark roots of mischief-making were supplied by them with far more nourishment than were the green shoots of a helping hand. Such men broke the tenth commandment in an instant on hearing of a neighbour's good fortune and went on to sink themselves into the comfortable cushion of plotting as to how the neighbour could be cut down to size.

As if to make a more conservative blip of colour in the midst of the fleet than the *Lilla* was capable of, a muted blue enhanced the superstructure of the fishing boat *Hope*, mastered by Mr Joey Thomas, known as Granfer Joey. His figure was so rotund that when he was clad in jersey and trousers he resembled an appendage-studded black sphere. Had Granfer Joey fallen over in the act of descending Back Hill he would probably have rolled all the way down to the primary school gate on Fore Street before stopping.

Granfer Joey was grandfather to my friend, and former Green Triangle associate, young Joey Thomas. The Thomas family resided on the left-hand side of New Road in a small terrace of houses (referred to for very good reasons as the "Thomas's Row"), located in between Mr Lansdowne's shoe shop and the ultimately ill-fated Dunoon guesthouse.

Granfer Joey and Gran Thomas (his astringently thin spouse) occupied a galvanised sheet-clad, rusty dull pink-painted cabin set immediately behind the top end of the Thomas's Row. The upper house in the row was where young Joey lived with his father Frankie Joey, his mother Nancy, his slightly younger sister Barbara and his much younger brother Keith.

Mr and Mrs Jack Hail Thomas resided in the middle of the Thomas's Row. Jack Hail was Granfer Joey's brother. Although time's ceaseless river had placed Jack Hail on the wrong side of his days as an active fisherman he remained a Town Platt regular, able to wield a tar brush and to spin yarns as well as anyone. Jack Hail's habit of carrying his personal effects of the day in a bucket slung loosely over one arm as he wended his way down and up between the Thomas's Row and the Town Platt gave due cause for certain of us to chant (from a safe distance behind him of course), "Jack Hail – pissed in a pail!"

The occupants of the lower house of the Thomas's Row were Mr Tommy Tabb and his wife Eliza. It was through marriage to Eliza, who was Granfer Joey's and Jack Hail's sister, that Tommy (known as "Tabber") had won his place in that exclusive Thomas enclave.

Tabber, a grand figure of a man, was extremely tall and blessed with the kind of lantern jaw that stuck out like a gallows arm over any boy looking up at him. He had a beaming countenance, a sunny disposition and could always be relied on for a tolerant word. Men like Tabber were among the salt of the earth.

Granfer Joey stored his fishing gear in the tar-stained, rickety-roofed cellar that opened onto the Wheelhouse side of the foot of the Town Platt. The beach terminated against the ledge along the lower outside wall of his cellar on which elderly fishermen habitually sat to contemplate the prospect of Lobber cliff and the breakwaters, relive past exploits with the comforting aid of chaws of baccy and hover in each other's faces like eager buzzards anticipating prey.

—

At the top right-hand side of the harbour beach the initial few of a conjoined group of a dozen or so fishermen's cellars, fronted by a walkway, leaned against the base of the Golden Lion's front wall and balcony in the manner of pub regulars anxious for opening time to arrive. A steep cobbled alley led up to the Bloody Bones yard and the pub urinal from alongside the lower wall of the first of the cellars.

The line of cellars thus originated continued on its way in a moderately steep ascending curve and in doing so provided ample buttress support not only for the Pentice on Fore Street but also for those who elected to set their elbows on the Pentice wall as a prelude to gossiping the day away. Their outward view from the Pentice took in a comprehensive panorama of the harbour, Roscarrock Hill, Lobber (cliff and field), Khandalla and the allotments. Their reverse view featured no more than the front door to Old Tair Bunt's fruiterer's shop and whoever happened to be passing by at the time.

Thanks to the said ascent of the line of cellars, the foot of the uppermost cellar door stood at a height of at least twenty feet above the level of the beach. All save the uppermost two or three cellar doors in line were screened from the harbour by a thick stone wall about six feet high that marked the beach side of the walkway. Sometimes, great waves broke over the top of the wall without mercy, pouring foamy green cascades down the scuppers of the walkway.

The surface of this protective wall, front and back, was decorated by the ooze of generations of the freshly tarred ropes that were hung on it to dry and cure. The sagging streakiness of congealed ancient tar put me in mind of the Christmas issues of comics, on which the titles so vital to my well-being were draped with symbolic snow, solid and entire at the top, fingering out towards the bottom.

———

Mr John Glover, elder son of the Dolphin Street patriarch Granfer Glover and skipper of the fishing boat *Amanda* (which was often abbreviated to "Manda"), lived in a cottage down in the heart of Middle Street, on to which thoroughfare his front door opened directly. As it was, that didn't matter much since John's cottage was invariably entered by the back door, accessed via a dark ope off to one side of the front door.

John was a true man of character honed by a lifetime of exposure to rough seas and inclement weather. He was a modest man of few words, which was a useful trait in one who existed amidst a clamouring household of large women and big girls over whom he erroneously assumed that he held mastery.

Not only was John as tough as bullock leather but he also looked the part of a man not to be trifled with. His overtly curt manner masked a totally even temperament that enriched the lives of all those who knew him. His reticence overlay a core of achievement, a rock-like integrity, and a sound ethic for the furtherance of meaningful day-to-day industry.

John's clothes were stained, his flat cap slouched and his boots heavily hobnailed. He walked with head angled and eyes slitted, one shoulder down. Hands that might have cracked rocks hung loose at his sides. He bore a stance appropriate to one who was a former champion of Cornish wrestling and who could still throw just about anyone foolish enough to try and match him.

John demonstrated his wrestling prowess in occasional exhibition bouts on Carnival days.

Mrs John Glover, weighty and aproned, emerged only occasionally from the ope leading to the back door of the Glover abode. Although the good looks of her youth had gone the way of several of her teeth, her gentle, giving nature had faded not a whit and endowed her with an aura of well-being.

Harriet, the youngest of the Mr and Mrs John Glover brood of strapping girls, was a pure model for the Glover breed. She was a few years older than me and made a sitting target in the primary school playground when the song, "All the cowboys want to marry Harriet" became popular on the wireless. Much to Harriet's fury, the song was regularly sung to her the instant she appeared in view – "All the cowboys want to marry Harriet! 'Cos Harriet's handy with a lariat! But Harriet doesn't want to marry yet! She's having too much fun!"

Harriet was equipped with muscular arms, and more than one of us who chose to sing to her received the unwelcome award of a thump from one or other of those weapons of offence if we let Harriet get too close. Any one who had the misfortune to be once smitten by Harriet was always twice shy thereafter.

In one celebrated year, Harriet was elected to the position of Port Isaac Carnival Queen following a ballot of the audience packing the Temperance Hall for the occasion. The whole Glover family and a host of its near relations were sown claque-like through the auditorium, a fact that made the eventual outcome of the vote no major surprise. The result was what counted, and Harriet carried the role off well enough, even though she looked as if she would have been more at home in the turret of a tank than she did being towed around on the Carnival Queen's float.

The availability of strong tea was a constant in the John Glover household, intended as much for the sustenance of visitors as for suiting the demands of *bona fide* family members. The time-saving habit of the returned master of the house after fishing excursions in the *Amanda* was to skip the unnecessary step of pouring tea into a cup, and instead to swig the brew directly from the spout of the teapot. The normal understanding behind the shortcut was that the contents of the teapot would be at best lukewarm.

Harriet entered the family home one day and, being nothing if not a dedicated follower of her father's fashion, lifted the teapot and sucked down a hard draught of freshly made tea at a temperature not far removed from boiling point. It said something for the hardiness of the Glover constitution that Harriet survived her trial by liquid fire and went on to conquer the equal challenge of becoming a successful Carnival Queen.

As a rewardingly lucrative sideline to fishing during the summer months, the *Amanda*, in common with a number of other boats of the fishing fleet, took parties of visitors on pleasure trips out into the Bay. The visitors were assured of catching a few mackerel and an odd pollock while admiring the perspective of the ruggedly scenic coastline.

On a fine summer morning the *Amanda* headed out through the Awn for a trip down along the Bay in the direction of Port Quin with a group of paying visitors on board. Mr Leslie ("Les") Honey, the father of my friend Leonard ("Buh") Honey, was skipper for the day. John Glover remained ashore. The *Amanda* took her punt on tow, perhaps to facilitate putting passengers ashore on Varley Sands in the lee of Varley Head.

In the course of the morning the sky clouded over quite abruptly, and with the arrival of the clouds the wind picked up and rose rapidly to near gale proportions. The sudden deterioration of the weather eliminated the possibility of a timely warning being gleaned from a perusal of the big barometer in the front wall of Pawlyn's cellars. The sea surged in huge waves under the running Atlantic swell. The Bay was a foam-wracked torment. The recently placid Awn turned into a crashing welter of white water.

The *Amanda* was caught out by the storm. News spread with the kind of alacrity that only a local misfortune could guarantee. A large crowd gathered along the cliff path leading towards Mr Hillson's house to observe (and in more than a few cases to revel in) the unfolding drama. It was a spectacle as good as anything seen on Friday night at the Rivoli. Many others, equally anxious to watch the fun, flocked to the top of Lobber field.

Les took the *Amanda* in under the lee of Varley Head where the sea was relatively less turbulent, intending to wait for the torment to ease. The storm, however, had other ideas and chose to intensify its fury. Vicious squalls of rain, one after the other, drove across the Bay like dark curtains.

With no apparent let-up to the tempest by early afternoon, Les must have decided that there was no alternative open to him other than that the *Amanda* should make a run for home.

The *Amanda* emerged from the relative shelter of Varley Head to make her crossing to Lobber Point and the Awn, violently pitching and rolling, now dropping out of sight into the back trough of a massive wave, now cresting and hanging for an instant on the crown of another wave prior to rocketing down the front slope. There were few among the onlookers ready to place a bet that the *Amanda* would stay the course.

Clearing Lobber Point and virtually enveloped in driving spray, Les lined the *Amanda* up on the tossing gap between the eastern and western breakwaters, and went for the goal. In my understanding, Les, allegedly a work-shy character with, like his brother Tom, a well-developed appreciation for a fag and a pint, was no doubt a long way removed from being a praying man, although it was possible that his predicament might have given him the motivation to become one.

The crowds lining the cliffs looked on as the *Amanda* plummeted through the Awn, now down in frighteningly deep wave-bound pits and then up on the curling crests, listing over at angles that seemed impossible to recover from until, to the accompaniment of resounding cheers, she burst through to reach the inner harbour and security.

Les's heroic feat probably marked his greatest moment in a life hitherto noted more for some of the low points that it was reported to have plumbed. The visitors were safe, although it was not known how many of them needed to change their underclothes as an immediate consequence of the experience.

The *Amanda* was also in sound shape, although in the pounding passage through the Awn her punt had fared less well by breaking free from its towrope. The punt had taken in a lot of water, but was still afloat and could be seen out in the stormy Bay being slung around as randomly as if it were a model boat made of cork.

John Glover, until that moment a helpless shore-bound spectator to the drama, then showed his mettle. Once Les and the visitors had disembarked, John single-handedly took the *Amanda* out again, running the terrifying gauntlet of the storm-lashed Awn. He retrieved the punt and brought both it and the *Amanda* back into harbour again.

Yea, verily was John a man forged of the finest steel.

*Rough seas in the Awn*

# 16

# Horses for Courses

*As tho' again — yea, even once again,*
*We should rewelcome to our stewardship*
*The rider with the loose-flung bridle-rein*
*And chance-plucked twig for whip.*

Rudyard Kipling (1865–1936)
"Rhodes Memorial, Table Mountain"

THE RESIDENCE OF Mr Frank Eade was a minuscule affair located in the middle of Middle Street. Frank lived alone. His front door stood two up from the John Glover family home and almost exactly the same number down from Mr Tom Saundry's shop adjacent to the Lake flush gate.

Frank was accustomed to sally furtively forth from his abode as the clock hands crawled towards that blessed moment (morning or evening it was all the same to Frank), when opening time at the Golden Lion would be declared. His clothes were often clean and his manners were generally gentlemanly.

Frank's appropriately hangdog face sagged around a lugubrious mouth in which a steady succession of fags held pride of place. He sidled towards his appointments with a waiting pint or two up in Harry Irons' public bar; his shoulders slouched in concentrated intent as he pored over the racing pages of his daily newspaper on the way.

Frank was getting on in years, but he wasn't so old that he could avoid being counted as one of the ranks of local men with exclusive access to dictionaries that didn't feature the word

301

"work" inside the covers. His reputation as an alleged waster (a word that was indeed included under the "W" section of Frank's personal lexicon) had taken him real effort to achieve. However, within the pantheon of Port Isaac's dedicated fellowship of idlers, Frank's position was fairly unique inasmuch as he exhibited no pretensions to appear to be anything other than what he was. Frank could take true pride in maintaining his status as an unabashed loafer. All in all, Frank merited respect.

Quite how he managed the means to get hold of what seemed to be an unfailing personal supply of fags and beer was an open question, particularly since the horse-racing bets that he placed so regularly they might have been subject to clockwork, tended to favour a succession of also-rans. The village's elite club of followers of form related to the sport of kings were advantaged by two local covert bookies. Frank succeeded without harming anyone, and that was all that was important.

Of course, for all any of us knew, Frank might have been submitting his gee-gee bets as entirely conventional and legal transactions with a nationally recognised bookie such as Mr William Hill. That kind of betting was carried out by post, with the stake money in the form of a postal order enclosed in a sealed envelope formally addressed to Mr Hill.

The problem with postal betting was that a postal order could only be bought at the Post Office, in which establishment the postmistress Miss Jinny Hills, well aware of what the postal order was required for, would be disinclined to cast an approving eye on its purchaser.

My father, in the mould of Frank, with whom for a time he enjoyed a crony-like relationship based on common tastes specific to the public bar of the Golden Lion, was a committed student of racing form. Now and then my father was lucky enough to win a little (but only a little) money with one of his bets. No winnings ever seemed to be grandiose enough to provide a material difference to our way of life at home, and at best they made no more than a temporary dent in the long-term cumulative losses to the bookies that my father incurred.

He found a racing-form debating partner in the person of the bedridden Mr Donald "Kenty" Kent when we moved up to Hartland Road and became near neighbours of Kenty and his mother, the leathery Em. Apart from their shared skills in picking non-winners, Kenty and my father had in common the contraction of TB during wartime submarine service.

Kenty frequently swept the formbook aside and allocated his couple of bob of stake money to no-hopers that he fancied the names of. He referred to a horse named Socrates as "Sock Scratch". If Sock Scratch ever won a race, I didn't hear about it.

My father and Kenty instructed me to purchase for their joint delectation a copy of the *Sporting Life Guide*, a weekly newspaper dedicated to horse-racing pursuits, both on the flat and over the sticks in season. That celebrated journal, possibly as a consequence of Port Isaac's prevailing downtown chapel mind set, was not available on Mrs Rowe's newsagent's counter.

However, the *Sporting Life Guide* was known to be on sale at Batten's, a more enlightened news-vending establishment in Camelford. Since at the time of the instruction I was a junior pupil at Sir James Smith's Grammar School, also located in Camelford, I was thereby well enabled to seek out and discover the elusive publication.

Unlike Kenty, who in order to join the Navy at the commencement of the recent war had declared himself to be a few years older than the under-aged youth that he actually was, I found that I wasn't able to falsify my age up to the point at which I could get my hands on a copy of the *Sporting Life Guide*. Prior to ordering me out of his shop, Mr Batten informed me, in tones as firm as they were scathing, that the *Sporting Life Guide* was intended for the consumption of adults only. Whether or not any of the said adults could read was immaterial to Mr Batten.

The one certainty to emerge from this debacle was that with

or without the *Sporting Life Guide* to point the way, my father and Kenty were always destined to continue to invest their coins in the bookies' account.

My mother once had a four-horse accumulator bet come up with Mr William Hill. On the basis of starting prices her anticipated winnings seemed to be an absolute fortune for us, calculated by my mother at three hundred and eighty pounds. Mr William Hill then sent my mother a letter in which he drew her attention to a small-print clause in his regulations governing postal betting which permitted him to make a calculation of his own on how much money should be paid out. He ultimately forwarded the sum of eighty pounds to my mother. Eighty quid was still not bad as a win and was enough to draw a couple of begging letters to my mother into its wake.

———

Mr William Hill's competition in Port Isaac, availed of by true betting men like my father, Kenty, Frank and a veritable host of others, was incorporated, quite literally, in the closed hands of two gentlemen whose respective Christian names were Jack and Jack.

One of this pair of eminent village worthies was Mr Jack Hicks, the Son in the equation of J. N. Hicks & Son Family Butchers. The other was Mr Jack Hobbs, an officer in the Port Isaac branch of HM Coastguard. This pair of Jacks plied their clandestine bookmaking activities so independently of one another that to all intents and purposes neither might have known if the other was drawing to a full house or was about to fold.

In order to place a bet with one or other of the two Jacks, the procedure to be followed was simplicity itself. Details, specifying the date, race meeting, time of race, horse's name, value of stake and intention (win or each-way, double or treble or whatever) were written out (usually with a blunt pencil, perhaps of the well-known Delabole, otherwise indelible, variety) on a small square of paper. The square of paper was then wrapped tightly around the stake money (strictly cash terms), and the small package was taken, clutched tightly in a fist, to the back door of the Jack selected to receive it.

I made bookie runs for my father, mother and Kenty many times, to place packaged bets as surreptitiously as possible into the ready hands of the particular Jack who appeared at the door following my knock. Few if any words were exchanged during the transactions.

If the bet brought in a winner, Jack (or Jack) paid out the winnings in full. If (as was more normal) the selected horses achieved neither wins nor places, Jack (or Jack) would pocket the stake and be so much the richer.

The one significant difference between the two Jacks in their part-time roles as secretive bookies was that Mr Jack Hicks, unlike Mr Jack Hobbs, could probably afford to pay up if an unexpected ace, not to mention a joker, was dealt to him.

Jack Hobbs took a large accumulator bet one day and, as I heard the story from my mother, omitted to lay off the risk. Each of the selected horses was first past the post. Jack was unable to honour the snowball of winnings. The outcome was unfortunate, the more so because all ensuing acrimony had (of necessity) to be indulged in with due regard to the lack of legality in the transaction. I never heard whether or not this Jack ultimately settled his obligations, as rumours relating to the sad affair emerged only after he disappeared from the parish in an alleged midnight flit undertaken without ceremony.

Mr Jack Hobbs was a man that I liked very much. In all my bet-clutching visits to his New Coastguard Station back door I found him to be quiet, steady and kindly. On more than a few occasions he gave me a threepenny bit when I handed a bet over.

Mrs Jack Hobbs was a lady that I also admired. She chose to remain in Port Isaac after her husband went away. Mrs Jack Hobbs' most distinctive characteristic was that she spoke through her nose. Until I got to understand her manner of speech she always sounded to me as if she was talking in a foreign language.

The shop premises of J. N. Hicks & Son Family Butchers (well established and highly proficient in the practice of butchery) stood at the back of an expanse of grass located behind a weathered cement block wall lining the elbow of lower New Road's sweeping bend. The grass was as successful in its endeavours to be recognised as a lawn as were both the aspirations of Mr J. N. Hicks and his Son (respectively John and of course Jack) to be acknowledged as gentlemen and the state of the internal facilities of their butcher's shop to be held up to scrutiny as being more pristine than Lanson jail.

John and Jack were known as men of means both on and off the turf in spite of their attempts to convince the restricted world in which they moved that they were not. Their protestations of impecuniousness fell on deaf ears, sounding like hollow pretensions. The pair of them always seemed to me to be most anxious to be tarred with the kind of respect that only money could buy.

They did their best to conceal the trappings of wealth behind the grime of their domestic facade, yet since their customers all knew that John and Jack had money and John and Jack knew that their customers knew that they had money that didn't mean anything. No kind of veneer could cover the fact that Jack and John were cut and assembled from rough wood. As men, they were less than couth – "the one so bad as the other" as the expression went. The public knowledge that they had money permitted them to make various breaches of acceptable social conduct, breaches that wouldn't have been tolerated had they come from less well off members of the general public.

If John and Jack's adherence to the rules of etiquette was not always what it should have been, the shortfalls were mostly glossed over and ignored by their customers who either owed them money or had designs on acquiring a piece of meat outside the limits set by a ration book.

Incidences of coarseness of language, crudeness of conduct or unkemptness of dress on the part of John and Jack, whether in or out of the butcher's shop, were dismissed from threat of censure by those whom such incidences affected with comments such as, "'Tis only John!" or "Damn the old Jack!"

John and Jack were beefy types, in keeping with their profession. They were both of no more than medium height, which served to accent what could have been construed as hints of corpulence. Their features were florid. In his vanguard Jack bore a big-bellied tribute to a succession of pints without number consumed in a galaxy of north Cornish public hostelries. John exhibited the facial characteristics and thrusting whiskery jaw of Desperate Dan from the *Dandy*.

The butcher's shop and associated cold room occupied one half of the ground floor of the house in which John and Jack resided. On the left-hand flank of the shop, one or two sides of meat hung suspended on evil-looking steel hooks. A few shiny little circles of occasionally fresh, many such of recently congealed and many more of long-since hardened blood spotted the tiled floor beneath. An overall patina of grease covered many of the self-same tiles. In those places where feet rarely trod, the patina seemed to be building up in the manner of the annual rings of a tree.

At the back of the shop a massive wooden butcher's block stood like a sacrificial altar, the surface of which was endowed with the smoothness of profile of Roughtor and Brown Willy as seen from the top of Poltreworgey Hill. Blood and bone splinters had been battered into the grain of the block via the repetitive imprecision of aim of the razor-edged cleavers that John and Jack used to hack Sunday joints into shape. Errant flecks of beef clung like shrapnel to the walls within range of the block.

Additional traces of indefinable animal products, accompanied by an extensive display of blood stains, transformed the once-white aprons of both John and Jack into gore-spangled banners redolent of the fact that such men were nothing if not masters of their craft.

---

Gran and my mother were regular customers of John and Jack in the context of butchery and, specifically in the case of my mother, for bookmaking needs as well. Their joint view on the characters of the Hicks father and son were consistent with those of the over-sympathetic, "'Tis only Jack (or John)!" brigade.

It fell to my lot, far too often for my liking, to be sent to the butcher's shop on Saturday mornings to collect what purported to be our Sunday joint. It was not only a duty that I did not volunteer for but also one that I had good reason to dread.

It seemed that whenever I arrived at the shop, no matter how much I tried to vary my schedule, it was to find it crowded with simpering, basket-clutching ladies all affecting an air of worldliness which in no way suited them. These ladies made a willing audience for the extended diatribes, far from subtle innuendo and blathering discourse that John ladled out in full measure, and which Jack always did his best to emulate.

The great bugbear for me was that John and Jack, in fronting up to the gathering of ladies in the shop, were ready to engage in any kind of activity other than one that had them actually serving someone. An hour might pass without any respite called to what for me was a Chinese torture-like ordeal by drip of badinage. If I had known what bullshit was, I would certainly have felt myself buried in that commodity both there and then.

Every Saturday a well-worn John and Jack double-act routine of anecdotes and repartee paraded in an all too familiar sequence, much as if it had been pinched from supporting comedians appearing at a canteen somewhere or other on *Workers' Playtime*.

On one particular Saturday morning I was immured in a seemingly interminable monologue from John concerning a lady for whom he went out on a limb to obtain a special cut of meat that she then declined to accept. Why she declined, or what the cut of meat consisted of, or whether the cut came from above or below the counter was not clarified. John declared that he was reduced to appealing to the lady's better nature.

He claimed that he pleaded with her, "Be British, Madam!" On the strength of John's plaintive delivery, I assumed that the lady must have been a foreigner, which went some way to explaining why she might have regarded what John obtained for her as being the unkindest cut of all.

"Be British, Madam!" was, I thought, a most telling catch phrase. It was nearly as good as anything of the kind that I heard on the wireless, and I felt it to be entirely suitable for John to cast directly in the face of double-dealing, unless it was his own.

Given considerably less than half a chance when the shop was groaning (both literally and figuratively) with Saturday morning customers, John and Jack were motivated to break into song. Each was an acceptable soloist in his own right, and together they formed a not altogether displeasing close-harmony duet that was more or less the equal of the sum of its parts. An alleged allegiance to the chapel ensured that they were adept crooners of Sankey-type numbers, although they were not above inserting an occasional popular ballad (as necessary) into the programme to relieve the monotony of what might otherwise have been an overwhelmingly pious repertoire.

Hymn singing in the shop probably provided a conscience-salving substitute for both John and Jack to set against the genuine non-appearance of either at chapel services. Listening to certain of their paeans and knowing something of their characters, I was easily able to imagine that chapel congregations (Wesley and Roscarrock alike) would be unlikely to object too volubly to the pair's absence.

On the other hand, a mighty oak-like chapel association by proxy was firmly set in their midst. Jack's sister Nellie had married that greatly respected true gentleman (and incidental local preacher and Castle Rock fancier) Mr Wesley Blake. The nature of Wesley's thoughts regarding his Hicks association were not known outside the family circle as Wesley was ever a man celebrated for his discretion. At the same time all was not lost, as Wesley and Nelly had a son named Tony (a little older than me) who gave every indication of being a chip off the old butcher's block of his grandfather John and his uncle Jack.

Mrs Jack Hicks was a lovely upstanding lady of refinement. She taught down at the primary school for some time, and it was to my regret that I was never one of her pupils. A glowing rose among thorns, Mrs Jack was a luminary of Roscarrock chapel, where she also taught Sunday school classes. The question, "Why ever did she marry he?" taxed the minds of many of John and Jack's customers, and as far as I knew it was a question that was never answered.

Whenever I was trapped in John and Jack's shop in the company of a host of powdered women by procrastination that for once was not of my own making, the flannel-ridden solos and duets emerging from the mouths of John and Jack ordained in my heart no strength because of mine enemies. Their renditions were far more than mere thieves of my time – they constituted aggravated robbery of too much of my day. Grievous bodily frustration ensued when the false hope that a few ounces of meat (rather than several hundredweights of words) would move in my direction came not to be met. The shadowed valley of the butcher's block lay between us and the meat did not walk in it.

One of John's party-piece solos was the Sunday school ditty, "Hear the pennies dropping". He performed it once in front of Roger and me with his little granddaughter Mary (Jack's elder daughter) in tow to provide an essential touch of theatrical pathos. At an appropriate moment during the show, John reached into one or other of his grease-rimed trouser pockets and withdrew a handful of change that he cast up into the air with a flick of his wrist.

310

We heard not only pennies dropping but also farthings, halfpennies, threepenny bits, tanners, bobs, florins, half-crowns and whatever other coins of the realm were contained in John's pocket on the day. The cash fell ringing and dinging, rolling towards the four corners of the shop.

Mary flitted hither and thither to locate and recover the scattered funds. I suspected that whatever Mary retrieved might be finders-keepers. I wished that we could have joined in. The debris of the butcher's trade that decorated the shop floor served to slow down the trundle of some of the coins and to halt a few others outright for Mary's easy retrieval.

It so happened that our local weekly newspaper, the *Cornish Guardian*, ran a story on the prowess of John and Jack as a butcher's shop duet.

The *Cornish Guardian* was in principle dedicated to publishing rural news items of stunning triviality, regularly reflecting the fact that not much had happened anywhere within its sphere of circulation during the preceding week. It was only on extremely rare occasions that a reportable event of sufficient interest to transcend the St Endellion parish boundary occurred. As a rule, anyone living in Port Isaac wasn't at all interested in stories about what took place in social circles in places such as St Kew and Delabole, and in all fairness vice versa applied as well.

The *Cornish Guardian* was required to walk a very fine line in the process of serving its readership. For the majority of readers the prospect of a ten-mile journey was regarded as an adventure into the interior. The newspaper's circulation figures in the parish were greatly enhanced of course by any report on the appearance of known personalities in court for the purpose of prosecution, especially when the offenders were subsequently handed down improbably punitive sentences by pompous magistrates puffed up by a surfeit of their own self-importance.

On the occasion of reporting on the vocal talents of John and

311

Jack, the *Cornish Guardian* touched a ripple of interest that went on to disseminate itself far and wide across the whole county of Cornwall before proceeding to achieve national and then international recognition.

John and Jack were dubbed the Singing Butchers by a national newspaper. My mother showed me a whole page about them, complete with a photograph, in the *Daily Sketch*. Other national newspapers covered the phenomenon of the Singing Butchers as well, but most of the dailies, apart from the *Daily Mail* that was taken by Gran and Granfer, were either too highbrow or too inclined in the direction of the Labour party for either my mother or my father to willingly peruse.

Reporters from such newspapers came down the line to visit Port Isaac and interview John and Jack. Whether or not the butcher's shop was tidied up for the occasion was not recorded. The Singing Butchers' fame certainly travelled all the way to Australia, as with my own eyes I saw a clipping about them that was cut out of an Australian newspaper. The clipping made a great talking point in the gossip centres of Fore Street after it arrived by air post.

The word went around that the Singing Butchers were offered a contract to sing professionally. The contract was intended, maybe, to turn John and Jack into butchers of innocuous songs rather than of much more innocent farm animal flesh.

The star of John and Jack's vocal success appeared to be twinkling ever more brightly. Then, suddenly, it flickered, dimmed and faded. One day the pair was believed to be ready to conquer the world, and on the next day the world looked as if it had conquered them.

The Singing Butchers could be taken out of Port Isaac, but Port Isaac couldn't ever be taken out of the Singing Butchers. On the premises of J. N. Hicks and Son Family Butchers, John and Jack were rough kings. Outside the shop they were merely rough.

----

John and Jack did, however, come to enjoy another moment of great popular acclaim when they undertook the preparation of a profusion of sausages (that rare and so highly desired commodity) for local consumption. Their brand type was not absolutely conventional, as their sausages were not equipped with skins and were rather longer and a little bit thicker than their well-known Plymouth counterparts. However, the shape of the sausages was all right, and, although it was not wise to query the nature of the ingredients, it all held together well enough for frying and the taste was pleasing.

John and Jack's sausage business might have gone from strength to strength, had it not been for the fact that one day a waiting customer happened to observe Jack in the act of creating a batch of the said items. It might have been the first-hand view of the raw ingredients that invoked the customer's subsequent reaction, or it could equally have been that those same ingredients were, when they failed to bind together, allegedly seen by the customer to be assisted to adhere more effectively by the addition of a medium personally generated by Jack. The observant customer was, in true Port Isaac tradition, not backwards in coming forwards to spread the word on the sausage-making technique. From that day henceforth John and Jack's sausage trade was as dead as were all of its ingredients – apart, that is, from the alleged binding agent.

For a while Jack and John's trade in Sunday joints declined in sympathy with the sausages, but time, expediency and the truism that money talked proved to be great healers as always. Customers returned anew and the affair of the sausages was never mentioned again.

---

The one thing that I could be sure about on any of my Saturday encounters with the erstwhile Singing Butchers was that eventually I would have to be served with our Sunday joint. Then I would be free to escape for another week from the sound of pennies dropping and ladies being implored to be British.

313

Those Saturday visits to the butcher's shop guaranteed that time spent in Jack and John's company hung just as long and as heavily on my shoulders as did the pervading aroma of raw red meat, blood, fat, fag smoke and splintered bone in my nostrils as it wormed its inexorable way into my clothes and hair. There was a sense of resignation about my pilgrim's progress to (at long last) the head of the queue.

Along the way I could only trust that the price of one song too many from the Singing Butchers' repertoire would not be too exacting a toll for me to pay.

The slicketing sound of Jack and John's shop door closing behind me and my descent of the few steps down to the non-lawn of the yard in front brought with it the kind of relief that only the onset of soft rain was able to provide to the exponent of the two-way family favourite, "Life Gets Tedious, Don't It?"

Ahead of me was the prospect of New Road, ennobled by its immediate context, beckoning me as if it were paved with yellow brick, inducing a skip in the step of one fleeing away from the Singing Butchers of the West.

# 17

# *Life at the Top*

*Such is the place that I live in,*
*Bleak without and bare within.*

Robert Louis Stevenson (1850–1894)
"The House Beautiful"

PORT ISAAC'S COLLECTION of council houses was constructed
under the auspices of the Wadebridge-based North Cornwall
District Council – a faceless organisation that, as a mark of the
general level of esteem in which it was held, was better known
as the "bleddy" Council. The council houses were rented out
to tenant families, *inter alia* my own family at Number Nine
Hartland Road.

A rent man was despatched by the Council to Hartland Road
one a week to collect (or attempt to collect) rent payment due
from the tenants, inclusive of the customary arrears. Trying in vain
to make himself inconspicuous, the rent man slunk from door to
door, secure in the knowledge that in spite of a multiplicity of
ongoing neighbourly feuds there was no one in the immediate
vicinity at that moment who was less popular than he was.
Sometimes his knock on the door was heeded, but more often
it was not. The imminence of the rent man's appearance caused
tenants to absent themselves from their properties if enough
forewarning had been received. Otherwise we hid downstairs
beneath a table or upstairs under a bed until the money-grubbing
official had moved on to try and ambush a more hapless target.

The principal image that the bleddy Council offered those of us who dwelt along Hartland Road was manifested in gangs of its workmen who turned up (unlike the rent man) when least expected and thereupon proceeded to do their level best to fill up the days by completing as little productive activity as they could get away with, apart from the key task of brewing up tea. The practice of imbibing tea was undertaken by Council workmen almost as assiduously as was their morning perusal of the racing pages of their daily newspapers of choice.

Shortly after we moved into Number Nine, a gang of Council labourers installed itself in Hartland Road and devoted the best part of the ensuing summer to the erection of a wire fence along the front of the row of New council houses. The gang foreman was a certain Mr Jones. He became so familiar to Hartland Road residents that he was affectionately known as "Jonesie".

Jonesie's professed willingness to be regularly disappointed by the performance of racehorses on which his stake money rode with a succession of losing jockeys ensured that he would fall into favour, as by no means the least of equals, with my father and "Sock Scratch" Kenty.

At a given moment during most of the mornings when the wire fence erection was enjoying its usual lack of progress, Jonesie, my father and Kenty (when he was permitted to leave his sickbed) assembled in the locality of where the fence was going to be (if ever it got finished) for the purpose of discussing the day's form and deciding on which horses the bets of the day were to be placed. To one side of them, Jonesie's gang worked hard at making and drinking tea and circulating a packet of fags.

The four constituent lines of the wire fence were designed to be strung at vertical intervals of one foot through holes drilled through a line of square concrete posts. Each post was about five feet high. The posts were set up maybe ten feet apart, securely cemented at the base in deep holes dug in the ground. Hinges on which to hang gates (on the by no means certain assumption that gates were forthcoming) were fixed to certain posts in appropriate positions.

On a late August morning of that fence-building summer of Council gang indolence, I looked out to behold the unprecedented scene of Jonesie and his gang engaged in energetic activity. It appeared that more progress had taken place in the preceding couple of hours than was achieved in the whole of the prior fortnight.

Much to the distress of my father and Kenty, the hive of industry caused Jonesie to be unavailable for the customary consultative meeting to review the day's racing pages. Asked about what could possibly have occurred to induce a gang of Council workmen to actually do some work, Jonesie advised that the Council had handed down a proclamation requiring that the wire fence must needs be completed before the end of August.

The news was not unwelcome. At long last it seemed that the New council houses of Hartland Road were going to get their wire fence. Jonesie told us that the fence had to be completed in a hurry because a demolition order against it was due to be executed at the beginning of September. It was essential for the fence to be finished in order that it could be properly demolished and replaced with a cement block wall.

The Council moved in mysterious bleddy ways, its wonders to perform.

———

Port Isaac's council houses were arranged in three rows consistent in orientation with the long axis of a rectangle of land bordered by a stretch of Trewetha Lane on the outside and Hartland Road on the inside

The outer row along Trewetha Lane was the oldest in terms of its construction date. As a result the row was known as the "Old" council houses, consisting of two contiguous terrace-like blocks separated from one another by a narrow wind-trap passageway. Each of the blocks contained four separate dwellings. The façade

317

of the Old council houses was essentially featureless, thereby of diminished architectural interest, and a martyr to weather and exposure both at the front and the back. In the grand tradition of the Old Coastguard Station, it was impossible to look the Old council houses over and prevent thoughts of a military installation coming to mind.

The other two rows of council houses faced each other across the inner leg of Hartland Road. The recently built "New" council houses, a row of three semi-detached edifices housing six families (including mine in Number Nine), occupied the left-hand side of the road in the sense of looking inland. From the windows at the back, the New council houses commanded a stupendous view of the Bay.

The council houses on the right-hand side of Hartland Road were neither old nor new in terms of date of construction, having been built a decade or so prior to the New grouping and much more than a decade after their Old counterparts, from which they were separated by two great expanses of well-tended back gardens.

This "Middle" row of council houses consisted of four semi-detached dwellings, providing space for eight families. If the designing architect had endeavoured to comply with the Council's architectural design he could be seen to have failed dismally since he had managed to achieve in the Middle arrangement an appearance of fairly pleasing elegance.

The peaked roofs of the Middle council houses were covered over with good grey Delabole slates. The edges of the roofs were outlined in red tiles. The lower front rooms were graced by fine bay windows containing sufficient space for adequate surveillance of Hartland Road to be conducted by the tenants within from a secure position of curtained camouflage.

No such aberrations of design were committed with respect to the New council houses, which were genuine classics of Council planning, incorporating not a whit of imagination. The New council houses were roofed with cement tiles and their outlines were replete with hard edges and sharp corners that the wind could rejoice in exploiting. All windows were rectilinear, flat-set and vacant of gaze.

---

Yet, for those of us who moved up to the New council houses from our former downtown lives in what we didn't know were cramped cottages, it was necessary to acknowledge that we had obtained houses that were so airy and full of space that we could easily lose ourselves inside them. The interior of our New council house even smelt of modern times, what with the freshness of wood, the barely dry distemper on the walls and a host of cupboards that would have made Old Mother Hubbard feel at home. As if an inside lavatory downstairs were not miracle enough for us, there was another of the same upstairs.

We could count on the magic of hot water emerging from a tap as well, provided that coal was burning in the fireplace so that the hot water tank in the airing cupboard could be heated up.

I found it curious that the back door and the front door were both set into the front of each of the New council houses.

On the other hand, at least at Number Nine, the front door was rarely used. It stood in the middle part of the lower front of the house and opened inwards onto a hallway from which a flight of banister-girt stairs on the right led to the upper floor where three bedrooms (and a bathroom) were located. A triangular-shaped cavity under the stairs was fitted with a door and established as a storage cupboard.

A door on the left side of the hallway provided access into our "front room", otherwise known as the "sitting" room, which was normally occupied only at Christmas and remained unused for very much of anything at any other time, inclusive of sitting. The interior of the front room, when it was not interrupted by the festive season, felt cold enough and grim enough to slow down the decomposition of a corpse.

319

The virtual abandonment of the front room to its own devices meant that it was necessary for my mother to keep a fire going only at the back of the house in what we called the "living room". The living room was the focus of our family congregation.

Our back door, left open by day and closed although never locked at night, opened outwards from its position in the face of a shed-like appendage tacked onto the far right-hand side of the house. The first feast for the eyes on entering through the back door was the downstairs lavatory door straight ahead, a contrivance of darkly stained soft wood. Then, with no more than a mere turn of the head to the right, two similarly constituted and decorated doors came into immediate view on the side. One of them accessed a small windowless chamber designated as a coal shed. The other of the two doors opened into a "washhouse", the main static and dynamic features of which were, respectively, a large copper and a compact mangle.

To ensure that our washhouse, provided with both a small window and a dimension slightly greater than those of the coal shed, should achieve an importance beyond that of a mundane wash-day facility, it was impressed into becoming a depository for out-of-date newspapers. Subsequently, in a natural process of creeping escalation, the washhouse took on the role of dumping ground for an ever-expanding inventory of unwanted non-perishable materials that finally went rampant and besieged the surrounds of the copper in a great drift of junk.

Our coalman, Mr Harold Spry, dumped an occasional hundredweight of damp coal in the coal shed when my mother had enough money to pay him for it. Sometimes Harold arrived with a sack full of soot-generating sustenance just as we were in the process of scavenging the coal shed corners for the final specks of cloying dust from his previous delivery. On other occasions we shivered in a web of noxious fumes around a small heater fuelled by paraffin as we waited for Harold to put in a belated appearance.

Boards could be dropped into twin vertically battened slots just inside the coal shed door to build up a frontage against which an increased volume of stored coal could rest. We didn't have due cause to bring the boards into play very often.

Another little window sat in the wall on the left across from the coal-shed door. It permitted such light as entered through the back door to be transmitted into a pantry, the flimsy entry to which was located just beyond a left turn at the downstairs lavatory door so as to proceed towards the kitchen and through to the living room beyond.

Our kitchen window looked over the eastern spread of the Bay, with Tintagel Head in the middle distance and Hartland Point at the rear, across a big back garden area and a hint of the roof of Mr Tom Saundry's pigsty at the bottom. In the kitchen, the sink was built in against the wall to the right of the window held in common with the downstairs lavatory. Our electric cooker, the fount of so very many of my mother's Sunday dinners past, present and yet to come, stood by the wall on the left of the window.

A door opened directly into the living room from the kitchen. Placed up against the wall underneath the living-room window, which was half as broad again as was the kitchen window, thereby making the view of the Bay seem ever more panoramic, was an oilcloth-covered wooden table at which we ate our meals, read whatever there was to read and did jigsaws among other things.

In the corner to the right of the table, a wireless, unaware that its eventual fate involved replacement by a television set, took pride of place on a cloth-covered card table.

The living-room fireplace formed the centrepiece to the inner wall that performed such sterling service by holding our next-door neighbours at bay. The fireplace was solidly framed and grated in a welter of cast iron that was induced to assume a bloom as ripe as it was deep through the daily application of black lead polish. It was the principal eye-catching feature of the living room below the jutting stretch of a mantelpiece.

321

A collection of brass ornaments gleamed in an array of glory on that mantelpiece. The inventory of brass consisted of two First World War front-line gift boxes (courtesy of royalty); the gift of Granfer's famous moneybox (same war) created from the two spent German shells and a Turkish soldier's badge; and a couple of small lidded urn-like devices that might at one time have been intended to contain tea. Polishing the five ornaments with the application of great gobs of Brasso or handfuls of Duraglit was a long-standing Sunday ritual for my father. The embossed details on the brass work had long since been blurred smooth by elbow grease.

Closed cupboards, as tall as the living room but not much deeper than a short arm's length, were recessed into the living room wall on either side of the fireplace. A few toys, a number of books, an occasional confiscated item, a compendium of games, plates and cups and a couple of bottles containing comestible items all resided in the cupboard on the left.

One of the cited bottles contained a celebrated quantity of Heinz tomato sauce from which a large, dead and absolutely genuine beetle emerged one day when my father shook the upended bottle over his plate. Care was essential in decanting tomato sauce as all too often a lot more slopped out of the bottle than was intended. The dead beetle was certainly surplus to my father's culinary requirements.

The likes of us didn't complain a great deal about anything much (not much!) outside our restricted local circles, but in the case of the invasive beetle an exception was considered worth making. Messrs Heinz, in receipt of a written complaint from my father, awarded him in a gesture of great magnanimity a full bottle of their illustrious tomato sauce to replace the beetle-contaminated product.

From that day on my father inspected every drop of sauce that he poured from any bottle in minute detail. He broadened the field beyond the relevant saucy members of the legendary fifty-seven varieties claimed by Messrs Heinz to include HP sauce (and Daddie's and OK sauces as less favoured alternatives if HP was not available). He discovered no further foreign objects and was thereby thwarted in his ambition to acquire another free bottle of sauce of any kind. Following a lengthy period of frustration he contemplated inserting an insect into a bottle in order to achieve his objective by pouring it out again but never quite got around to doing the deed.

I took my first faltering steps into learning the words of a foreign language by reading the French version of the inscription on HP sauce bottle labels and comparing it with its English translation. Bilingualism was an added advantage brought into so many homes by that most excellent table companion of high quality, containing no artificial preservatives and, according to the label, being ideal when served with meats, hot or cold.

The cupboard on the right of our living-room fireplace enclosed the hot water storage tank, and as a consequence it was used as a clothes airing cupboard. Its customary contents consisted of stacked sheets, pillowcases, towels and clean apparel. A constant exotic object up on the top shelf was my father's copy of *The Pilgrim's Progress*, which like Tate and Lyle's granulated sugar, was untouched by human hand.

At the back of the living room a bulky sideboard standing by the wall took up most of the space. In keeping with the auxiliary function of the washhouse, the interior of the sideboard was a repository for any items that were not only not needed in the here and now but were also unlikely to be needed in the future. Such items, many and varied but united in a common quality of being appreciably small, were thrust into the sideboard for retention "just in case". Opening either of the sideboard's two doors tended, as often as not, to release an avalanche of debris every bit as precipitately and as gloriously manic as the cascade of bodies that poured from the Marx Brothers' ocean-liner cabin in *A Night at the Opera*, which I saw down at the Rivoli.

323

Attempts to stuff the overflow back into the sideboard invariably highlighted the supremacy of a poured quart over the volume containable in a pint pot. It was only fortunate that the washhouse was always there to manage the excess.

On the wall above the sideboard hung an original painting (or possibly a print of an original painting) of the cruiser HMS *Jamaica* on which my father served for a period during the war. In one impenetrable area of his mind my father still remained at sea. He was a torpedo gunner on HMS *Jamaica* in the battle that resulted in the German pocket battleship *Scharnhorst* being sunk.

One of each of a pair of well-worn easy chairs stood at either flank of the fireplace on what were almost certainly their last legs. The positioning of the chairs marked the outer rim of the tight sphere of radiant warmth thrown out by the fire. The chair at the right of the fireplace was my father's domain. The rule was that anyone else could sit in it provided my father was not in the house at the time. When I chose to occupy his chair in his presence the action implied that I was anxious to receive a clip around the ear.

The second chair was nominally available for first come first served occupation but was more usually taken up by my mother. That left the rest of us free to sit on hard-backed chairs pulled in from the side of the table. We endeavoured to insert our selected chairs, jigsaw-like, into the glow of the fire-cast halo, but there was only so much space to use, and frequently it was in the sight rather than the feel of the fire from which comfort was drawn.

A door in the corner of the living room at the left of the sideboard led to the front hallway and provided through access from the living room to the front door, the sitting room and the stairs. Up at the top of the stairs three bedrooms and a bathroom were linked to a wooden-floored landing, protected on the outside by a line of banisters. The main bedroom, which was used by my mother and father, and a small bedroom, nominally the demesne of my sister, were both at the front of the house.

The bathroom and the third bedroom, which I shared with my brother, were at the back. Has it not been for the panes of the bathroom window being made of frosted glass, it and the back bedroom window would both have covered a view of the Bay superior to that obtained in the living room down below.

My mother's first cousin Maureen Collings occupied the small front bedroom for the best part of one year. Maureen was the third in line of the six daughters of Gran's alleged card-sharping sister Eva (hence my Aunt Eva) and her husband Jack.

Maureen's status as our houseguest was occasioned by her eviction, on the express orders of Uncle Jack, from Uncle Jack and Aunt Eva's residence down in the first of the Middle row of council houses adjacent to the corner of Hartland Road's dogleg. Uncle Jack's word was the gospel according to himself. His will was always to be done forever and ever amen except when he was out of sight (even if he was never out of mind).

As a result of Maureen's departure from the family home, the early days of her presence among us at Number Nine gave rise to numerous fireside discussions laden with a stuck gramophone record-like assertion concerning Uncle Jack's antecedents to the effect that "He can't be human!" Uncle Jack, who perhaps fortunately for all concerned in his character assassination was not there to defend himself, was judged in the court of Number Nine and sentenced in absentia.

Maureen worked behind the counter in the grocery section at the Co-op shop over at the top of New Road under the managerial command of Mr William Auger. Swapping Uncle Jack's subjective will for the parade-ground crispness of Mr Auger had Maureen jumping from the fire to the frying pan, so her place of work was not as bad for her as it might have been.

On each working day Maureen walked the three hundred yards or so between Number Nine and the Co-op (and of course back again), during the course of which she had no alternative other than to pass by Uncle Jack and Aunt Eva's residence. It seemed improbable, considering the institutionalised nature of front window surveillance on all movements in Hartland Road, that Maureen's travel to work and back went unrecorded by Uncle Jack when he was at home. When he who allegedly couldn't be human was not in the house, Aunt Eva placed a pre-arranged signal in her front window to alert Maureen to the fact that it would be safe for her to drop in.

Every story had two sides to it, however, and in Uncle Jack's case (even if he was identified by some of his familiars as lacking in certain mortal qualities), he probably was sinned against at least as much as he himself might have sinned.

In the back bedroom at Number Nine my brother and I shared a large double bed. My birds' egg collection was secured within a small chest of drawers placed against the wall to the left of the foot of the bed. The bedroom window and the edge of the guttered eaves above it bore the brunt of the gales off the Bay.

Our bedroom floor was covered by linoleum, more familiarly known as lino. It was a substance possessing a supreme capability of storing and concentrating coldness and transmitting the same in an icy surge to any bare foot that dared to step on it, particularly a foot emerging from the protection of warm bed covers. No matter how cold our bedroom was, its floor felt much colder.

When I got into bed, the bedclothes often seemed slightly damp and not a little clammy at the initial encounter. It took me a long time to warm up, especially where my feet were concerned. The lino made an effective deterrent to any pressing impulse for me to arise during the night to go and pee, even though the bathroom was so close by.

In our bathroom a white-enamelled cast-iron bath stood against the wall to the right of the (frosted glass) window. A hand washbasin was in place directly below the inner windowsill. Both the bath and the hand-basin were fitted with twin hot and cold-water taps, each of which served as cold taps when there was no fire burning in the fireplace down in the living room.

As a rule we had a bath once a week. That was quite enough, and it was always good to get it out of the way. There seemed to be no point in us breaking all the hard-won bathing tradition of Six Canadian Terrace. Bath-day was celebrated every Sunday. Since it required most of the contents of the hot-water tank to charge the bath once, there was no option for anyone other than the first in line to experience water that was clean when he or she stepped into it. We were used to that of course. The sequence of bathing flowed the Canadian Terrace order of precedence, namely, first of all my father, then my mother, then me, followed by my brother and finally my sister.

Sometimes if I was lucky it was possible to top up the temperature of the bath water, cooling as it was when I got it, with the dregs of any hot water remaining in the hot water storage tank or perhaps with the contents of a specially boiled kettle or saucepan. It was miraculous to watch the tidemarks on my wrists and ankles ebb and vanish at the touch of soap. I assumed that the tidemark around my neck was similarly affected.

A wood-framed mirror hung on the wall to the left of the bathroom window, set at a suitable height in between the wash basin and the length of chain attached to the overhead lavatory cistern. The mirror was my own handiwork, made at Sir James Smith's Grammar School in woodwork classes.

Woodwork fitted well into the grand list of Grammar School subjects for which I had neither aptitude nor talent. Mr Perry, the woodwork teacher, recognised at the outset that my mind was an impervious membrane as far as absorbing his instructions was concerned. He correctly decided not to waste his time on me. A wing and a prayer held the chiselled dovetails of my mirror's frame together.

My lack of prowess at woodwork generated a series of unflattering observations from a classmate who was none other than the incidental air pistol possessor and fortunate son of a

Port Isaac chip shop owner, Arker Keat. He was proficient at woodwork and knew that my mirror was Hillson's dump material when he saw it.

In the wake of Arker's forceful critique one thing led to another, and in an impulsive reaction that I instantly regretted, occurring at a moment when Mr Perry had left the woodwork room, I kicked out at one of Arker's shins. As Arker was not wearing shin pads at the time, Arker's shinbone took the brunt of my kick.

That fisticuffs did not immediately ensue owed thanks to the fortuitous return to the woodwork room of Mr Perry (who had presumably been out at the back smoking a hasty fag when the altercation between Arker and myself took place).

With the exception of the Grammar School's self-styled headmistress, who bore the ominous name of Miss Battle, the teachers tended not to smoke in the classrooms. They were forced, as in the case of Mr Perry, to seize a suitable opportunity for a drag as and when it presented itself. The school staff room was a prime location for such opportunists. Billows of smoke rolled outwards as if fleeing from an inner fug whenever the staff room door was opened.

The *modus operandi* of Miss Battle, who taught Latin, was to set her class a reading or translating task for the duration of the lesson, park herself behind the big desk out at the front, swing her legs up onto the desk, light up a cigarette, open up a newspaper, and read through it. Sometimes she completed her perusal of the newspaper before the bell sounded for the end of the lesson and sometimes she didn't.

The newspaper hid Miss Battle from the class and vice versa. Curls of fag smoke rose from behind the newspaper screen to signify that she had not yet gone to sleep. It would have been interesting to know how many once-eager pupils she managed to alienate from the subject of Latin for life. Miss Battle's lessons were enlivened only by an occasional glimpse of her voluminous bloomers as she adjusted her legs on the desk for comfort.

A further confrontation with Arker came hard on the heels of the end of the woodwork lesson during which I kicked him. He wanted to fight me there and then. Luckily (for once) we were required to proceed from the woodwork room to another classroom for the next lesson and so there was insufficient time available to us to be able to trade meaningful blows. At Arker's behest, since we were both Port Isaac boys, we agreed to meet to settle the matter down on the Town Platt at seven o'clock that same evening.

Arker's enthusiasm for the evening meeting was considerably greater than mine. He was able to hold on to a desire that an injustice needed to be avenged in a way in which I couldn't. I thought about not going along but dismissed that option right away and was there at the Town Platt at the appointed time, sick to my stomach with dread. I wasn't opposed to fighting when blood ran momentarily hot, but I saw little point in doing anything other than apologising when situations cooled down immediately afterwards.

Arker turned up shortly after me. He emerged like a phantom from the darkness of the narrow passage that ran along the lower side of the Wheelhouse to link through to the Bloody Bones courtyard where the Golden Lion's urinal was festering away in silence.

I was keen to apologise for the kick and approached Arker to do so. However, Arker's nature was not yet set to forgive, as without preliminaries he swung a fist and hit me solidly on the side of my head. I suddenly understood what it meant to see stars. My view of the visually imposed firmament was so spectacular that I fell to the ground in awe and was unable to rise.

I lay on the ground for a little longer than might have been justified by Arker's blow, as I didn't want him to follow it up with a second one. I didn't intend to fight back anyway, knowing I was in the wrong. When I finally stood up, Arker was gone.

On the following morning at school the boys in my class came

329

to seek information on the outcome of the preceding evening's combat.

"I lost," I told them.

Much to my surprise, by that simple admission, ungarnished with excuses, I was received into their fold at once and with evident warmth. Arker, the true conqueror, curiously seemed to be accorded the second place. It seemed that the world liked a repentant loser.

No wonder the bathroom mirror that I made was wonky.

————

The loft under the eaves of Number Nine Hartland Road was entered through a push-up hatch set in the ceiling directly above the centre of the upstairs landing. In order to ascend into the loft, since we didn't own a ladder, my practice was to climb onto the banister rail, push up the hatch, grab the edges of the opening and pull myself through. This whole brute force and ignorance exercise was the work of a moment to anyone who, like myself, was accustomed to climbing up, down and around the cliffs of the Bay. Up in the loft I was standing under a pitched slope of not particularly well-fitted cement roofing tiles. The wind whistled and wafted through a multitude of chinks that permitted the penetration of just enough light from the world outside for me to be able to see my way around, once my eyes became accustomed to the relative gloom.

The loft was a space of church-like proportions, having a pointed vault and a floor, all shaped by splintery new pine-scented beams and trusses. Against the outer sidewall our cold-water storage tank lurked in the twilight looking like a mighty altar.

The cold-water tank was covered over at the top with loose planks of wood. Its lagging-free exterior extended an open invitation to Mr Jack Frost to bless it with his touch whenever he chose to pay us an extended visit. Jack always obliged by calling in.

Important elements of the creed of council-house tenants,

whether of the New, Middle or Old variety, were, "I believe that the cost of maintaining my council house in good order is the responsibility of the bleddy Council. I believe that no bugger on the Council will ever get a penny from me outside of the rent money, and they won't even get the rent if I can get away with it".

This confirmed belief considered that the cost of maintenance included repairs to roof, walls and woodwork (no matter who caused the damage in the first place), painting and distempering, and replacement of windows broken by flying objects originating both from within and without the house.

Unless the Council came along to do it, such maintenance didn't take place. The scope also covered the installation of any form of lagging aimed at deterring Jack Frost's touch not only on the cold-water storage tank but also on associated piping. Consequently, a prolonged cold spell in winter guaranteed that pipes would freeze and the flow of domestic water would be suspended until more equable temperatures returned. The Council would then be roundly cursed for causing so much inconvenience.

When the frozen pipes thawed, water began to flow once more. Unfortunately, much of the flow emerged through ruptures in the pipes and from there proceeded to invade the bedroom ceilings. Thus did we receive an annual lesson that when water froze in a copper pipe, it expanded to create a volume that was greater than the volume of the pipe. That rule never seemed to apply to the good old lead pipes that we had before the copper versions came along. The shortcomings of copper piping were something else to blame on those miserable buggers at the bleddy Council.

The wall held in common with our next-door neighbours on the inner flank of the loft was constructed from cement blocks, and was one block thick. Against its upper edge by the roof there were gaps large enough for me to peer through into the adjoining loft. It would have taken a very little effort to create a hole big enough for me to have squirmed through. I might have done it if I thought I could have got away with it.

Those next-door neighbours were Mr and Mrs George Williams. Mrs Williams was named Dorothy but was known as "Dar". George and Dar had three children, all of them younger than me. Georgina ("Gina") was the eldest of the three, Marlene ("Mars") was the one in the middle, and Caroline ("Car") was the youngest.

Dar was a hugely fleshy lady who ruled her roost with a proverbial rod of iron gripped at the end of an all too realistic arm that resembled one of Mr Jack Hicks' rarely seen legs of pork in both colour and texture. The volume of Dar's voice was comparable to the weight of her figure, both quantities being equally able to crush whomsoever they fell on. George, by contrast, was short of stature, light of figure, mild of manner and as sweet as treacle. He was a man made for henpecking.

Dar's voice in full flight of fancy made it evident that New council house walls didn't incorporate soundproofing elements in their design. Even if the walls had been so equipped, however, Dar's vocal prowess was capable of penetrating any obstacle. The walls were as thin on substance as Dar was not.

It was possible that in their wisdom the Council had decided that an audible appreciation in one New council house of whatever was taking place next door would provide a form of home entertainment that could be enjoyed when there was nothing worth listening to on the wireless.

For what seemed like time interminable in our living room at Number Nine we were less than enthralled by Gina's performance of exercises and scales on a not very well-tempered clavier in Dar and George's front room. A strong doubt over the veracity of the proverb that practice made perfect surfaced in my breast as I listened to Gina's endless search for the lost chord.

George constantly scurried hither and thither, engaged in the commission of one errand or another mandated by Dar, all the while clutching hold of a shopping bag as if his life depended on it, which it possibly did. George carried the mark of a man whose life was subject to so much harassment that he had thrown in the towel and come to terms with it. He was a man of true fortitude.

Of George and Dar's three children, Gina was cast in the mould of George. Mars and Car showed every sign of bearing Dar's ponderously sharp-tongued tradition well on into the future.

When she was in Dar's vicinity my mother trod as carefully as if she were walking on eggshells, not that we saw too many of those. She didn't want to make an enemy of Dar, easy though that might have been, or to provide Dar with soft ammunition that Dar could toss back hard in my mother's direction.

Dar's preferred method of chastisement of the young was what she referred to as a "smack around the chacks". My mother abhorred the expression. I didn't know what chacks were, but imagined they were whatever part of the body of a victim that Dar was able to reach when the need to smack a chack arose.

One summer afternoon Dar, from a position behind the lace-curtained security of her living room window, spotted me wandering about with a few other boys on the far side of the Port Gaverne Main. It wasn't so much that Dar possessed superhuman eyesight but rather that she was using a pair of binoculars at the time. The Main in the summer was a happy hunting ground for binocular-equipped remote scrutiny.

As a result of her observations, Dar formed an instant opinion that I was messing around in too close proximity to the cliff edge. She waddled around to inform my mother of what she had seen and suggested in strong and direct terms that I should receive a handsome smack around the chacks immediately following my return home. My mother was not moved to comply, but she did tell me about it.

I imagined Dar handing me such a smack, her open hand making contact with my chack, powered by the flesh that rolled right up to her shoulder. I had a vision of my head sailing off to bounce on the floor and end up at the feet of a Port Isaac version of Madame Defarge knitting and nodding away sagely from a vantage point on one side.

Dar's parents, Mr & Mrs Reuben Brown, lived in the Old council houses – not too far from their well-fleshed daughter. Reuben was affectionately known as "Rubie". Dar walked in her mother's equally weighty footsteps, since, with all due allowance given to the moderating characteristics (for better or for worse) wrought by time, George and Dar matched the image of Rubie and Mrs Rubie almost as well as any mirror might have done.

Rubie and Mrs Rubie's immediate Old council-house neighbours included the families of Mr William John Honey, Port Isaac barber and friend to the multitude; Mr Anthony Provis, harbourmaster and Town Platt *éminence grise;* and that reluctant hero of the storm-bound voyage of the *Amanda*, Mr Les Honey.

Among Anthony's family still living at home was his son (and stalwart of the Wesley chapel) Mr Harold Provis. I was delighted to look on Harold, a young man of totally even disposition, as my friend. On what could have been its penultimate (if not its terminal) outing, Harold invited me to carry the Port Isaac Band of Hope banner with him in procession, and thereby, as we marched in step through the village, set both the icing and the marzipan on the Christmas cake of respect I had for him.

Les and his good wife Ada were blessed with five children named, in descending order of age, April, Leslie (young Les), Pearl, Leonard (known as Buh) and Jeanette. The heavily asthmatic Buh (in the same class as me at the Port Isaac County Primary school) was ever a set piece in the jigsaw of my days. He was famous both for the balaclava helmet that he wore as a year-round remedy against earache and for a supremely impressive ability to summon up gargantuan belches on demand.

In her working partnership with Rubie, Mrs Rubie subscribed to the apple-sharing principle that hers had to be the biggest half. Her effective collar was as white as a sheet whereas Rubie's neckband was figuratively as blue as blue could be. Mrs Rubie provided substance, and Rubie bore the burden. George, looking at Rubie, could well have had cause to speculate on the extent to which his own advancing years would bend him ever further to Dar's will. Although George performed the function of hunter-gatherer for Dar alone, Rubie's role had progressed beyond that of being a mere slave serving Mrs Rubie to promote his submission to certain other heavyweights of the family on Mrs Rubie's side, not excluding Dar.

Rubie, in the manner of George, was constantly on the go, nipping around hither and thither at the whim of hefty Amazons. He deported himself with dignity, an endearing man, greatly liked and respected but even more greatly sympathised with.

Rubie might not have been the master of his fate, but he was surely the captain of his soul whenever I met him. I found in him a kindly manner that was always at the forefront. His soft voice was ever ready to bestow a greeting. I imagined that Rubie had come to be not quite as discontented with his lot in life as most people thought he was.

———

Port Isaac laid claim to having no resident dentist. That was all to the good, as a dentist out of sight was happily out of mind as far as I was concerned. However the shortfall of dental facilities wasn't all good news, as an itinerant member of the profession turned up every once in a while in order to inflict long needle and pincer generated pain on far too many of us for my liking – especially when one of us was me.

For his visits, the dentist set up his surgery in a front room in the lower block of Old council houses, from which chamber of torture he dealt with highly fearful and much less than willing patients. His stock in trade as I saw it was vested in ripping out rotting teeth and spilling blood from mangled gums.

It was something of a toss-up for me to decide if a raging toothache was preferable to the dentist's administrations, and usually the toothache won. The throbbing pain could be held at bay by a fragment of cloth or cotton wool soaked with drops of either oil of cloves or whisky, placed on the infected tooth and held tight by biting down on it. The strategy could be employed until such time as the infected tooth was loose enough for either me (if I was brave enough) or a gleefully eager member of my family (if I was not) to pull out.

Once a week down at the primary school each teacher inspected the hands (palms and back) of all the pupils in his or her class and followed this up by having a look at the teeth as well, which we were required to expose for the occasion in a lupine snarl. For the inspection we stood side by side in a line, our teeth bared and our hands held extended as if a one-foot ruler was about to fall on them. Ranked in this way we looked like a row of candidates waiting to be interviewed by Dr Frankenstein. Only our front teeth were scrutinised, and those only perfunctorily as the teacher flipped by, anxious to get the task out of the way.

Immediately prior to the inspection we devoted much effort into ridding ourselves of remnants of the day's breakfast menu still residing in gaps and cavities between (and in) our teeth. Anyone who had a handkerchief (generally referred to as a snot rag for reasons that were only too obvious when it was produced) used the same for the purpose of feverishly scrubbing his or her teeth. Anyone who didn't have a handkerchief made do with a shirtsleeve as a substitute.

It was open to debate as to whether or not this examination of our teeth made any difference in controlling or even slowing down the locally rampant decay of the same. We were just as unenthusiastic about cleaning our teeth as we were about having a bath. Decay mainly affected the back teeth in any case so was kept well out of sight. In my case the teacher was usually more interested in the condition of my fingernails than in my teeth. If the teacher expected to see black half moons when looking at my fingernails, he or she was seldom disappointed.

I was once forced to attend the visiting dentist at the Old council houses thanks to a severely aching back molar with an abscess at its roots. To ensure that I honoured the appointment my father conducted me to the premises. The dentist extracted the troubled tooth with the assistance of a local anaesthetic, referred to as cocaine, which he injected into my unsuspecting back gum with a syringe-mounted needle of such huge proportions that the pain-killing quality of the drug was almost obviated by my passing out with fright at the sight of the implement carrying it.

The subsequent relief from torment after the effects of the local anaesthetic had worn off gave me a feeling that would have been close to euphoric had the dreadful vision of the needle and the awful squishy sound as it entered the gum not still been branded on my brain.

The dentist declared himself to be unhappy with the condition of my teeth in general and waxed irate on the subject with my father, not that that did either of them much good. "I suppose you know," he told my father, "that your son has a foul breath". I didn't know, or care, what the dentist was worried about. It was only teeth. Everybody's teeth were going to fall out eventually. People with false teeth had all the luck as they didn't have to worry about dentists ever again.

At the top end of the Middle row of council houses those recognised luminaries in residence included Mr and Mrs Frank (hedge trimmer extraordinaire) Gilbert; Mr and Mrs Robert Smith with Charlie, Stanley and Clarence (their three far from little boys who were less likely to sing to you than their five namesakes did on the wireless); and Mr and Mrs (the queen of front-room curtain twitchers) Arthur Dinner.

Aunt Eva and Uncle Jack (he can't be human) were located right down at the bottom of the Middle row, with Mr and Mrs Charlie Couch and their daughters Sybil (doyenne of blackberry pickers) and Pamela as their immediate next-door neighbours.

337

As a couple, Charlie and Mrs Charlie were patently modest and well respected. Sybil and Pam both tended to adopt the example set by their parents. Aunt Eva and Uncle Jack and their array of female offspring, who were all endowed with great skill in the art of striking sparks from one another, fell short of being as tranquil as Charlie and Mrs Charlie by a considerable margin.

Mrs Charlie had to contend with being an inadvertent audience to many secrets passed through thin walls on the occasions when vocal renditions from members of the Collings family, focused on giving Uncle Jack something not to be human about, rose in volume. Mrs Charlie could, or could not, have been an unwilling recipient of such transmitted intelligence, although anyone who believed that she was not would probably believe anything.

Pam, Mongolian and as such singular in Port Isaac, was a few years older than me. In contrast to Sybil's thin-bodied razor-edged characteristics, Pam appeared as being plump and simple-minded, although none of that affected her mobility.

Pam roamed all around the village, ranging perhaps too broadly as her customary availability coupled with her handicap ensured that she made an easy target for teasing. It would be nice to reckon that teasing Pam was not done with malicious intent, but since Port Isaac people were involved, some unkindness at least must have been at the heart of it.

Any incidence of mental illness or related incapacity was certain to place a profound stigma upon the whole family of the person afflicted, to be visited by the fathers upon the children unto at least the third or fourth generation. A family associated with any member who was popularly acknowledged as a "loony" or a "nut case" found it well nigh impossible to live down the applied shame. The stain on the family circle was traditionally countered by not being spoken about. It was simply swept under the carpet, as often as not by shutting the cause of the problem away in a place where he or she was out of sight, out of mind and thereby conveniently ignored if not forgotten.

338

On the near outskirts of Bodmin (the capital of Cornwall not because it used to be, or ought to be, but because it was) the St Lawrence's Mental Hospital lurked behind fearsomely high walls of stone. St Lawrence's was commonly known as the "lunatic asylum" or "loony bin". It was a notorious repository for the mentally ill of the district whose sundry ranks were known to include people like Pam.

Bodmin and the loony bin were, by long-standing tradition, held to be essentially one and the same thing. Those who, like me, had been told repeatedly that we belonged there, were well aware of this enduring linkage.

Pam, however, always lived at home. She was fortunate in her choice of parents. Within the kaleidoscope of Hartland Road residents, Mr and Mrs Charlie shone as true graces.

---

The Middle council house next up above the one housing the Couches and the Collings was occupied on its lower side by Mrs Emmeline ("Em") Kent, her son Kenty (the ever-hopeful student of racing form) and her daughter Amanda. On the upper side the occupants were a certain Mrs Mitchell plus Leonard, Diane and June, who were three of her four children – the other one being Walter who had flown the nest. It was a case of "Walter, Walter, lead me to the altar!" as Gracie Fields' cracked falsetto told us.

Em and Mrs Mitchell were related via branches in the Glover family tree, although I wasn't sure how closely Mrs Mitchell fit into the foliage. She might have been more closely related to Mr Andrew Mitchell, who, with his wife Vera, lived in the lower half of the next house up in the Middle row alongside Mr and Mrs Arthur Dinner.

The respective husbands of Em and Mrs Mitchell had both been lost in wartime action. The shared misfortune seemed to affect each of them differently, however. Em became much harder, tougher and even more independent than the durable Glover mould cast had made her in the first place. Mrs Mitchell appeared

339

to be rather reclusive and over-protective where her family was concerned.

Kenty eventually won his fight against TB, although he never enjoyed the state of health thereafter that his wartime sacrifices merited. He gained in both weight and geniality and ambled around in a manner suggesting the receipt of instructions in personal deportment from Boris Karloff. Since Kenty had done his duty in theatres of war, post-war work, in his view, was a duty incumbent on people other than him.

Kenty married a girl named Frances. She came from somewhere outside the village. Frances' mind wasn't nearly as sharp as her nose. She and Kenty eventually moved into the council house formerly occupied by Mr and Mrs Charlie Couch, thereby further extending the scope of the Middle row Glover enclave. There they raised an extensive brood of girls and cared for them passionately.

Em was tall, thin and withered. Her skin, which looked like cracked leather tanned by fag smoke, seemed as impervious to punishment as it all too obviously was to soap and water. Em entered Sherratt's bakery shop one day and asked for a bar of Sunlight soap. "What?" exclaimed John Sherratt from behind the counter, "Don't tell me you're actually going to have a bleddy wash!"

Em wore her hair at shoulder length, severely parted on one side. The hair was as lank as it was greasy. I wouldn't have cared to touch it, and I thought it unlikely that either of the two bookies named Jack would have been prepared to lay off a bet (even from Kenty) on when Em's hair's most recent wash was celebrated, let alone when the next one would be.

Em's neck collected grime every bit as assiduously as did the nape of the pride of upper Roscarrock Hill, Captain (retd) Roy May. She favoured wearing wrap-around aprons that were themselves no strangers to dirt and a few other stains that were best not investigated.

I knew Em well and was always glad for it. She often came up to us in Number Nine to ask if I could run an errand or carry out one small task or another for her, always promising me that I should be the ultimate recipient of "a few bobs" for my services. My mother nodded her head sagely, knowing as well as Em did that no few bobs, not even one bob, would ever pass from Em's hand into mine, but that was no matter, I liked Em and always did what she wanted.

Em was more than able to outlast any man in a job where hard labour was concerned, in which capacity she was always greatly in demand by farmers for tetty picking in the autumn. With no complaint about the backbreaking nature of the work, Em, ankle-deep in mud, tramped up and down fields tirelessly filling sodden sacks with freshly turned up tetties washed white by the rain.

Any money that Em made, from tetty picking and elsewhere, was probably spent principally on packets of fags. It was rare to see Em without a fag in her mouth, and on those occasions when such an object was *in absentia* it was only because she was either in the process of reaching for another or in the process of cadging one from someone else.

Em gave an impression of kippering her body from the inside out. She manifested a crackling cough and was never shy about gobbing up great rafts of evilly streaked phlegm when the mood took her.

As far as I knew, Em feared neither man nor beast. However, both using the telephone and receiving a telegram were, for Em, a phobia that she could not conquer. Telegrams were understood to bring to their recipients only the worst kind of news. Em had been informed of the loss of her husband by telegram. As far as the telephone was concerned, it had assumed guilt by association with that dreadful telegram in Em's mind.

I spent a lot of time with Em when I did weekend work for Mr George Moth at the Lawns, his hotel on the Terrace. My duties for George involved cleaning up the bar and public surrounds, and bringing in and setting up barrels and bottles of beer to replenish the depletion from recently expired boozing sessions.

Em worked in the kitchen and residential section of the Lawns, washing dishes and sweeping floors. Even though no critical premium was placed on the maintenance of culinary hygiene at the Lawns, Em was kept well away from activities involved with the handling and preparation of food.

The kitchen linked to the back bar area through a curtained-off opening to the left of the sink. The proximity of the kitchen sink to the bar ensured that it was used as much for the washing up of used bar glasses as for the dirty plates and cutlery coming from the dining room. The upshot of all of this juxtaposition was that Em worked on the kitchen side of the curtained opening and I worked on the bar side. We communicated through the opening. Em's regular grouse focused on how little she felt she was being paid and how badly she thought she was being taken for granted.

I couldn't really reciprocate with Em on the second count as mine host George always treated me with the greatest of kindness. George was a jolly, beaming man whose consideration for me reached its heights when my St Peter's PT Club boxing activities were at their peak.

Regarding the amount of my wages, George didn't pay me too little, since he didn't pay me at all. He let me know (repeatedly) that business was pretty bad, placing him in a position where he was temporarily not in possession of the kind of funds that could properly recompense me for my work. Yet, George went on, business was bound to pick up before too long, and when it did he would be sure to pay me all that was owed.

I didn't get to know if business fared better at the Lawns, since no payment ever came. I continued to trust in George, assuming that his business was permanently forced to languish somewhere in the doldrums.

One day I was impelled to run from the bar through the

kitchen to answer the telephone when it rang and rang at its location out in the Lawns hallway. Em held fast at the kitchen sink and showed no sign of moving to pick the receiver up, and there was evidently no one else in the immediate vicinity ready to oblige.

The caller asked to speak to Mrs Emmeline Kent. I called to Em to come and take the call, but she must have been riveted to the kitchen sink as she either wouldn't or couldn't pull away from it. Her sink–attached posture was as hunched as if she was preparing to fend off an anticipated onslaught of blows. To the extent that Em was ever able to break into a cold sweat, she did it then.

Em wouldn't only not answer the telephone, she would also not approach it. She seemed to regard the telephone as a Flash Gordon ray gun type of secret weapon that would destroy her if she got within close range of it.

The duration of Em's telephone call was mercifully short-lived. There was a message for her, fortunately of no significance, which I relayed to Em by yelling it through the hall into the kitchen. Em screamed an acknowledgement back to me, which I then passed on to the caller, who I thought was Kenty but wasn't sure as he didn't say.

The telephone receiver went back on the hook, and Em went back to her dishes, releasing a number of hitherto suppressed emotions in a clatter of dirty crockery.

———

Of Em's neighbour Mrs Mitchell's three children still at home, June was the same age as me, Leonard about six years older, and Diane in between the two.
Leonard was therefore more of a young man than a big boy. Stanley, youngest of the aforesaid three Smith brothers and equally as big as Leonard was the latter's regular sidekick.

However, Leonard's body was a lot more mature than was his aptitude. Leonard could have served as a model for his namesake

343

Lenny as interpreted by Lon Chaney Jr in *Of Mice and Men*, a great but immensely sad film that came one Friday night to the Rivoli.

I didn't know if Leonard knew how to read and write – if he did he held the light so securely under a bushel that only an act of faith could provide him with the benefit of the doubt. I also wasn't too sure what Leonard's feelings might have been with respect to keeping a hutch containing rabbits.

Leonard took more pleasure in the company of smaller boys like me than he did from being with youths of his own age. For our part we welcomed Leonard's attentions and were proud to be seen as his associates. Our parents were a little more reticent about the arrangement, but we put that down to them not knowing Leonard as well as we did.

Leonard told us about a lot of things that we hadn't heard of before, and moreover he had no hesitation in passing them on to us. His company gave us more of the kind of status that we enjoyed from the companionship of the ever-endearing Mr William (Gaggy) Hosking when Gaggy joined the church choir.

Leonard was both tall and rangy. He affected an impressively unkempt style of attire from the worn rim of his shirt collar all the way down to the hobnails on the soles of his boots. His hair was naturally wispy, and if a comb had ever tried to tame it, that comb had surely failed to achieve its objective.

Leonard leaned backwards while he walked. Although the reverse angle of his back was fairly acute, the inclination was sufficient for the eye to easily appreciate. The propensity for Leonard to topple over was accentuated by a further tendency that he had to tilt his head even further to the rear, so that he always appeared to be staring at a point with an azimuth somewhere above the distant horizon.

He had a slack, open-hanging mouth in the depths of which a flickering tongue could be glimpsed. His nose was large and turned slightly to one side as the possible result of a playground fight, although in my experience I never once saw Leonard involved in aggressive activities of that kind.

The most notable aspects of Leonard's facial features were his eyes. They were bright and bulged like convex mirrors. They had no depth – all of Leonard's personality lay on the surface. His left eye was usually clenched in a squint that, as a direct result, made his right eye appear even more protuberant. The overall effect was one of controlled wildness.

Not inconsequentially, Leonard acquired the nickname "Cockeye". Mrs Mitchell was as enthusiastic about Leonard being called Cockeye as she was regarding June's receipt of the appellation of "Monkey Face". Her opposition to the name of Cockeye guaranteed that it came to be popularly enshrined with absolute finality.

Later on, Leonard chose to award himself the nickname "Cap'n". The ranking title stuck to him like glue. Cap'n and Cockeye were from then on to all intents and purposes interchangeable nicknames for Leonard, although of the two, Cockeye was always my favourite.

Cockeye took to being Cap'n so wholeheartedly that he talked about himself as Cap'n in the third person. When we met up with him we would ask, "Where have you been to Cap'n?" and Cockeye would reply, "Cap'n just come from home".

Cockeye wasn't much inclined to range the cliffs, but he knew the valleys like the back of his hand and was adept at spotting birds' nests in season and telling us where they were. His preference for getting around was to use the roads and lanes of the parish and parts beyond, in the consummation of which wandering activity he had no peers.

Cockeye roamed far and wide accessorised by a short length of stout stick and a well-worn lorry tyre scavenged from a dump. The tyre bore tread of such limited sufficiency that even Granfer might have been unwilling to cut boot soles for me from it.

With the ancient tyre rolling ahead of him, Cockeye trotted

along, maintaining its forward momentum by batting it ever onwards with the stick. He pursued the tyre ceaselessly, up hill and down dale, along open roads and tight lanes for mile after mile after mile. One day Cockeye might chase the tyre all the way to Wadebridge and on another day appear behind it up at Delabole.

Cockeye and his tyre were able to leave Port Isaac at the same time as the National bus and reach Wadebridge before the National did. The National had to make stops but Cockeye didn't. Cockeye's triumph of will over distance was a wonder to behold. I was sure that there were lesser long-distance runners who had competed in the London Olympic games.

When Cockeye started working, his enthusiasm formed a buoyant counter to his slowness on the uptake. The latter characteristic tended to ensure that the men he worked with were less tolerant of Cockeye's perceived deficiencies than the boys were.

In the great society of the working man Cockeye was usually vested with the role of whipping boy. He was expected to stand as the butt of jokes that were as lacking in good intent as they were in humour.

Cockeye was taken on as tea maker at a building site, where the daily jibes from some of his fellow workers became so oppressive that Cockeye was induced to take what for him was the unheard of action of complaining about it at home. Mrs Mitchell brought Cockeye's concerns to the attention of an avuncular relative, none other than Mr John Glover. John, a man unaccustomed to taking prisoners, was motivated to express his personal disapproval in a forthright manner to Cockeye's said fellow workmen.

Anyone taken aside to be spoken to by John in this way rarely showed any hesitation in mending his ways afterwards. On the following day Cockeye received an abject apology from his former tormentors. They assured Cockeye that they would never again upset him in any way.

"All right," said Cockeye, "Then Cap'n shan't piss in your tea any more when Cap'n makes it!"

———

Mr Andrew Mitchell, whose Christian name was rendered in speech as "Andra", would never have found it necessary to piss in the teapot of unpleasant workmen to exact revenge. For a start, anyone seeing Andra on the warpath would be well aware of the need to keep his head well down if he wished to remain in a condition sound of wind and limb.

Andra was tall, rounded and burly. The cumulative effect of these characteristics endowed his gait with a deceptively gentle roll. He dressed smartly enough, obviously mandated to do so by his very proper wife Vera.

Vera dolled herself up to the nines for all of her appearances in public. On more than one occasion I heard her referred to in terms of mutton dressed as lamb. She wore outfits and combinations that looked expensive and clung on to her as thickly and as heavily as did her face powder. The quantity of the clothing that she possessed appeared to suggest that Andra had discovered a secret fountain spurting out clothing points.

Vera was quite slim and presumably elegant with it, although in terms of my judging Vera's elegance there were not a lot of local yardsticks around with which I could compare her. Most Port Isaac people dressed in what they could get – hand me down or hand me over, it made no difference. Clothes were first and foremost things to keep warm in.

Vera, with her hair crisply permed, glided through the streets with an air of languid imperiousness that would have done credit to Bette Davis. Had she been asked if her shit stank, and as far as I knew she never was, Vera would definitely have responded in the negative.

For all of that, Vera didn't appear to consider that she was a cut above her neighbours, as a mere cut would have fallen well short of her pretensions. Andra, a man caught in the frame of

Vera's ostentation, confirmed his support for her couture down in William John's barber's shop in Fore Street when he said, "The better her do dress, the pleasder I are."

Andra's hands were huge and square. His fingers resembled an array of Mr Jack Hicks' sausages of chequered career. The backs of his hands bristled with hairs that looked stiff enough to scour a saucepan of burnt milk. They were hands that I instinctively knew would have the capability of knocking someone's block off before breakfast and of crushing rocks to surface Miss Jinny Hills' back yard with fresh gravel before dinner.

A further feature of note about Andra was his flat cap and the jaunty manner in which he wore it. It was unusual enough at the outset that Andra's flat cap always seemed to be clean. He wore it in a "wide awake" position, unbuttoned in front so that the brow rose above the peak like the blunt bow of an advancing barge. The flat cap was Andra's trademark, a gaping symbol of his mighty guffaw, which was as loud and infectious as some of the costumes Vera wore when the two of them went out on parade together.

Andra's facility with the rules of etiquette fitted him less well than did his best suit. He was fundamentally a good man with a common touch who was putty around the window of Vera's whims and whimsies. Vera knew what was best for Andra and was prepared to accept nothing less than that.

# 18

# *Tetty War*

*You left us in tatters, without shoes or socks,*
*Tired of digging potatoes, and spudding up docks*

Thomas Hardy (1840–1928)
"The Ruined Maid"

WHERE EACH MET Trewetha Lane, both Lundy Road and Hartland Road ran for a hundred yards or so on similar headings pointing at the Bay, prior to making respective left and right turns to bear towards one other, presumably in the hope of uniting. That they didn't meet was entirely due to the intervention of the garden wall at Number Nine Hartland Road. The two cited Roads dead-ended against this wall, Lundy Road down at the bottom of the garden, and Hartland Road up at the top.

From the lower part of our garden at Number Nine we could step onto the grassy track that formed the death rattle of Lundy Road. Mr. Hillson, proceeding down Lundy Road on his milk round after leaving his farmyard, always used our back garden to make a shortcut through to Hartland Road

Between the stony surface of the upper part of Lundy Road and the testing teeth of a gale arriving from the Bay and all points west, nothing stood that could possibly be regarded as representative of a windbreak. The few houses on Lundy Road may have been eternal homes providing shelter from the stormy blast, but as their degree of exposure offered no improvement over that of the

New council houses, amelioration of the worst excesses of the elements was not something they achieved easily.

My bedroom window at Number Nine, looking out as it did over the Bay, ensured that I was no stranger to the skill of the wind to hammer, boom and rip the sharp edges away from masonry corners.

In a probable consequence of the predisposition of the wind to blow a gale at them at will there were only a few brave souls residing by choice in Lundy Road. As council tenants, the power of such choice was not something we knew much about in Hartland Road. Neither could those other beggars who lived in the prefabs be adequately characterised as choosers, although the prefabs were of such restricted height that the adjacent Trewetha Lane hedge protected them from the wind fairly well.

Eyesnot lived in Lundy Road. His father, Mr Steve Bate, was made of stern stuff. Steve's stalwart three-storey house reared up in a bold left-hand side presence at the foot of the said Road, almost hanging onto the brink of the valley slope that dropped into Port Gaverne across Mr Tom Saundry's pig, chicken and rat infested field.

Tom never took a shortcut to his field through the Number Nine back garden, much to my relief, since whenever he set foot on our property, a stiletto-aided despatch of a chicken won by my mother as a whist-drive prize was likely to be in the offing and I didn't much like to witness that. (My leading role in the unauthorised elimination of one of Cogsy's bantams was then but a fading memory.)

In a dead straight line, the back door of Steve's house, behind which Eyesnot lurked somewhere, was no more than twenty yards distant, if that, from our back door at Number Nine. Unfortunately, it wasn't possible to walk directly between the respective back doors owing to the intervention of a bungalow and its private grounds. There was always a problem, as the old song had it, with "the houses in between".

Of course, in keeping with the feelings of my friends in general, I didn't recognise the right of private property to form an inviolate barrier to our intentions to cross over. Any declaration of property being "off limits", especially when it was associated with an emphatically signposted decree that "trespassers will be prosecuted", was judged by us to be no more than a gauntlet cast down to be picked up; as a welcome challenge to be both tackled and overcome.

On countless occasions in the primary school during the week and twice or even thrice on Sundays at both Sunday School and in church we ritually mumbled in unison about having our trespasses forgiven as we forgave those who trespassed against us. On the strength of this clause from the famous prayer, we felt reassured that our trespasses on private property would eventually be forgiven by "Our Father who charged into heaven" if not by anyone else.

The key rule of trespass, a lesson learned through experience, was that the danger of our not having our trespasses forgiven would increase in direct proportion to the proximity of our trespasses to our back doorsteps. A farmer on the warpath chasing us off his land was a thrill to be savoured. An irate neighbour bearing down on us was a fright to be avoided. Hence, we generally accepted that taking a shortcut to Steve's house from the inner end of Hartland Road by way of the intervening bungalow grounds was off limits, unless it was dark enough for us to slip through unseen.

The bungalow was home to Mr and Mrs Frederick ("Freddie") Ford. Freddie, after a lifetime of close association with youth activities including the boy scouts and their famous "Gang Show" (it was said that Freddie was a personal friend of the "Gang Show's" Mr Ralph Reader) was a gentleman imbued with the quality of tolerance not only for his fellow man but also for his fellow boys.

I could easily imagine that Freddie looked on the construction of the New council houses with some dismay. He already had the residents of the Middle council houses to contend with as neighbours, and New council house runners-in could only serve to heap insult on injury for Freddie as far as the declining quality of the general neighbourhood was concerned.

As a keep-out measure the perimeter of Freddie's property sported a tight grove of dark and bushy cypress trees on the Hartland Road side, each tree being from six to eight feet tall. The trees formed an impenetrable screen for whatever was taking place behind them. Freddie could stroll around his property in complete freedom from the ever-questing eyes peering from behind the front-room curtains of his immediate Hartland Road neighbours.

—

In one good year, with Guy Fox (Fawkes) day an all too imminent prospect, I was given a present of a brightly caparisoned (if small) box of fireworks. The benefactor behind the windfall was none other than Mr Harry Hackett, the barman at the Port Gaverne Hotel. Harry's motivation for the dispensation of such largesse related to the high level of regard that he had for Granfer and bore little or no relationship to any admiration for me that he may or most likely may not have entertained.

A box of fireworks of any size wasn't something to be received by my mother with any sentiment of approval, however, as she was a non-believer in the religion of inspecting the mouth of a gift horse, she accepted Harry's fireworks with as much good grace as she could muster in the circumstances, much to my delight.

The contents of the box included a Catherine wheel, a pair of Roman candles, some sparklers, one rocket, two cones of Vesuvius, a concertina-like squib, and last, but absolutely by no means least, four bangers. Alongside the bright new dawn of the bangers, the first of the breed that I had even come remotely close to laying my hands on, the balance of the firework inventory paled into the dimmest twilight.

Pending its availability to me only following nightfall on Guy Fox Day, Harry's pyrotechnic donation was placed, supposedly out of my reach, up on the highest shelf of Number Nine's airing cupboard, where it made a strange bedfellow for that abandoned copy of *The Pilgrims Progress*.

A pre-Guy Fox assault on the top shelf of the airing cupboard was a simple matter to achieve for one like me who regularly scaled local cliffs. It was the bangers I wanted, and therefore it was only the bangers that I took from the box when I made the ascent during my mother's absence from the house on a shopping expedition.

I had heard a story told about a boy in Camelford who once tied a banger to a stone, lit the blue touch paper and dropped the combination into the River Camel in the manner of a depth charge. The underwater explosion stunned a small trout that the boy recovered from the river and took home, where, it was alleged, it was fried for his supper.

I was anxious to try out the fishing technique for myself and did so in Port Isaac harbour at a period of low tide. I must have lacked the touch of the Camelford boy, as my stone-bound banger immediately expired with barely a hiss on first contact with the water, on the strength of which I surmised it to be probable that the detonation would only work under fresh-water conditions and concluded that salt water was antipathetic to damp squibs. The lessons learned from the debacle were not only that my stock of four bangers was depleted by a quarter but also that there was no value in experimenting.

With three bangers remaining, I felt the need to look around for more productive targets. A hardheaded cabbage in our back garden at Number Nine offered one attractive option. I pushed the banger into an incision made for the purpose in the cabbage head, lit the blue touch paper, and then, as recommended, I retired. The outcome of the cabbage demolition exercise was immensely satisfying. The banger detonated with a pleasingly solid thump, a lot more muffled than I was anticipating, and the cabbage head sundered in an instant. Fragments of smoking cabbage were scattered far and wide.

Cresting on the joyful wave of the moment, a second cabbage was a direct, but unfortunately anticlimactic recipient of my third banger. The banger exploded, but the cabbage remained intact, a wisp of smoke from the aperture where the banger had been installed emerging to offer the only evidence that sabotage, not to say cabotage, had been attempted.

One and one only of the four bangers was then left in hand. The question of how best to use it greatly taxed my mind. I recalled a cops and robbers film that I saw down at the Rivoli in which a safe door was compelled to open by attaching a small quantity of explosive to a strategic location on the door and causing it to go bang. It offered an example worth emulating.

Adjacent to the Hartland Road flank of his bungalow, close to the cypress hedge and therefore within relatively easy reach to me, Freddie Ford had erected a wooden shed in which, among other things, he maintained a stock of garden tools. I was well aware that the door to the wooden shed was under lock and key when Freddie was not around as I had tried the handle on a few such occasions.

Freddie's shed door lock was equipped with a big keyhole, broad enough to permit the insertion of a banger.

I checked carefully to make sure that Freddie was not at home, climbed over the wall, slipped between the cypress trees and approached the shed door. There, I shoved the banger into the big keyhole, lit the blue touch paper, and stepped back. The banger produced a loud "crack!" and a blossom of acrid fumes. Nothing else occurred for what seemed to be a very long moment.

Then the shed door swung open, slowly and steadily, emitting a shrill creak of hinges that gave me a chilly sensation of standing outside Bela Lugosi's castle. What lay inside the door suddenly appeared to be relatively unimportant. I pushed at the door to close it, but the banger had sprung the lock too well, and the lock refused to catch. In the manner of all good criminals when the dreadful deed was done, it seemed prudent for me to absent myself from Freddie's property and hope that justice would not come to claim me, which in fact it never did.

———

On a morning of the late summer of the following year, at a time when tetty tubers were swelling in the ground and the long school holidays still had at least a week or more to go, Freddie's property lay at the heart of a theatre of war across which an epic battle surged to and fro for several hours. The conflict involved invading armies with such numbers of combatants that they could barely be counted in the heat of the moment.

As it was, not one among the mighty host of belligerents could have been subsequently judged as being without sin. It was a matter of conjecture as to just who it was that threw the first figurative stone (in the form of a tetty) into Hartland Road from Lundy Road so as to set the train of combative events in motion.

The overall area covered by the field of battle was approximately two hundred yards long by one hundred yards wide. The long outer edge was formed by the section of Trewetha Lane in between the right-angled junctions of Hartland Road and Lundy Road, partially fronting on the Old council houses. The Lundy Road junction was located directly across Trewetha Lane from the field, formerly the property of Mr Hillson, in which the prefabs were put up.

In the noble tradition of most of the good tussles that took place in Port Isaac, the tetty war was rooted in insignificance. It began as a harmless pimple that was induced to turn into a ripe and festering boil by those who believed they had a vested interest in scratching at it. When battle was finally joined the originally light malaise had been heaved over the Hillson's dump of memory to be swallowed up totally by the forgiving sea and replaced by a raging plague.

It so happened that on that fateful morning a small group of boys were gathered up at the top end of Hartland Road for the purpose of playing marbles. The inoffensive pastime took place in the shadow of the bastion of Freddie's cypress hedge. At a given moment, the marble enthusiasts, intent on a game in hand, were at first startled and then intrigued when a small tetty dropped from the sky and came to ground within their midst.

It was not recorded whether any boy (or marble) was actually struck by the descending tuber, although it was subsequently assumed that a sudden impact with something present (boy or marble) could well have been the case.

One of the marble players picked up the fallen tetty, stared at it for a while, and hefted it up and down in his hand. His marbling companions "look'd at each other with a wild surmise" and rose from their knees to move as one in the direction of the little gate to Freddie's property set amid the cypress trees from behind which it was assumed that the vegetable missile must have been expelled.

From the vantage point of the little gate an uninterrupted view through to the back door of Mr Steve Bate's house on the far side of Freddie's wooden shed and the top end of his bungalow was obtained. Eyesnot plus one companion were spotted standing at the back door. Eyesnot, by virtue of his observed demeanour, appeared to be neither any more nor any less innocent than he normally did.

Linking the sighting of Eyesnot with an assumed direction of flight of the thrown tetty caused the stalled marble players to reach a rapid conclusion that it must have been Eyesnot who slung the self same tetty at them. On the other hand, Eyesnot's companion could have been the one responsible. The judgement was based on purely circumstantial evidence, but that gave no good reason not to consider retaliation.

So it was that the tetty at the heart of the matter was forcibly returned in Eyesnot's direction by one of the marbling fraternity in the eager anticipation of scoring a direct hit on Eyesnot's person. That was sadly not to be, yet the heaved tetty did manage to strike the side of Steve's house with sufficient force for it to split up into a few juicy pieces, one of which appeared to come to ground right alongside Eyesnot's feet.

As if galvanised by the near miss, Eyesnot and his associate retreated from the field of view at a fair clip. With honour having provided every impression of being satisfied and the players having recovered from their not entirely unwelcome disturbance, the Hartland Road marbles game recommenced.

The implied truce was, however, not one of a long duration. All too soon three further tetties came soaring in succession over the shivering peaks of Freddie's cypress trees. Eyesnot, irrespective of whether or not he threw the original tetty, was clearly engaged in raising the stakes.

Name-calling from both sides, mingled with expletives not meant for the vicar's ears to pick up, enlivened the air above Freddie's property. The three tetties were picked up and promptly hurled back towards Eyesnot. A few more tetties travelled back to Hartland Road from Eyesnot's redoubt. The increasing stridency of tone coming from all who were involved up to then attracted the attention of several more boys. It was holiday time and they were ever ready to home in a honeyed hive bearing a buzz of excitement.

The glad tidings were spread. Boys turned up on both the Hartland Road and Lundy Road sides of Freddie's property in ever increasing numbers. Eyesnot took on the semblance of a gang leader, a landmark chequer in his otherwise not always eventful career.

The exchange of tetties and taunts across the no-man's land of Freddie's property made satisfying sport for a while, but its repetitive nature staled with time, much in the way that a loaf of Sherratt's new bread did after a couple of days in the bread bin. If the waning enthusiasm for the day was to be regenerated, it was deemed essential to devise some means of holding on to the freshness of the earlier moments.

A realisation that the twin assemblies of raucous assailants were surrounded by well tended back vegetable gardens containing abundant supplies of potential ammunition beneath lush, neatly banked rows of tetty stalks, appeared to dawn on a number of the combatants simultaneously.

It needed a mighty act of faith for the first among them to make the great leap forward into one of the back gardens, there to commence ripping up tetty stalks and lifting exposed tetties for hurling into the engagement, but once the initiative was taken, it was clear that there would be no shortage of willing followers. The revelation that enhanced action was under way rippled outwards to pull ever more recruits into the fray.

Flying tetties filled the air like a winter flock of starlings. Back gardens were successively cleared out of their tetty crops in a ravaging and seemingly unstoppable wave of acquisition heading down Hartland Road and up Lundy Road. My father's back garden at Number Nine was an early casualty.

Immaculately cared for rows of tetties planted by Mr Frank Gilbert, Mr Charlie Smith, Mr Arthur Dinner, Mr Andrew Mitchell, Mr George Williams and Mr Jack ("Jack Tar") Thomas fell to the onslaught like dominoes.

At the height of the battle, the sacrosanct nature of Freddie's cypress-lined hedge was overturned. A mass invasion of Freddie's property took place from all quarters. Tetties that fell short of target were picked up and hurled in whatever direction the invaders happened to be facing at the time. Freddie's own back garden was denuded of tetties in short order.

Close combat became the order of the day, each one seizing and pummelling at whomsoever he was closest to. Taking sides no longer mattered. The adversaries threw themselves like berserkers through the mesh of cypress trees, intent on drawing blood and creating mayhem.

Eyesnot was then seen to be wearing a wartime tin helmet and to be holding in one hand what appeared to be a rather ancient cutlass. A phalanx from Hartland Road, heedless to the deterrent effect of Eyesnot's weaponry, bore down on him. He retreated apace to leap through the open front doorway of his house and slam the door shut behind him just in time.

As Eyesnot crouched in behind the front door, peering through the keyhole to check on what his pursuers were up to, one of his said pursuers poked a stick through the keyhole, which not unnaturally made contact with the vicinity of one of his eyes.

It was a decisive moment in the tetty war. Thereafter, the flow of action, which was threatening to overwhelm the tub of conflict, commenced dissipating down the plughole. Members of the opposing sides joined together to desert in droves. The sight of our village policeman advancing up Hartland Road with a slow yet implacably metronomic tread following an urgent summons by an unidentified third party, could also have influenced the melting away of hostilities.

The field of battle was abandoned. The owners of devastated back gardens contemplated the desecration of their respective tetty crops as if to query what could be salvaged before recognising that the answer was bugger all. They could only exclaim that they hadn't (at least some of them hadn't) fought a war to permit such outrages to happen. Uncle Jack Collings' garden wasn't touched, giving him no excuse not to be human about it.

At intervals during the following week the policeman interviewed many of us who were allegedly involved in the tetty fracas. He called on some at home in the evenings, and arranged for others, including me, to be pulled out of class at school during the day. His objective was to establish not only what had happened and why but also to flush out and bring the ringleaders to justice.

All of us who were interviewed, and probably some of us who weren't, were recipients of good hammerings – the customary

359

form of good old homespun punishment. Some might even have been smacked around the chacks. Such retribution needed to serve as justice sufficient unto the day, because no subsequent charges were laid at the feet of any one that I knew of.

A rumour was passed around that Eyesnot was in a serious condition as a result of the injury to his eye. It was said that he was forced to lie immobilised in bed, under strict doctor's orders to keep his damaged eye perfectly still. Someone said that if Eyesnot rolled the eye he would go blind. If the rumour was designed to scare those of us who took part in the tetty war, it achieved its objective. All of us were on tenterhooks in the anticipation of hearing more bad news about Eyesnot.

As it was, Eyesnot eventually showed up in the school playground looking not much the worse for wear. A slight scratch near one of his eyes was much admired, and continued to be much admired, right up to the time that it faded away, healed up and disappeared. I heard that Eyesnot had accidentally nicked himself alongside the eye with the cutlass he was seen wielding. The cutlass never appeared again and so may well have existed only in our imagination.

The critical question remaining unanswered was, who threw the first tetty? Eyesnot was adamant in maintaining that it wasn't him, and therefore he was believed. Any boy who caused the tetty war to erupt would have been more than happy to gain the fame of having the responsibility for it known by his peers. It spoke volumes that Eyesnot owned up to nothing.

As with the crew's disappearance from the good ship *Marie Céleste*, the identity of the first tetty thrower was forever destined to remain one of life's great mysteries.

# 19

# *Wholesale Co-operation*

Three for the rivals,
Two, two, the lily-white boys,
Clothed all in green O,
One is one and all alone
And ever more shall be so.

"The Dilly Song"

ONCE UPON A TIME, a bulky hotel cum guesthouse, Dunoon by name, dominated the left-hand side of the steep part of New Road. "Dunoon" was located just above the Thomas's row, about half way up from J. N. Hicks & Son Family Butchers at the bottom of the hill and the National bus garage adjacent to the Co-op at the top.

In the dark of one dreadful night, Dunoon vanished from the local scene owing to its being entirely consumed by fire, fortunately without human casualties. Unfortunates like me, who missed all the fun through being asleep in bed at the time, felt cut to the deep quick. We became even more distraught about our absence from the scene when we heard Charlie Smith's eyewitness account of fire-riven slates on Dunoon's roof exploding "like bleddy machine guns".

Miss Cassie Saundry, who lived in a neatly kept bungalow on the side of New Road straight across from Dunoon, suffered from no such sleeping-through-it-all disadvantage and therefore probably enjoyed a ringside seat for the conflagration. Cassie's bungalow stood behind a longish front garden, so that she, albeit perhaps not her floral display, was reasonably clear of most of the heat, if not quite out of reach of the radiant warmth as Dunoon blazed away.

It was not reported whether or not Cassie actually took up a position in her front garden to become a *bona fide* spectator of Dunoon on fire – more probably force of habit triumphed and her personal association with the excitement was effected from behind a front-window curtain – her customary location for examining the nature of traffic passing up and down New Road when she was at home.

It was necessary only to throw a passing glance at Cassie to recognise in her features certain of the well-known Saundry family characteristics. She was blessed with a directness of gaze that lagged at the rear of boss-eyed obsession by no more than the balance of a hair trigger. In keeping with the trait, it required an economical employment of truth for Cassie to be described as handsome. For all that, she was one who quite obviously took pains to moderate her inherited aspect by means of regular cosmetic maintenance.

As if to offset the fact that she was not entirely gifted with good looks, Cassie dressed well. Her naturally frizzy dark hair was often constrained as trimly as it was possible for it to ever be. Cassie's figure erred in the direction of weightiness, but she bore it with resolve.

In the context of place and time, Cassie's critical attribute was manifest in the position of power that she held in the village community. She established her dominion over the works of others up at the Co-op, where she was in charge of the section of that enduring shopping establishment in which drapery, with a sideline in footwear and clothing, was available (under certain conditions) for purchase by the general public.

Given a choice between exercising her supremacy objectively for the benefit of Co-op customers and of applying the same authority subjectively in order to strike fear into the customer's hearts, Cassie (so it was said) had originally elected to commence on the straight and narrow path. Yet, power was power, and, perhaps in spite of herself, it seemed to me that Cassie (as I knew her) leaned inexorably away from having any truck with altruism.

Cassie governed her part of the Co-op demesne with a rod and sceptre made of pure iron. Her style was what whatever she wanted it to be on the day. It could never have been said of Cassie in what she did that she was merely "following orders". Co-op customers holding ambitions to successfully conclude a purchase in Cassie's area of the Co-op needed to take great pains to stay in Cassie's good books.

The Co-op building in which Cassie held court was a solid, single-storey feature constructed from cement blocks coated on the outside with roughcast mortar. Its front was adorned with two large plate-glass windows and a couple of entry doors, one at each flank. The inner precincts were long, deep and chunky.

In comparison to the National bus garage alongside it, the Co-op made, all things being relative, nothing less than a slightly attractive prospect. Its face looked out across Charlie Smith's "No refuge here" signposted field in the foreground on an impressive view taking in Homer Park at the top of Church Hill on the right and the grand sweep up to the crest of Lobber field and cliff away to the left.

Since, as was the case with Cassie's bungalow, the Co-op stood twenty feet or so back from the verge of New Road, the National bus garage obscured it from the view of anyone coming up New Road from below, including Cassie of course.

The superstructure of the National bus garage was characterised by a surfeit of galvanised sheeting. A formal plan presumably supported the construction, although the completed arrangement gave an impression of having been thrown up in a hurry to provide cover for an unwitting National bus parked on open ground. Whatever the plan may or may not have been, the National bus garage was (at least in my eyes) undoubtedly Port Isaac's most unlovely building. Placed as it was in such a prominent location, it could do nothing other than constitute the village's greatest eyesore.

The National Bus Company was familiarly known to one and all as the "National". The National favoured painting its buses in an unpleasant shade of glossy green. The slightly bilious effect thereby provided was accentuated rather than relieved by a narrow yellowish trim that circled the sides of the bus in the manner of a plimsoll line below the windows, as if submerging out of sight were a pending option.

Be that as it may, the National was a local institution. A National bus plied to and fro between Port Isaac and Wadebridge on a daily schedule that was noted more for travelling hopefully than for arriving on time. On the Wadebridge route the National ran in competition with a Prout Brothers bus service, but since it was competition of a kind that neither participant appeared ready, willing or able to win, any sense of genuine rivalry between the two giants of public transport was rarely obvious.

The National bus garage therefore was effectively regarded by many people as being much less of a monstrosity than it actually was and was viewed more in terms of its being the stately home of a faithful retainer. Within the garage National buses rested up every night when their day's work was done.

The crew running the Port Isaac National consisted of two men, both of more or less local extraction. One of the said worthies drove, while the other conducted. What the National got from the pair was both a known and familiar quantity, as pure as it was simple.

He who drove the bus was Mr Maurice Renowden. The conductor was Mr Raymond Polkinghorne. Although neither of the two gentlemen was born in Port Isaac, they were married to local girls (sisters in fact), which provided local credentials for them that were good enough for nearly everyone. The sisters espoused to Maurice and Raymond were respectively Beryl and the palindromically named Anona (Nona) – incidentally the eldest and second-eldest daughters of Aunt Eva and Uncle Jack (he can't be human) Collings. Thereby Maurice, Raymond and I became familiars by proxy.

Maurice and Beryl lived in one of the Old council houses. Raymond and Nona resided not far away in one of the establishment of new prefabs. From either of the two specified domiciles, the walking distance to the National garage troubled Maurice and Raymond with the effort of no more than a few minutes.

As couples, the Renowdens and the Polkinghornes exhibited a number of considerable contrasts. Some might even have specified the contrasts as dramatic. Beryl was tall and slim. By her own lights she was anxious, to the limited extent that it was feasible in a rural retreat, to ferret out the latest fashions and to be favourably judged for the elegance of her appearance. It said much for Beryl that she quite often managed to live up to the image of what she thought she ought to be. In the tradition of her mother, Beryl was gifted with a serrated edge to her tongue that she was ever ready to bring to bear on the good wood of any fitting target. However, she rarely applied the talent in public, probably because her sense of modish identity would not permit her to do so.

Nona was both shorter and dumpier than Beryl. She made no secret of the fact that she was relatively unconcerned with the image of how she was perceived by the general public. The cutthroat razor of Nona's tongue flashed regularly and the hot embers of her wrath were zealously maintained, ready to be fanned into flame at the first gentle puff of the bellows of any personal slight, whether real or imagined.

Raymond made a tall and brooding presence at any given moment of the day. He was a taciturn man who gave every appearance of having been shaped at the anvil of Nona's pre-fabricated forge. As a bus conductor Raymond took on the singularly miscast role of primary interface with travelling members of the general public. He angrily cranked out tickets from a machine he carried slung around his neck as if he believed implicitly that he was doing passengers a great favour by taking their fares.

By contrast, Maurice invariably showed a bright and cheerful demeanour to the world in which he moved. Whatever his life may or may not have been behind the scenes at home, Maurice never relaxed his bubbling spirit when he was in the driving seat at centre stage. He was short and wiry, walking head down as if he was out with a clear sense of purpose.

Maurice had a quip, a joke or a gag of some kind or other for every boarding passenger. Lesser comedians than Maurice appeared on *Worker's Playtime* on the wireless. He was on Christian name bantering terms with most of his passengers, and even with passengers he didn't know, the repartee he dished out flagged not a whit. As the National threaded and scraped its way to Wadebridge and back through narrow lanes overhung with blackthorn and brambles, Maurice yelled pithy observations through the driving cab window at motorists, walkers, bicyclists and anyone at all who had nothing better to do than stand around on a grassy verge and try to look half-way intelligent as the bus went by.

Maurice lifted passengers' spirits and thereby mitigated the dismal aspects of their encounters with Raymond in the nether regions where they sat. If Maurice and Raymond had had similar characters, competition between them would have been certain and conflict may have followed. As it was, their disparities dovetailed to make a perfect fit. Together they were, like Messrs Bud Abbott and Lou Costello, much more than the mere sum of their parts.

The National was too good an institution to last for ever, and so it came to pass that eventually its Port Isaac-based services were discontinued. Maurice took a job driving for the Prout Brothers, in which capacity he not only carried on with his loveable, cheerful and cheeky chappie career on the Wadebridge route but also applied his monologues to other Prout Brothers bus destinations, not least among which was Sir James Smith's Grammar School at Camelford. In conjunction with the demise of the National, Raymond seemed to follow the example of old soldiers and simply faded away.

What Beryl and Nona thought about the break up of the celebrated National team was not known, but jealous self-interest must have been a feature somewhere in their minds.

At the back of the National garage and the Co-op, an open patch floored with oil-stained cement was just large enough to permit vehicles to pull in for the purpose of discharging cargoes of goods, comestible and otherwise, for replenishment of the Co-op's solid and liquid stock inventory. On the upper side of the open patch adjacent to a sword-stroke straight and weed-ridden through pathway linking New Road to Tintagel Terrace, a low cement block retaining wall, not much more than a foot high, ensured that all arriving vehicles would come to a stop irrespective of the efficiency of their brakes.

Screened off as it was from New Road, the open patch was very nicely secluded. It enjoyed great popularity as a playground for us on warm evenings when the National had made its last run of the day, the Co-op was shut and the members of staff of the said establishments were all observed to have marched off on their separate ways homewards.

It needed only a minor leap of imagination for us to convert the open patch into a semblance of a theatre. The cement floor made an acceptable stage. The low retaining wall constituted the stalls where the audience sat.

Uniquely, this rudimentary theatrical facility was patronised by girls as well as boys. Girls and boys combining for purposes of play under any other circumstances or conditions were not only unknown, they were unthinkable. A theatrical pursuit offered common ground on which boys and girls were equal, no matter whether they believed it or not.

Performances by boys at the theatre behind the Co-op were characterised by physical presence rather than by artistic talent. Our contributions were for the most part re-enactments of thrilling action scenes recalled from recent cinematic offerings at the Rivoli. The best that could be said about them was that we invariably kicked off with good intent. We normally wound up in a free-for-all roughhouse, something that was hugely enjoyed by the performers, although it was probably not appreciated at all by the audience of girls.

Presentations by the girls were oriented towards either dancing or singing, or a combination of both, none of it managing to enthral the boys. Our attention span was not extensive, and at a given moment when enough had become enough and the pleasures of barracking the girls on stage had palled, we were ready to rise as one from the stalls to get another *mêlée* going in order to spice up the proceedings.

Cockeye Mitchell's sister June was among the more ardent of Co-op theatrical performers. Her star turn was a rendition of the song "Little Mr Baggy Britches, I Love You", to which she gave vent in a duet with little Ann McOwen (a Glover in all but name), complete with an impressive range of undulating hand movements. June deserved much better than the catcalls that she generally got from us.

June was tall and very good-natured. Her face seemed to be composed of angles, a geometric trait shared by many in her family that gave rise to her being known to some of us as "Monkey Face". Using the insensitive nickname within audible range of June's mother provoked a reaction from the said Mrs

Mitchell at least equal to and maybe even surpassing the one triggered in the breast of Mr Ted Robinson when he heard his son Tony referred to as "Bollicks".

On leaving home at Number Nine Hartland Road one day I spied June leaning out of an upstairs window of her house across the way and called out to her, "Hallo, Monkey Face!" The front doors of Old, Middle and New council houses alike were opened only on special occasions, and my addressing June as "Monkey Face" precipitated just such a special occasion for Mrs Mitchell.

Her front door burst open. Mrs Mitchell sprang through it, leapt down the short flight of adjoining steps and sprinted towards Hartland Road with clearly signalled non-benign intentions regarding my person. I didn't wait to find out what those intentions were and took off in the direction of Tintagel Terrace at the best speed that I could muster. I wasn't sure when Mrs Mitchell ceased pursuing me as I didn't dare disadvantage myself by looking back, but I was certain that I had passed my Uncle Sam's cottage half way down along Tintagel Terrace before Mrs Mitchell gave up.

Uncle Sam was Gran's eldest brother. He was married to Auntie Barbara, who was goodness personified. They had two sons, both of whom were lost in the war. Uncle Sam was my godfather and so I should, from a sense of duty, probably have visited him more often than I actually did when I passed by his cottage and wasn't being chased by anyone.

The three things that Uncle Sam did promise and vow in my name at my baptism probably never departed from either his or my subconscious but were too deeply submerged in my conscious beneath a wave of more pressing priorities including birds' egging, wrecking, ranging the valleys and wondering what was the next thing I could do that my elders and betters had fought a war to prevent me doing.

----

At the front of the Co-op the door on the left (the one that was closer to the National garage) opened into the shop's grocery section. The door on the right provided access to the drapery section where Cassie worked. Inside the Co-op, God's good daylight held sway on the left, whereas twilight pervaded to the right. In essence therefore, the Co-op was something of a department store. It was possible to walk between the grocery and the drapery sections through a passage at the rear.

The Co-op's stock, which arrived on the floor of our theatre behind, was stored in back rooms adjoining the passage. The bulk paraffin storage tank was located close enough to the grocery area to make its existence no secret.

It wasn't essential for anyone who wished to shop at the Co-op to be a member of the parental Co-operative Wholesale Society, although membership of the same undoubtedly offered an advantage to those who held it. Both Gran and my mother were among the many who had joined the CWS and had in consequence been assigned personal membership identification numbers in recognition of the same.

Gran's membership number was 1137 (eleven-three-seven) and my mother's was 654 (six-five-four). The cost of purchases made by a member was recorded against the specific membership number, so that at a given moment the cumulative value of purchases could be used to calculate a dividend, or "divvy" due to the member. Both eleven-three-seven and six-five-four were numbers drummed into my mind, never to be forgotten. In an errand to the Co-op on behalf of Gran or my mother it would be considered a most serious offence if I failed to record one or other of the two membership numbers against the value of the goods purchased.

As a pure matter of fact, the Co-op's long-standing manager was a certain Mr William Auger. He was known to his customers one and all as Mr Auger and was never addressed in more familiar terms. He bore an air of strict formality as if it was a cloak of office. Mr Auger was not Port Isaac-born, but he lived locally in the middle member of a row of three bungalows set on a terrace above Mine Pit Corner where Trewetha Lane and Back Hill came together.

Mr Auger bore a strong resemblance to the celebrated actor Mr Raymond Huntley in one of his definitive characterisations of a pompous civil servant. As such, he seemed to play the part of Co-op manager as if he was created to do nothing less.

It was unlikely that Mr Auger would have acted to dissuade anyone who regarded him as having graduated to Co-op management via a spell in military service. From his conduct and bearing, it might be surmised that Mr Auger would surely have outranked Captain (retd) Roy May.

Some of us called him "Mr Ogre", although not to his face of course. We might, depending on how ill used we felt by him at the time, also be inclined to refer to Mr Auger with slightly less respect as "Auger the bauger". Mr Auger was a man whose aspect was best contemplated by us from a safe distance.

Mr Auger managed the Co-op with brisk authority and paraded his functional skill in the manner of a martinet towards the young and trembling girls who staffed the grocery counter. In the dim and mutinous precincts of the drapery section, however, the shadow of his command of the Co-op's overall establishment had, unfortunately for him, lost itself beyond recovery.

Mr Auger dared not invade the fortified empire of drapery unless defeat was his objective. The empress of drapery, the much-cited Cassie, was suffused with territorial imperative. The drapery section in her view was hers and hers alone to govern. Since an association with assistants would only have served to dilute Cassie's ability to exert her influence on Co-op customers for good or for ill, Cassie in the drapery section was a one-harridan show.

We were inured to never referring to the drapery section as anything other than "Cassie's". The fact that a sign heralding this title did not come to be erected over the right-hand entry door of the Co-op did not imply that Cassie hadn't contemplated erecting one.

"Cassie's" was a maze of dark shelves and gloomy corners that light of any kind seemed not to have touched. Only Cassie knew what manner of stock lurked back there. It was rumoured that there were forgotten pre-war items gathering dust on the shelves. Cassie considered the whole kit and caboodle of her fiefdom, right down to the last shoelace and ultimate stray thread of cotton, to be her personal property, not to be liberated lightly to customers.

It was mandatory for customers to justify themselves to Cassie if they were to be permitted to buy anything from her. It wasn't enough that a customer would have the ready funds, points and ration coupons in hand to make a purchase. A customer's face had to be acceptable to Cassie on the day in hand, even if the same face might have been *non grata* yesterday and might be the same again tomorrow. Cassie's customers had to show her the deferential humility that were the due accord of her regal presence.

When push came to shove, Cassie decided whether or not a customer was worthy of being allowed to buy from her hoard what the customer wanted. It was said that were some items in her domain that she was unwilling to let go at any price, and there were identified people, both high born and low, to whom Cassie was not prepared to sell anything, come what may. In the matter of social class Cassie stood on blessedly neutral ground.

Her power was acquired much in the manner of Topsy's origins in "Uncle Tom's Cabin". Unchallenged, it simply "grow'd".

———

Mr Auger could possibly have curtailed the snowballing ascent of Cassie's sovereignty once upon a time, but that time was gone. He was deemed to have failed in that duty. On the other hand, I imagined that Mr Auger's trepidation in Cassie's presence was similar to my own.

The passage at the back between the grocery and drapery sections of the Co-op became a variety of no-man's land that Mr Auger seldom left the trenches to invade. "Cassie's" functioned beyond the pale as an independent state bolstered by a wild-eyed resolve on the part of Cassie to rule it and continue to rule it irrespective of the impact on the Co-op's balance sheet.

Mr Auger, frustrated by the denial of success in marking his authority over "Cassie's", elected to impose his will with extra vigour in the grocery section of the Co-op that he indisputably controlled. There, he flitted hither and thither, subjecting customers to a probing scrutiny from a safe distance and the girls on the counter to such close-order review that they might have been puppets activated by strings at his behest.

Mr Auger's staff tended to be recent school leavers. They were impressionable and relatively inexperienced girls (my mother's first cousin Maureen being an exception), hence they were subordinate putty in Mr Auger's hands. Their function was to hand over to customers whatever customers wanted, although if bacon had to be sliced, cheese cut or butter patted, Mr Auger was impelled to involve himself in the transaction.

His vigilant hovering presence was not designed to put the girls at ease; it rather increased any propensity they had to make the kind of anxiety-generated mistakes that Mr Auger loved to identify, pounce on and proceed to berate the perpetrators for in front of an audience of waiting customers.

In spite of their having finished at school, or possibly because of it, Mr Auger wouldn't permit any of the girls to add up bills, receive money or hand over change. He and only he did that. He did it slowly and painstakingly, lingering over every last farthing and leaving each customer in no doubt that he was doing them a considerable personal service for which they ought to be most grateful.

Mr Auger appeared oblivious to the fact that no matter what heights of education and literacy might have been scaled, or for

373

that matter what respective depths might have been plumbed, there was not one among the Co-op's customers who wouldn't know in an instant if he or she had been short changed.

Receiving more change than was due was quite another matter for a customer of course. Few were ready to calculate it, and even fewer were prepared to acknowledge it. Perhaps this was the inevitable consequence of the war of rectitude that Mr Auger had set out to win, having lost his battle with Cassie.

# 20

## *All a Matter Hov*

*Forty years on, when afar and asunder
Parted are those who are singing today...*

E. E. Bowen (1836–1901)
Harrow School Song

AS NIBS WAS WONT to observe, when it came down to it, it was all a matter hov.

Half way through the opening decade of the twenty-first century, neither the village of Port Isaac nor the green and pleasant rolling lands of the parish of St Endellion of its hinterland look radically different from the way they did to those of us who knew them as they seemed to be in the middle of the dearly departed twentieth century.

In between the stipulated dates there were, to be sure, many scores (not to say tons and tons), of new dwelling places built in the village, inclusive of shacks, bungalows, would-be mansions, and houses of the council variety. It would be churlish not to observe that quite a few of these recent creations don't look out of place.

A similarly spruce quality can be applied also to the current state of the classic slate-invested jumble of downtown cottages – the inevitable consequence of most of them having been bought up, painted on the outside and refurbished on the inside by modern invaders for whom tank traps on the Port Gaverne beach would have proved no deterrent. The renovators came and

375

continue to come from up the line, among them one or two bearing the cachet of celebrity. In the good old post-war days the majority of them would have been recognised by us as being foreign enough for the forcible despatch of half a brick in their direction to be justified.

In the year of grace 1948, my Uncle Sam sold two examples of downtown cottages that were located towards the foot of Rose Hill. Both cottages were the inherited property of Uncle Sam's deceased father (and my great-grandfather). The two cottages together went for the then princely sum of two hundred and eighty pounds. Uncle Sam's eventual departure to a final resting place up at St Endellion could well have been hastened had he known at the time of the sale that at a certain point in the future (following the expiry of an equivalent amount of years to that of Messrs Heinz' number of well-publicised varieties – any contained beetles notwithstanding) the two cottages would be priced at around a thousandfold more than what he got for them. A matter hov indeed!

During the recent half-century or so of progress involving the local arrival of not only all kind of things mammon but also unimaginable technological advances, not a few of which passed Port Isaac by on the run, the population of the village remained very constant. In the best *Grand Hotel* (on screen at the Rivoli) tradition, people came and people went. Life moved on, oscillating like the tide in the harbour.

Steady replacement of those who went by those who came served to ensure a continuity of census, although the net effect has been achieved to the comparative detriment of both village character and the distinguishing features of individuality.

The personality of any village like Port Isaac is, for better or for worse, a function of the colour of the characters that inhabit it. On that reckoning, Port Isaac in 2005 is in considerable arrears when set against its counterpart of 1948. The arrears are such that no council rent man would be equal to the task of collecting them.

Perhaps somewhere at this very moment in the impressively orderly depths of the present-day village, a boy or a girl of an age that would be unlikely to appeal to sentiments of the late Mr Jack Short is either consciously or subconsciously engaged in storing away memories of life as it is now lived – memories destined to rise to surface in whatever format will define a book fifty years from now. Who will such budding scribes identify as the current Pharisees gracing their childhood? Locating more than two currants in a shop-bought yeast bun would be an equally onerous task for them to tackle.

In fairness, the vein of character existing to be mined is likely to contain nuggets as rich as they are sporadic, not dissimilar in distribution to the incidence of "proper" pasties among the present day plethora of shop-bought mediocrities that feature in the take-away outlets of any Cornish town, village and parts beyond.

Now, however, there will be no-one of the calibre of John and Jack the Singing Butchers to identify – none of the substance, strength, wit and peculiarities of the likes of Tom Brown, Ningy Short, John Glover, Tom Saundry, Wesley Blake, Jack Short, Frank Eade, Jim Creighton, Jess Steer, Dr Sproull, William John Honey, Old Tair Bunt, Em Kent, Cockeye Mitchell, Charlie Smith, Jimmy Baker, Rueben Brown, Jim Honey, Boss Richards, Freddie Honey (and so on and so forth almost *ad infinitum*) to celebrate and place in the thin present-day ranks of those whose useful toil, unlike that of yesteryear, was not mocked by ambition, as the poet Gray tells us. The likes of such as they were will not be looked on again in anyone's actual or future lifetime.

As the great comedian Alfred Marks sang with great relevance in one of his wireless programmes, in a lyrical tribute to the tune of the "Toreador Song" from *Carmen* (thereby bringing the ire of the toffee-nosed elite down on his head), "I yoo-hoosed too-hoo be like Errol Flynn, now I'm like Godfrey Winn!"

———

One day, not long after the end of the war when I was still living at Number Six Canadian Terrace, my mother came in through the back door in a high old state of excitement. There was an aura of anticipation about her that stretched out to encompass me. I had never before seen her looking quite that happy.

I trembled. The moment seemed to be poised on the edge of something memorable, and I couldn't even imagine what it was. My mother's hands were held behind her back. I half expected her to go into the tried and not very true playground mantra, "Close your eyes and open your mouth and see what God will give you!" I knew only too well from experience that that way lay disillusion – some pretty awful things had gone into my mouth down at the school as a consequence of placing too much trust in the donor's intentions.

However, "You won't ever guess what I've got!" my mother said to me.

"What? What is it?" I wanted to know, by then almost beside myself with eagerness.

My mother drew her hands from behind her back. In the right hand she held a very strange looking object, which she held out towards me. It was nearly as long as my forearm, and just about as round as the same limb although it was also slightly curved. It was smooth to the extent of appearing glossy, and coloured overall in yellow with an occasional black dot on it here and there.

I backed away. "It's a banana!" said my mother laughing.

I knew the song "Yes, we have no bananas!", having heard it lots of times on the wireless, but had never seen a banana before and had consequently never been motivated to bother about what such things might look like. Whenever we heard that song my mother would say, "If we had some ham we could have some ham and eggs, if we had some eggs!"

The sight of something that yes, nobody had, pushed my sense of nervous agitation to new heights. I burst into tears and refused all entreaties from my mother to touch the exotic object.

My mother had obtained the banana from Jim May at his greengrocer's shop down in Victoria House after standing in a queue for as long as it took. As with so many of her contemporaries she was accustomed to queuing and was ever ready to join a line-up of any length without even knowing what lay in wait at the far end. Whatever was up there at the head of the queue, albeit of animal, vegetable, mineral or abstract derivation, not one out of a possible twenty questions was ever wasted on worrying about it. Getting into the queue and travelling hopefully, one step at a time along its snaking path, was all that mattered.

The reward at the front of Jim May's banana queue was one banana per customer. One banana wasn't much, but one was more than bugger all. What was of paramount importance to those who queued for their banana was the symbolism of the moment.

That first post-war delivery of bananas to Port Isaac provided the queuing public with the clearest possible signal that the corner had truly been turned on the road to better times ahead. That was it at any rate for everyone. No one had seen bananas since before the war. The historical significance of Jim May rationing the over-ripe fruit out one at a time slipped by me in the manner of a swallow on the wing.

The Co-op building, from which the darkling precincts once held under Cassie's iron rule were flushed away and dispelled from the foreshore of memory as effectively as if Ned Cowlyn had directed the Lake through the premises, houses a present-day supermarket that is as brightly illuminated as it is well stocked. When two oversized shoppers approach each other in one of its Temple Bar-like tight aisles in the manner of opposing cars at the bend in Fore Street, one of them must needs engage reverse gear to allow the other to move on.

Both Cassie and Mr Auger have long since gone the way of the undeclared cold war that they engaged in against one another with such dedicated assiduity. The Berlin-styled virtual wall dividing Co-op drapery from grocery has fallen to the forces of mercantile enlightenment, although probably not without the involvement of some resistance along the way.

In this existing co-operative monument to deposed despots, bananas aplenty are freely available in multiple hands at various stages of ripeness, all carefully arranged within a display of other fruit and vegetables over on the right-hand side of the aisle to the immediate right of the Co-op's entry door, facing towards the stacks of bread loaves and saffron cakes across the way on the left.

One can almost sense Chad's fingers and pendulous nose drooped over the Co-op's checkout counter next to the array of scratch cards (the very concept of which would have horrified Mr Auger's cramped sensitivities) above the caption, "Wot, no queues?"

Yes, at the Co-op they do not have no bananas today. What makes the Co-op almost unique in the Port Isaac of the early twenty-first century is that it performs (more or less) the same role in serving the public with comestibles that it always did. For that alone, with honourable mention given to those who staffed the establishment through the years as well as those who stood and waited, the Co-op merits commendation.

The one great pity is that my mother's and Gran's respective Co-op membership numbers six-five-four and eleven-three-seven no longer cut any ice up there.

The situation with respect to many others among Port Isaac's post-war commercial establishments does, however, have rather less of a happy outcome.

The Co-op's stalwart neighbouring feature, the National Bus garage, was demolished in its entirety and replaced by a mansion-like edifice of Roy May styled proportions. Although there is little of Usher about this recent palatial construction, it does make a statement more redolent of overt opulence than of humility. To a degree it epitomises the less gentle mood of the Port Isaac of today as compared with past times.

Further down along New Road, the Singing Butchers and the bloody but endowed facilities in which they conducted their trade have all gone the way of the felled grove of bushy fir trees linking them with Mr Lansdowne's former shop – which is now the office of an estate agent.

Time has levelled both the noble and the ignoble of Port Isaac with an even hand.

The butcher's shop down by the Lake flush in Middle Street is also no more. John and Jack may well look on from wherever they are at present and give full vocal vent to "Abide with Me", since in commercial terms "Change and decay are all around to see". I trust that the Singing Butchers found a good home in heaven. If they didn't, then the consolation is that I can look forward to meeting them again at my assigned destination on Judgement Day.

The commerce of Fore Street has inexorably fallen victim to a time-associated scorched earth type of dynamic. Chapman's, once the famed grocer's shop, is currently an art gallery displaying canvasses of such dimensions that they could qualify as sails for a fishing boat, given a favourable wind. The canvasses are daubed in vividly coloured compositions that are almost as garishly abstract as was Mrs Lynwood Cowling's pancake application of facial makeup at the Old Drug Store.

A bit further down Fore Street from the Chapman's supplanting art gallery, William John's original barbering emporium is dedicated to an additional art studio, although its artistic exhibits fortunately reflect the character of William John in being gently conventional.

The public lavatory adjacent to Little Hill was demolished

many years ago. Its loss was very keenly felt and was not entirely offset by the provision of a successor in lower Roscarrock Hill, set into the back of the old Pawlyn's cellars behind a barred gate that offers no suggestion of welcome to anyone taken short and far from home.

The Old Drug Store of the aforementioned Mrs Cowling, located up in Fore Street at the corner with Back Hill, is now a fast food take-away specialising in outstanding offerings of fish and chips. By contrast, the run-of-mill pasties on offer on the premises are unlikely to win similar plaudits.

The nearby Liberal Club, verging on its centenary year, looks pretty much as it always did, subject still to an ever-thinning veneer of political affiliation. Curios and *objets d'art* are sold in its annex by a genial couple who additionally edit and publish an excellent monthly parish newsletter under the banner name of "Trio", a boon alike to subscribers and Fore Street's ever-diminishing cadre of true disciples of Paul Revere.

In a relatively recently created functions room under the eaves of the Liberal Club an occasional art exhibition or jumble sale (the two not being mutually exclusive) is held, and much tea is drunk when members of specified local organisations, not least the Port Isaac Historical Society, assemble to bemoan the undisputed assertion that, "things aren't what they used to be!" Beyond that, apathy invariably rules the day to optimum effect.

Aficionados of the Liberal Club's billiard room are sadly getting to be few in number and far between. All that is left of their once substantial company is a group of ageing reprobates, each one irreplaceable by his own lights. The great billiard table with its baize-covered slate playing surface seems destined to become a monument to silent balls, racked cues and an empty spittoon.

Curiously enough, although Sherratt's bake-house was overtaken by the groundswell of demand for holiday accommodation in the downtown area – and in the process underwent a conversion that had little in common with a similarly categorised event on the road to Damascus – the tradition of bread in the immediate locality has not yet fully succumbed to the developers.

In what was once Sherratt's shop, it is still possible to purchase loaves of bread (ready-sliced even though without a bacon machine in sight), as well as saffron cake and buns. Indifferent pasties are again prominent among the usual suspects, and (perish the thought) quiches are available as posh versions of good old egg and bacon pies (not forgetting the parsley).

On the whole, the cited fare on offer is not bad stuff, being brought in daily from its point of origin in Wadebridge. Whatever the pasties may contain, they are not only immensely popular with visitors, especially in the summer months, but are additionally much fancied by each and every herring gull in sight.

These gulls, deprived of the fruits of the Lake by both the manifestation of internal cottage plumbing (with a mighty sewage treatment plant disfiguring the heart of the Port Isaac valley down below the ruins of Top Shed to prove the point) and also a regular garbage collection round by council operatives, have directed their invaluable clean-up attentions to feeding on the not inconsiderable mess of leavings that many visitors strew in their wake.

The ingenious birds are self-taught experts in opening up unattended black garbage bags put out for the attention of those same council operatives (who were known as dustmen in the days when they took a pride in the service they provided) and are not averse to stealing fragments of the said pasties directly from the hands of visitors in a full feathered dive-bombing assault.

Needless to say, the airborne mugging technique of the gulls has tended to give the species a bad name with many people who should really know better. The gulls' destructive reputation is accentuated by their current propensity to build nests and rear their young on rooftops and chimneys of cottages surrounding the harbour, Canadian Terrace being not exempt.

A certain amount of destabilising damage to brick and slate is a consequence of the gulls' feet scrabbling on takeoff and landing. The key beneficiaries of this clog-footed activity are the host of Port Isaac's builders and decorators, who are guaranteed a steady demand for services they are unlikely to provide in good time.

The cry of gulls, particularly in the early morning, is such an essential facet of the Port Isaac *ambiance* that it has taken on an institutionalised status. Its absence from the scene would not only be intolerable, it would be unthinkable.

"Gulla, gulla, gulla!" we used to call to the gulls, and they answered us in kind. Long may they rain over us, and if they should choose to shit on the pretentious from a great height, what a proper job they do!

———

In Victoria House's long-term chamber of greengrocers both halt and fleet of foot, virtually all traces of fruit and vegetable produce are expunged from the scene. In its place, the vending of hot beverages, chiefly of coffee, stands supreme. However, the flavour and texture of the coffee on offer today far transcends its ancestors in the days when tea was the only serious game downtown and such coffee as existed was prepared from the viscous contents of a bottle with the word "Camp" printed on its label.

Present-day tastes in coffee are catered for in Victoria House in terms of *espresso*, *latte*, *cappuccino*, *frappuccino* and *macchiato* preparations among others, to the extent that an Italian pocket dictionary may well need to be consulted by a customer in preparation for placing an order. The presence of common or garden filter coffee on the menu (both literally and figuratively) may go some way to comfort the customers whose facility with foreign languages leaves a little to be desired.

Then, of course, there are various shades of cakes, pastries and ice creams on the side to act as a further sop to the palate of the less discerning coffee drinker.

What Clokie would have made of it all could pose a useful

question for a panel discussion. What the "dish-o-tay"-addicted denizens of Pawlyn's cellars would have thought about this coffee regime will never be known, which is probably all for the best as any comments might not bear repeating in mixed company.

---

Rowe's the newsagent, is also a defunct enterprise. Its twilit empire of printed periodicals has been usurped, renamed "Fearless" for reasons best known to the new proprietor, and turned into a gift shop ablaze with light, colour and a certain appeal to visitors with *avant-garde* tendencies.

Come to think of it, some of the items on sale in Fearless do look as if they were designed to scare the innocent, thereby providing the name above the shop front with some justification. One could be forgiven for wondering who in the hell buys such stuff, but clearly there are enough people ready, willing and able to do so to make the business all worthwhile.

It would not be out of line to imagine that Fearless' stock contains examples of that left-handed screwdriver and tin of black and white striped paint that Tom Brown was ever ready to despatch us boys up to Old Tair Bunt's fruiterer's shop to enquire after – a matter of Tom riling up Old Tair by proxy.

Old Tair's is now also a gift shop, although it is rather more standard in character than Fearless, specialising in a range of seaside souvenirs of the "Kiss Me Quick" quality and style. The name "Port Isaac" is to be found inscribed in one way or another in a prominent place on the surface of many of the items. A saving grace for this so-named "Lucky Piskey Gift Shop" is that it is owned and managed by Old Tair's granddaughter Eileen, thereby preserving a welcome bond of continuity over the years.

No doubt Old Tair's dead watch motto of "No tick here" still applies to those who step across the Lucky Piskey's threshold.

---

Whether or not the particular piskey in question was (or is) actually lucky is immaterial when faced with the enduring presence of the good old Pentice wall over there on the opposite side of Fore Street, no more than a chaw of baccy spit away from the Lucky Piskey entrance.

The view over the Pentice wall is eternal – Roscarrock Hill still rises to meet Lobber field. With the whole of the harbour intervening, Lobber cliff continues to soar a sheer slate face above the western breakwater. Roy May's house may have been upgraded to an extent that the unkempt Roy never contemplated in all his life, but it manages to look as grim as ever when the long shadows of the hill behind it bleed across its roof as the sun goes down.

By contrast, Khandalla looks as stately as it always did. At Khandalla's foot, the bramble-swamped allotments barely exhibit the boundary lines of subdivisions in which dedicated men once dug for victory.

In the former Pawlyn's cellars, recreated as the demesne of the "Port Isaac Fishermen's Association" (PIFA), old distinctions have become equally blurred.

Fresh fish can be obtained from a fish jouder's stall just within the PIFA entry. The jouder is Mr Dennis Knight, a successful local entrepreneur who commenced his local career as a ragged-assed boy ward of the three Misses Abbot out at the Old Mill. His fish is as famous for its variety as for its quality.

On the far side of the PIFA from Dennis' stall, another maritime merchant specialises in fresh and cooked shellfish – crabs and lobsters as prime as they seem to be overpriced.

In the innermost sanctum of what was Pawlyn's, where bullshit baffled brains every time under Tom Brown presiding as Master of Ceremonies, and into which multitudes of withies from the Mill Pool proceeded with religious fervour for baptism by clasp knife and conversion to crab pots in numbers beyond the ability of man to estimate, an aquarium open to paying members of the public is to be found.

The aquarium would be sure to strike a chord in the late lamented breast of Mr P. T. Barnum, standing as a testament to that great man's dictum that as far as the said paying members of the public are concerned, there's a sucker born every minute.

Down in the harbour the number of fishing boats is not that many, to the extent that applying the term "fleet" to their assembly would smack of hyperbole. However, each of the current group of fishing boats is bigger by far than the flagship *Winifred* of former fleet-leading glory, and all of them are so fast and have motors so powerful that they make Tintagel Head reachable with ease and even render accessing Lundy Island a not unconquerable challenge.

As a consequence, each of the modern fishing boats is capable of handling and controlling almost as many crab pots and of covering as much if not more oceanic territory than could the whole of the post-war fleet put together. So far so good, yet the overall result is that the give and take balance of conservation of the natural resources of the Bay has been tilted towards the point of diminishing returns, depleted by rapacious fishing practices that seem set to continue as if there is no tomorrow or until the stocks run out, whichever comes sooner.

'Arr Oaten's pithy observation on the whereabouts of the fishermen being up at St Endellion can be seen with hindsight to have endowed 'Arr with St Paul's oft-quoted gift of prophecy, even if any association with the same saint's favoured quality of charity was as elusive a commodity in the grand tradition of 'Arr's time as it is today.

Behind Black Doors, as solid and secure as they always were, the wheel has moved full circle in lifeboat containment terms. Fishermen's classes may no longer be an attraction within, and could indeed even be seen as a current irrelevancy under the circumstances, but the echoing hallowed spaces in which the classes were so much appreciated are again being used to house a Port Isaac lifeboat.

This lifeboat is an inshore version, inflatable, nippy and invaluable as much in fair weather as in foul for the wellbeing of carelessly straying foreigners who, heedless of time and tide, test the patience of the rim of the Bay.

The Old Lifeboat House, which was Chapman's warehouse in another life up at Little Hill adjacent to the old primary school's out-around playground, contains today, among other things, the village Post Office.

The Post Office counter, for those who can manage to worm their way to it through a maze of racked guernseys, flourishes of postcards, cascades of souvenirs and mountains of bric-a-brac, not to mention a side-on display of newspapers and selected magazines, lurks in the rear of the edifice.

The probity of those who serve the public across the present Post Office counter is suggestive of Miss Jinny Hills without rancour – and in all likelihood with zero recourse to a back-up bay tree at home. Jinny's venerable bay tree (or a replacement of the same) still stands, a little ragged in the wind, against the outside wall of Jinny and Wilfred's former residence half way up Front Hill – as attractive as ever to the attention of any cook intent on marinating a mackerel or two.

Chapel as an umbrella under which to conduct life, so beloved of Jinny and of so very many others of both the Roscarrock Hill and the Wesley persuasion, has long since been crushed out of existence in Port Isaac by the creep of secularism. The once mighty congregations have faded away like tussocks of sea pinks browned to brittle crispness by autumn gales.

The intensity of mutual distrust that characterised the pair of chapel sects probably ensured that neither would ever yield its self-assumed supremacy to the other, with the result that divided they fell, surrendering to stubborn inertia.

The post fall-of-faith Roscarrock chapel buildings are home to a pottery, known with perceptive unoriginality as the Port Isaac Pottery. The items it produces are of porcelain, unique in style and design, tasteful in aspect and splendid in tone, ringing like bells when tapped. The key motif set thereon is an image of silvery mackerel.

The Wesley chapel building was partially demolished for conversion into a garage and dwelling house by Mr Peter Rowe, younger son of Mr and Mrs Frank Rowe the newsagents. Much to Peter's credit, the general character of that well-loved place of worship has been carefully preserved.

Improbable though it might seem, given the calibre of local chapel opposition of half a century ago to the church, as manifest in St Peter's, the church must be deemed to have won Port Isaac's crusade of religious factions. It is only unfortunate that, at the end of the road to ultimate victory, St Peter's must be classed in terms of walking wounded.

The spirit of St Peter's and the concept of the church moving like a mighty army do not always sing from the same hymn sheet these days. There is no longer much point in anyone sneaking into St Peter's to make surreptitious alterations to the posted numbers on the hymn boards, as there may not be a congregation to come in that really cares.

My mother always told me that the church functioned on the strength of "two or three gathered together", although I never imagined that St Chrysostom, who included that minimum expectation in one of his prayers, ever intended the thought to be taken at face value.

St Peter's continues to function in the intent if not the practicality of local ecumenism, being a rallying point for the faithful few of all shades of religious belief, including that of the chapel, the odiously born again and other budding virtual nearer-my-God-to-Thee deck chair arrangers on the SS *Titanic*.

The current vicar now resides at the outer edge of the parish in the old rectory backing on the church at St Endellion under cawing rooks and shady trees. This location somehow epitomises Port Isaac's demographic thrust, a sort of rippling exodus spreading ever outwards from an increasingly barren downtown core towards the promised land of more elevated parts.

In the natural course of things, old characters pass on, some certainly going to a better place, some probably not. Younger people have tended to leave Port Isaac for other reasons, heading up the line largely in search of work and educational opportunities denied to them locally.

Cottages that fall vacant and then stumble into disrepair are placed on the market and evolve into so-called second homes for foreigners who wear body warmers and sensible shoes. The men among them sport yachting caps and the ladies push their sunglasses to the tops of their heads and favour heavy strings of beads around their necks. They all converse in loud and plummy-accented voices, consider themselves quasi-gentry and sip beer from half-pint glasses either in the saloon bar of the Golden Lion or out at Port Gaverne hotel, or both – but not at the same time.

To accommodate those of local birth who yet remain in the village, in numbers fast dwindling against the pressure of time, the council estate that celebrated its post-war renaissance in the New council houses of Hartland Road as well as in the prefabs has spread, like the dendritic blight in the corners of the great mirror on the wall of William John's old barber's shop, around the rim of the Port Isaac valley on the Trewetha Lane side and onwards half way up to Trewetha itself.

In so doing, the council estate has completely blotted out what was Mr Hillson's farm beneath an array of bricks, mortar, concrete, tarmac and neighbourly intrigue. The prefabs were early casualties of the expansion. They deserved a better fate but didn't get it, not unlike what happened to most of the likes of us.

Standing stark on the rim of the valley, the council buildings look like a half-vast (rather than a vast) rampart, something of the antithesis of Poe's proud tower looking gigantically down on the mute grey jumble of downtown roofs and tangled streets on which, in the closed season of the year, barely a soul (or for that matter a sole) steps willingly out.

Former rent-paying tenants own some of the houses in the council estate. These worthies chose to exercise an option to purchase when the council offered it. Others among the houses exist under a policy of rent, and a few, out where the edge of the estate threatens to head towards Trewetha, are devoted to housing members of a local underclass, some of whom can be defined as deserving cases.

The core of this broad conglomeration that the council built is Port Isaac's current primary school buildings and facilities, set in a top-of-the-hill location that reflects the inescapable fact that very few children live downtown any more. This present-day school is a sound institution of learning and gentle recreational pursuits, where rough conduct may exist only in the minds of an easily suppressed minority.

The teaching staff has enjoyed great success in eradicating all but rare vestiges of the once prevalent Port Isaac accent from the speech of their charges, as effectively as the back wheels of Mr Harold Spry's coal delivery truck under full load might extract the juice from a tetty if they accidentally ran over one.

The buildings and playgrounds of the original primary school, attended by Freddie Honey as a founder pupil (and attended by me as, well, a pupil at any rate) haven't gone away in substance of course, but they have been subjected to a quite dramatic change of use in which formal education plays no part.

The old school complex has been converted into a rather pleasant hotel retaining many original features and no small part of the character that we once knew under the headmastership of Boss Richards and didn't realise until we had left school that we also loved.

The casual visitor to the hotel, known as the Old School Hotel, can enjoy a drink in a comfortable bar incorporating the very classroom in which Boss flourished his cane and taught his charges. Moreover, as if to prove that banana-deprived years really have been put to rest, an excellent meal featuring local maritime produce can be partaken of in the atmospheric dining room that the former infants' classroom has turned into.

The ghosts of past glories drift along the hotel corridors, and echoes of excited voices shiver in corners, a passing parade that like Khayyam's moving finger wrote, and having writ moved on.

---

In the company of short cinematic gems such as the "Pete Smith Specialties"; witty episodes from the lifetime experiences of Mr Robert Benchley; the ultra-severe *Crime Does Not Pay* as presented by the depressingly morose Mr Edgar Lustgarten; manically narrated out-of-date newsreels; and an occasional leavening from Tom and Jerry, *The Passing Parade* ranked quite highly in the Rivoli's "Full Supporting Programme" preceding big films on Friday evenings.

Like the rudiments of progress that came to Port Isaac, a full supporting programme, passing parade and all, was a useful means to an end. Remodelled and converted to holiday flats, the Rivoli was very much of its time and stepped aside when its relevance to everyday life faded under the onslaught of television. Like Sir John Moore after Corunna, the Rivoli was buried and left alone in its glory.

---

And we boys? Some of us merely got old and in a few cases were converted by the process into the kind of miserable old buggers that were once the love-hate banes of our lives.

Some of us – Roger, Syd, Maxie, Eyesnot and Tibby among their number – are no longer with us. They will be forever young, the hall of their memory filled with endless sunlight. Mr Walter

Glover put it best, "Their clothes is shabby, but their bellies is full".

Port Isaac calls back its exiles, since after all family roots remain not only to be nourished, but also to have nourishment drawn from them. The exiles return, stay a week or so, and then go back to whence they came, usually (if the truth be told) with few genuine regrets.

New riders hold the reins of local society today, and notwithstanding laments for pleasures past and gone, it is right and proper that it should be so.

We tend to compare the retained rose-coloured image of what we think Port Isaac was then with what we all perceive it to be now, and even if we don't find the present day wanting, the feeling that it is not really what we want or can cope with is difficult to suppress.

Whenever exiles meet it seems that they relive the past in conversation to the exclusion of all else. Thoughts of Custer's last stand may well enter the minds of uninvolved observers.

Looking at the Port Isaac of today it seems that all those men who told us that they hadn't fought a war so that we little buggers could act in accordance with our own lights weren't exactly right, but it is fair to admit that their philosophy has endured.

When it comes down to it, we were all just a matter hov.

# *Acknowledgements*

THIS BOOK WAS designed and prepared in every detail by Corinne Orde and Romilly Hambling who together form Special-Edition Pre Press Services. Their kindness, style and expertise and the patience they brought to the work were exemplary. Corinne's skill in editing and improving the text and the finished work as a whole added so much to the final product and could not have been of greater benefit.

The digital files for the book were registered for print-on-demand orders with key trade and Internet booksellers and distributors by Lightning Source UK Limited of Milton Keynes. LSUK's total commitment to its clients demonstrated consistent professional excellence and personal consideration that could not be bettered.

I am very much in the debt of each and every person named in the book. It has been a lifetime privilege to know them all and an everlasting pleasure to commemorate them in print.

Finally I would like to thank my dear wife Maria for her unfailing support.

Any qualities that my book has are to the credit of all who are mentioned above. Any shortcomings are entirely to the detriment of me.

*"We boys. O them haunt companyeros."*

Frederick Manfred (1912–94) — *Lord Grizzly*

Printed in the United Kingdom
by Lightning Source UK Ltd.
108102UKS00001B/43-48